Applications in Basic Marketing

Clippings from the Popular Business Press

2003-2004 Edition

William D. Perreault, Jr.
University of North Carolina

and

E. Jerome McCarthy
Michigan State University

Boston Burr Ridge, IL Dubuque, IA Madison, WI New York San Francisco St. Louis
Bangkok Bogotá Caracas Kuala Lumpur Lisbon London Madrid Mexico City
Milan Montreal New Delhi Santiago Seoul Singapore Sydney Taipei Toronto

APPLICATIONS IN BASIC MARKETING:
CLIPPINGS FROM THE POPULAR BUSINESS PRESS 2003-2004 EDITION
Published by McGraw-Hill/Irwin, a business unit of The McGraw-Hill Companies, Inc., 1221 Avenue of the Americas, New York, NY, 10020.

This book is printed on acid-free paper.

1 2 3 4 5 6 7 8 9 0 QPD/QPD 0 9 8 7 6 5 4 3 2

ISBN 0-07-286469-9
ISSN 1099-5579

Publisher: *John E. Biernat*
Executive editor: *Linda Schreiber*
Coordinating editor: *Lin Davis*
Managing developmental editor: *Nancy Barbour*
Marketing manager: *Kimberly Kanakes*
Media producer: *Craig Atkins*
Senior project manager: *Christine A. Vaughan*
Manager, new book production: *Heather D. Burbridge*
Director of design: *Keith J. McPherson*
Lead supplement producer: *Matthew Perry*
Senior digital content specialist: *Brian Nacik*
Compositor: *Electronic Publishing Services, Inc., TN*
Printer: *Quebecor World Dubuque, Inc.*

www.mhhe.com

Preface

This is the fourteenth annual edition of *Applications in Basic Marketing.* We developed this set of marketing "clippings" from popular business publications to accompany our texts—*Basic Marketing* and *Essentials of Marketing.* All of these clippings report interesting case studies and current issues that relate to topics covered in our texts and in the first marketing course. We will continue to publish a new edition of this book *every year.* That means that we can include the most current and interesting clippings. Each new copy of our texts will come shrink-wrapped with a free copy of the newest (annual) edition of this book. However, it can also be ordered from the publisher separately for use in other courses or with other texts.

Our objective is for this book to provide a flexible and helpful set of teaching and learning materials. We have included clippings (articles) on a wide variety of topics. The clippings deal with consumer products and business products, goods and services, new developments in marketing as well as traditional issues, and large well-known companies as well as new, small ones. They cover important issues related to marketing strategy planning for both domestic and global markets. The readings can be used for independent study, as a basis for class assignments, or as a focus of in-class discussions. Some instructors might want to assign all of the clippings, but we have provided an ample selection so that it is easy to focus on a subset which is especially relevant to specific learning/teaching objectives. A separate set of teaching notes discusses points related to each article. We have put special emphasis on selecting short, highly readable articles—ones which can be read and understood in 10 or 15 minutes—so that they can be used in combination with other readings and assignments for the course. For example, they might be used in combination with assignments from *Basic Marketing,* exercises from the *Learning Aid for Use with Basic Marketing,* or *The Marketing Game!* micro-computer strategy simulation.

All of the articles are reproduced here in basically the same style and format as they originally appeared. This gives the reader a better sense of the popular business publications from which they are drawn, and stimulates an interest in ongoing learning beyond the time frame for a specific course.

We have added this component to our complete set of **P**rofessional **L**earning **U**nits **S**ystems (our **P.L.U.S.**) to provide even more alternatives for effective teaching and learning in the first marketing course. It has been an interesting job to research and select the readings for this new book, and we hope that our readers find it of value in developing a better understanding of the opportunities and challenges of marketing in our contemporary society.

William D. Perreault, Jr. and E. Jerome McCarthy

Acknowledgments

We would like to thank all of the publications that have granted us permission to reprint the articles in this book. Similarly, we value and appreciate the work and skill of the many writers who prepared the original materials.

Lin Davis played an important role in this project. She helped us research thousands of different publications to sort down to the final set, and she also contributed many fine ideas on how best to organize the selections that appear here.

The ideas for this book evolved from and built on previous editions of *Readings and Cases in Basic Marketing.* John F. Grashof and Andrew A. Brogowicz were coauthors of that book. We gratefully recognize the expertise and creativity that they shared over the years on that project. Their fine ideas carry forward here and have had a profound effect on our thinking in selecting articles that will meet the needs of marketing instructors and students alike.

We would also like to thank the many marketing professors and students whose input have helped shape the concept of this book. Their ideas—shared in personal conversations, in focus group interviews, and in responses to marketing research surveys—helped us to clearly define the needs that this book should meet.

Finally, we would like to thank the people at McGraw-Hill/Irwin, our publisher, who have helped turn this idea into a reality. We are grateful for their commitment to making these materials widely available.

W.D.P. and E.J.M.

Contents

Getting Information for Marketing Decisions

Product

Place

Promotion

Price

Marketing Strategies: Planning, Implementation and Control

Ethical Marketing in a Consumer-Oriented World: Appraisal and Challenges

Marketing's Role in the Global Economy and in the Firm

What's Wrong With This Printer?

Believe it or not, it's too solid. So Hewlett-Packard spent $1 billion to replace it with new machines that won't hold a person's weight. But they sell for less—and can squash rivals.

■ *by Noshua Watson*

The bet-the-company project that came to be known within Hewlett-Packard as the Big Bang started out with a whimper. And with grumbles and complaints that it shouldn't and couldn't be done. That was how the printer engineers who gathered for a kickoff meeting in Vancouver, Wash., three years ago reacted to the mandate laid down by their boss, Vyomesh Joshi. The mandate was to build a $49 printer—one $30 cheaper than HP's least expensive model at the time. Making a cheap printer was not itself an earthshaking proposition, but how Joshi intended to go about it certainly was. He didn't want just one low-end model; he wanted the engineers to conjure an entire new line of more than 50 consumer products—inkjet printers, digital cameras, "all in one" printer/fax/copier/scanners, and more. He wanted the engineers to ignore the models then being sold and start from scratch.

He wanted HP to be able to introduce the entire product line in one fell swoop. And he wanted to take it from concept to store shelves in less than three years—18 months faster than HP had ever accomplished a product launch.

The designers in the conference room that day, however, weren't in a history-making frame of mind. They were justifiably proud of the high-quality printers they'd been building, and if high quality meant higher prices, so what? Quality was what HP was known for.

To explode their complacency and focus their attention on the real need to build a frugal machine, manager Tom Alexander finally grabbed an HP printer and set it on the conference room floor. Then he stood on it, all 200 pounds of him. The point behind his grandstanding? Customers aren't going to use printers as step stools, so don't add costs by building them strong enough to withstand the weight of a grown man. Instead, design them to fit in the kitchen and print nice pictures.

Alexander's Stand helped open the way to a project that was audacity itself. Manufacturers often dream about reengineering an entire key product line, but few actually dare try. The risk is enormous not only because of the direct capital expense, but also because the market moves on. While the manufacturer is tied up getting the new line out the door, customers stray and competitors pounce.

With Joshi's Big Bang, the $47-billion-a-year company (before its merger with Compaq) was betting more than $1 billion: $125 million for R&D, $900 million for manufacturing, and $200 million for marketing. More important, HP was gambling its crown jewel. Printers, ink, and related products accounted for 43% of HP's sales and 65% of HP's profits. If the new product line stalled or flopped when it debuted, it would sap HP's strength and very likely hammer the stock.

The gamble didn't scare Joshi, 48. The greater risk, he felt, was to maintain the status quo. HP had gained preeminence in the printer market by relying on the "waterfall" or "cascade" method of product development. Engineers would design a printer, put it on the market at a high price, and then gradually tweak the design to reduce the manufacturing cost. Meanwhile they'd also work on developing the next-generation machine. When the new generation eventually hit the shelves, HP would lower the prices on the old machines. The waterfall method worked: It put the emphasis where HP was strongest—on its superior engineering and allowed it to dominate the inkjet-printer market during the 1990s. But in late 1997, HP got a shock when competitor Lexmark introduced the first inkjet printer to sell for less than $100. By mid-1999 Lexmark had doubled its market share

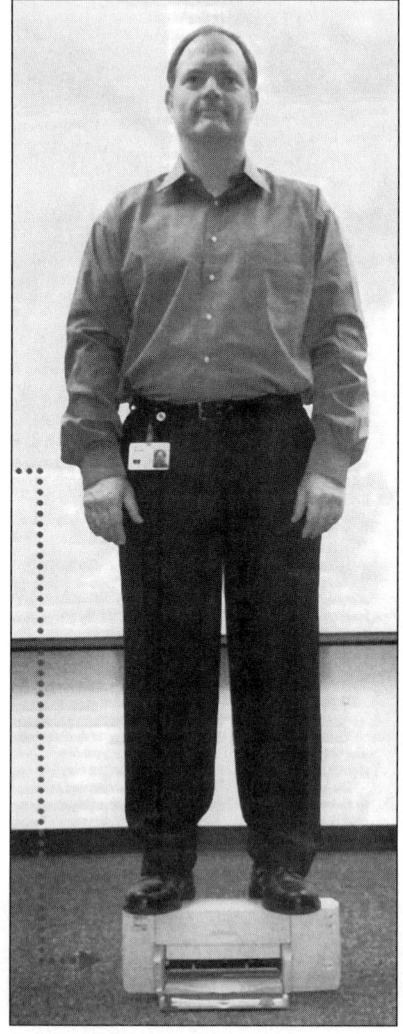

to 14%, according to market researcher ARS. The price pressure was on.

Joshi predicted that HP's low-end printer business would slowly but surely erode unless HP abandoned the waterfall practice and went head-to-head with Lexmark on price. That meant the cost of making printers had to come down—way down.

When Joshi came to that conclusion in 1999, he was not yet in charge of the printing group, and CEO Carly Fiorina was new to the company, having come from Lucent just four months before. The head of the printing group, Carolyn Ticknor, then Joshi's boss, saw the urgency in his proposal and pushed for the massive capital investment. Other division heads objected—it was a risk they felt HP could not afford—but Joshi and Ticknor prevailed. Convinced that the imaging business would be a high-growth area and merited a billion-dollar investment, Fiorina overrode the objections, cut the check, and gave Joshi free rein.

Joshi's cost-cutting concept was this: He wanted his engineers to build 14 inkjet printers and seven all-in-ones using two new, cost-efficient platforms while he squeezed productivity from every link in the supply chain. The printer platforms consist of the main chassis and printer carriage on which the plastic casing and output trays rest. The Malibu mechanism was developed for high-performance, top-of-the-line models like the 7350 and the 5550 that start at $150. But the key to the Big Bang's low-end strategy was the Crossbow platform, a design that taxed the Vancouver engineers' ingenuity.

In developing the Crossbow line, HP engineers had to count pennies for the first time. To make money on low-end printers, HP would have to make more than a million Crossbows a month. At that volume, each additional cent in unit manufacturing costs adds up quickly. For three months the engineers brought design after design to management only to be told that it wasn't cheap enough. And the heat was on: The old waterfall cycle had taken about four years. "We wanted to do it in less than three years," says Joshi, "because Lexmark was already there."

Finding the solution, the designers finally realized, depended on a kind of printer-engineer Zen. To clear their minds, they began to conceive of the printer not as a complex mechanism but rather as an empty box. It was perfectly light and inexpensive but would get heavier and costlier with every new feature. The object of the exercise was to think simply, adding only what the customer would absolutely need. Suddenly bells and whistles like the ability to print on glossy paper or card stock seemed easy to live without.

The engineers brought design after design to management only to be told that it wasn't cheap enough.

But frugality had its limits. One of the fiercest debates broke out over the power switch. Technically there is no need for an on-off switch, since a PC can turn on a printer automatically, and installing a manual switch adds about $1 per machine in cost. The engineers thought they had hit on easy savings until the marketing department got wind of it. The marketers argued that the average customer wouldn't understand how the printer could turn on and off without a power button and would become frustrated looking for it. The power switch stayed.

While the Vancouver engineers were perfecting the Crossbow mechanism and case designs, engineers in Corvallis, Ore., were racing to overhaul the most technologically complex part of the printer: the cartridge. "If a printer is a car, the cartridge is the engine and the gas tank," says Keith Bartlett, a cartridge group vice president. HP's intellectual-property stronghold in cartridges is formidable: Each cartridge is supported by nearly 100 patent applications, and in their own extension of Moore's law, HP's engineers have succeeded in doubling the number of ink drops per second every 18 months.

The little jewel boxes are also big money. For every printer on a store shelf, HP makes ten to 20 cartridges. Some go in the printers, and the rest go to retail stores as replacements, where they sell for between $20 and $35 each. A customer spends more on cartridges over time than on the printer itself. Not surprisingly, cartridges and other supplies account for half of the imaging group's revenues and a higher percentage of its profits.

Because of the high volumes, savings on the manufacturing cost of the cartridges would be even more significant than savings on the printer itself. The cartridge engineers shaved off "nickels and dimes," says Bartlett, by using thinner plastic on the cartridge casings and covering the top with a paper label rather than a plastic cap.

The biggest savings were to be found by altering the cartridge's engine head, the most important part of the inkjet system. The head consists of a silicon plate perforated by ink nozzles and glued to a piece of flexible plastic embedded with metal circuits. The flexible plastic wraps around the bottom of the cartridge, which skims back and forth above the paper's surface. When it's printing at full speed and top quality, the nozzles fire eight to ten million drops of ink a second.

The more ink-shooting nozzles on the engine head, the better the printing speed and quality. But engine heads are cut from pricey silicon wafers. The HP engineers' challenge was to make the heads smaller, thus using less silicon, without sacrificing the number of nozzles. In the end they managed to shrink the engine head to half its original size and still squeeze 30% more nozzles onto it by making each nozzle narrower. (They also refined the ink.)

By early 2001 Joshi, now head of the imaging and printing group, was ready to move the new line into the plants. To guard its cartridge-making secrets, HP designs and manufactures the little boxes almost entirely in-house, at a design and fabrication facility in Corvallis and high-volume manufacturing plants in Ireland, Singapore, and Puerto Rico. Printers, meanwhile, are farmed out to contract manufacturers in Southeast Asia, China, and Mexico.

HP's contract factory owners were in for a big surprise. After test runs were complete, Joshi wanted to increase production from zero to one million units a month within three months, ten times faster than any previous ramp-up for an HP product. To support the huge volume, HP's manufacturers would have to build factories, and do it faster than ever. Under the old system, engineers would design the production line in the U.S. to get out

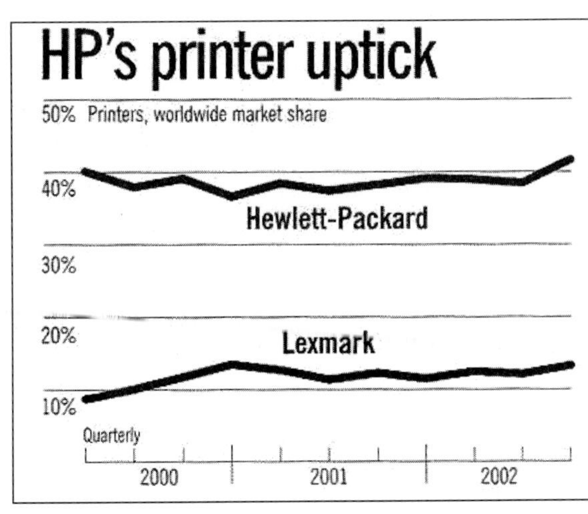

the kinks before sending the plant blueprints overseas. That process typically took about 18 months. But under the pressure of the Big Bang, Joshi gave them only one year. To speed up building the plants, engineers passed along tooling specifications to the factories before the printer designs were final. There wasn't a minute to lose, and everyone felt it. Paul Speer, who supervises the Vancouver engineers, recalls debating alternatives in his cubicle with two program managers when the fire alarm went off. Sent out into a rainstorm, Speer and his staffers huddled behind a passenger van in the parking lot to continue their discussion.

To support the huge volume, HP's suppliers would have to build new plants, and build them faster than ever.

Building printers from just two platforms—the Malibu and the Crossbow—made the production line more efficient. Before the Big Bang, HP had built printers using multiple platforms, and the production line had to shut down and retool when switching from one platform to the other. Now several different models could be built from the Crossbow alone. The line could run continuously, splitting into smaller lines to finish off different products. The Crossbow printer's compact dimensions doubled the number that HP could pack on a shipping pallet, saving shipping costs. Even a 20-year veteran like Speer was awed by the millions of machines spilling from the production lines by early 2002. "I walked into a factory in Singapore and looked all the way down the line to the curvature of the earth," he claims. "All I could see were Crossbow printers."

Back home, HP's marketing department was preparing to sell this sea of Crossbows. The timing couldn't have been worse. HP's merger with Compaq had just been announced. The tech sector was in a slump. Still, the marketers knew they had to go all-out to make sure Big Bang wasn't a bust. After mailing one million direct-mail "magalogs" and outfitting three tractor-trailers with HP products and demos to tour the U.S., the company invited major retailers, including Circuit City, Office Max, and Best Buy, to Cupertino, Calif., for product demos. The retailers were hesitant to commit to buying the Big Bang line. HP was making a lot of demands: It wanted better displays, with all its new printers lined up together in a single aisle. At the same time, HP had disappointed many retailers by failing to keep them stocked with its old products. Without a guarantee that the new machines would be in the stores on time, the retailers wouldn't advertise the Big Bang printers in their Sunday circulars.

HP marketers promised to supply more than 8,000 stores by July 28, 2002. To make that date, the printers would have to be shipped from Asia in May or June at the latest. Most of the factories kept to the schedule, but by June it was apparent that thousands of printers weren't going to make it onto ships because of manufacturing problems in Singapore. Rather than jeopardize its relationships with retailers, HP paid a huge sum to transport tens of thousands of printers from Southeast Asia by air. By July 28, HP had put more than one million printers on store shelves.

Joshi had been waiting for that moment for three years. Despite the economic slump in general—and the tech slump in particular—he was optimistic. "I was extremely confident," Joshi says. "I felt like a proud parent." In the next few months the market justified his pride. In a year when overall printer sales fell 10%, HP's printer sales increased by 3% between June and December. Shipments of color inkjet printers to stores grew by 18%. Joshi was particularly pleased by the results in the high-margin all-in-one market: After the Big Bang, HP took 20 percentage points of market share—most of it from Lexmark—to grab nearly 70% of the market. In June, Joshi had promised Wall Street that his $20 billion business would grow 10%, with 12% to 15% margins. In the fourth quarter his results made analysts purr—record revenues of $5.6 billion, representing 12% year-over-year sales growth. His margins: 16.5%.

Joshi's lieutenants now brag that he wants a Big Bang every year. "We're improving our cost structure all over HP," says Larry Lesley, senior vice president in the imaging and printing group. "This isn't an endgame; it's an ongoing philosophy." Leveraging its new competitive advantage, HP plans to launch new products in June and to continue to make the existing Big Bang line faster and better. As John Solomon, printer category manager, summarizes the success of the new line, "It's much cheaper to make, much better in terms of image quality and speed, and it's half the size." But success does have its price: "Of course, you can no longer stand on it."

"What's Wrong with This Printer?," *Fortune,* Feb 17, 2003, p. 12OC–12OH.

Selling Cellphones with Mixed Messages

By Gabriel Kahn

In China, a special karaoke-enabled cellphone plays music and scrolls lyrics while you sing into the mouthpiece. A phone in South Korea allows you to download video clips and exchange them with friends. And in the U.S., there's a phone from Verizon Wireless that lets users play games.

These devices are all made by **Motorola** Inc.—and they also happen to be practically the same phone, known as the T720 in the U.S. and the V730 elsewhere. The thing that separates them is Motorola's multipronged sales strategy, which targets different markets with different phone features.

The mixed message reflects a new trend sweeping the $60 billion cellphone industry. At the moment when technological standards for cellphones are becoming more universal, marketing campaigns for the phones are becoming more local. Giants such as Motorola of Schaumburg, Ill., **Siemens** AG of Germany and Sony Ericsson Mobile Communications Ltd., a venture of **Sony** Corp. of Japan and **Telefon AB L.M. Ericsson** of Sweden, once rolled out ads globally; now, they tailor their messages to different audiences.

Driving the change is the evolution of the cellphone itself, from phone to fashion item and now to a vehicle for content, such as music, news or games. And content is extremely local.

"The industry is moving from a device-centric approach to an experience-centric approach, and that is making it a lot more local," says Brian Holmes, Motorola's Asia Pacific marketing manager.

So, for example, Motorola opted to play up the karaoke capability of the V730 in China. A special China ad campaign designed by **WPP Group** PLC's Ogilvy & Mather depicts a latter-stage Elvis impersonator crooning into a V730 mounted atop a microphone stand. The specially designed phone, which comes preloaded with two songs, was born of an alliance with Chinese cellular operator **China Unicom.**

Karaoke would seem a natural selling point for South Korea, too, where amateur singing is a popular pasttime. But Motorola's research in South Korea showed that karaoke took a backseat to other functions, such as downloading video clips from soccer matches.

For people like Mr. Holmes, brought up in a design-based culture that emphasized sleeker cellphones, the shift to content means he has to move even faster than he did when he was following the latest fashion trends. "It means our product is radically changing by the minute," he says.

So is the research. "In the '90s, you could just have a focus group with a few phone owners, and the discussion was who had the smallest phone," says Pasi Jarvenpaa, **Nokia** Corp.'s Asia Pacific director of marketing for mobile phones. "The scope is now much broader and the answers a lot less obvious. We now look for a psychographic orientation, such as people who are open to change."

The shift in cellphone marketing tactics also can be seen in the demise of ad campaigns that touted just technology—even as the phones themselves continue to become more sophisticated. Instead of throwing around acronyms for the latest messaging technologies, "now we put a lot of focus on what's on the street and what's in the stores," says Philip Vanhoutte, London-based vice president for marketing of Sony Ericsson.

That change in focus is forcing companies to rejigger more than just marketing. The cellular division of Siemens strengthened its marketing and research operations in Asia so that it can now feed back local consumer insights to headquarters in Germany while a new phone is still in the planning stage. More input upfront means less retooling later on, says Mark McCallum, vice president for product and marketing for mobile phones.

In both Europe and Asia, Siemens is targeting the same group for its C55 phone: the "social-centric set," a mostly teenage, female audience focused on friends and dating. But based on its research it has two distinct marketing plans. In Europe, it is promoting the phone's ability to record sounds and play them back or send them to friends. In Asia, it is shipping the same phones with special luminescent covers that glow in the dark, which emphasizes the phones' romantic or "puppy love" feature, says Mr. McCallum.

FINALLY, COKE GETS IT RIGHT

The company is finding its footing in India after years of missteps

You might think selling in India would be a romp for beverage giant Coca-Cola Co. The country has a billion-plus consumers, a growing middle class, and the climate is hot, hot, hot. Look a little more closely, though, and this market is more minefield than mother lode. Sure, Coke's various beverages have more than half the market. But its flagship brand—Coca-Cola, the ur-soft drink—remains a distant third, with an estimated market share of 16.5%, far behind arch rival Pepsi-Cola's 23.5%. Almost as embarrassing, No. 2 is Thums Up, a sweeter local cola that Coke acquired in 1993, then proceeded to neglect. "The environment in India is challenging," says Alex von Behr, a Briton who is president of Coke India. "But we're learning how to crack it."

The learning curve has been steep. In 1993—15 years after being thrown out by India's socialist government—Coke stormed back into the country with big plans to wrest control from Pepsi and the local beverage marketers that had risen up in its absence. Instead, the company spent years on the defensive after overestimating the size of the market, misreading consumers, and battling with the government. A semi-farcical tussle in which Coke bottlers hoarded empty Pepsi bottles gave the company a black eye until the dispute was resolved last November. And Coke India has been hurt by a revolving door in the executive suite. In 10 years, it has had five expatriate heads. Pepsi, by contrast, last year appointed its third Indian chief executive in 14 years. The result: In 2000, Coke wrote down the value of its Indian bottling assets by $ 405 million. It has suffered losses in India for years—although its execs won't reveal financial details.

Finally, Coke is starting to inject some fizz into its Indian operations. On Feb. 28, the company plans to sell 49% of its Indian bottler, Hindustan Coca-Cola Beverages, for $41 million. The sale won't be the domestic stock listing that some in New Delhi had sought. Instead, the shares will be sold in a private placement with institutional investors and employees. But it puts to rest a thorny issue that had chilled relations with the government, which wanted Indians to have a substantial ownership stake in Coke's local operation. Better yet, Indians appear to be developing a taste for Coke products: The company's overall sales in India jumped 24%, to $ 940 million, last year. "Coke lost a number of years over errors," says Jagdeep Kapoor, chairman of Samsika Marketing Consultants in Bombay. "But at last, it seems to be getting its positioning right."

That will come as a great relief at Coke headquarters in Atlanta. India, with soft-drink consumption of just seven 8-ounce (250 milliliters) servings per capita annually, holds more potential for growth than just about any other market on earth. By contrast, neighboring Pakistan hoists an average of 14 servings per year; in China, it's 89; and in Mexico, the world's hottest soda market, it's nearly 1,500 servings. Determined to consolidate its position and boost growth, Coke this year cut prices on all of its beverages by an aggressive 15% to 25%, forcing Pepsi to follow suit. "India is the beverage battlefield for 2003," says Ronald S. McEachern, Pepsi's Asia chief.

Key to Coke's battle plans is operations chief Sanjeev Gupta. After being promoted from marketing director three years ago, the boyish, straight-talking Gupta persuaded his Coke bosses to change the way they do business. "He bravely stood up to Atlanta and told them their strategy in India was wrong," remembers a former Coke exec in New Delhi. Gupta's first step: revitalizing Thums Up, which led the market in 1993 with more than 60% of carbonated beverage sales but had slipped to just 15% by 1998. After Atlanta gave the green light to pushing local brands as much as Coca-Cola, the 41-year-old Gupta spent $ 3.5 million to beef up advertising and distribution for Thums Up. Within a year, he built it into India's No. 2 soda.

Then Gupta—a veteran of marketing juggernaut Hindustan Lever Ltd.—persuaded Atlanta to revamp pricing and advertising for Coca-Cola. In 2001, he launched a new size, a 200-ml. bottle that sells for 10 cents and is aimed at rural areas and lower-income urban markets. This year he dropped the price of a 300-ml. bottle to 17 cents from 24 cents. The price cuts were key to boosting sales and the little bottle was a big hit. Gupta expects it to represent 50% of sales by volume this year.

In 2002, after years of lackluster ad campaigns, Gupta's team settled on an advertising strategy that caught the imagination of Indians. Breaking with Coke tradition, he hired a celebrity spokesman, Bollywood movie star Amir Khan. The campaign equates Coke with "thanda," the Hindi word for "cold," a commonly used term for a generic soft drink. "Coke had to break a lot of its rules for India," recalls Ashok Jain, the former head of Cadbury Schweppes PLC in India, who quit Schweppes after Coke bought it in 1999.

LOCAL HERO Operations chief Gupta stood up to U.S. bosses and changed pricing, ads, and products to appeal to local tastes

The company has been cutting costs, too. Although Coke owns 70% of its bottlers, many of them were outdated operations inherited from the Thums Up purchase. Over the past three years, it has shut down eight of them, which helped trim the payroll by 23%, to 5,000. Employee costs have fallen to 4.5% of revenues from 7% in 2002. Coke got rid of about 80 managers, including high-priced top execs, earning Gupta the moniker "Prince of Darkness." It saved 57% on import duties by using more local raw materials. And by upgrading its bottling technology and improving maintenance and training, Coke has improved plant efficiencies by 40%. Says Gupta: "We were saddled with chaotic operations, but that's all changed."

At the same time, Coke is branching out into other products. In 2001, it introduced Kinley bottled water, which has grown to a leading market share of 37% by building on Coke's

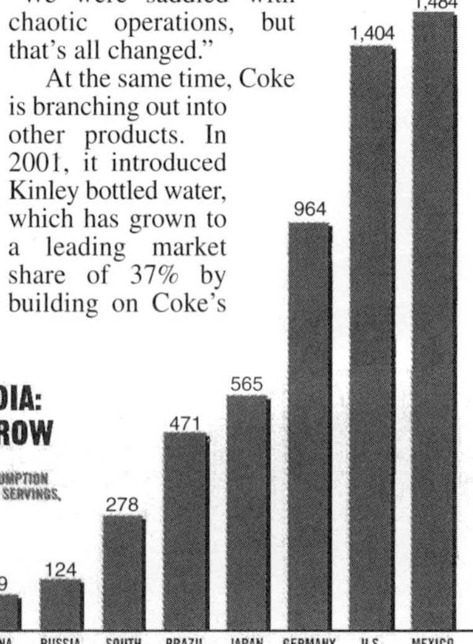

distribution network to reach far-flung villages. Key to Kinley's expansion have been ads depicting village life and military families that, given India's constant security concerns, have "built an emotional connect with the Indian consumer," says consultant Kapoor. Encouraged, Coke is now copying the success of its ready-to-drink coffee in Japan and test-marketing the concept in India.

Finally, it has settled its long-standing dispute with Pepsi over bottles. Last November, Pepsi accused Coke of hoarding more than 5 million of its bottles, which had ended up in Coke's hands from recyclers. Without them, Pepsi had difficulty meeting demand for its drinks. On Nov. 26, after Pepsi called the police and a court ordered Coke to return the bottles, the two companies agreed to regular exchanges.

The changes are paying Coke dividends. Execs at Coca-Cola India say the company is no longer losing money. "We have turned a corner," says N. Sridhar, Coke India's finance director. "This will release our energies to concentrate on building market share." Now, Coke is planning on investing $150 million more to expand its bottling and distribution network. That will make India Coke's second-largest Asian investment after China. The subcontinent hasn't become a mother lode for Coke yet. But the company sure is trying to make it one.

Could This Be the Next Disney?

Electronic Arts makes one of every four videogames sold in the world (and that's before it took The Sims online). CEO Larry Probst says he's just getting started building "the greatest entertainment company ever."

By: Geoff Keighley

Until her boss showed up, Hecubah, queen of the undead, was having a pretty good day at work. It was the 1999 Electronic Entertainment Expo (known in the industry as E3), and the villainess of the chop-'em-up role-playing PC game Nox had young men flocking to the Electronic Arts (ERTS) booth in Los Angeles's Convention Center. Some undoubtedly came to hear about EA's lineup of new videogames, but many stayed just to stare at the actress playing Hecubah—in devil horns, red contact lenses, and a dominatrix corset just a few threads shy of a misdemeanor rap.

As the gamers milled and gawked, Larry Probst, CEO and chairman of Electronic Arts, pushed his way through. The sight of the queen stopped the 52-year-old executive in his tracks. Blanching, he turned to an assistant, and within seconds one of his minions had backed Hecubah into an inconspicuous corner while another raced off to get her some clothes. When the queen returned to work, she was wearing a skirt. "We want the focus at E3 to be on our products," Probst says about the incident, "not on scantily clad women."

Dressing the "booth babes," as they're inelegantly known at E3, may not be the most significant branding initiative of Probst's 18-year tenure at Electronic Arts, but it's a perfect metaphor for his vision of his company. In an industry that was born catering to adolescent male fantasies, Probst has turned EA into the runaway market leader by mining a largely PG audience. One of every four digital games sold worldwide this year carried the EA logo, despite the fact that the company has no product to compete with raunchy titles like the Grand Theft Auto series, unquestionably the hottest console franchise in the business. EA's gentler focus is evident in its lineup for the all-important 2002 holiday season. Of the 35 titles being rolled out, several are all-but-guaranteed blockbusters—Harry Potter and the Chamber of Secrets, Lord of the Rings: The Two Towers, James Bond 007: NightFire, NBA Live 2003, and the highly anticipated The Sims Online, the Web version of the best-selling PC game. The last, which goes live on Dec. 3, could bring EA as much as $100 million a year. But not one is rated M, for a mature audience. As Bing Gordon, a co-founder of EA and now its chief creative officer, puts it, "Management only wants to sell stuff that we'd be proud to have in our homes in front of our families."

If that brings to mind another media power built on wholesome entertainment, the resemblance is wholly intentional. "We've looked at Disney (DIS) as a model," Probst says. "It is the gold standard for us." Of course, it's almost absurd to compare a $2 billion software maker with a $25 billion diversified media giant. But that's what visions are made of. That, and the $920 million of cash on EA's balance sheet—money Gordon hints could be used to expand into movies or music. In any event, Probst is clearly way beyond thinking of EA as merely a creator of software toys. "Our goal," he says with no hint of self-consciousness, "is to become the greatest entertainment company ever."

If any gamemaker has a shot at realizing such ambitions, it's Electronic Arts. Based in Redwood City, Calif., the 3,800-employee company has more than twice the sales of Activision (ATVI), its biggest rival, and its expected revenues for this year are around $2.3 billion, a 35 percent increase over 2001. The stock market seems to believe in EA's future: During the past 30 months—a period

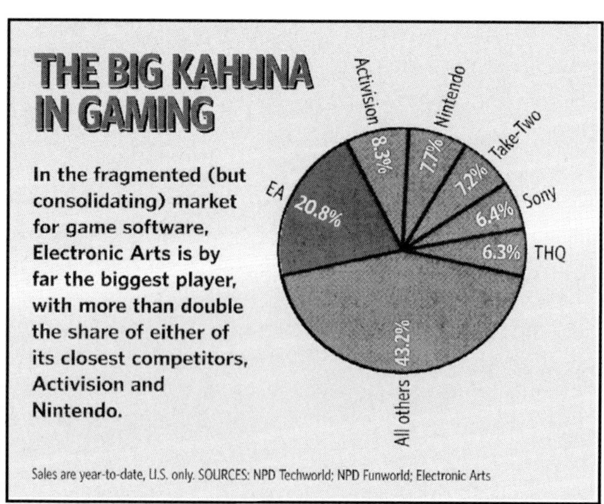

that left most tech stocks in smoking ruins—EA's shares are up more than 80 percent.

Mike Wallace, an analyst at UBS Securities, calls EA "the Microsoft (MSFT) of the gaming business," in part because of its portfolio of seemingly indestructible franchises, such as Madden NFL Football, James Bond 007, and The Sims. These titles produce revenues year-in and year-out and give the company a breadth and stability that are the envy of the industry. That, in turn, has enabled EA to assemble a massive internal studio system—2,500 game developers in five countries—that produces games that are consistently considered the best in their categories. "In terms of overall lineup, no one else comes close to EA," says John Davison, editorial director of Ziff Davis Media Game Group.

The man at the helm of this success story started his career a long way from Redwood City. A sales director for Clorox in St. Louis, Probst had never even thought about computer games until the early 1980s, when he first played Pong. In that primitive ricochet game, Probst says, he saw the future of entertainment.

Packing up his wife and two boys, Probst traded the Midwest for Silicon Valley in 1984 and joined Trip Hawkins, the former director of product marketing at Apple (AAPL) who had launched EA two years earlier. Back then Pac-Man was the most popular videogame and Electronic Arts's portfolio was limited to a handful of products for the Apple II and Atari computers. Hawkins hoped that Probst would bring the fledgling company some practical business smarts, and he did. As Don Valentine, the Sequoia Capital VC who bankrolled EA, puts it, "Unlike Trip, who is far more evangelical and visionary, Larry was the down-to-earth businessman who really set EA on its course."

Within months of arriving, Probst began to shake things up. At that time, game publishers distributed their titles to thousands of independently owned stores through a handful of big manufacturers' representatives. "I just didn't think that was very effective," Probst recalls. He set out to bypass the distributors and sell directly to retailers, as he had done at Clorox. The benefits, he reasoned, were too good to pass up: higher margins, better market intelligence, and, most important, he says, "the guarantee that your reps aren't also selling competitive product."

The move was risky, expensive, and unprecedented. "Who are you to think you can change the rules of the industry?" demanded Valentine at the board meeting in which Probst outlined his proposal. But Probst promised that it would work, and EA began to put a sales network in place, one store at a time. The distributors howled, but at a board meeting six months later, Probst reported better orders. Today, EA deals directly with 20,000 retail outlets, even those that are part of a national chain—a unique strategy among gamemakers. Instead of shipping exclusively to Wal-Mart's (WMT) distribution centers, for example, EA also ships directly to individual Wal-Mart stores as often as three times a week. Ken Williams, former CEO of Sierra Entertainment, which published Leisure Suit Larry, calls EA's sales force "unrivaled and a huge competitive edge."

In the late 1980s, EA stumbled upon another of its key competitive advantages: sports games. The beauty of

FOCUSING WHERE IT COUNTS

Electronic Arts makes games for every platform, but it has built its dominance by emphasizing titles for Sony's PlayStation 2 console and the PC. As well it should: PlayStation 2 titles make up 66 percent of console games sold and 38 percent of all games. The PC is the next-largest platform, with a 26 percent share, and it has the added benefit of stability: It isn't subject to the disruptive hardware upgrades that occur with consoles.

TOP-SELLING GAMES IN 2002, BY PLATFORM

	PLAYSTATION 2	PC
1	Grand Theft Auto 3 (Take-Two)	WarCraft III: Reign of Chaos (Vivendi Universal)
2	**Madden NFL 2002 (EA)**	**The Sims (EA)**
3	**Medal of Honor Frontline (EA)**	**Medal of Honor Allied Assault (EA)**
4	Spider-Man: The Movie (Activision)	**The Sims: Vacation Expansion Pack (EA)**
5	**Final Fantasy X (Square EA)**	Neverwinter Nights (Infogrames)
6	**NCAA Football 2003 (EA)**	Star Wars Jedi Knight II: Jedi Outcast (LucasArts)

	GAMECUBE	XBOX
1	Super Mario Sunshine (Nintendo)	Halo (Microsoft)
2	Super Smash Bros. Melee (Nintendo)	Spider-Man: The Movie (Activision)
3	Sonic Adventure 2: Battle (Sega)	Max Payne (Take-Two)
4	Resident Evil (Capcom)	**James Bond 007: Agent Under Fire (EA)**
5	Spider-Man: The Movie (Activision)	Elder Scrolls III: Morrowind (Bethesda)
6	**James Bond 007: Agent Under Fire (EA)**	WWE Raw (THQ)

Sales are year-to-date, U.S. only. SOURCE: NPD Group, courtesy of EA

these titles is that fans will buy essentially the same program year after year simply to get updated team rosters. EA has been selling sports games since 1989, when John Madden Football first hit the shelves. Since Probst became CEO in 1994—replacing Hawkins, who left to found console and software maker 3DO—EA Sports has grown to 11 franchises, including NBA Live Basketball and FIFA Soccer, and has matured into a virtual annuity, contributing 40 to 45 percent of EA's revenue in any given year. Add in other popular series, such as The Sims and the World War II-themed Medal of Honor, and the share of revenues from such annuities figures to hit 70 percent this year. "In the end," Probst explains, "each year we only have to drive about 30 percent of our revenue with new things."

Minimizing the need for "new things" is no small matter. New games—as opposed to updates of existing games—can take two years and $4 million each to develop, twice the time and money needed just five years ago. For a product like Harry Potter, the license alone can cost as much as $25 million. Most games need to sell at least 400,000 copies to break even. Hits that sell more than 1 million copies are vital, but elusive. In 2001, only seven titles hit that mark—including EA's Madden 2002.

As the stakes climb and costs mount, the industry has gone through spasms of consolidation, leaving fewer independent one- or two-hit companies like Take-Two Interactive (TTWO), the creator of Grand Theft Auto. Meanwhile, a handful of major publishers like EA, Activision (Tony Hawk's Pro Skater, Quake, Star Trek franchises), Nintendo (Zelda, Super Mario, Donkey Kong), and THQ (THQI) (WWE Wrestling, SpongeBob SquarePants, Blue's Clues) swallow up smaller developers and publishers to keep the pipelines flowing.

Few acquisitions, though, have paid off as well as Probst's purchase of Maxis for $125 million in 1997. At the time, that company had a series of popular reality simulation games such as SimCity and SimAnt. Two years later EA translated the format to a single simulated suburban neighborhood and called the game The Sims. The worldwide take since then has been a breathtaking $658 million—and The Sims Online is one of the most eagerly awaited launches in the online world.

For all that has gone right for EA, however, it is not infallible. EA.com, launched in 2000 as an online game hub supported by advertising and subscriptions, ran head-on into the advertising recession. A number of newer online subscription games, such as the sci-fi conspiracy title Majestic, also met with lukewarm reactions. To date, EA.com has lost a cool $368 million. That dotcom experiment could come to a very happy conclusion, of course, if The Sims Online proves to be as big a hit as some industry observers predict.

Even as Probst sorts out the struggling online business, he will also have to prepare for every gamemaker's least favorite event, the rollout of a new generation of game consoles. In the game industry, the hardware is upgraded every five years or so, as inevitable as El Niño, presenting gamemakers with a perilous choice: Bet on the right platform and you can get rich; bet wrong and you're a goner. Two console generations ago, in 1990, the then-new 16-bit platforms, Sega Genesis and Super Nintendo, caught Activision low on suitable titles. Activision filed for Chapter 11 (the company emerged from bankruptcy in 1992). By contrast, when the Sony PlayStation 2, Microsoft Xbox, and Nintendo GameCube appeared in 2000 and 2001, EA bet correctly on the Sony system (see "Focusing Where It Counts.") But when the next generation of consoles appears in 2005, there's no guarantee that EA will be so lucky, and Probst knows it. "We're really paranoid around here," Probst says. "Every time we think we have things figured out, an atomic bomb goes off."

Analysts worry that one such bomb—Grand Theft Auto 3—went off last year and that Probst doesn't appreciate how serious it is. That game, wherein players assume the role of mobsters, kill each other over cocaine, and consort with prostitutes, sold 8 million units in the last year and took in $400 million for its creator, Take-Two. The title's success marked the arrival of the "mature audience." Consider this: 60 percent of the original PlayStation audience was younger than 18; 70 percent of PlayStation 2 users are over 18. M-rated games will account for 15 percent of the market this year, and some analysts predict they will grow to a full 25 percent in the next two to three years.

As if to prove the point, the latest Grand Theft Auto title—GTA: Vice City, which is set among drug lords in a Miami-esque city during the 1980s—is expected to break all sales records. Other publishers are chasing the audience. Acclaim Entertainment (AKLM) released BMX XXX, a sports game that incorporates digital video of strippers (using the company's new "jiggle technology"), while Nintendo (NTDOY), the home of Pokémon, is fielding Eternal Darkness, a gory mystery, and Conker's Bad Fur Day, a South Park-like game starring a foulmouthed squirrel.

EA has published mature-rated games in the past—last year it brought out American McGee's Alice, a twisted version of the Lewis Carroll tale, and Clive Barker's Undying, a horror game—and it will again. But relatively speaking, EA's mature material tends to be tame. "Culturally, our executive team just can't get comfortable with the content in a game like Grand Theft Auto," Probst says. "I think there's a spectrum of M-rated content. We're on the M-light side and [Take-Two is] on the M-dark side." Still, EA has no M-rated games slated for this year, and some analysts say Probst is making a big mistake. "It's totally foolish of Larry to have the view he does of mature-themed games," says Michael Pachter of Wedbush Morgan Securities. Not so, Probst says: "We have an obligation to get EA's share price as high as we can, but that doesn't mean we have to prostitute ourselves or violate our code of ethics."

Indeed not. After all, Probst's role model Disney already addressed a dilemma not unlike EA's and found that it could eat its wholesome apple pie and have some edgy products too. In the early 1990s, when the audience for G-rated movies was shrinking, Disney purchased Miramax, the independent film distributor that had made its mark with sophisticated foreign releases like The Crying Game. Under the Disney aegis, Miramax went on to produce mature fare like the gay-themed Priest and the blood-soaked Pulp Fiction, adding hundreds of millions of dollars to Disney's top line—without any apparent damage to its brand image.

That lesson hasn't been lost on Probst. Earlier this year he toyed with buying Take-Two but rejected it. He's not ready to venture that deeply into M territory. But it's still reasonable to expect him to spend some of EA's cash to branch into other forms of entertainment. While industry analysts guess that EA will buy back stock (as says James Lin of Jeffries & Co.) or snap up more game-development houses (as Mike Wallace of UBS suggests), Probst is thinking hard about Disney. "They have the world's most impressive catalog of intellectual property," he notes, "and they have found ways to exploit that intellectual property in more forms than you could have ever imagined."

So how would EA exploit its own bank of intellectual property? Probst won't speculate beyond games, but Bing Gordon will: "In 10 years EA will unquestionably be in entertainment fields other than videogaming." EA's 2,500-strong internal studio is actually twice as big as Disney's animation group, and, Gordon notes, it includes a small army of accomplished Hollywood-expat musicians, writers, animators, and special-effects experts who have worked on movies like Shrek and Titanic—"the guys who know how to make bit hits." Gordon says EA will probably start producing game soundtrack CDs; music videos that tie into EA games are another possibility. And he even hints that EA could someday form a digital animated movie studio à la Pixar. Walt himself would be proud.

"Could This Be the Next Disney?," *Business 2.0,* Dec 2002/Jan 2003, p. 110–118.

THE DELL WAY

Michael Dell's famous business model made his company the world's premier computer maker. Now he's branching into new fields and taking on virtually every other hardware manufacturer. Can "the Model" stand the strain?

By Kathryn Jones

AT DELL THEY CALL IT, SIMPLY, "THE MODEL."

You can see it in action inside the Topfer Manufacturing Center, a squat, white factory a few miles south of Dell Computer's headquarters campus in Round Rock, Texas. The newest of Dell's seven plants worldwide, it is cavernous—big enough to enclose five and a half football fields—and a blur of activity: Market domination in motion. Boxes of Intel (INTC) microchips and electronic components from Taiwan and Korea skitter by on double-decker conveyor belts. Workers read orders off a monitor and assemble a new Dell OptiPlex desktop computer every three to five minutes. The finished boxes, more than 25,000 on a typical day, then trundle off on other conveyors to be shipped directly to customers. The whole fandango is choreographed so tightly that the factory rarely needs more than two hours' worth of parts inventory. Two hours. Parts storage takes up roughly the space of an ordinary bedroom.

Nobody, but nobody, makes computer hardware more efficiently than Dell. Operating costs soaked up just 10 percent of Dell's $35 billion in revenue last year, compared with 21 percent of revenue at Hewlett-Packard (HPQ), 25 percent at Gateway (GTW), and 46 percent at Cisco (CSCO). No unnecessary costs: This is an all-but-sacred mandate of the famous "Dell direct" business model. No inventory, no middlemen to eat into profits, no agenda other than giving the customer what he or she wants. Crucially, the Dell model also insists on no more than minimal spending on research and development (1.3 percent of revenues last year, compared with 15 percent at Intel and Microsoft) and no proprietary technology of the company's own. The goal is to offer computers at irresistible prices—and to leave the cost and the risks of innovating to others.

In other words, the Dell model allowed the company to reinvent the PC industry—without inventing anything.

Now the Model faces its biggest challenge.

Dell is moving into markets where it has never been before. In some of these new fields, Dell's PC success has opened doors; in others, the company is starting from scratch. In one market, success has nothing to do with Dell's specialty of cranking out good hardware at great prices but instead hinges on providing that ephemeral thing known as services. Every inch of the way, the Model is being challenged, tweaked, tested, and pounded on. And surprisingly, its defenders say, the thing is stronger than ever.

On a December morning, Michael Dell, eponymous founder, multibillionaire, and at the ripe old age of 37 the longest-tenured CEO of any U.S. PC maker, is trying to put all this into a simple metaphor. "Some people say we're like Wal-Mart," he ventures. Dell seems to find the comparison distasteful, but it's not far off. Starting with $1,000 in seed money in 1984, the company has grown from its founder's University of Texas freshman dorm room into a force that, like the Bentonville, Ark., behemoth, dominates its industry. Dell is No. 1 in desktop PCs, No. 1 in the United States in low-end servers, and the country's No. 1 Internet retailer. The PC industry sank into the worst slump in its history 18 months ago, but Dell's revenues have nevertheless grown 14 percent to more than $35 billion, and the company is on track to earn $2 billion this year, even as its competitors run hundreds of millions of dollars in the red.

No wonder shareholders regard the Model as just short of Revelation. As of mid-December they were willing to pay 36 times earnings to own a share, a sign that they expect gangbuster growth for years to come. To Michael Dell and his right-hand man, president and chief operating officer Kevin Rollins, it is clear that those expectations can't be met with profits from PCs alone.

So, like Wal-Mart (WMT), Dell has had to expand into new businesses. During the past 18 months, the company has announced its entry into a host of new fields: network switches, PDAs, and printers, as well as the sophisticated hardware at the heart of corporate computing networks. Says Dell: "The best way to describe us now is as a broad computer systems and services company."

With the territory, however, comes a whole new set of enemies. Dell isn't just competing against the floundering

(Cont.)

The Wisdom of Chairman Dell

Michael on "the Model"

"All technologies, over time, commoditize."
The IBM PC started out as a unique product, until cloners like Compaq sprang up, driving prices down relentlessly. DVD players took off once the price dropped below $200—and the resulting economies of scale lowered prices further. Dell believes all technological products will eventually follow a similar path.

"Standards-based hardware and software is the future of the data center."
The main standard he's talking about is the Wintel duopoly. Just as Microsoft (MSFT) Windows and Intel processors took over the desktop PC and low-end server markets, Dell expects them to continue their march into the "data center"—back-office operations of corporations.

"Be direct."
Dell's PC-making competitors sold their wares through retailers and resellers, which required them to produce months' worth of inventory and kept them at arm's length from consumers. Dell uses direct customer relationships to keep a lid on costs and stay in tune with buyers' desires.

"There are two kinds of research in our industry—the kind that actually benefits the customer and the kind that doesn't."
Dell engineers have filed almost 1,000 patents, but they tend to be for process improvements, not product innovations. Dell contends that most R&D helps companies develop proprietary technology that locks customers in, instead of actually making their products better.

"If you have high margins, that means you have this big, soft underbelly."
Most businessmen like healthy margins, Dell included. His move into the enterprise market is fueled by a quest for higher margins. But Dell has succeeded over the years by making his margins thinner than the competition's and relying on pumping up volume. He sees a rival's high margins as an invitation to attack it by drastically undercutting its prices.

"Dell is all about improving the value-chain cycle."
The company's physical factories and virtual data warehouses have transcended the prosaic supply chain; what he now calls the "value chain" still moves computers and parts around the world more cheaply and efficiently than anyone else can. But more important, it offers perfectly transparent information about sales, orders, and shipments to employees, customers, and suppliers.

PC industry. Now it's Dell against everyone who's left. Already competitors are talking trash. "Look at where they came from and where they want to go," says Tim Dougherty, director of strategy for IBM's server group. "Expertise in enterprise computing is not in Dell's skill set." Mike Winkler, HP's chief marketing officer, predicts that his company's archrival has finally overextended. "The closest analogy," he says, "is Napoleon's invasion of Russia."

Michael Dell has heard all that before. Competitors once dismissed him as an underage computer geek who'd never amount to anything against the likes of Compaq and IBM, and clucked that Dell's direct model could never move off the desktop into the complex world of corporate computing. Both predictions were wrong. The point is, Dell says, that the Model, like the company, is broader than people give it credit for. "We have a pretty simple system," he says. "The most important thing is to satisfy our customers. The second most important is to be profitable. If we don't do the first one well, the second one won't happen."

MOVING IN FROM THE EDGE: SERVERS

Opportunity: $50 billion
Competitors: HP, IBM, Sun

Until the mid-1990s, Dell existed almost exclusively at the edges of business computing, its desktop PCs and laptops the last stop between the information core of an enterprise and its employees. Now Dell wants a much larger share of the industrial-strength hardware at the heart of corporate systems, where the stakes—and the profit margins—are higher. These are the machines on which entire businesses rise and fall.

In the mid-1990s, Dell took its first steps in from the desktop, tackling low-end servers, $5,000 to $25,000 machines just powerful enough to serve up webpages or run small-office e-mail systems. Like PCs, they ran Microsoft Windows on Intel chips, and Dell could build them cheaper than anyone. "When it comes to assembling servers, we enjoy all the same advantages from our procurement, logistics, and manufacturing capabilities as we do making PCs," says Randy Groves, vice president and general manager of Dell's enterprise systems group. Dell's enterprise revenues, almost nonexistent in 1994, accounted for 13 percent of the company's total intake in 1998. Three years later Dell passed Compaq as the top provider of Intel-based servers, with 31 percent of the market.

There is more at work here than the tendency of recession-squeezed IT managers to choose a cheaper alternative. Many of the servers that Dell replaced ran on proprietary technology, like IBM's Power4 microprocessors or various proprietary flavors of the Unix operating system. If you wanted upgrades or new applications, you had little choice but to get them from the manufacturer. Dell's model eschews these arrangements, which the founder calls "proprietary prisons." Instead, Dell machines stick with the de facto industry standards, like Intel microprocessors and Windows or Linux operating systems, which don't lock users into any particular hardware.

That was a key selling feature to Jeff Davis, a senior systems programmer at the oil company Amerada Hess (AHC), where he runs a cluster of several hundred Dell workstations to model undersea geological features in search of oil deposits. Although Dell is his vendor of choice, he likes the fact that the company's machines are built from standardized parts, so he can mix and match boxes from a variety of vendors to hold down his costs. "We can pretty much pick a vendor based entirely on the merits," he says, "and on whether they've got the right price." He spends $300,000 a year upgrading and maintaining the cluster of workstations; they replace an IBM supercomputer that cost $1.5 million a year to lease and operate.

In the Dell model, sticking with industry standards is not simply a matter of building customer goodwill. It's more like obeying the Second Law of Thermodynamics: You don't really have a choice. "In the long run, all technology tends toward low-cost standards," Dell explains. The Model is predicated on it. After all, in a world dominated by standard platforms, the hardware running the platform becomes a commodity, and the most important reason to choose one vendor over another is price. And when it comes to price, Dell can compete with anyone.

LAND WITHOUT STANDARDS: STORAGE SYSTEMS

Opportunity: $22 billion
Competitors: EMC, Hitachi, HP

Having made inroads into servers, the next logical step for Dell was into storage systems, the advanced computers that house an enterprise's most crucial data. But in contrast to the PC and server industries, there are no standard storage technologies, and Dell floundered as it tried to apply the Model. The company first tried unsuccessfully to develop a system in-house but quickly realized that it didn't have the expertise. It then tried reselling other companies' systems. In a rare acquisition, Dell purchased network storage specialist ConvergeNet Technologies for

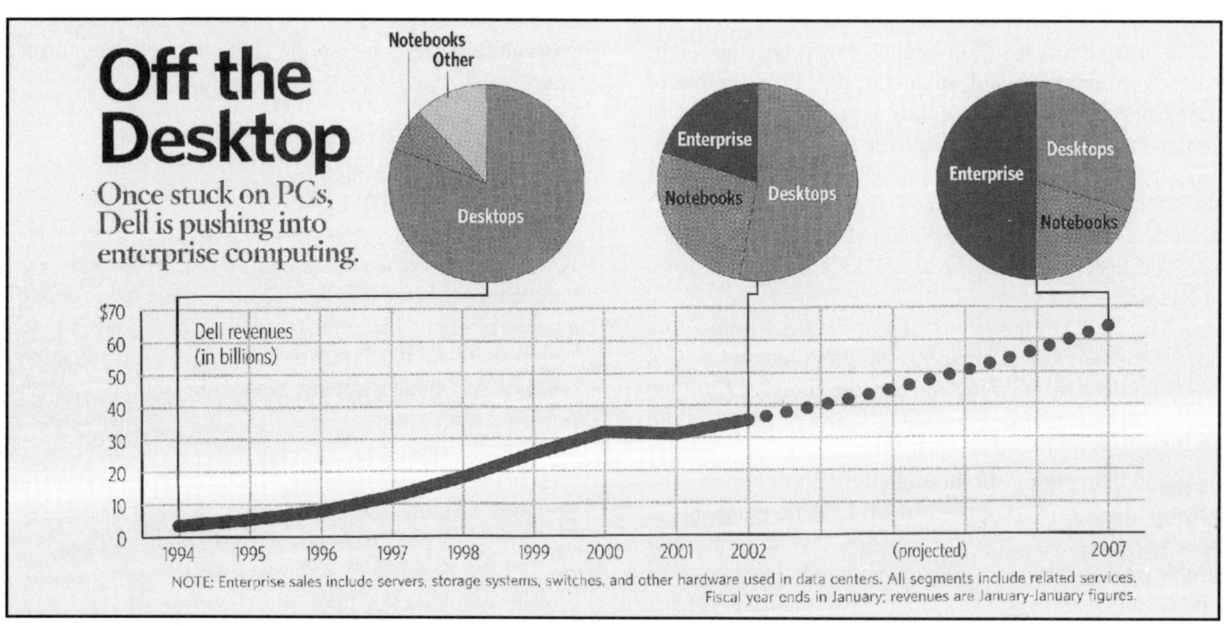

(Cont.)

The Way Here

Dell has always had doubters.
So far, they've always been wrong.

1984

Michael Dell founds PC's Limited, the forerunner of Dell Computer.

1988

Initial public offering of Dell stock: 3.5 million shares at $8.50 each (9 cents, adjusted for splits).

"Dell has just about tapped out the mail-order business." *Technologic PC Letter" editor Richard Schaffer,* ***1998***

1993

Dell becomes one of the top five computer system makers worldwide. It starts selling its machines in Japan.

1996

Customers begin buying Dell computers over the Internet at www.dell.com.

1997

Dell opens a production and sales center in Xiamen, China. In 1999, Dell is ranked No. 6 in China in PC shipments. By September 2002 it eclipses IBM as the top foreign PC seller. (Domestic PC maker Legend still outsells it 6 to 1.)

"You can't sit on your laurels. You must keep moving forward, and that is where Michael Dell is falling down." *Compaq CEO Eckhard Pfeiffer,* ***1993***

1999

Dell grabs the top spot in the U.S. PC market.

2000

Dell stock hits its all-time high of $58.13 a share in March.

2001

Dell overtakes Compaq in worldwide PC and U.S. server sales. It loses both leads when Compaq announces plans to merge with HP.

"Dell has a great business model, but that dog won't scale." *John Shoemaker, head of Sun's (SUNW) server division,* ***2000***

2002

Dataquest reports that Dell has reclaimed the top spots in both worldwide PC and U.S. server sales from the merged HP-Compaq.

$332 million in 1999, only to find that ConvergeNet's elegant but complex technology made a poor fit with Dell's commodity-producer business model. Within a few years, Dell had written off the entire investment.

In October 2001, Dell accepted that the closest thing to a standard was the systems built by industry leader EMC (EMC), and agreed to co-market its midrange ($30,000 to $500,000) Clariion storage systems until 2006. The deal brought EMC a partner in a sector where it had been hard-pressed by Compaq; Dell got into a key enterprise market without the cost of (any further) R&D. The partners say the deal is working: They've added 1,500 customers so far.

As Dell ponders the lessons of jumping into a sector without clear standards, the storage industry seems gradually to be moving exactly as the Model would predict. Standards are winding their deliberate way through industry committees, but in the meantime, the technology is taking matters into its own hands and loosening the hold of proprietary systems. New technologies that link small devices to storage networks are beginning to replace the proprietary big iron of companies like EMC. If cheap networked boxes become the storage standard, Dell is the logical winner. Indeed, in a December survey conducted by investment research group ChangeWave, 17 percent of Dell's current corporate clients said they expected to buy Dell storage systems in the next six months.

LOOKING TO SUPERSIZE: NETWORKING

Opportunity: $13 billion
Competitors: Cisco, Enterasys, Nortel, 3Com

In the networking world, Dell's natural targets are the routers and switches that shunt information through corporate networks. Here, Dell is moving more cautiously. Its sole offering in the category is its PowerConnect switch family, so-called Layer 2 devices, the simplest, most commodity-like of their kind. At $20 per port, their positioning is all about price. (According to the Yankee Group, Cisco's entry in Layer 2 costs $100 per port, while a 3Com switch costs $38.) So far, most sales have been add-ons to other deals, a tactic that Dave Smith, 3Com's vice president for sales and service, derides as the "Want fries with that?" ploy. "If you buy a bunch of servers," Smith says, "they'll ask, 'Want some networking gear to go with that?'" Still, Smith is taking Dell seriously: He has instituted a "Match Dell" program, in which 3Com grants its resellers discounts of as much as 25 percent in return for their offering 3Com goods at prices that match Dell's.

Many analysts say Dell will have trouble moving beyond basic networking hardware. While standard protocols like Ethernet determine how data flows through networks, the software and chips that distinguish the smartest switches from the rest are jealously proprietary. To challenge Cisco in higher-end equipment, Dell would have to build its own, and that would be folly, says Jim Slaby, an analyst at the Giga Information Group. "You'd have to duplicate 15 years of software development and thousands of man-years of R&D. It would be like creating a word processor to compete with Microsoft Word."

But big R&D investments are not part of the Model anyway. And as is happening in storage, the industry's leaders could well be on the verge of losing their proprietary grip on networking hardware. Intel and Broadcom are building instructions into networking chips that make the equivalent of years of R&D available to any interested hardware maker. Dell is waiting.

THE HUMAN TOUCH: SERVICES

Opportunity: $350 billion
Competitors: Accenture, HP, IBM, others

Perhaps Dell's biggest enterprise challenge lies in applying the Model to services. The company has a big services group—some 8,000 employees strong—and Dell sees it playing an expanding role in future growth. But how? Everyone from IBM to the newly independent consulting arms of disgraced accounting firms wants in on the $350 billion IT consulting game. And at first blush, the Model offers no real competitive edge. "Dell has amazing production efficiencies," says Gary Chapman, head of the 21st Century Project at the University of Texas at Austin. "But managing a workforce of consultants is a whole different thing. It's much easier to control costs when you're only dealing with widgets."

But when asked whether Dell can do in services what it did in PCs, Kevin Rollins says, "Absolutely." The Model isn't just about making cheap boxes; it's also about freeing customers from overpriced relationships. "Our direct model has basic principles: Don't let anyone come between us and the customer. Keep clear communication, and no extra costs." Those tenets apply even when Dell is selling services, Rollins says, and they enable the company to give service customers a better experience than the competition. That is an opportunity Dell is programmed to seize.

There's a difference, though, between principles and experience—particularly in services, where knowledge is the only asset that counts. There's no reason to suppose that mere principles can make Dell a success when it's literally years behind its competitors.

No reason but one: Betting against Dell has been a fool's errand for nearly 20 years. And if the company succeeds in dominating enterprise services as it has dominated PCs—well, Rollins will have been right. It must have been part of the Model all along.

"The Dell Way," *Business 2.0,* Feb 2003, p. 60–66.

Think Nevada, Think Haven for Daredevils

BY CHRISTINA BINKLEY

Nevada is trying to turn to its advantage one of its less-than-flattering features: thousands of miles of desolate desert.

Figuring that it can't compete with the likes of Colorado and Wyoming when it comes to luring nature lovers, Nevada hopes to entice sand surfers, rock climbers and other diehard adventurers to its arid reaches through a new $1.5 million print-ad campaign. The pitch to potential visitors: "A nice quiet place to get in touch with your inner masochist. . . . Ready to get medieval?"

No false advertising there. Nevada's 70.2 million acres are the driest in the nation and the most rugged, with 314 separate mountain ranges. Most of the state is uninhabited. In decades past, these characteristics allegedly put the state's deserts in competition with New York's East River as the preferred dumping ground for mob corpses. A current federal proposal would make rural Nevada a prime depository for nuclear waste.

The ads, which describe Nevada as "a primal playground with more . . . tear-yourself-to-shreds terrain than any other place in this great nation," feature unshaven, decidedly not pretty men, in a state of howling or panting. Developed for the Nevada Commission on Tourism, the ads are set to begin running in coming weeks in adventure magazines such as Outside, National Geographic Adventurer and Blue. They also will run in Western newspapers to reach nearby drive-in markets.

The tourism commission didn't initially set out to tout Nevada's barrenness. The agency has been running "Discover the other side of Nevada" campaigns for 15 years in its mission to get visitors to look past the glitz of Las Vegas and Reno and move on to the state's rural reaches.

But the panel's ad agency, Las Vegas-based **R&R Partners,** got discouraging news last year when it ran 16 focus groups in places including Phoenix and Portland, Ore. For one thing, plenty of states play up their Old West flavor—and many of those are more visually appealing than Nevada. Few people gave Nevada credit for its own pristine wilderness. Shown photos of beautiful Nevada scenery, the focus groups insisted the shots were taken in other states like Wyoming and Utah.

A hiker howls *in the desert in an ad extolling Nevada's arid ruggedness.*

Rather than argue that Nevada isn't just a wasteland, the agency settled on an altogether different tactic: It decided to embrace the state's bleakness. "OK, it may not be for everyone," acknowledges Tim O'Brien, R&R's creative director.

What Mr. O'Brien is banking on is that those who do find the message appealing will prove to be big spenders. A 1997 study by the Travel Industry Association found that adventure travelers have average household incomes of $49,000, compared with $42,200 for the population as a whole. The harder core they are, the more they seem to spend. The study reported that "soft adventurers," who favor activities such as camping and skiing, spent an average of $820 per trip, while "hard" adventurers—who hang glide, kayak and rock climb—spent $1,275.

Still, it's a long haul to take public perceptions from total wasteland to daredevil haven. In the focus groups, in fact, "very few people thought of us as an adventure state," says Bruce Bommarito, the tourism commission's executive director. He says hardly anyone knows of areas such as Nevada's Ruby Mountains, which must be reached by foot or horseback, or the Blackrock Desert, where people windsurf on wheeled vehicles.

To shoot ads that would appeal to adventurers, the agency hit the road for nearly a month last September and October. They hired just one professional model—the only woman who appears in the ads. Mostly, the group grabbed anyone they could persuade to pose.

Thus, R&R's balding Mr. O'Brien makes an appearance as an exhausted mountain biker in one ad. "I'm not a pretty boy," he concedes. Even the photographer's Norwegian assistant is featured. He appears shirtless, clad in a rabbit-fur hat that Mr. O'Brien once bought in Russia, with his head thrown back in mid-howl. "You are not well," the caption reads.

That one went too far for some on the Tourism Commission. The parched terrain and the unshaven visage of the fur-hatted Norwegian reminded several panel members of photos they have seen out of Afghanistan. Concerned it might offend some people, they decided to hold that ad for several months until Americans become less sensitive about the search for terrorists and members of Afghanistan's former Taliban regime. "We're a commission," Mr. Bommarito notes, "and we're subject to some politics."

eBay's Secret Ingredient

If your customers gladly held your inventory, shipped your products, and did all your marketing, you'd make money online too. Only question: Can eBay keep growing and not destroy the social capital that is its unique competitive advantage?

By: Erick Schonfeld

After all these years, Lu Matis, a housewife in Flemington, N.J., has finally figured out how to "monetize eyeballs" on the Internet. Her secret? She sells them on eBay (*EBAY*). Glass eyeballs, that is, handblown and hand-painted by German artisans at the end of the 19th century and kept as prosthetic inventory in doctors' offices. Matis got 700 of them a year and a half ago from a dealer for about $7 a pop, but on eBay they fetch anywhere from $20 for a brown eye to $40 for a blue, gray, or green one. "I pay my son's college this way," Matis says. "They are gory to look at, but once you realize the work involved, it is like having a piece of Tiffany glass." Her customers range from collectors to jewelry makers to a guy who glued them to his steering wheel. "Where else could you possibly sell these?" she asks.

Matis's ocular oddities are proof positive that eBay has come a long way on its quest, as CEO Meg Whitman explains it, "to build the world's largest online trading platform where practically anyone can trade practically anything." eBay has gone well beyond collectible Elvis prints and Beanie Babies—or glass eyeballs, for that matter. A motorcycle is sold on eBay every 18 minutes, a laptop every 30 seconds, and a book every 4 seconds. You can buy time-shares in Hawaii, restaurant equipment, gardening tools, or your pick of goods in 18,000 other categories. eBay traded $9 billion worth of goods in 2001—equivalent to roughly 20 percent of all consumer e-commerce that year. More than $1 billion of that total was estimated to come from autos alone, a category that did not even exist on eBay two years ago.

"If you had asked me in September 1998 [when eBay went public] if eBay would be in the used-car business, I would have said no," Whitman observes. Today, eBay is the largest online seller not just of autos and collectibles but also of computers, photo equipment and supplies, and sporting goods. To further promote the brand, it is developing with Sony a TV show profiling eBay users and the items they buy on the site. It is beginning to attract larger corporate sellers such as Disney (*DIS*), IBM (*IBM*), and Home Depot (*HD*). And the company is expanding internationally, with operations in 18 countries. In 1999, for instance, eBay Germany reached only 6 percent of the country's Internet users. Now, one out of every four German Web surfers visits the site. Back when she was gearing up for the IPO, Whitman would tell investors that she was going after a $100 million slice of the U.S. collectibles market. Today she estimates the size of the markets that eBay addresses at $1.7 trillion.

At one level, this success is easily explained. eBay has come closer than any other creation of the Internet boom to realizing the promise of the virtual corporation. With no inventory, no warehouses, and no sales force, eBay's electronic bazaar, run properly, is a profit-spewing machine.

Far less understood, however, is the invisible fuel that powers that machine: eBay's unique ability to attract vast amounts of what economists call social capital. The rest of us might call it trust, or goodwill, or credibility. Whatever you call this resource, eBay, in its vast community of buyers and sellers, deploys more of it than almost any company in memory. Social capital is what enables eBay to harness the creativity of the millions of entrepreneurs on its site striving to meet the most capricious demands of the even more numerous buyers who also congregate there. eBay's own customers do much of the company's work, bringing it countless new products and marketing techniques, picking up shipping costs, handling customer service. The high octane of eBay's social capital explains how, even in a down economy, with its dotcom brethren wounded and dying, eBay nearly doubled its profits in 2001 to $90 million. Revenues—bolstered by healthy online Christmas shopping—were $750 million, or equivalent to about 8 percent of the value of all the goods that were traded on its site. By 2005 the company expects to be raking in $3 billion in revenues and $1 billion in operating profits.

But getting there is far from a sure thing. To reach that goal, the company will have to more than triple the number of its registered buyers and sellers to 150 million. Yet some of the very steps eBay is taking to drive growth and keep its stock at a lofty price/earnings ratio of about 80 (on 2002 estimates) are straining the vital bonds between the company and its core customers. Out in the eBay community, it turns out, it's hard work to keep the social fabric from tearing.

As has been well chronicled, eBay takes advantage of the low communication and transaction costs of the Internet to bring its buyers and sellers together. The company takes a commission—typically 1 to 5 percent—on every trade on its electronic exchange; the rest of its revenues come from listing fees and other charges. eBay is considered the classic example of a company benefiting from so-called network effects. The more buyers who go to eBay, the more sellers they attract, who in turn draw even more buyers as the site becomes a larger source of supply with more competitive prices. This positive feedback loop magnifies the volume of trade on the site, and thus revenues to eBay, while making it increasingly difficult for other auction sites to survive.

But there is more to it than that. "eBay's business is so new that it's not well understood," says Rajiv Dutta, eBay's chief financial officer. "There is an enormous amount of subtlety and complexity underneath." eBay, according to Dutta and other eBay executives, is not so much a conventional company as a self-regulating, complex system. And indeed, eBay has few of the characteristics typical of traditional corporations—especially rival retailers such as Wal-Mart. "We have no real cost of goods, and customer acquisition is largely driven by word of mouth," Dutta says. Wal-Mart has nearly $16 billion in long-term debt; eBay has virtually none. Free of many of the costs that almost every other corporation must bear, eBay's business throws off an increasing amount of cash, reflected in operating margins that have gone from slightly negative in 1999 to 19 percent in 2001. (Wal-Mart's operating margin is about 5 percent.) Dutta expects operating margins to hit 30 to 35 percent by 2005, which is how he gets to that $1 billion operating-profit target.

Such an achievement would be pretty spectacular, but it cannot be reached on the strengths of new-wave financials alone. Social capital is the crucial hidden asset that could make it possible. The forms of capital that most people are familiar with are physical (stores, factories, machinery), human (education, skills, expertise), and financial (cash, debt, equity). Social capital flows from social relationships—things like membership in old boys' networks, trust, reputation, and social norms that allow people to do more work (such as coffee breaks). eBay's network effects are an extremely valuable form of social capital, but there are others. What eBay has figured out how to do is tap into the social capital created on its site by the millions of people who trade there, and convert it into profits.

One source of eBay's social capital is its feedback system, whereby buyers and sellers can rate each other. People need such confidence-building mechanisms to buy stuff from faceless strangers. Negative feedback is posted very rarely (less than 1 percent of the time, according to a study by University of Michigan economist Paul Resnick), but sellers are afraid of getting any negative comments and go to great lengths to avoid them. It's not uncommon for sellers to be brutally honest about their wares, going so far as to describe every nick and scratch. "Every time you get a negative feedback, your sales go down," says Howard Getz, who does 600 auctions a week in collectibles such as Barbie dolls and *Star Wars* figures. Displaying a buyer's negative comment by a seller's name is like letting a disgruntled customer leave a sign in a store for all subsequent customers to see.

Like other kinds of capital, social capital earns a return. One of the unique ways it pays off at eBay is in the thousands of small pricing and product selection innovations its members make that keep eBay's merchandising always in tune with the whims of the economy. "No single company could react as quickly as our millions of users do," Whitman explains. MIT economist Erik Brynjolfsson concurs: "If you had a central purchasing department, you would not have all the creativity that the millions of people have who are posting on eBay trying to meet unmet needs and develop products that might otherwise have gone unnoticed." Glass eyeballs, unused vacation real estate, even packing supplies for other eBay sellers—eBay users create markets where none existed before. They then absorb expenses, such as inventory, marketing, and shipping, that eBay itself would have to eat if it were a conventional company. Users even help out with customer support, as anyone who has ever visited an eBay discussion board knows. "Here you have people who are volunteering their time," notes Dan Ariely, a behavioral economist at MIT. "That is the amazing thing."

To keep the community of users happy, Whitman and her lieutenants spend a lot of time listening to their customers and observing trends on the site. Every morning, for example, Whitman is handed a report excerpting comments posted on eBay's discussion boards. And the company regularly conducts intense all-day focus groups, called Voices, with representative buyers and sellers.

The most important way that eBay manages its marketplace, however, is by organizing itself as a collection of startups. Each major category (books, collectibles, music, real estate, tickets) has its own manager. So does every country (eBay runs the number one auction sites in Australia, Britain, Canada, France, and Germany, among other nations). These managers are the stewards of the social capital on their turf. They must be experts in their particular markets and make sure nothing impedes trade there.

They are also responsible for the growth of their niches. When they notice that activity around certain items, such as tickets or automobiles, is growing organically, they signal up the chain that it's time to carve out a new category. "We decide to expand the trading platform based on where users want to go," Whitman explains.

Sometimes, that is away from auctions. So eBay is adding fixed-price components to its site as well, an unabashed challenge to Amazon's (*AMZN*) business. In 2000, eBay acquired Half.com, a fixed-price online store for discounted commodity goods that is being integrated into the regular eBay site. "Half.com is bringing the Amazon buyer into person-to-person trading," says Jeff Jordan, head of eBay's U.S. operations. And about 45 percent of all eBay auctions now have a "Buy It Now" button that lets the first bidder end the auction by agreeing to a preset price. All told, about 19 percent of sales on eBay are now fixed-price rather than auction.

One of the most promising avenues for future growth hinges on eBay's ability to court a whole new class of customers: big corporations. Disney, IBM, and Home Depot, among others, are dipping their toes into eBay's market for discontinued goods, excess inventory, and returned items. Even Dell (*DELL*), which arguably does not need any help with online commerce, sells refurbished off-lease PCs on eBay. It's just another sales channel. Governments are getting into the act too. Seventeen state governments, up from zero in 1998, are using eBay to liquidate foreclosed assets.

The giant sellers are proceeding cautiously and so far account for less than 3 percent of eBay sales. But eBay is working on them—and urging them to expand their offerings to the types of fixed-price, in-season items that make up the bulk of the economy. In a pitch to the Gap clothing chain, for instance, eBay would say, "We have 10,000 Gap items on eBay right now, so whether you like it or not, we are a channel." Or, as eBay marketing VP Bill Cobb likes to tell reluctant corporate sellers, "We have the technology, the marketplace, and the buyers. Why are you going to do it on your own? Nobody visits your site."

Disney uses eBay to auction collector's items such as ride vehicles from its theme parks, animation cels, and movie props. Recently a statuette used by animators during the making of the film *Monsters, Inc.* went for $3,556. "We create archival items every time a park or a new movie opens," says George Grobar, the head of auctions for Disney's Internet group. Many of the objects used to end up in landfills, but by using eBay, Grobar says, Disney can sell them cost-effectively—and generate promotional buzz.

IBM has gone further. By selling mainly laptops that are reaching the end of their product cycle for about $1,000 each, Big Blue has become eBay's single largest seller (although it accounts for less than 0.1 percent of the site's total sales). The computer giant is finding that rather than stealing sales from IBM.com or other channels, eBay auctions are bringing new clients into the IBM tent. Some 79 percent of its eBay customers—half of which are small businesses—are new to IBM. "We see eBay as an incredible growth engine for us," says IBM.com auction manager Paul Canham. Indeed. Canham's sales on eBay are growing more than 40 percent per *month.*

But the question remains: Will the forces pulling eBay in so many different directions undermine its social capital? After huge surges in 1999 and 2000, eBay's listings growth (a major contributor to revenues) has slowed dramatically. To meet its dramatic financial goals, eBay must continue to expand aggressively into new categories, geographies, formats, and customer types. But the faster eBay grows, the greater the risk to its social capital.

There are already signs that its expansionary strategies are beginning to alienate existing users. For instance, one of the basic principles that eBay has tried to maintain is neutrality. The company avoids taking sides between buyers and sellers whenever possible. That is what the feedback system is for. But the Switzerland stance increasingly does not wash with the people who are the source of all of eBay's revenues: the sellers. The most vocal are those who sell more than $2,000 a month on eBay, known as Powersellers.

Eric McKenna of Pittsburgh quit his sales job at a paging company about two years ago to sell guitars on eBay for $500 to $3,500 apiece. When he had a problem with a deadbeat buyer and wanted eBay to yank him from the site, customer service reps kept explaining to him that they could not do that, and that eBay was a social phenomenon where different rules applied. "I don't want any of your socialistic b.s.," McKenna would tell supervisor after supervisor. "You are a company. I am a goddamn Powerseller! I am paying you 1,000 bucks a month, and I want service." To eBay's credit, the deadbeat was finally barred from the site. But if McKenna wants preferential treatment from eBay for his BoogieStreet Guitars, imagine what IBM will want.

eBay insists that it will maintain a level playing field. "Our vision of eBay consists of a marketplace where your

(Cont.)

next-door neighbor can compete side by side with large corporations," Whitman says. Indeed, if you search for IBM laptops, you will see IBM's listings alongside auctions from other sellers. From the prominence of the listings, it's impossible to tell which are the next-door neighbors and which is the $86 billion corporation.

The level playing field approach, however, can create another problem. If customers stop benefiting from the relationships they make through eBay, all of the company's accumulated social capital goes out the window. In the original collectibles and antiques categories, for instance, eBay has created such an efficient market that average selling prices have declined 30 percent during the past year, according to the Internet Antique Shop. Gary Sohmers, an appraiser on *Antiques Road Show* and Boston radio host who has been selling pop culture collectibles online for years, is not happy about this trend. He says of dealers' feelings for eBay: "We all hate it. They leveled the playing field, but unfortunately they leveled it underwater."

Another uproar centered on the controversial checkout feature that eBay introduced last fall, which automatically exchanges information between the buyer and seller after an auction. eBay says it is meant to standardize the old procedure, in which buyers and sellers e-mailed one another after an auction to arrange delivery and payment. But many sellers despised the imposed feature, not only because they felt it was clumsy but also because they thought that eBay was trying to come between them and their customers—a violation of the social compact. "I was mad as a wet hen," says Frances Neale, a seller of used books on eBay. eBay responded to sellers' concerns by making the feature optional, but Neale still sees the new checkout system as symptomatic of eBay's larger push to embrace corporate sellers and to further automate the interaction between customers. "I think they want to be the complete system for the large brick-and-mortar companies that want to be on the Web," she speculates.

eBay would be wise to quash that fear quickly. The company derives much of its social capital from the fact that its site is a place where people transact with people, not with large, impersonal corporations. The irony is that, so far, the corporations on eBay are typically the ones adjusting the way they do business. Buyers are just so much more demanding on eBay. Winning bidders expect an e-mail response the next day, not in six weeks, and shipping had better not cost half as much as the entire product.

Some observers argue that eBay could afford to be at least a little less solicitous of its buyers and sellers (as a recent price hike demonstrates). After all, where else are they going to go? But the company knows deep down that its future hinges on figuring out how to continue to grow and appeal to multiple constituents without depleting its crucial social capital. At one recent Voices focus group attended by people who trade in autographs, car stereos, and Renaissance gowns, Jordan acknowledged that "the challenge is expanding eBay to car stereos and all the other things you sell without leaving behind the core." Indeed, the difficulty of relying on a resource that does not appear on your balance sheet is that you won't know it is missing until it is already gone.

"Ebay's Secret Ingredient," *Business 2.0,* Mar 2002, p. 52–58.

Finding Target Market Opportunities

BILL HAS DESIGNS ON YOUR WRIST
Microsoft's Spot: Clever technology but goofy gizmos

It was 2 in the morning a year ago, and Microsoft Corp. Chairman William H. Gates III was still banging out e-mails. That's nothing strange, but instead of operating systems or game consoles, he was focusing on technology of a smaller and humbler order: refrigerator magnets, watches, and key chains. Gates was prodding his developers to turn scads of such gadgets into tiny information devices. He shot them such ideas as how users could get horoscopes and lottery numbers transmitted to their watches.

Not all of Gates's ideas made the cut. But on Jan. 8, he unveiled prototypes of a host of new smart devices at the Consumer Electronics Show in Las Vegas. Microsoft's idea is to equip all sorts of gear to receive gobs of information via FM radio waves. The first gizmo: a new take on a Dick Tracy-like watch that can be set to track such things as stocks and traffic snarls. Other items in the lab are refrigerator magnets that display up-to-the-minute sports scores and alarm clocks that ring extra early when commute traffic is a mess. Some of the ideas sound downright silly, but Gates insists the possibilities of the technology are "just mind-blowing."

The technology that makes this possible is Spot (Smart Personal Objects Technology). The breakthrough uses a chip developed by Microsoft and National Semiconductor Co. The plan is to create a host of information services and transmit them to a growing galaxy of smart devices. "Our goal is to get these things so inexpensive that you can put them anywhere," says Richard F. Rashid, senior vice-president for research at Microsoft.

But before Spot runs, Microsoft faces stiff challenges. The toughest: creating services so appealing and convenient that people will pay for them. For years, watchmakers and tech companies have trumpeted computer watches, only to wait for consumers to buy them. They'll have another chance in September, when watchmakers Fossil, Citizen, and Suunto, a Finnish sports-watch company, will introduce Spot watches for $ 120 to $ 300. While Microsoft hasn't yet priced the service, Gates expects it will be "on the order of $ 99 a year"—a price that is too steep, says Michael Gartenberg, research director of Jupiter Research.

For Microsoft, the financial risk is minimal. The software giant has spent a mere $50 million on Spot—pocket change for a company with $ 40 billion in cash. For Microsoft to break even, 500,000 consumers must buy the service. But, in truth, Spot's bottom line matters far less than the technology and lessons that Microsoft draws from the venture.

This is Microsoft's step into so-called ubiquitous computing, a holy grail for the tech intelligentsia. For years, companies have toiled to develop technology to pack computing smarts into all sorts of devices. The ideas, often utopian, feature legions of machines communicating with each other, and streams of information following customers nearly every step of their lives. Most have fallen short. One is Jini software, developed by Sun Microsystems Inc. to make it easier for consumer devices—from refrigerators to cars—to connect to the Web so their operations could be monitored. But four years after its launch, Jini is still struggling to catch on.

Microsoft's own track record launching new consumer businesses is, well, spotty. Microsoft has long labored to get interactive television software out of its labs. Digital stereo speakers and PC-connected phones each lasted less than a year. "Spot has all the signs of a Microsoft launch of 'ready, fire, aim,'" says Gartenberg.

One trouble is that most of Microsoft's potential customers already lug around ubiquitous information devices: cell phones, pagers, and handheld computers. New mobile phone services, for example, already provide lottery numbers, traffic reports, and storm alerts. Smart watches "are going to be nothing more than a novelty item unless they offer something you can't get from the other devices," says Todd D. Slater, a retail analyst with Lazard Freres & Co.

Gates is convinced he has something unique to offer. With Spot, users can get up-to-the-minute information without ever having to dial their phone or find a Web connection to use their handheld. The technology's well suited, he says, for one-way instant messages.

Microsoft launched work on Spot in 1999. First, the company needed to come up with a chip to process data and receive radio transmissions. It had to be tiny and cheap. Microsoft gave basic design ideas to chipmaker National Semiconductor, which takes custom orders. National ginned up the new chip for about $ 10 each.

To transmit the data to the devices, Microsoft researchers looked to a little-used portion of the FM radio band. The information will be sent by satellite or Internet to radio stations, which in turn will broadcast the data to the FM receivers in each gadget. Microsoft inked deals with six broadcasting companies for coverage in every major city in North America. It plans to offer Spot in Europe and Asia but has yet to sign on any broadcast partners there.

For all of Microsoft's clever technology, though, the success of the Spot wristwatch and other devices will come down to whether Gates & Co. can persuade consumers to pay for data delivered to everyday devices. Otherwise, it may not amount to much more than a spot on the technology horizon.

SPOT ON? Microsoft's Spot (Smart Personal Objects Technology) lets tiny gadgets receive gobs of data such as stock prices and sports scores. Microsoft is starting with a watch but has other ideas.

WRISTWATCH Push a few buttons for data about the commute. Fossil, Citizen, and Finnish sports-watch designer Suunto will have watches this summer, priced from $120 to $300.

KEY-CHAIN FOB Microsoft figures that women won't be comfortable with a large-faced digital wristwatch. So it has come up with a key-chain fob to deliver the info.

ALARM CLOCK When travelers unpack, their clock would automatically change to the local time zone. It could also synchronize with their calendars.

CALL IT THE PEPSI BLUE GENERATION

So much for the one-soda-fits-all strategy

When 130 million viewers tune into Super Bowl XXXVII this year, PepsiCo Inc. won't disappoint those who are counting on it to deliver a parade of glitzy and entertaining ads. What viewers won't see, though, is a single commercial devoted to Pepsi's flagship cola. Instead, three of the four slots, purchased for a cool $ 2 million apiece, will go to newer and narrower brands such as lemon-lime Sierra Mist and lemon-flavored Pepsi Twist.

It's the latest sign of how the soft-drink giant has reformulated its mission from bolstering core brands like Pepsi-Cola and Mountain Dew to peppering the market with niche products and brand extensions. Why the change? Pepsi's market has splintered and big brands no longer have universal appeal. To attract a younger, less cohesive generation, Purchase (N.Y.)-based Pepsi has had to rethink the way it develops and markets its wares. "The era of the mass brand has been over for a long time," says David Burwick, chief marketing officer of Pepsi-Cola North America. "It took our category longer than most to accept that."

Pepsi's response has been a raft of new products, most bearing the Pepsi or Mountain Dew names. So far, its biggest hit has been cherry-flavored, caffeine-loaded Mountain Dew Code Red. Pepsi Twist and berry-flavored Pepsi Blue have developed more modest followings. Sierra Mist is a youth-skewed challenger to Cadbury Schweppes PLC's 7 Up. Beverage execs expect to see at least one or two more launches this year—possibly including an orange-flavored Dew extension called Monsoon. Burwick says no decisions have been made, but adds that Dew, in particular, has been underexploited for too long. "It was like we had millions of dollars in the bank and had never written a check," he says.

Are these new entrants likely to become Diet Pepsi-like blockbusters? Probably not, but Pepsi isn't expecting that. Code Red, Twist, Blue, and Mist account for barely 5% of Pepsi's soft-drink sales. In the past, Pepsi might not have bothered with such small fry. Today, though, it's looking for products that can crack a hard-to-reach demographic group. Code Red, for example, has reeled in urbanites, women, and African Americans who had not previously shown any impulse to do the Dew. That could help offset flagship Pepsi's 2% volume sales decline last year.

Because these new drinks are more narrowly targeted, Pepsi has had to refine its marketing techniques. To launch Code Red in 2001, the company handed out a million samples at youth magnets like the Winter X Games and the NCAA Final Four basketball tourney before the brand was available in stores. That helped create a buzz that got Code Red off to a brisk start. For teen-oriented Pepsi Blue last fall, Pepsi went beyond hiring rock stars to appear in ads. Instead, it worked out an innovative deal with Universal Music Group: Pepsi premiered songs by Universal artists Sev and Papa Roach in ads, then made longer music videos for the studio's use. "It used to be TV, TV, TV," says Burwick. "Now, it's TV-plus."

That logic will extend to Pepsi's most mainstream TV time slot, the Super Bowl. Pepsi will use three of its four ad spots for new products. Sierra Mist, just rolling out, will get two, and Pepsi Twist will get another (with an ad starring rock paterfamilias Ozzy Osbourne). Only one will go to an established brand, Diet Pepsi. To get more bang for one of the Sierra Mist ads, Pepsi let consumers preview and vote on two versions of the ad online, with Pepsi promising to air the more popular one.

Of course, playing the niche-marketing game is full of risk. The new drinks may siphon off customers from the older brands. Code Red, for example, gets a quarter of its volume from existing Dew drinkers. Then there's execution. The last time Pepsi embarked on a new-product frenzy, a decade back, it brought out Crystal Pepsi, Pepsi AM, and Pepsi Max—all expensive flops. Burwick, though, shows no signs of wavering. With flagship Pepsi stalled, he has little choice.

Carmakers Design For Generation Y

Honda and Toyato Work Hard To Banish the 'Really Uncool'

BY MICHELINE MAYNARD

Among younger buyers, Honda and Toyota are chasing Hyundai . . .

AVERAGE AGE OF VEHICLE BUYER, 2002	
Hyundai	35.8
Toyota	41.1
Honda	43.5
Industry average	*44.0*

. . . which has a hipper image with young adults . . .

CONSUMERS AGE 18-24 WHO CONSIDERED THE FOLLOWING BRANDS STODGY:

	CARS	TRUCKS
Hyundai	19.5%	11.1%
Toyota	63.0	47.0
Honda	44.7	61.0

. . . but Honda and Toyota, due to their overall size, still rank among the most popular brands for young buyers.

MARKET SHARE OF TOTAL VEHICLES SOLD TO BUYERS 25 AND UNDER, 2002	
Ford	17%
Chevrolet	14
Honda	12
Toyota	9
Volkswagen	6

DETROIT, Jan. 15 — The **Honda** Element looks like a sport utility vehicle that married a Brink's truck, with as much headroom as a Greyhound bus. Inside, Honda calls it a dormitory room on wheels, with seats that can be turned around, pulled out, folded flat, stacked with gear and hosed off.

The **Toyota** Scion xB seems like a time-warped homage to Chrysler's 1980's minivans, shrunken and brought down to curb level. There are no gauges in front of the steering wheel to distract the driver; they are off to the center, above an ear-blasting Pioneer stereo prewired for satellite radio.

Ye Chen, 25, a graphic designer in Brooklyn, loves the Honda. "The Element is different," he said. "It's not pretentious. It's not trying to look good. It's a box. I like it."

But Alisha Broberg, 24, who works in sales while she finishes her college degree, hates the Scion xB. "I think the Scion is awful," she wrote in an e-mail message from San Antonio. "When did designers start thinking that boxy equals cool for the under-30 set?"

These opposite reactions hint at the gamble that auto companies are taking as they set out to sell cars to Generation Y, the under-25 group that marketers associate with extreme sports, blaring techno music and a zealous individuality.

Led by Honda and Toyota—both otherwise known for lineups of fairly conventional-looking cars and trucks—some automakers are building cars meant specifically for young drivers, hoping that the attempt to be cool does not brand them as hopelessly not.

Toyota's Scion is a new nameplate that will eventually house a collection of vehicles aimed at the trendiest Gen Y drivers. Honda is selling the Element at a base price just under $17,000 alongside the rest of its vehicles, where it stands out like a Frank Gehry building in an industrial park.

> The Honda Element, which the company plans to introduce at a base price just under $17,000, emphasizes headroom, utility and something of a departure in design. Along with Toyota and others, Honda seeks to appeal to a youth sensibility.

Others are making less severe departures, with demonstrable success. **Mitsubishi,** which lacked much of an identity in the 1990's, has built the youngest customer base of any auto company, not with a new vehicle but with sharp marketing. Its ads feature the music of rock bands like Barenaked Ladies. And its financing terms are extremely liberal, at times zero percent loans with nothing down and no payments for a year.

The Korean automaker **Hyundai,** meanwhile, has plowed the time-proven path to winning young drivers: its vehicles are among the cheapest in America, and are backed with a 10-year, 100,000-mile warranty. Sales have quadrupled over the last four years, and the age of the average Hyundai buyer has fallen to 35.8, just a few months older than the typical 35.5 of a Mitsubishi owner.

Finbarr O'Neill, chief executive of Hyundai America, is skeptical that vehicles can be aimed at an age group. "You can slice and dice the market too thin," said Mr. O'Neill, banging his hand on a conference table for emphasis during an interview last week.

But most carmakers, like nearly every maker of consumer products, say their future success lies in winning the loyalties of young customers today. "If we can capture them at 15 to 24, we can enjoy their business for years to come," said Fujio Cho, Toyota's president.

Toyota's research shows that while the company was successful at attracting baby boomers in the 1970's and 80's, the children of those customers consider Toyotas to be their parents' cars—"really uncool," as Mr. Chen puts it.

(Cont.)

People of his generation bought just 5 percent of the 17.2 million cars and trucks sold in the United States last year. Within seven years, though, buyers born after 1977 will make up 25 percent of the car market, and by 2020 they will be 40 percent, according to Toyota's estimates.

Auto companies have spent decades chasing such young buyers. Ford and General Motors succeeded in the 1960's, when the Mustang and the Pontiac GTO were resounding hits with the first baby boomers who could afford to buy cars. Some other efforts may best be forgotten, like the fire-prone Ford Pinto and the bulbous AMC Pacer.

More recently, the **Pontiac** Aztek, a sort of minivan-sport utility amalgam, was supposed to appeal to young outdoor enthusiasts, but its thick polymer cladding and enormous rear end secured its standing as an Edsel for the new millennium.

Indeed, vehicles that auto companies say are aimed at young people often become means for parents to relive their own youth, as with **Volkswagen's** revived Beetle and the Toyota Matrix, both of which have been bought primarily by boomers, said Art Spinella, an industry analyst with CNW Marketing Research of Bandon, Ore.

So far, Generation Y buyers, like generations before them, have gravitated to small, relatively inexpensive models. In 2002, the top sellers in this age group in 2002 were the Honda Civic, the Volkswagen Jetta and the Chevrolet Cavalier, according to J. D. Power & Associates; all have base prices well below $20,000, compared with the average $25,000 price tag last year for a new car or truck.

But that does not mean these customers will remain satisfied with such vehicles for long. Toyota's market research has found that baby boomers' primary buying criteria are peace of mind and luxury, while Generation X buyers—those born from 1960 to 1977—seek fun and variety. Generation Y buyers, Toyota says, want to flaunt their personal style.

There is no better evidence of that than in California, where legions of young consumers have turned to the Honda Civic—which began life as a plain-vanilla compact—into the centerpiece of a customizing craze called tuning. The term is borrowed from the process of tweaking the valves of an engine so that it has a distinctive roar.

Tuners tweak their cars with all manner of options, from wheels and rims to sidelights to radios, spending as much as $3,000 on extras. Featured in the 2001 movie "The Fast and the Furious," the tuning movement caught Honda and the rest of the auto industry by surprise. Now, car companies are scurrying to exploit the phenomenon—an effort that experts say will be tricky.

"The youth market is a lot more savvy than the car companies give them credit for," said Todd Turner, president of Car Concepts Inc., a consulting firm in Thousand Oaks, Calif. "If it's specifically meant for them, they're not interested. If they adopt it and discover it, they like it."

"A GENERATION'S PICK"

The most sought-after car among Generation Y buyers was the Honda Civic. It sold for under $20,000, well below the average $25,000 price tag for a new car or truck.

MOST POPULAR VEHICLES AMONG BUYERS 25 AND UNDER, 2002	
Honda Civic	7%
Volkswagen Jetta	4
Chevrolet Cavalier	3
Ford Focus	3
Chevrolet small pickup	3
Ford F-Series	3

Source: J.D. Power & Associates

Tuners' influence shows up strongly in the first two models in Toyota's Scion lineup, the xB small van and the xA hatchback. The Scions, which will carry a base price under $16,000, are versions of vehicles already sold by Toyota in Japan, where the xA is known as the Ist (pronounced east) and the xB is marketed as the BB.

Toyota is aiming Scion at a thin slice of Generation Y that it calls trend leaders, who it says make up less than 15 percent of the youth market. These are the people, according to James Farley, a Toyota vice president in charge of Scion sales, who have gone to the movies more than seven times in the last six months, spend up to 30 hours a week listening to music and 7 to 10 hours playing sports, eat out three times a week, and visit a museum maybe once every six months.

They want their vehicles to be as luxurious as possible for as little money as possible—old news to Mr. Farley, 41, who spent several years working at Lexus during his 14-year Toyota career. Despite their penchant for brightly colored sportswear, like Lexus buyers they favor muted paint hues when it comes to cars.

But the base vehicle is just a canvas, because Scions can be tuned.

Along with choosing a manual or automatic transmission, buyers pick the style of the wheel covers, reflector lights and seat covers (leopard print or gun-metal polka dots, for example), and the color of the lights behind the dashboard gauges (choices include amethyst, passion pink and tangerine). They can add 40 other accessories, including color trim on the steering wheel and gearshift knob.

Dealers, who are investing a modest $125,000 apiece to sell Scions from a specially designed corner of their showrooms, will then relay the choices to Toyota, which will build the cars in Japan. The completed vehicle is supposed to be tuned to customer specifications at the port of entry and delivered to the dealership in seven days.

Toyota hopes to sell as many as 100,000 Scions a year. The cars go on sale in California this summer and on the East Coast a year from now, but do not roll out nationally until the summer of 2004. That schedule allows the company to hedge its bets: If Scion is an immediate failure, Toyota can scrap it.

Joseph Phillippi, the president of AutoTrends, a consulting firm in Short Hills, N.J., said Toyota had little at risk except a red face if Scion failed. "They can afford to experiment and you have to give them credit," he said. "This is a pretty conservative company."

But others retain their doubts about such generational carmaking. Helmut Panke, the chief executive of **BMW,** believes in focusing on vehicles with a broader appeal. He has had a hit with the Mini Cooper, an updated version of the British cult car, that sells for $20,000.

"People who are 96 years old are buying the Mini, as well as 20-year-olds, and I'm happy with it," Mr. Panke said. "It's good to have a customer. What's wrong with that?"

Is That an iPod in Your Pocket?

More Clothing Makers Target Gadget Users; a Ski-Jacket With a Remote Sewn In

By Walter S. Mossberg

Digital products are taking over our lives in many ways. They're also taking over our clothing. People walk around with as many as three devices—a PDA, a cellphone, and a pager or e-mail receiver—jammed into various pockets, or dangling from belts, or crammed into purses that lack good compartments for them.

You know the scenario: A cellphone rings and someone scrambles to find the phone in a bottomless purse or bag. She detangles and then attaches her "hands-free" headset to the phone and finally starts talking if the caller hasn't hung up yet. Or someone who uses multiple digital devices can't seem to remember in which pocket he crammed his Global Positioning Service-enabled Palm Pilot in time to turn right on Michigan Avenue.

But now, the clothing industry—or a tiny branch of it—has come up with garments specifically designed for toting all these gadgets and using them conveniently. These items range from marketing gimmicks to impressive new technology, and my assistant, Katie, and I have been trying out some of them. To our surprise, they didn't make us look as geeky as we'd feared they might.

The techno-garments break down into three categories: clothing designed with specific compartments and places for holding high-tech products; clothing designed with such pockets, but also with conduits for the wires so things such as earbuds are easier to use; and truly futuristic clothing with wiring and even control buttons actually sewn right into the material.

The most basic category includes coats from **Sanyo Fashion House** Inc. and **Palm** Inc. These coats have a special pocket for Palm devices, lined with static-shielded material, as well as a cellphone pocket lined with antimagnetic material. Coats with such pockets range from $225 to $750, though I have never had a static-electricity or magnetic problem with Palms and phones in regular old coats.

Even Dockers pants are getting in on the action. The Dockers Mobile Pant, which costs about $52, has several special pockets that conceal technological gadgets. The Web site advertises that, "Now men can carry their gear without the world knowing it. Style is the only thing you can't hide."

Dominating the second, more elaborate category is something called the SCOTTeVEST. These are jackets, with removable sleeves, that are available in various colors and in several models ranging from $79 to $149.99.

At first glance, the SCOTTeVEST, by **SCOTTeVEST** LLC, looks like a normal windbreaker. But once unzipped, its true purpose is revealed. The jackets sport as many as 22 different compartments inside, covering almost every inch of available material. You can vary the sizes of some of the pockets by attaching and detaching hidden Velcro seals. There's even a place in back for a flat water pack, with a drinking tube that can be snaked up toward your neck.

Extra Padding

The most useful pockets are made so that your phone, MP3 or CD player can be carried comfortably while the wires connecting to earbuds can run from the device through a thin, long compartment in the coat and up to your ears. There are even tiny, convenient hidden pouches that hold your earbuds while you're not using them. All models come with extra padding in the shoulders so that when you fill the pockets with gadgets, water bottles, magazines and other items, the weight is evenly spread across your shoulders.

We were actually surprised by the attractiveness of the Scott jacket. Katie walked around the office in one and didn't look like a woman toting an Apple iPod, a Palm, a book and a large bottle of water, without her purse. I briefly wore one on the streets of Las Vegas, during last week's Consumer Electronics Show, and didn't attract undue attention (although both the trade show and Vegas itself are settings where it's pretty hard to look odd). However, when you start to pull things out of the jacket, you risk looking like either a shady watch dealer, or a circus clown who yanks miles of scarves from his pocket.

If you really want to draw attention, you can now buy special backpacks with speakers mounted in the sides and compartments for your choice of audio player. The combination allows any hiker to destroy the serenity of nature with really loud music. One such backpack, the **Osiris** G-Bag (www.osirisgbag.com), has a battery-powered amplifier built in and internal Velcro tabs for securing the wires that connect the player, the amp and the speakers. We didn't test it, but various models sell for $100 to $200.

But the most interesting garment we tested falls into the third, techiest category—clothing with electrical connections and controls physically integrated into its fibers. We tested the Burton Amp, from **Burton Snowboards** and **Apple Computer,** a jacket that is made for use only with Apple's iPod MP3 player. It's a handsome, perfectly normal-looking winter jacket, with one difference—a fabric panel on the left sleeve with a set of raised audio-control buttons.

The 'Brains' of the Jacket

The iPod fits snugly into a stiff, custom-shaped outer compartment near where the left breast pocket would normally be located, and connects to a tiny black box that zips into its own pouch. This interface module, which Burton calls the "brains" of the jacket, is essentially a reconfigured iPod remote control. A white cloth data cable, a ribbon with conductive fibers in it, is sewn down the inside of the sleeve of the jacket to the forearm area, where the five raised circular buttons appear on the outside material of the coat. Something called SOFTswitch technology allows these flexible, fabric buttons to replace hard plastic.

These SOFTswitch buttons are made for snowboarders or skiers who don't want to take their gloves off to play, pause, skip songs or adjust volume while listening to music. And they do work. But there are some drawbacks. We didn't get it hooked up properly on the first try, and had to wiggle around and reconnect the iPod's earbud cable to the black box to get it all to work. And, because the iPod's screen and its wheel-shaped song-selection control aren't replicated on the sleeve, your only option for changing songs is to skip ahead and back. So, you may be unable to pick out the perfect psyche-up song before tackling a black diamond slope.

The Amp can be washed by removing its interface module and, of course, the iPod and earbuds—which snake up to the neckband of the coat via various custom openings.

The Burton Amp costs a hefty $499 (the iPod is sold separately for $299-$499), but music-loving downhill die-hards might be able to justify the price.

This spring, **Philips Electronics** hopes to continue this textile tech trend by introducing cloth neck lanyards with embedded audio controls similar to those on the Amp jacket. The lanyards will be an accessory for a new line of tiny MP3 players, which plug right into them and dangle on your chest. I tried one on and it seemed comfortable. The volume-adjustment buttons are on the left-hand strap and song-seeking buttons are on the right. A jack for earbuds is near the nape of the neck. The player with lanyard will cost $30 more than a player with normal controls. The lanyard can't be washed because of the earbud port.

(Cont.)

Well-Equipped

It's likely there will be more and more of these wearable products with integrated technology. The Pentagon is driving a lot of the research in the field, in a quest for high-tech uniforms for its digitally equipped troops.

Before you stuff one more gadget into your pocket, you might consider trying one of these garments. Some of them border on the geeky, but they might also make using your gadgets more convenient and comfortable.

Apple Thinks Big, And Small

By DAVID POGUE

SAN FRANCISCO — The number 128 is important in personal computing. Because it's a tidy power of two, it often defines quantities of things like megabytes, megahertz and megawatts. But for Apple at the annual Macworld Expo trade show, 128 was a more important number. It was the number of times the audience interrupted Steve Jobs's keynote speech with applause.

Part of that reaction, to be sure, had to do with Mr. Jobs's legendary onstage charisma. Part of it, however, was also that his company had a lot of products to unveil.

The parade began with gracefully improved versions of Apple's flagship multimedia programs: iPhoto 2 (for organizing and exhibiting digital photos), iMovie 3 (for editing camcorder video) and iDVD 3 (for turning those finished videos into Blockbuster-style DVD's), all to reach the market on Jan. 25. There were new programs, too, like Final Cut Express, a $300 junior version of the $1,000 Final Cut Pro editing software beloved by professional video and film editors.

Then Mr. Jobs dropped a pair of software bombshells sure to thrill Mac fans, and infuriate Microsoft.

First, he introduced a Web browser called Safari (a free download at **www.apple.com,** for Mac OS X only). Its three most important features are speed, speed and speed, loading Web pages in a third the time of Microsoft's Internet Explorer. Next, he introduced Keynote, a presentation program like—or, rather, unlike—Microsoft's PowerPoint. The new Apple program is a graphics powerhouse, not as full-featured as PowerPoint but with far superior typographical and visual effects.

These programs may make life even easier for Mac fans, but may not persuade many Windows users to leave what, at this trade show, is known as the Dark Side. Yet Apple did show off something that might: two new laptops that lay claim to superlatives like "biggest," "smallest" and "first."

Over the last year, Windows laptop makers have introduced models with 16-inch screens (measured diagonally). These behemoths, weighing up to 10 pounds and going dark after only two hours of battery life, are too unwieldy to use on airplane tray tables—or even, paradoxically, on laps. Their makers (like Hewlett-Packard, Toshiba and Sony) call them "desktop replacements," implying that these babies have all the power of a standard PC, with just enough portability to move occasionally to another location.

Anything they can do, Apple figures it can do better. In early March, Apple will begin selling the first laptop with a 17-inch screen—1,440 by 900 pixels, or enough to view two side-by-side Web pages with room to spare. According to Apple, it's the same screen used on its best-selling desktop model, the 17-inch iMac.

This 17-inch PowerBook G4 is a beauty, clad in unpainted, finely textured aluminum alloy, rounded at the edges and completely flat (and very hot) underneath. At 15.4 by 10.2 inches and only one inch thick when closed, it's gorgeous and shockingly big, like a sterling-silver cafeteria tray from Tiffany's.

Apple's engineers no doubt had a field day dreaming up cutting-edge technologies to cram inside; you've never seen such a long laptop feature list. In addition to the usual PowerBook amenities (Ethernet, S-video, modem, two U.S.B. jacks, a PC card slot, and a drive that plays and burns both CD's and DVD's), the new PowerBook offers several technologies that are not only firsts for Apple, but, in some cases, for the computer industry as well.

First, a Bluetooth transmitter is built in, so that the PowerBook can communicate wirelessly with a similarly equipped Palm organizer or cellphone (for an Internet connection). Second, one of its two FireWire jacks can connect to a new breed of hard drives with so-called FireWire 800 connections, which can transfer data about twice as fast as regular FireWire (and U.S.B. 2.0).

Third, the new PowerBook introduces 802.11g, a new version of the Wi-Fi wireless networking technology that has become popular among laptop lovers in coffee shops and airports. (Apple, understandably, gave it a less user-hostile name: AirPort Extreme.)

The beauty of this new standard is that it is compatible with all existing wireless "hot spots"—but if you buy Apple's new, $200 AirPort Extreme base station, you can transfer files five times as fast.

Apart from its Montana-size screen, the new PowerBook's most glamorous feature is its hidden light sensor. When it detects that you are working in, say, a darkened movie theater, the screen automatically dims slightly to save power. Then, amazingly, a fiber-optic light glows beneath the keyboard. The light spills out around the keys and, in fact, through the transparent letters on the keys themselves.

Frankly, the whole thing is a little silly; finding your way around the keyboard just isn't much of an issue when a 17-inch floodlight is towering above you. Still, the effect is undeniably spectacular. PowerBook owners will soon be dragging loved ones into dark closets and basements for demos.

You should also know four important statistics about this machine. It weighs 6.8 pounds, it contains a 1-gigahertz G4 processor, it manages 4.5 hours of battery power per charge (according to Apple), and it costs $3,300.

Apple points out that no Windows "desktop replacement" laptop has a bigger screen, lighter weight, better battery or slimmer profile—and that's all true. But if you don't need state-of-the-art features like Bluetooth, FireWire 800, and 802.11g wireless, some rivals come relatively close. Sony's Vaio GRX600, for example, is thicker and heavier (eight pounds), and the battery life isn't as good. But when equipped like the PowerBook (60-gigabyte hard drive, 512 megabytes of memory, CD-DVD burner), it costs $600 less. And don't tell Apple, but its 16-inch screen actually reveals more of your spreadsheets and Web pages, because it has more pixels (1,600 by 1,200) packed into that space.

The other new PowerBook is another story. This time, Apple outdid itself in the opposite direction. Apple calls its 12-inch PowerBook G4 the smallest laptop it has ever made—and the smallest, lightest full-featured laptop on earth. ("Full-featured" means that the CD burner and a full complement of jacks are built in.)

The keyboard is identical to the one on its 17-inch counterpart. So how could a full-size keyboard fit on a mini-notebook? Simple: Ingeniously, Apple let it run all the way across, edge to edge. Without a millimeter of margin, the keyboard just fits in the laptop's 10.9-inch width. (The other dimensions: 8.6 inches deep and 1.2 inches thick.)

As it turns out, the little PowerBook inherits only some of the 17-incher's hot new features: the aluminum case, 802.11g wireless transmitter (this time, a $100 option), and built-in Bluetooth. It lacks the FireWire 800 jack, PC card slot, and the light-up keyboard. On the Internet some are already calling it the "G4 iBook," as though it's just a faster, slightly smaller and lighter version of Apple's inexpensive, ice-white iBook (which runs on a slower, G3 chip) rather than a true sibling to the original, 15-inch widescreen PowerBook G4 (which is still available).

But that's not fair; this little powerhouse is in a class by itself. You can pick it up with one hand—it weighs only 4.6 pounds—and hide it from jealous co-workers under a sheet of typing paper. Best of all, it costs only

(Cont.)

$1,800. (For $200 more, you can get a CD-DVD burner instead of the CD burner-DVD player.)

As Apple's latest big-and-small experiments illustrate, designing laptops is no picnic. The trouble is that the world's wish list contains two mutually incompatible kinds of specs. On one hand, everyone says that the perfect laptop should be small, light and inexpensive; on the other hand, it should also be rugged and powerful, with a big screen and full-size keyboard.

Most people will probably find that the new 17-inch PowerBook grants plenty of wishes in the second category at the expense of the wishes in the first. But in the 12-inch PowerBook, Apple has found a sweet spot bigger than a sugar plantation. It's worth 128 rounds of applause all by itself.

Time for Marketers to Grow Up?

By Cris Prystay and Sarah Ellison

If demography is destiny, then consumer products companies are facing an aging future. As the world's birthrates slow and its population ages, multinational companies are being forced to reconsider strategies for selling diapers, arthritis medicine and everything in between.

But some remain reluctant to let go of their fixation on youth. Lois Coleman, who organizes focus-groups for consumer companies, says she is almost never asked to study people over age 50. Even for the bran flakes she helped launch in Mexico, she was asked to talk to consumers under 35. "It was a bran cereal," she says, pausing. "Now who do you think really needed that product—the kids in their 20s?"

For now, many companies find themselves straddling a widening gap between the relatively young populations of developing countries and the aging populations of the developed world—and trying to find growth opportunities in both.

"For decades, our industry took for granted that population growth in the developed countries would deliver a substantial part of the sales growth," said A.G. Lafley, chief executive of **Procter & Gamble** Co., at a recent conference on laundry detergent. "Few imagined the day would come when we would see zero population growth—let alone decline—in major markets. Yet that is what we are facing today."

Growth has to come from developing markets, Mr. Lafley says—so, the company built a low-cost diaper factory in Vietnam, where it sells diapers for 15-cents a piece, less expensive than in the West. Population growth in other "young" countries such as Mexico and Brazil are a critical source of sales growth, providing the extra bodies to buy more toothpaste and laundry detergent and other staples. But pricing is an issue, too: On average, prices of laundry products in developing countries can be half or even less than half the price in developed markets, P&G says.

Meanwhile, P&G has focused on one of the clear advantages of selling in developed markets: affluent, albeit aging, consumers. In the fall, P&G launched a toothpaste for aging women, called "Rejuvenating Effects" in the U.S. One of P&G's latest blockbuster beauty products is its Olay anti-aging cream, which it rolled out first in Western Europe and the U.S. The best opportunties for its $500 million osteoporosis drug, Actonel, are (in descending order) Japan, Italy, France, the rest of Western Europe and then the U.S.

Some big multinationals are still clinging to dated ideas about the demographic makeup of new markets. "There is a big gap between the realities of demographics and the way advertisers approach it," says Mike Townsin, regional director of MediaCom Asia Pacific, the media planning and research arm of ad agency Grey Worldwide.

In Asia, for example, the young adults that attracted multinational marketers in the 1980s now have grown up and become so-called empty-nesters—that is, people from the age of 40 to 59 whose youngest child is nearing financial independence, according to research company Asian Demographics Ltd., of Auckland, New Zealand. At the peak of their careers and newly dependent-free, empty-nesters are a fast-growing group in powerful economies such as Hong Kong, Singapore, Korea and Taiwan. Their numbers are forecast to grow by 30% to 10.9 million in the next decade. Meanwhile, the youth market will shrink by 10% to 11.4 million in the same decade, according to the research company.

Half of Japan's population will be over 50 by 2025, yet multinationals keep romancing Asia's youth.

Yet multinationals are, for the most part, still obsessed with romancing Asia's youth. Coca-Cola Japan, for example, isn't yet targeting Baby Boomers, says a spokesman. The company has been making canned teas and coffees for years but hasn't yet created ads pitching them to seniors.

Motorola Inc. makes phones with features that aging consumers like, such as a zoom function to bump up the font size on the tiny screen and even internal speakers that can connect with hearing aids. But still the company hasn't developed ad campaigns highlighting these features or targeting seniors. "Our strategic direction is to focus on the youth," says Mabel Tay, Motorola's director of brand and consumer communications for Asia Pacific.

In Japan, several domestic companies have already begun to get with the program, reorienting their marketing to the senior set. They have little choice: Half of Japan's population will be over 50 by 2025, according to the U.S. Census Bureau's International Database on Aging. In the U.S., in comparison, 36% of the population will be over 50 by that time.

Toymaker Takara Co. Ltd. is trying to gain a foothold in the growing adult market with creations including a two-seater mini electric car, home karaoke systems and robots that open beer cans. Two years ago, Meiji Dairies Corp., which had long pitched its yogurts to children and health-conscious young adults, started making a yogurt for people over 40, called LG21. The product contains a bacteria that kills off another type of bacteria that many older Japanese carry and that is believed to cause stomach ulcers and even cancer. The company forecasts LG21 sales will make up 25% of its total expected yogurt sales for the year ending March 31, 2003. Says Seichi Sato, manager of Meiji's yogurt-marketing department: "The advantage of the [older] market is there is virtually no competitors."

Yamaha Corp. recognized Japan's ranks of teenagers had thinned over the past decade. Two years ago, the company created an easy-to-play electronic guitar for Baby Boomers who grew up on the Beatles and Japanese folk rock and always wanted to play.

"The population of younger people is decreasing in Japan, and at the same time there's many entertainment products, like Playstation and Nintendo, competing for their interest," says Yasuhiko Asahi, of Yamaha's EZ EG Guitar product. "We're now looking at people 50 years old and up. They'll retire in the near future, and generally have more money and more time."

Of course, there are many good reasons why global marketers have learned to shy away from older consumers, in Asia and other places. Young adults do spend more freely than older adults: They are quicker to pick up on new technologies, and quicker to open their wallets. And children exert a strong influence over their parent's spending.

Young people "don't hesitate to buy new products compared to elderly people, who take time to consider and closely examine any new purchase," says Setsuo Sakamoto, executive director of Japanese ad agency Hakuhodo Inc.'s "elder business development unit."

Pitching products to Asia's elders means learning more about the cultural and historical nuances shaping their values, says Richard Pinder, regional managing director at ad agency Leo Burnett. Asia's middle class youth, on the other hand, all speak MTV. "They are easier to understand," says Mr. Pinder. "They're more willing to spend. They're more Western."

Still, he notes, sooner or later the demographic reality will force a change. "It's going to become a major issue" he says.

How To Sell XXXL

With more Americans overweight, smart firms aim to sell them things to make their lives more comfy

by Unmesh Kher

Pierre Sabourin, a venture capitalist and former amateur hockey player, has been so successful at losing weight, having dropped 165 lbs. on a rice diet, that he wants to share his secrets with others. But at 435 lbs., he is still keenly aware how hard it is for a wide body to navigate the many narrow armchairs and undersize seat belts of daily life. So even as he works excitedly to promote his just opened weight-loss camp, the Living Center, in Durham, N.C., Sabourin, 43, is operating a complementary business. He sells hard-to-find products to other folks his size at *overweightpeople.com*. Looking for a scale that measures up to 500 lbs.? Sabourin's your man. Belly won't let you reach your ankles? Check out the extra-long shoehorns.

Sabourin has set up shop at a profitable crossroads. Today 65% of U.S. adults are classified as overweight, up from 46% two decades ago. And nearly a third of adults are considered obese (say, 190 lbs. or more for someone 5 ft. 6 in.), up from 14% in 1980. Any way you look at it, heavy Americans represent a fast-growing market with special needs. Until recently the business world's primary response was to pitch diets, workouts and potions to those determined to melt off the pounds. The weight-loss market grew to about $40 billion last year, from $33 billion in 1999, according to Marketdata Enterprises of Tampa, Fla. Even drastic measures are catching on. Last year 63,100 obese patients—including celebrities like *Today* show weatherman Al Roker—underwent surgery to have their stomach capacity reduced, an increase from 23,000 such operations in 1997.

Few weight-loss efforts, however, show long-term success. So a new business is building for mainstream firms that aim to make a profit by accommodating XXXL Americans and making their lives easier rather than trying to change them. "I'm not handicapped by my body," asserts Elizabeth Fisher, 42, a 350-lb. computer programmer in Baton Rouge, La., who made headlines when she tried (and failed) to force Honda to provide her with seat-belt extenders for her new Odyssey. "I'm handicapped by stuff that's too small." That situation is beginning to change as more companies modify their products and services to win business from bigger customers. Among the shifts under way:

AUTOMOBILES Despite Fisher's experience, most automakers are highly attentive to changes in demographics and consumer preferences. The wider profile of the U.S. buyer is cited as one reason that suvs and other so-called light trucks outsold passenger cars in 2002. "The quickest way to alienate customers is to have them rubbing against something," says Michael Arbaugh, a top Ford interior designer. The seats in Ford's already spacious Lincoln Navigator were widened an inch for the 2003 model, and the room between driver and steering wheel was opened up considerably. In its 2003 Focus compact, Ford narrowed the center console, armrests and map pockets in doors to accommodate wider seats.

DaimlerChrysler and Ford have for years offered systems for extending seat belts. Honda has made the seats of its Civic and Accord two inches wider in response to customer requests. Car companies are starting to think ahead about this trend, perhaps because dealing with design problems after a product has been brought to market can be costly. Volvo recalled 65,000 station wagons for repairs when it learned that heavy passengers might short-circuit a heating mechanism in their seats, starting a fire.

FURNITURE While studying census and medical data in 2000, designers at mattress-maker Simmons noticed that the average American is 10% larger now than when its king and queen sizes were introduced four decades ago, according to Don Hofmann, senior vice president of marketing. So Simmons placed a 66-in.-wide platform on the 60-in. queen box spring, making room for a wider mattress dubbed the Olympic Queen. Hofmann believes the model has fueled an 8% growth in sales of his firm's larger mattresses. His hunch that Americans need more room in the sack is borne out by industry figures. Although the trend has not been directly linked to the fattening of America, between 1997 and 2001 the U.S. market share for queen-size mattresses has grown from 31% to 34%, while king sizes (76 in. across) have claimed an 8% share, up from 6%.

Chairs of all sorts seem to be matching the expansion of the American backside. "If I take the seat of a recliner from 21 in. to 24, it will be more popular," says Cabot Longnecker, vice president of merchandising at Berkline, based in Morristown, Tenn. "There are just a lot of wide-bottomed people out there," Longnecker is constantly pondering design tricks to help him broaden his recliner seats without making them look like love seats. He is also putting the finishing touches on a 500-lb.-capacity lift recliner—which lifts and tilts forward to help the obese stand up. It will be out in April and priced between $899 and $999.

Steelcase, based in Grand Rapids, Mich., makes a 500-lb.-capacity office chair, Criterion Plus, that is 5 in. wider than the 18-in. standard and sells for $1,500. Countless hours of watching people at work and noticing how much larger they had become, says product manager Ken Tameling, convinced Steelcase engineers that the seat of their ergonomic Leap chair should be set at 20 in. They engineered its backrest to produce greater resistance when heavy people lean back, as well as attached arms that move laterally. All this, says Tameling, has helped make sales of the $1,299 chair the fastest-growing of any chair Steelcase has ever sold.

CLOTHING Lane Bryant has targeted full-figured women for more than a century, but its new owner, Charming Shoppes, a plus-size retailer, opened 60 outlets last year, for a total of 696. Today 70% of the parent firm's $2.5 billion in revenues flow from the purses of the Rubenesque. "Our customer is the average woman;" says Dorrit Bern, Charming Shoppes CEO, "not the minority."

Half of all U.S. women today wear size 14 or larger; in 1985 the average size was 8. "You don't have to be a rocket scientist to see the opportunity here," says Ceslie Armstrong, editor in chief of *Grace Woman,* a lifestyle magazine for the full-figured. Marshal Cohen, an analyst at NPD Fashionworld, a market-information service in Port Washington, N.Y., estimates that the retail market for plus-size apparel is worth $17 billion and accounts for 20% of the total women's clothing sales. It's one of the industry's fastest-growing segments, up 11% in 2001. (During sluggish 2002, when clothing sales dropped 4.3% overall, plus-size sales were down only 1%.) "Retailers that take this segment of the market and bring it front and center," says

Cohen, "are the ones who will succeed."

In 1999 J.C. Penney started a separate special-sizes division that caters to full-figured women. Kmart has expanded the floor space devoted to plus-size clothes 25% and added a junior-plus-size department in 400 stores. Over the past three years, the retailer's plus-size sales have grown more than 15% and make up about 30% of its women's clothing sales. "Customers have been demanding it," says Nick Just, a general merchandise manager. "Why should plus-size clothes be dumpy?"

That's precisely what designers like Tommy Hilfiger, Liz Claiborne and Carmen Marc Valvo have been asking themselves. "Beauty comes in all shapes and sizes," observes Valvo, who made a name for himself designing evening gowns for such slinky stars as Kim Cattrall and Halle Berry. "The conventional wisdom was to cover big women up. I asked, 'Why can't she wear a sexy, low-cut neckline?'" So he carefully cut his patterns to flatter large women and provided balance to minimize the waistline—or create one if it was lacking. The effort, he says, has flattered his bottom line, contributing an estimated 10% to company sales.

The plus-size movement has gathered sufficient momentum to inspire a full-figured doll, a replica of size-14 fashion model Emme; about 12,000 have been sold since October. Still, some advertisers have a tough time adapting to the subtleties of promoting their products to any but the most svelte of women. Editor Armstrong says she returned submissions from a couple of advertisers who used thin, young models to display their wares. *Grace Woman,* she explained to them, is aimed at a more realistic (and moneyed) audience: primarily women in their mid-30s who wear size 12 to 14 and up. The young model promoting cosmetics wouldn't connect with them. The advertisers have since customized the material they submit to the magazine. And *Grace's* investors have decided to capitalize on their understanding of the plus-size market and move up the date of the launch of a boutique creative agency the company had intended to open in the fall.

MEDICAL EQUIPMENT Few are benefiting as directly from the increase in obesity as equipment manufacturers that cater to the bariatrics market—a branch of medicine that treats the severely obese. Michael Dionne, a physical therapist in Gainesville, Ga., who specializes in bariatrics, says more and more hospitals call on him for help in reducing injuries to nurses and orderlies who must move an increasing number of greatly overweight patients. One Detroit hospital attributed 23 back injuries in two months to moving the obese.

Medical-equipment manufacturers such as Hill-Rom of Batesville, Ind., and Kinetic Concepts of San Antonio, Texas, rent and sell everything from heavy-duty commodes and wheelchairs to mechanized beds that can hold 500 lbs. to 1,000 lbs., help turn patients and feature air-circulation mattress systems to help prevent bedsores. The market for bed surfaces and accessories alone is estimated to be $150 million a year and is growing 15% annually. "As the obesity epidemic grows, so does our revenue," says Lynne Sly, vice president of marketing at Kinetic Concepts. Rental rates are steep—up to $200 a day for a bed—but worth it. Before such products were available and widely covered by Medicare and private insurance, recalls Joe Sacco of Central Medical Supplies in Long Valley, NJ., "we'd see patients sleeping on top of plywood propped up on cinder blocks." CMS's sales of heavyduty beds have doubled in the past year.

TRAVEL AND ENTERTAINMENT Walt Disney theme-park managers say they haven't made specific changes to accommodate fat customers, but company staff members say they are now trained to deal sensitively with the obese. As a result, the company has won kudos at the many websites where overweight activists share their experiences and advice. When a customer approaches a turnstile that is obviously too small, Disney employees move quietly to open wheelchair gates. They discreetly pass out seat-belt extenders on some rides and steer large folk away from others, like Indiana Jones, that might prove dangerous to them. The company also stocks scooters and wide electric wheelchairs. "Disney World may not be perfect, but it's as close to heaven as a fat person can get," says Wanda Sykes, 33, a health-care administrator from Atlanta who weighs 285 lbs. "I visited the old Spanish fort in St. Augustine and got stuck in this dungeon room. It was horrible!"

Southwest Airlines announced last June that it would enforce a long-standing policy of requiring the obese to buy an extra seat based solely on the judgment of staff at the check-in counter that a particular passenger wouldn't fit in a single seat. Southwest says most people who have contacted the airline have supported the policy. And it doesn't seem to have hurt business. Southwest is the only one of the top five airlines that is in the black. But advocates for the obese are livid over the policy. "It infuriates both men and women;" says Allen Steadham, 33, director of the International Size Acceptance Association,

GOING AFTER FAT PROFITS

Americans are putting on pounds—and here's how companies are adapting

CLOTHING

Kiss the muumuu goodbye. Today full figured fashionistas can opt for outfits from Lane Bryant's annual fashion show. Big men can find extra-large garments at retailers like *kingsizedirect.com*

FURNITURE

Steelcase offers a desk chair that can carry 500 lbs. Berkline will soon introduce a recliner with similar capacity that lifts and tilts to help obese people stand up

MEDICAL

The market for bariatrics, a branch of medicine dedicated to caring for severely obese, is booming. Manufacturers that make equipment for such patients produce everything from heavy-duty commodes and wheelchairs to high-tech beds and lifts like this model from Kinetic Concepts, used by caregivers to hoist and turn patients who weigh up to 1,000 lbs.

AUTOMOBILES

Elizabeth Fisher lost her battle with Honda for seat-belt extenders, but many automakers are widening car seats and making interiors roomier to appeal to bigger drivers. Accessories also help, like the leg-lift strap from *amplestuff.com*

HANDY GEAR

Online retailers, like *amplestuff.com* and *overweightpeople.com,* sell hard-to-find items such as a supersize umbrella or a heavyduty 500-lb.-capacity scale and extra-long shoehorns to accommodate the growing girth of their obese customers

(Cont.)

based in Austin, Texas, "but it seems like it's particularly devastating for some women." In fact, the airline industry has pretty much ignored the needs of the fat. Aside from catering to the widespread preference for king-size beds, hotels have also made minimal adaptations. Aware of this, entrepreneur Sabourin—who used to travel with 4-x-4 wooden blocks to prop up rickety hotel beds—sells vacation packages to resorts that qualify as fat friendly.

Still, marketers and manufacturers have only begun to address the needs of America's obese, let alone the merely fat. Bill Fabrey, co-owner of Amplestuff, the pioneering online and catalog retailer that sells more than 100 products to the obese, says fat customers represent "a reluctant market." They are, he notes, often too embarrassed to make demands. Another obstacle to better service for the fat market is that many national and global brands—whether cars or sneakers—want to be seen as young and hip and fear that any association with overweight customers will muddy their expensive imagemaking.

Attitudes are changing, though, as Americans grow heavier. Three-quarters of 8,000 people surveyed by the NPD Group felt that it's O.K. to be overweight, up from 45% in a similar survey in 1985. Sabourin, for his part, doesn't doubt there's new opportunity in the bloating of America. "I've seen the future," he says. "I've lived the future."

Upper Crust

Fast-Food Chains Vie To Carve Out Empire In Pricey Sandwiches

Mr. Lynch Likes the Bread At Panera, While Zell And Kravis Back Cosi

Starbucks as a Role Model

BY SHIRLEY LEUNG
Staff Reporter of THE WALL STREET JOURNAL

For years, growth-obsessed fast-food chains expanded around the world without noticing the potential of a 75-cent item on their own menus. Only after that item—the humble cup of coffee—became the high-priced beverage behind Starbucks Corp. did fast-food executives search their kitchens for other undiscovered stars.

Now they think they've found one: the sandwich.

Lately, small restaurant chains with big ambitions have been racking up impressive sales by offering Americans upscale sandwiches as an alternative to burgers and fries. Some of those outlets, such as Cosi and Briazz, have names designed to convey European sophistication. Others, such as Corner Bakery Cafe and Panera Bread Co., have names that emphasize their use of fresh bread. All of them hope to win a big following among the nation's aging and increasingly health-conscious baby boomers.

Their success so far, especially during the current recession, has captured the attention of many on Wall Street, who see an opportunity for at least one such chain to grow into a national brand, pioneering a mass market for made-to-order sandwiches much the same way that Starbucks did for premium coffee.

Above 99 Cents

Though overall fast-food sales growth has been waning for years, growing numbers of American consumers have proved willing to pay as much for a sandwich as for the $4 cappuccino to go with it. That's big news in an industry long accustomed to promoting 99-cent hamburgers or chicken nuggets. And it is making even some fast-food veterans rethink their marketing strategies. For example, roast-beef specialist Arby's Inc., a unit of Triarc Cos., has launched a new line of Market Fresh sandwiches, which are served on thick slices of bread, instead of a bun, and cost about $4 apiece, about 50% more than its average fare.

Already such financial heavyweights as deal maker Henry Kravis, market guru Peter Lynch, real-estate baron Sam Zell and hamburger giant McDonald's Corp. have invested in the sandwich-shop concept. "There's an opportunity . . . to elevate the experience" of eating a sandwich, says Starbucks founder and Chairman Howard Schultz, who also is backing two fledgling sandwich chains.

Nor is the enthusiasm limited to the U.S. A popular new sandwich chain in London, for example, is named for the owner's 18th-century ancestor, the Earl of Sandwich, who is credited with having first stuck meat between bread. "We have a brand that already has 250 years of heritage and literally global recognition," says company founder Orlando Montagu, whose father is the 11th Earl of Sandwich.

Rising Sales

In the U.S., sales of custom-made sandwiches are rising 15% a year, much faster than the 3% growth rate for hamburgers and steaks, says Technomic Inc., a Chicago food-consulting firm. That helps explain why Panera Bread Co., the largest player in the premium-priced sandwich category, has seen its share price nearly triple in the past year.

Panera, which is based outside St. Louis, rang up sales of $529.4 million for 2001, up 50% from the previous year, and it is expected to report an about 80% increase in net income for 2001. The company had average sales per store of $1.75 million in 2001, compared with McDonald's $1.6 million. In 4 p.m. trading on the Nasdaq Stock Market yesterday, Panera's shares rose $3.28, or 5.3%, to $64.65 on volume of 758,500 shares, more than double its average daily volume for the past three months.

Panera and some other high-end sandwich chains also sell gourmet coffee, meaning that success on a national scale could steal sales from their role model, Starbucks. But the chains vying to carve out an empire based on sandwiches face a challenge that Starbucks never did—a field of well-funded competitors. Starbucks, which expanded to roughly 4,100 stores in North America in little more than a decade, was helped by a dearth of big-chain competition. Even today, its largest U.S. competitor, Diedrich Coffee Inc., based in Irvine, Calif., has a total of only 380 outlets.

"The probability of any of these sandwich chains becoming a Starbucks is a major question," says Dennis Lombardi, Technomic's executive vice president. "It is going to be very difficult."

Yet the prospect of spinning prosperity out of a commodity long taken for granted, of dotting the landscape with a recognizable logo, of becoming synonymous with a particular product, is proving seductive. After investing in one sandwich chain that is struggling, Starbucks's Mr. Schultz recently put "several million" dollars into another: Potbelly Sandwich Works Inc.

Until recently, the sandwich was hardly considered cuisine. According to popular lore, it was invented solely to allow the Earl of Sandwich to eat without leaving the gaming table. Its culinary status sank even further when the fast-food industry began to tout it as a low-cost meal, available at most big purveyors for as little as 99 cents.

By contrast, the new sandwich shops treat sandwich-making as an art. Fresh-baked bread is the basis of their strategy for improving the sandwich's image. Sure, the tomato slices are fresh, and the meat is carved off homestyle roasts. But the big difference is what some of the chains call "artisan bread."

Panera employs professional bakers at $13 an hour to make bread from scratch throughout the day. Together, Panera and Smyrna, Ga.-based Atlanta Bread Co. offer more than two dozen kinds of bread, including asiago cheese, nine grain, kalamata olive and sundried tomato. At New York-based Cosi Inc.'s restaurants, bread that's been out of the oven for 30 minutes or more is tossed away unused.

The finished products feature names as fancy as the coffee specialties at Starbucks. The menu blurb describes Panera's Frontega Chicken Panini as: "Smoked and pulled white-meat chicken, red onion, mozzarella, tomato, chopped basil, and our chipotle mayo, on our rosemary focaccia." Compare that with the Big Mac: "Two 100%-beef patties, sesame-seed bun, American-cheese slice, Big Mac sauce, lettuce, pickles, onions, salt and pepper."

Demographic Shift

Of course, the price of the Frontega is $5.75, about $3 more than for the typical Big Mac. The average check is $6.25 at Panera and $8 at Cosi, more than twice that at most burger joints. But the chains can make these prices stick because of a major shift in the demographics of fast-food customers.

The industry's traditional diner is male, between five and 24 years old, and typically short on cash. But now that youthful segment of the population is expected to grow by only 5% over the next decade, while the 45- to 64-year-old population will grow about 30%, according to the U.S. Census Bureau. And compared with previous generations in their current age group, baby boomers are less likely to eat at home. Pressed for time, they want food fast. Moreover, the growing availability of healthier and higher-quality sandwiches has eroded their loyalty to fast-food burgers.

"If the value is there, I'll certainly pay the price," says Karen Davis, a 45-year-old Chicago real-estate developer and self-described former burger fan who says she, her husband and nine-year-old daughter visit Panera about five times a week.

Subway Restaurants still dominates the sandwich arena, with more than 13,200 U.S. outlets. Until lately, the privately held chain competed with other fast-food purveyors on price, charging about $3 a sandwich. But 18 months ago it, too, started going after more affluent consumers. The chain now offers as many as five different breads, including Asiago Caesar and Sourdough. "We made the food more interesting," says founder Fred DeLuca.

Likewise, some of the nation's other fast-food chains are seeking to rev up their sales growth by adding gourmet sandwiches or premium breads to their menus. But some of them are finding that many of the new sandwich diners also want atmosphere, something that Subway and many other more traditional fast-food chains may be ill-equipped to provide.

Some sandwich chains have learned the hard way about the importance of ambience. Boston-based Au Bon Pain was among the first bakery-style chains to offer high-quality meat on fresh-made bread. But its sales growth faltered, and the company sold its namesake division in 1999 in order to focus on Panera, whose predecessor it acquired in 1993. Former Au Bon Pain Chief Executive Ron Shaich blames the chain's minimalist decor. "We thought the paradigm was to be like McDonald's," recalls Mr. Shaich, who is now Panera's chairman and chief executive.

McDonald's itself has joined the contest to attract the high-end sandwich eater. Last year, it paid an undisclosed sum for a 33% stake in Pret A Manger, an upscale British chain now embarked on a massive invasion of New York City. A typical Pret A Manger offering is the Coronation Chicken, a $5.25 chicken-breast sandwich with curry dressing and mango chutney on malted-grain bread.

Custom-Made vs. Prepackaged

But Pret A Manger, which makes its sandwiches fresh each morning, may be learning a different lesson—that its U.S. growth potential is limited by its strategy of selling its sandwiches prepackaged in cellophane and cardboard, not made to order. Consider the fate of Briazz Inc., a Howard Schultz-backed competitor whose sales growth has sputtered and whose stock price has collapsed to $1.50 a share from $8 last May. One problem, competitors say: Many of its stores continue to sell only prepackaged sandwiches.

In other stores, to pump up sales, Seattle-based Briazz has begun offering pricier hot, custom-made sandwiches—and the harried office workers it caters to are eating them up. As much as 35% of some stores' sales now come from the grilled sandwiches. "We have found that many of our guests want hot food and are willing to wait five or six minutes for a prepared hot item," says Chairman and Chief Executive Victor Alhadeff.

Starbucks also found that high-quality sandwiches packaged fresh each morning didn't meet customer expectations. After launching a much-publicized effort to sell prepackaged sandwiches in 1999, Mr. Schultz says that Starbucks, whose stores aren't equipped to prepare sandwiches on site, doesn't plan to emphasize food. "We recognize more than ever our core competency is roasting and selling the best coffee in the world," he says.

Mr. Schultz's latest bet is on Chicago-based Potbelly Sandwich Works, whose custom-made sandwiches are so popular that devoted customers often have to stand outside in the cold waiting to get inside the company's nine stores.

But many other investors regard the field of possible sandwich all-stars as narrowed to a field of two, Panera and Cosi.

Panera's robust net income, sales and market-value growth may qualify it as the restaurant industry's hottest company. And that growth is only expected to accelerate this year, because Panera, which hoarded cash during the boom years in anticipation of a downturn, plans to take advantage of lower commercial rents to add 100 stores to its current 369. Former Fidelity fund manager Peter Lynch, a longtime investor in Panera, says he is also a loyal customer. "Nobody had done bread," he says, "I thought there was a market for it."

Panera serves its sandwiches on real plates and with real flatware in rooms furnished with fireplaces and upholstered couches. Its locations include suburban strip malls that feature discount stores such as Wal-Mart. Mr. Shaich, Panera's CEO, says the chain, originally conceived for neighborhoods with average household incomes above $50,000, also is thriving in blue-collar neighborhoods.

Cosi's chairman and co-chief executive, Andy Stenzler, believes that his will be the more famous sandwich chain. Similar to Panera in its gourmet sandwiches and decor, Cosi offers one twist of its own. It sells alcohol in the evening, which helps in attracting dinner customers. "Our vision is to define what an American cafe is," says Mr. Stenzler.

Cosi now has 66 stores. But this year, it plans to add 40 more. Among the privately held chain's investors are Messrs. Kravis and Zell, as well as Terry Diamond, whose Chicago venture-capital firm made a fortune as an early investor in Starbucks. Recalling how Starbucks became "part of the landscape of America," Mr. Diamond says: "I think Cosi can do the same thing."

Something Stylish, Something Blue

JetBlue's sleek, sophisticated look, on everything from its advertising to its uniforms, sends a message that low fares don't preclude high style.

By: Amy Goldwasser

In late 1998, when Amy Curtis-McIntyre joined the founding team of JetBlue Airways as vice president for marketing, she knew she had her work cut out for her. "We had a list of the 10 most hated industries in the United States," she recalls, "and sure enough, airlines were up there." That JetBlue intended to be a low-fare, all-coach carrier made it even more challenging. Most people associate such brands with inept customer service, dingy waiting areas, and cramped seats upholstered in leftover 1970s fabric.

Not anymore. As JetBlue turns two this month, flying coach has never been more hip. *Vanity Fair* named JetBlue the "It" airline of 2000, and readers of Conde *Nast Traveler* and *Zagat* rated it the number two domestic airline of 2001, behind Midwest Express, an all-business-class carrier that charges far more. (The cheapest Newark-San Francisco round trip, for example, is $437 on Midwest; New York-Oakland is $298 on JetBlue.) The airline's 42-year-old CEO, David Neeleman, has succeeded Southwest's (*LUV*) Herb Kelleher as the industry's celebrity executive, and no wonder: Despite the triple whammy of simultaneous recession, terrorism, and war, JetBlue reported profits of $10.5 million on $82.6 million in revenues for the third quarter of 2001.

Innovative positioning has been crucial to the company's success, and the carrier's distinctive style—what Curtis-McIntyre dubs "cheap-clever"—is at the heart of it. From the beginning, says the 35-year-old New York City native, the brand has combined low fares with high style and high-touch service. Its strategy has been to excel at the things that can really distinguish the brand but cost relatively little—such as comfort, punctuality, and courtesy—while dispensing entirely with things that can't, like airline grub.

What travelers resent most about airlines, JetBlue realized, is being treated like cattle: packed in, kept in the dark, denied real choice—what Curtis-McIntyre refers to diplomatically as "issues of communication and control." JetBlue addressed the problem, in part, by gambling on a hub at JFK Airport, even though most New Yorkers fly out of LaGuardia or Newark for travel within the United States. The upside was that JFK is far less congested for domestic routes. "We knew it was our opportunity to have phenomenal on-time performance," Curtis-McIntyre says. So far it has paid off: JetBlue's on-time record of 83 percent tops the industry. When delays do happen, moreover, JetBlue goes out of its way to keep passengers informed. By company policy, no more than 15 minutes can pass between updates on a flight's status, and if the delay stretches to more than four hours for any reason other than crummy weather, passengers get credit for a free flight.

Another part of the brand's positioning is an air of sophistication that carries over even to the flight attendants' uniforms. For these, Curtis-McIntyre sought out fashion designer Stan Herman—known for FedEx's uniforms, among other things—and asked for what she called "classic New York black." After Herman gently reminded her that her company, after all, was named Jet*Blue,* they settled on tailored almost-black navy-blue attire that is functional at 30,000 feet but chic enough to fit in at a Soho bar. "People don't necessarily point to one thing—'I'm flying JetBlue because the uniforms look good,'" Curtis-McIntyre admits. "But it's all part of the effort to make everything feel sort of generous and interesting and valuable."

JetBlue's decision to buy brand-new Airbus A320 planes was another inspired trade-off. The jets are more expensive up front than used models, but they require substantially less maintenance over the years. The A320s also have the added benefit of being 8 inches wider than comparable Boeing 737s, meaning that aisles can be roomier and all seats can be 18.5 inches wide, just a half inch shy of standard business class. Adding to the all-business-class feel of the cabin, the airline upholstered the seats in leather and gave each one its own video screen with access to as many as 24 channels of live TV, beamed in by satellite.

JetBlue looked to the Internet as another way to offer high-touch service at bargain costs. Hip New York advertising agency Merkley Newman Harty translated the brand's clean, blue line over to JetBlue.com. "We really wanted to make something that didn't look or feel like any other airline's [website] and that [visitors would find] utterly simple and user-friendly," Curtis-McIntyre says. The site is spare, with just a few navigational options, but the customers use it. While the major carriers sell an average of 10 percent of their tickets online, JetBlue books fully half of its fares on the Web and saves about $5 in transaction costs for each ticket booked online.

In getting the advertising message out, Curtis-McIntyre again looked for something "very un-airline." In this case, that meant losing the standard it's-a-small-world sap and introducing some big-city swagger and wit. Last summer, the airline's cheeky slogan was "Somebody up there likes you." The message changed after Sept. 11, to address people's anxieties about flying, but Curtis-McIntyre was careful to maintain JetBlue's distinctive voice. Less than 24 hours after the terrorist attacks, she had met with the Ad Store, a New York agency, and written the "Reasons to Fly" TV and radio campaign, which featured individuals sharing motivations sentimental and unsentimental for continuing to fly. "Because I want to see my family," one says. "Because I want to get away from my family," another retorts. Says Curtis-McIntyre, "I felt that it would be untrue to our brand to deny our sense of humor or personality."

Future campaigns will continue to reach out and reassure customers. Ads will dwell less on amenities like roomy seats and more on punctual arrival times and safety. (JetBlue was the first national carrier to install bulletproof, dead-bolted cockpit doors after Sept. 11.) After all, that's what travelers are interested in these days, and as a result, that's what interests Curtis-McIntyre. "The day I stop viewing the business as a consumer does is a bad day."

"Something Stylish, Something Blue," *Business 2.0*, February 2002, pp. 94–95.

Evaluating Opportunities in the Changing Marketing Environment

Here's the Beef. So, Where's the Butcher?

BY CONSTANCE L. HAYS

Over the summer, a new Pathmark supermarket opened in a fast-growing corner of Staten Island. From the outside, it looks unremarkable. But inside, it holds the latest in supermarket meat—steaks and cutlets that are not merely someone's future meal, but byproducts of the industry's battle to keep up with Wal-Mart, its biggest rival.

There in the meat section are small white tubs holding pale pink pork chops, their profiles distinct beneath the layer of plastic that seals them off from the world. They, too, look unremarkable except that they were not prepared by the store's butcher. This is "case ready" meat, which differs from traditional supermarket fare in that it is delivered, with its cutting, packaging and labeling complete, to stores in a process that has grown rapidly in popularity among retailers in the last 18 months.

It has also brought controversy. Some of the meat is injected with a saline solution to keep it both good-looking and fresh, and some shoppers complain about the taste. Many of the steaks and chops sold at Wal-Mart note, on their packages, that they contain up to 12 percent liquid. Do they shrink on the grill? Yes, say people who have cooked them. Union leaders anxious to preserve jobs have called for regulations on case-ready meat to make shoppers more aware of what they are buying.

A saline treatment 'keeps the bloom on the meat,' Wal-Mart says.

The main difference between case-ready meat and store-handled meat is that the former is cut, trimmed, packaged and labeled at a plant, not in the back room of a supermarket. The shelf life of case-ready meat is said to be longer, because the package is "flushed" with gas, usually combinations of oxygen and carbon dioxide, to keep everything inside looking fresh. The saline treatment "keeps the bloom on the meat," as a spokesman for **Wal-Mart Stores** put it.

Since September 2001, Wal-Mart has sold only case-ready meat. The change followed a vote by workers at a Wal-Mart supercenter in Texas who voted to join the United Food and Commercial Workers, a unit of the A.F.L.-C.I.O.

Pathmark is the first supermarket chain in New York City to serve meat to shoppers this way, but New York may be the final frontier. In the last year, meat packers report a surge in orders for case-ready meat as supermarkets eagerly follow Wal-Mart's lead.

Chickens have been case-ready for decades; 25 years ago, they too were split and packaged inside the stores' back rooms. But case-ready meat is a newer development, the biggest revolution inside the meat department since 1961, when boxed beef replaced the hanging steer that had to be wheeled into the back room.

Various competitive concerns have pushed stores away from the meatcutters and toward case-ready meat. The entry of Wal-Mart, the retail giant based in Bentonville, Ark., into the grocery business has made all supermarkets eager to trim costs. In recent years, Wal-Mart has made its supercenters, which combine groceries with general merchandise, the cornerstone of its expansion, and will open at least 200 new ones this year on top of the 1,258 already doing business, said a company spokesman, Tom Williams.

There are no meatcutters in the Wal-Mart stores, and they are likely to disappear from supermarkets that switch to case-ready meat, said John Niccollai, president of Local 464-A of the United Food and Commercial Workers in New Jersey. But beyond that, he said, the union objects to the absence of information about the meat in stores that sell case-ready products.

"This will cost us jobs, so we have a vested interest," Mr. Niccollai said. "But there are also a great many concerns we have about case-ready meat. There are additives and preservatives put in it. A number of people are allergic to what they put in the meat." Spokeswomen for the Food Allergy Network and the American Dietetic Association said they could not confirm whether people were allergic to the substances in case-ready meat.

In the New Jersey Legislature, a bill is pending that would require stores to post signs notifying shoppers if more than half the meat they sell is case-ready. Mr. Niccollai said supermarkets were largely opposed to the legislation. "When we send our union agents into the stores and they talk with people, the people have no idea that this product they are buying was not cut and weighed and wrapped in the back room," he said.

The cost savings for Wal-Mart include the elimination of meatcutters in stores (the experienced ones typically earn $1,000 a week) as well as reduced waste and improved efficiency. "It flows really, really well," Mr. Williams said. "The biggest savings we realize is in the efficiency of handling the product and moving it. You have so much more control over what you're ordering and what you need." Most of Wal-Mart's meat comes from **Tyson Foods,** a large Arkansas-based processor that acquired IBP, a beef and pork processor, in 2001.

Other supermarkets that find themselves up against Wal-Mart are turning to the same technique.

"Business is really, really growing," said Michael Queen, chief executive of **Pennexx Foods,** a Philadelphia processor that supplies many supermarkets and is half owned by **Smithfield Foods.** Pennexx, with $60 million in sales this year, will probably triple its sales by next year, he said, as supermarkets, which he described as having "tremendous fear of Wal-Mart," seek to cut costs.

Of course, prepackaged meat costs more than the unadorned raw material. "You are paying for the product and the packaging and the labor," said Mark Greenberg, vice president of meat for **Wakefern Food,** a cooperative that runs ShopRite supermarkets and buys from Pennexx, among other suppliers.

Wal-Mart's ubiquity has pressured all supermarket chains, putting some in unusual difficulty. The **Great Atlantic and Pacific Tea** Company, owner of the Food Emporium and A.&P. chains, announced last month that it would be forced to examine ways of cutting costs to improve profits. "We are probably operating in one of the worst possible retailing environments," A.&P.'s chairman and chief executive, Christian W.E. Haub, said, alluding to "tough choices" that would have to be made later this year. A few months ago, **Albertson's,** another major supermarket chain, retreated from Houston and several other parts of Texas where it competed with Wal-Mart; **Kroger** and regional chains remain.

Some executives say that it is not Wal-Mart, but the need to satisfy customers, that has made them introduce case-ready meat. "Wal-Mart has done it for other reasons," Mr. Greenberg said. "Our position is, we are looking to determine what the customer is looking for."

Shoppers have altered their buying patterns, he added, which means they may be browsing for ground chuck at 9 o'clock in the morning on a Sunday, instead of 4 o'clock on a Friday afternoon. If there is no butcher working at that morning hour, they might be disappointed. But with case-ready meat, the

(Cont.)

product will be there waiting for them.

"A lot of our stores are 24-hour stores, but the butchers aren't working 24 hours," he said. "We want to make sure that when the customer comes in, the full variety is there." In ShopRite's 200 stores around the Northeast, case-ready is available along with store-handled meat, he added.

Mr. Niccollai said wholesale prices for case-ready meat were as much as 25 percent higher than for store-packaged meat. "You're going to save money, they feel, in terms of labor because you are not paying meatcutters," he said. "If you eliminate that, you can operate for less money. But what are you doing to your operation?" He believes that customers will go elsewhere for meat.

That has not been true at the Pathmark in Staten Island. "In this store, it's all case-ready," said Art Whitney, Pathmark's regional manager, as he stood near the meat case. "Over all, the acceptance is very good." A few shoppers have complained, he said, that the deep tubs take up too much room in their refrigerators, compared with the flat trays that chops and other kinds of meat used to come in.

Chris Cossean, who was checking out a cartful of groceries in the store, is not one of them. "I have no problem," she said. "They're fine."

Dueling Diapers

Think big companies can't innovate? Look how Kimberly-Clark and P&G are fighting over disposable training pants. ■ *Matthew Boyle*

The battle for your baby's bottom—a brutal slugfest that makes the Coke-Pepsi showdown look like a playground tussle—took an even nastier turn last year. Procter & Gamble's overhaul of its $4-billion-a-year Pampers product line sparked a knockdown, drag-out price war with the Huggies line from Kimberly Clark, P&G's archrival in the $19-billion-a-year global baby-care market. (The price war took such a toll on Kimberly-Clark that new CEO Thomas Falk said it was largely to blame for the company's depressed fourth-quarter earnings.) The most interesting fight between Kimberly-Clark and P&G is taking place on one specific front: disposable training pants.

Worn by toddlers while they're being potty trained, the elastic diapers are pulled up over the legs like ordinary underpants, rather than being fastened at the sides—and they're the fastest-growing, highest-margin diaper product around. Kimberly-Clark invented the category in 1989 with its Huggies Pull-Ups brand and has dominated it ever since. But in the past 12 months P&G's Pampers Easy Ups have come from nowhere to grab 15% of the $1 billion U.S. training-pants market, reducing Pull-Ups' share from more than 50% to 41%, according to year-end data from Information Resources in Chicago. (Private-label brands and other products like nighttime pants make up the rest of the category.) P&G's sudden success shows the power of product and marketing innovation even late in the game.

In the 1980s, as parenting experts such as Dr. T. Berry Brazelton began counseling parents not to rush the potty training process, Kimberly-Clark—long known for product innovation—sensed an opportunity. Delaying potty training meant that kids would increasingly be in nappies longer. So why not create an entirely new category of diaper: disposable training pants that protected against accidents but also let the growing child feel as though she were wearing underwear just like a big kid? To help give that feel, Kimberly-Clark developed a clothlike outer cover and a breathable nonwoven material called stretch-bonded laminate. It also built new machines to attach the sides of the pants, a step not required for regular diapers.

To help sell parents on the concept, Kimberly-Clark argued that "switching out of diapers and into training pants help[s] speed the potty training process along," a claim made on Parentstages.com, a parenting site sponsored by Kimberly-Clark. That assertion isn't endorsed by the American Academy of Pediatrics, though. Some doctors say that the products are unnecessary and may even delay or prolong potty training. (In 1961, 90% of children were potty trained by age 2 1/2; by 1997, only 22% were.) Training pants give diaper makers the opportunity "to sell into the market two or three years longer than before ... and triple the life cycle of that consumer," says Ryan Mathews, a consultant who follows retail trends.

Whether or not training pants were strictly necessary, they took off. A dozen years later demand is still growing at a 15%-a-year clip. And there's plenty of room to expand, since only about half of the nation's 3.5 million training-age toddlers—defined as kids 18 to 48 months—wear disposable training pants, according to Dudley Lehman, group president of Kimberly-Clark's infant and child care division. (Some parents choose cloth training pants, some keep their kids in regular diapers, and some intrepid souls go right to underwear.) Pull-Ups are big moneymakers too. Training pants are typically 35% more expensive per unit than regular diapers at retail, giving them margins north of 20%, an analyst estimates (neither company will disclose its diaper margins).

If training pants are such an attractive category, why didn't P&G enter the market sooner? Well, it did. Pampers Trainers launched in 1994. But a combination of poor design and high production costs conspired to do them in. The company quietly killed Trainers in 1996. While Kimberly-Clark gloated, Procter went back to the drawing board.

Three years later P&G unveiled a new training-pant design. It chose to introduce it in Japan, the Land of the Rising Pant, where pant-type diapers command about half the market. (One reason: Japanese kids are changed while standing up.) P&G's product, called Pampers Suku-suku, looked and felt much more like underwear than Trainers had without sacrificing absorbency, according to P&G global baby-care president Deb Henretta. Its clothlike exterior was softer and, Henretta hoped, more appealing than that of Pull-Ups. The design held its own in Japan and convinced P&G that it was on to something.

P&G soon moved to test markets in Scandinavia and Greece; a full rollout of what it was now calling Easy Ups followed across Western Europe and Britain in 2001. Europe posed a special challenge, partly because kids there are toilet trained earlier. So P&G positioned Easy Ups as an extension of its premium diaper line rather than as a training pant. The strategy worked, and P&G says Easy Ups are now twice as popular as Pull-Ups in Western Europe. (Kimberly-Clark disputes this.) "They are a godsend!" says

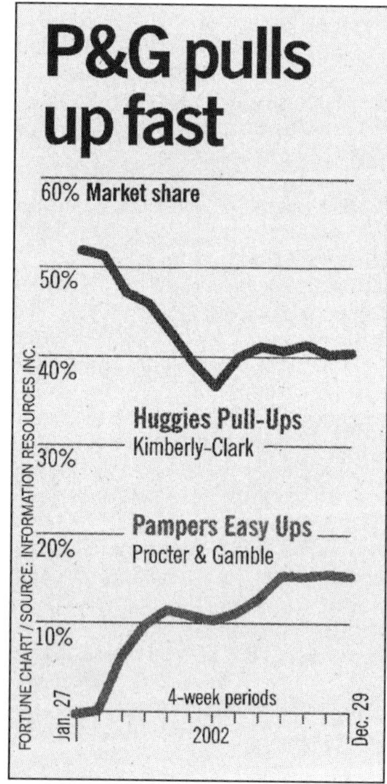

(Cont.)

Kate Beard, a resident of Weston, 30 miles north of London, whose 3-year-old, Molly, wears Easy Ups at night.

The stage was finally set for Easy Ups' North American debut in February 2002. Kimberly-Clark execs, who had seen P&G try and fail in the U.S. market before, pooh-poohed Easy Ups' prospects. "Kimberly-Clark was trashtalking that P&G wouldn't even get a 7% share," says Tom Vierhile, executive editor of *Productscan Online,* which tracks the packaged-goods industry.

In fact, P&G got 7% in less than three months. That share has since more than doubled, thanks to a well-orchestrated attack on Pull-Ups' position. First, P&G threw buckets of advertising and marketing dollars into the Easy Ups launch. According to ad-spending tracker CMR in New York City, P&G spent $19 million on ads for Easy Ups in the first ten months of last year, more than the company spent on all other Pampers products combined. Meanwhile, through aggressive couponing and other promotions, P&G cut the price on its training pants so that they cost only 15% more than regular diapers rather than 35% more. Shoppers buying Kimberly-Clark's Pull-Ups at Krogers would turn over their receipt to find a coupon for $4.50 off a jumbo package of Easy Ups, which usually sold for about $11.50. This wasn't exactly a new trick: "The easiest thing to do is to buy share by lowering the price," says Vierhile. And $40-billion-a-year P&G has much deeper pockets than $15 billion Kimberly-Clark.

On the production side, a new global manufacturing system (in which modular machinery can quickly be added to or removed from the diaper line) enabled P&G to release four product improvements to Easy Ups in just seven months. The upgrades included adding Elmo graphics, a thinner core, and a wetness indicator. Normally a single change could take a year or more. "That's stunning," says Bill Steele, an analyst at Banc of America Securities. "That should have their competitors worried."

Still, Kimberly-Clark insists it's not fazed. Lehman told *Advertising Age* last summer that "the jury's out" on Easy Ups' success, and he stands by that opinion. Kimberly-Clark has rolled out improvements to its Pull-Ups, making them 30% thinner and, more recently, adding refastenable sides. The company claims that consumers prefer its newest PullUps three to one over Easy Ups. And, Lehman boasts, it has the highest margins in the diaper industry.

Analyst Steele, for one, thinks Kimberly-Clark should worry: "If a 15% share doesn't indicate that P&G is here to stay, is Kimberly waiting for 40%?" he asks. "I was surprised that Kimberly didn't defend its position as aggressively as it should have. Perhaps they underestimated P&G." If Kimberly continues to do so, it will have quite a mess to clean up.

"Dueling Diapers," *Fortune,* February 17, 2003, pp. 115–116.

Cracking China's Market

Adapting to Chinese Customs, Cultural Changes, Companies From U.S., Europe Find Profit

BY LESLIE CHANG AND PETER WONACOTT

Beijing

Long-held perception: China is a perpetual market of tomorrow, sucking money from foreign companies tantalized by visions of a billion new consumers, even as hope of profit recedes year by year.

Dawning reality: China has turned into a profitable market for foreigners in relatively short order.

Capitalizing on dramatic changes that include the emergence of urban consumers, more open local governments, the spread of modern retail outlets and the entrepreneurialism of the Chinese, a critical mass of foreign companies are now making money in China. According to an August report by the American Chamber of Commerce, 64% of about 200 companies surveyed in China say they are profitable.

China is now **Eastman Kodak** Co.'s second-biggest film market after the U.S., and sales here are growing faster than in any other major market, the film firm says. Food conglomerate **Groupe Danone** SA of France has in the past six years built a $1.2 billion business in China that is profitable in all its divisions. Germany's **Siemens** AG, selling everything from washing machines to high-speed railways, saw double-digit profit growth last year in China, now its No. 3 market after the U.S. and Germany. **Procter & Gamble** Co. has invested $1 billion in China and says its operation here is profitable. The KFC restaurant chain, owned by **Yum Brands** Inc., opens a new store every other day in China, all funded by its Chinese profits. "China is an absolute gold mine for us," Yum's chief executive David Novak told analysts recently.

China continues to be one of the most challenging markets around, owing to brutal price wars, backstabbing business partners, widespread counterfeiting and a slow-moving judicial system. But here is how some of the most successful players in China are turning a profit:

Kodak: Just $12,000 to Run an Outlet

Under a tropical evening sky in Xiamen, executives from Eastman Kodak pile out of a minibus to be greeted by hundreds of cheering workers. They climb to a stage festooned in red-and-gold Kodak colors, and a worker reads a poem commemorating production of the 20-millionth Kodak disposable camera in this seaside city. "Kodak, I love you," he gushes.

Kodak is loving China back. "There were a lot of people that were burned and hurt and called China a shattered dream," says one of the executives, Ying Yeh, a vice president for Kodak. "But I never had any doubt."

Kodak, which is based in Rochester, N.Y., has nearly 8,000 photo stores across China, one of the country's largest retail networks in any sector. The company taps the desire of many Chinese to run their own businesses while helping them negotiate the ins and outs of setting up shop on their own. Because of China's vast size, foreign companies seeking national reach must rely to an unusual extent on such a far-flung network of people, then find ways to tie their interests to the company's own.

One Kodak campaign, "99,000 Will Make You a Boss," offered all the necessary photo-development equipment, training, and a store license for the equivalent of a one-time fee of 99,000 yuan, less than $12,000. Kodak negotiated a deal with the Bank of China and other big banks to arrange financing for individual operators lacking capital. As its numbers of distributors and outlets boomed, Kodak factories have fed these "minibosses" with competitively priced cameras and film. That's thanks to a big bet Kodak made on manufacturing in China in 1998, when it picked up three debt-laden state firms and many of their workers for over $1 billion. In return, Beijing barred new foreign-invested film factories for four years.

The gamble helped Kodak, a distant fourth when it arrived in China in 1994, leapfrog rivals including Japan's **Fuji Photo Film** Co., which relies on imports to stock its stores. Today, Fuji's market share has shrunk to 25% compared with Kodak's 63%.

Kodak is now expanding in China's poorer west. In a country where fashion and new lifestyles spread at warp speed, many are buying cameras for a first time to record the change. Says Paul Walrath, a plant manager in Xiamen and a 26-year Kodak veteran, "We're counting on great performance in China to drive the company where we want to go."

Danone: Master of Piggybacking

Like Kodak, France's Danone was a relative latecomer when it started building its

Opening Doors for Big Business

Multinational companies are expanding their operations in China and turning profits. Some examples:

COMPANY	SCALE OF OPERATIONS	EMPLOYEES	TOTAL INVESTMENT	PROFIT DETAILS
Coca-Cola	31 bottling plants with three joint-venture partners and two concentrate plants	20,000	$1.1 billion	Profitable for eight years
Danone	More than 50 manufacturing plants for biscuits, beverages and dairy products	25,000	NA	Operating profit margins higher than the company's global average, amounting to at least $140 million in 2001
Kodak	Five manufacturing plants for cameras, chemicals and film and more than 8,000 outlets	5,000	$1.2 billion	Company says it's profitable
Motorola	Two manufacturing plants for mobile-phone handsets, cellular networks and semiconductors	12,000	$3.4 billion at end of 2001	Company says it's profitable
Procter & Gamble	Five plants for food, personal care and household consumer goods	4,000	$1 billion	Company says it's profitable
Siemens	40 companies with businesses including telecommunications, machine automation, power, transport and home appliances	21,000	More than $610 million	Profit grew at double-digit rates in 2002
Yum Brands	Close to 800 KFC restaurants and 100 Pizza Hut restaurants	40,000 to 50,000	More than $400 million	China is expected to account for 29% of international profits for 2002

Source: The companies

China business around 1996. It decided to piggyback off the successes of domestic brands rather than to build all its businesses from scratch, in 1996 buying a controlling stake in Hangzhou Wahaha Group Co., an enterprising maker of vitamin-enriched milk drinks targeted at children.

Danone embarked on a massive expansion for Wahaha—building multiple plants across the country, backed by a huge advertising campaign—that pushed annual sales from 800 million bottles when it bought the company to four billion bottles within two years. It then quickly leveraged that scale, distribution network and brand-name recognition into a new business: bottled water, for China's increasingly health-conscious population. Through the same obsessive focus on scale and speed, Danone has built Wahaha into China's biggest water company—and made China into Danone's biggest water market, with $908 million in revenue in 2001.

In launching a new drink, Danone expects that prices will collapse by 50% within three years, thanks to local competition. Only through investing heavily upfront is it possible to achieve economies of scale and, hence, profitability. "You need to recover your investment before the price wars start," says Simon Israel, Danone's Asia-Pacific chairman. "I've never seen anything move so fast as it does in China."

Rare for multinationals, Danone acquires Chinese companies but continues to sell their products under their own brands. The strategy has smoothed the way for a steady diet of acquisitions and curried favor with Chinese executives and officials, who are loath to see national brands go under.

Today, 80% of Danone's sales here are under Chinese brands. The company has so played down its multinational origins that it was asked by the government to help Wahaha manufacture a "domestic" cola to take on Coke and Pepsi. Thus did Danone, which does not sell soft drinks anywhere else in the world, become the parent of Future Cola, which holds the No. 3 spot in China and is known as "the Chinese people's own cola."

The moves have handed Danone dominance despite its late start. The company had $1.2 billion in sales here in 2001 and is one of China's largest food and beverage concerns. Danone has more than 50 plants and 25,000 employees around the country, all built up in the past six years.

Coke: 12-Cent Strategy

Coca-Cola Co., which has seen eight straight years of profit in China, says sales are growing faster here than anywhere in the world. The Atlanta-based company already reaches 600 million consumers in China's large and medium-size cities, but its latest drive focuses on reaching the other half.

A survey the company conducted in Yunnan, a largely rural province in the southwest, revealed that most consumer offerings, from ice cream to drinks, cost between six cents and 36 cents, which meant a 30-cent can of Coke was too expensive for many. Coke's solution: ramp up its business in returnable bottles, in which a customer drinks a Coke on the premises of a shop or restaurant. The business, which drives down costs because bottles and crates can be reused many times, brings the price of a Coke serving down to a single yuan—about 12 cents.

> As multinational consumer-products companies such as Coca-Cola, Eastman Kodak and Motorola make further inroads—and more money—in a rapidly changing China, their logos are becoming an integral part of the nation's landscape.

"We're looking for this to be a solution for our rural markets," says Nick Moore, region manager for the North and Southwest China Region.

Such minute price distinctions are crucial in China. At an Internet cafe in Tangshan, where customers can surf the Web for an hour for a mere 24 cents, 2,000 cases of Coke sold last year, compared with 300 cases in 2001, before Coke launched its cheaper drinks in returnable bottles. "Customers always want the cheapest thing to drink," says the cafe's owner. "Now, the Coke is the same price as the water."

Yum Brands: Localize, Localize

When KFC set up its first China store in 1987, the venture was seen as so politically sensitive that the site required the approval of the Beijing mayor, and foreign novelty was a big part of its appeal. Recently, it took Yum Brands only a day to get most of the approvals it needed to set up a new Pizza Hut restaurant in the central city of Zhengzhou.

Globalization is taking hold in China faster than anyone expected, and fast food has become part of the Chinese landscape. Catering to national tastes, KFC offers soup, rice and Chinese breakfast porridge. It does its own tests and product launches with minimal input from the home office in Louisville, Ky. "We're free to create our own products. Our company is not a company that micromanages from a distance," says Sam Su, president of Greater China for Yum Restaurants China.

KFC now has about 800 restaurants here and plans to open 200 a year for some time to come, and China is the company's biggest source of profit after the U.S.

Who's Blocking the Xbox? Sony and Its Games

BY MATT RICHTEL

XBOX, the video game console that **Microsoft** introduced nearly 14 months ago, is technologically sophisticated and, by many accounts, the best way to play games against competitors over the Internet.

But the advantages have not translated into the returns Microsoft had hoped for. It has sold nine million Xbox consoles, on the low end of its projections; it continues to lose money on each one it sells; and it remains desperately behind **Sony,** whose PlayStation 2 is selling at a record pace. Wall Street analysts have mixed opinions about whether Microsoft's early effort has been successful, but they agree that it has a way to go.

Avid game players like Brian Green, 26, who spends hours each week on both consoles, have a simple explanation for why Microsoft has yet to make the inroads it sought. "The Xbox is cool," he said, "but the PlayStation is where the games are at."

That is not good news for Microsoft, because people tend to buy electronics based on the amount of software they can use. Sony learned that lesson two decades ago, when its technically superior Betamax video recorders were swamped by VHS machines that had more tapes available.

Makers of video games are starting to produce more games for Xbox, but the 2-to-1 gap with PlayStation will take some time to close. And while Microsoft, which has more than $40 billion in cash on hand, can afford to be patient, analysts and investors wonder how much time and money it is willing to invest before it starts to turn a profit.

The issue is of no small significance. The market for consoles and video games is worth more than $9 billion a year. Even while losing on selling consoles, Microsoft could still make a lot of money from game makers. They pay the console makers about $10 for each copy of the games they manufacture—and they made well in excess of 50 million games in the United States last year. Games typically sell at retail for $50.

For now, though, there are only losses for Microsoft. It declines to say how much it loses on each console, but industry analysts estimate the figure at close to $100. Sony, by contrast, does not sell PlayStation 2's below cost.

Part of Microsoft's problem is the ambitious design of Xbox: its chipsets and other electronic components are more expensive than those of the PlayStation. Microsoft has also been unable to realize certain economies of scale because sales have not been as robust as expected.

Joseph Osha, a semiconductor analyst at Merrill Lynch who follows **Nvidia,** a company that makes the graphics processing chips for the Xbox, said Microsoft had had to "pull back sharply" on its orders. He estimated that Microsoft had 1 million to 1.5 million unsold Xbox chipsets, which are the brains used in Xbox consoles.

Larry Davis for The New York Time

Robert J. Bach, above, the executive in charge of Xbox, says it is on track. Xbox games were displayed at a video-game show in Los Angeles last spring. Consumer testers tried the games at Microsoft in Redmond, Wash.

Microsoft is too big to have its stock price move significantly on sales of Xbox. But the effect of all that idle Xbox inventory is evident on its profit-and-loss statement. In a recent filing with the Securities and Exchange Commission, Microsoft said its home and entertainment segment, which includes the Xbox and television divisions, lost $348 million in its most recent quarter on sales of $1.28 billion. In the period a year earlier, the home and entertainment unit lost $180 million on sales of $833 million.

On a micro level, investors "don't like it because they lose money on every piece of hardware they sell," said Michael P. Wallace, a video game industry analyst at UBS Warburg. But, he added, "on a macro level, they're in the No. 2 spot."

In addition to overtaking **Nintendo,** which makes the GameCube console, as the second-place console maker, Microsoft has put itself in a position to compete with Sony for years to come, Mr. Wallace said.

When Microsoft introduced the Xbox in January 2001, it promised to put $2 billion into the product—$500 million in advertising alone. It may well need to spend it all. In 2002, according to UBS Warburg, Sony sold 18.3 million PlayStation 2 consoles, while Microsoft sold 5.2 million Xbox machines and Nintendo sold 4.7 million GameCubes. These figures reflect consoles sold to consumers, not consoles that the manufacturers ship to wholesalers or retailers.

The good news for Microsoft is that industry experts expect it to widen its lead over Nintendo this year. **Electronic Arts,** the world's largest game maker, is projecting that in North America in 2003, Sony will sell 9 million to 10 million PlayStation 2's, Microsoft will sell 2.5 million to 3 million Xbox consoles and Nintendo will sell 2 million to 2.5 million machines.

Electronic Arts also projects that Microsoft will beat Nintendo in Europe, the second-biggest market after the United States. Still, Microsoft is particularly struggling in Japan, where it has been virtually shut out of the market, selling a mere 300,000 consoles, according to the company. Throughout all of Asia, Microsoft has sold only 500,000 Xbox consoles, according to UBS Warburg, compared with Sony's sales of 3.67 million PlayStation 2's.

Microsoft officials say they are hampered in Asia because Sony and Nintendo, both Japanese companies, have entrenched positions and great control over distribution and sales channels there. But industry analysts say Microsoft should come up with more than excuses.

"If Xbox has any chance of closing the gap against PlayStation, Microsoft is going to need a better Japanese strategy," said Michael Gartenberg, an analyst at Jupiter Research. He said it needed to have better games and to burrow into the Japanese distribution channel.

Microsoft said it was already making progress on games, introducing in Japan a game called DOA Xtreme Beach Volleyball. The 80,000 games sold out within two days.

Robert J. Bach, a senior vice president for the home and entertainment division, acknowledged that the Xbox was continuing to lose money, but he said that such losses were natural with a new business. A better picture of the situation, he said, is how the company is performing relative to its business plan. "We're doing very well on that basis," he said.

(Cont.)

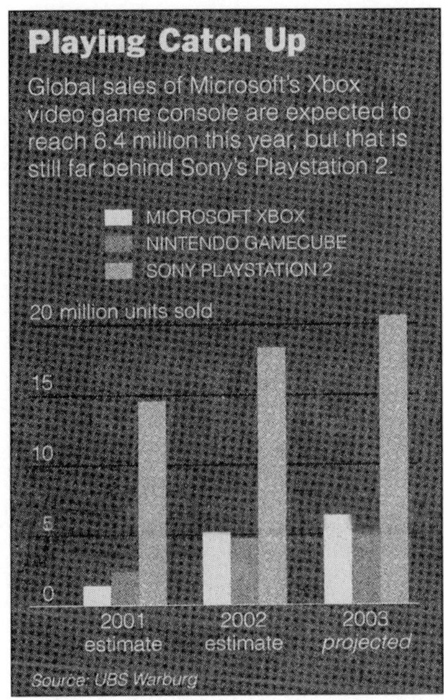

Analysts said Microsoft must also persuade video game makers to produce versions of their products for the Xbox. According to figures provided by Microsoft but compiled by NPD Funworld, an industry research group, there are 458 games available for the PlayStation 2, versus 207 for the Xbox and 168 for the Nintendo GameCube.

Microsoft faces a chicken-and-egg problem: makers of video games won't make versions of their games for a given console unless the machine has a wide installed base, but it is hard to build a base without a lot of games.

Some big game makers have made versions only for the PlayStation 2. Most notable has been Grand Theft Auto, the most popular game the last two years. Microsoft said it is in discussions with the game's maker, **Take Two Interactive,** to persuade it to produce a version for the Xbox.

Xbox also suffers because video game publishers will sometimes release a PlayStation 2 version of a game first, then deliver an Xbox version months later. That happened last year with Medal of Honor, a top-selling game from Electronic Arts that came out some six months earlier on the PlayStation 2. Jeff Brown, a spokesman for Electronic Arts, said, however, that the company was increasingly releasing games concurrently for the two platforms.

Industry analysts like Mr. Wallace of UBS Warburg said Microsoft needed to find video game makers that would produce hit titles exclusively for its console.

To bolster its game portfolio, Microsoft has been in discussions to buy **Vivendi Universal Games.** Microsoft would not comment on the issue.

In the meantime, Microsoft has quietly begun to make inroads with a feature that cuts across individual games: Xbox Live. This is a $50 attachment that lets console owners play games against one another over the Internet. Microsoft, citing figures from NPD Funworld, said it sold 350,000 Xbox Live kits since introducing the service in November. Sony has sold 438,000 of its own online kit, said Microsoft, citing NPD Funworld figures, but Sony has been selling its kit for almost twice as long, since August.

Mr. Bach said that these kinds of numbers showed that Microsoft, by sticking to its plan, could succeed, and he has said so to Microsoft's chairman, Bill Gates, and its chief executive, Steven A. Ballmer. "In the conversations I have with Bill and Steve, they want to know where we are on that plan," he said. "We're on that plan."

The question is whether Brian Green and other gamers are on board, too.

For This Delicacy, Brand Recognition Is a Problem

BY NEIL MACFARQUHAR

BASRA, Iraq — The hundreds of packages of dates stacked on the cement factory floor and metal shelves of the venerable Al-Moosawi Company are remarkable for one curious absence.

The label does not mention they are Iraqi. The brand itself, "Dubai Dates," is misleading enough, but the name "United Arab Emirates" runs up one side of the package decorated with a drawing of a date bouquet.

Anyone handling the packages—and their predominantly Russian labels signal their ultimate destination—would have no idea they were grown around this southern port city.

That is the whole point, of course. Iraqis resort to subterfuge to avoid United Nations sanctions preventing exports of a product once viewed by the cognoscenti as more desirable than even the country's crude oil.

"Nobody wants to hear about anything called Iraqi dates, or for that matter about anything made in Iraq," lamented Fathi Atallah Raja, the Baghdad spokesman for the Iraqi Date Processing & Marketing Company, a semiprivate collective that handles all sales.

To a certain extent, the story of Iraq's dates mirrors the Iraqi experience since Saddam Hussein assumed control. What was once a thriving industry finds itself inexorably fading after 23 years filled with war, economic sanctions and a negligence driven by the pursuit of industrial development and other, more lethal projects.

Iraqis crow that the reputation of their dates was once such that Americans set sail with a whole shipload of date palm saplings to plant in California in the 1930's. Exports of the dates spanned the globe.

War wrought the first devastation. Millions of trees in what Iraq boasts was once the largest date forest in the world, on the Fao peninsula, just south of here, were either burned or felled by shrapnel during the raging battles of the 1980-88 war with Iran.

What were once majestic stands of palms are gone, replaced by a stunted, nightmarish landscape of decapitated trunks and blackened stumps. The former population of 16 million date palms around Basra is now estimated at 3 million.

The Persian Gulf war also took its toll, with a mysterious outbreak of disease afterward that some trace to depleted uranium shells.

Iraqi scientists identified the disease as a fungus, fusarium, that attacks the crown of the tree, causing it to topple and leaving the flaccid trunk weirdly twisted. It is known around here as Mad Palm Disease.

"The heart of the palm turns from white to black and it creates a bad smell," said Abbas Mahdi Jassim, director of the Center for the Study of Date Palms at the University of Basra. "We link it with the war because we didn't know this disease before."

The only way found to prevent the spread has been to fell the trees and burn them. Mr. Jassim, who earned a doctorate in horticulture from Kansas State University in 1988, is trying to regenerate tens of thousands of trees through tissue culture in test tubes. On several occasions, the chemically intensive process has attracted the attention of United Nations weapons inspectors trying to determine whether the medium in which the tiny sprouts grow might have a more sinister use.

Dates have long been a staple around the region's deserts—they are rich in minerals and vitamins and last for months without refrigeration. The Koran includes no fewer than 18 mostly laudatory references to dates.

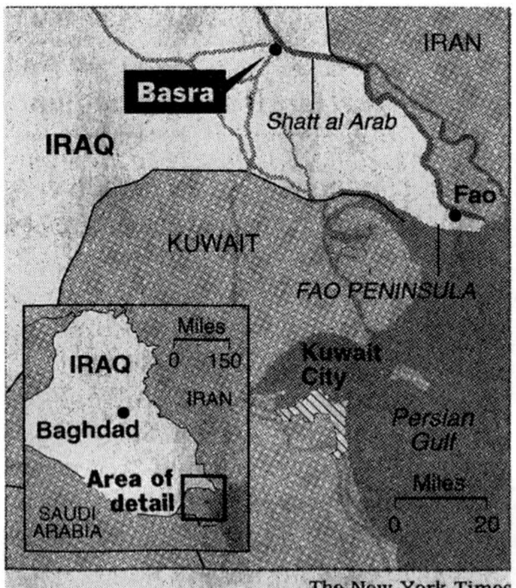

The New York Times

War and disease have ravaged Basra's date industry.

Sitting around the lunch table with a group of Iraqis talking about dates is vaguely reminiscent of, say, the French discussing cheese. The official date encyclopedia lists 627 varieties in Iraq, and everyone champions a favorite.

Great nostalgia for the finest Iraqi dates lingers throughout the Arab world. A Saudi household wishing to show a guest particular honor will bring out a basket of the exquisite Barhi variety, now cultivated there. Egyptians of a certain age, when hearing that a traveler is going to Iraq, will urge, "Bring back dates."

Growers in the Emirates and Saudi Arabia have bred millions of Iraqi date palms, becoming the main suppliers of the finer varieties that have all but disappeared in Iraq. Growers here sniff that others can never replicate the combination of conditions that give Iraqi dates their luscious, chewy quality.

"Sure other countries can grow the trees, but the dates of Basra have a special taste," boasted Sayid Abdel Rida al-Moosawi, the patriarch of the clan that founded Basra's first date processing factory in 1959.

Mr. Moosawi rails against what he calls American piracy in the gulf, stopping Iraqi products like dates—exports are now less than one-fifth what they were before the Iran-Iraq war.

He demurs on the subject of the bogus labels, however. "I seem to remember they are marked as made in Iraq," he said during an interview in the sprawling, turquoise-domed mosque that his family built in downtown Basra. "Besides, the Americans watch any ships moving from Iraq's territorial waters and they can confiscate the cargo whatever the trademark."

But Mr. Raja of the collective says Iraqis gamble on a variety of methods to evade the blockade, including phony labeling or shipping the dates on Iranian-flagged ships. (Similar methods have been used with oil.)

The United Nations bans all exports from Iraq except under the oil-for-food program.

A Western envoy in Baghdad acknowledged that the United Nations did not pay terribly close attention to contraband dates. It interdicts much of what leaves Iraq by sea, but the land borders are fairly porous, especially for products that are not exactly going to supply the secret wealth Iraq would need to develop weapons of mass destruction.

As with other fields where they excelled, Iraqis dream that after the sanctions are lifted and peace returns, they will reassert their domination of the market in fine dates.

"One day we will regain the same reputation, the same position," predicted Mr. Moosawi. "It will probably take 25 years to get back where it was."

Is Fat The Next Tobacco?

For BigFood, the supersizing of America is becoming a big headache ■ *Roger Parloff*

On August 3, 2000, the parody newspaper *The Onion* ran a joke article under the headline HERSHEY'S ORDERED TO PAY OBESE AMERICANS $135 BILLION. The hypothesized class-action lawsuit said that Hershey "knowingly and willfully" marketed to children "rich, fatty candy bars containing chocolate and other ingredients of negligible nutritional value," while "spiking" them with "peanuts, crisped rice, and caramel to increase consumer appeal."

Some joke. Last summer New York City attorney Sam Hirsch filed a strikingly similar suit—against McDonald's—on behalf of a class of obese and overweight children. He alleged that the fast-food chain "negligently, recklessly, carelessly and/or intentionally" markets to children food products that are "high in fat, salt, sugar, and cholesterol" while failing to warn of those ingredients' links to "obesity, diabetes, coronary heart disease, high blood pressure, strokes, elevated cholesterol intake, related cancers," and other conditions.

News of the lawsuit drew hoots of derision. But food industry executives aren't laughing—or shouldn't be. No matter what happens with Hirsch's suit, he has tapped into something very big. Seasoned lawyers from both sides of past mass-tort disputes agree that the years ahead hold serious tobacco-like litigation challenges for the food industry—challenges that extend beyond fast foods to snack foods, soft drinks, packaged foods, and dietary supplements. "The precedents, the ammo, the missiles are already there and waiting in a silo marked 'tobacco,'" says Victor Schwartz, general counsel of the American Tort Reform Association.

Junk food may not be addictive in the same way that tobacco is. But weight, once gained, is notoriously hard to lose, and childhood weight patterns strongly predict adult ones. Rates of overweight among small children—to whom junk-food companies aggressively market their products—have doubled since 1980; rates among adolescents have tripled. In 1999 physicians began reporting an alarming rise in children of obesity-linked type 2 diabetes. Once an obese youngster develops diabetes, he or she will never get rid of it. That's a lot more irreversible than a smoking addiction.

Though many people recoil at the idea of obesity suits—eating habits are a matter of personal responsibility, they protest—the tobacco precedents show that such qualms can be overcome. Yes, most people know that eating a Big Mac isn't the same as eating a spinach salad, but most people knew that smoking was bad for them too. And yes, diet is only one risk factor out of many that contribute to obesity, but smoking is just one risk factor for diseases for which the tobacco companies were forced to fork over reimbursement to Medicaid. (The industry's share of the blame was statistically estimated and then divvied up among companies by market share.) The tobacco companies eventually agreed to pay $246 billion to the states, and juries are now ordering them to pay individual smokers eight-digit verdicts too.

By the Surgeon General's estimate, public-health costs attributable to overweight and obesity now come to about $117 billion a year—fast approaching the $140 billion stemming from smoking. Suing Big Food offers allures to contingency-fee lawyers that rival those of Big Tobacco, and the implications of that are pretty easy to foresee. While the food industry is not apt to be socked with anything like the penalties that hit tobacco, companies will face consumer-protection suits that might cost them many tens of millions of dollars and force them to significantly change marketing practices.

THE TRIGGERING EVENT OCCURRED in December 2001. That's when the Surgeon General, observing that about 300,000 deaths per year are now associated with overweight and obesity, warned that those conditions might soon cause as much preventable disease and death as smoking. The report prompted journalists to call John Banzhaf III, an antismoking activist and a law professor at George Washington University School of Law, to see whether tobacco-style litigation might be in the offing. "I said, 'Well, no, there are important differences,'" Banzhaf recalls. But even as he talked, he began to change his mind.

Another key academic strategist in the tobacco wars, Northeastern University law professor Richard Daynard, was soon drawn into the fray. At a conference last April to discuss Marion Nestle's new book, *Food Politics,* he was asked to talk about possible obesity-related litigation. (Nestle, who chairs the nutrition department at New York University and whose name is pronounced NESSel, is not related to the founders of the food company.) Daynard, like Banzhaf, at first saw no analogy to tobacco. But as he read Nestle's book, he, too, began to change his mind.

Here's Nestle's argument. For at least the past 50 years public-health authorities have wanted to deliver a simple, urgent message to the American people: Eat less. They have been thwarted from doing so, however, by political pressure from the food industry. The meat industry alone spends millions a year on lobbying, apparently with great success. Instead of forthrightly saying, "Eat less red meat," government health authorities are forced to say, "Eat more lean meat." Food companies compound the confusion by advertising that their products can be "part of a balanced and nutritional diet," even though they know that their products are not typically consumed that way Any food can theoretically be part of a balanced diet if you keep the portions tiny enough and eat lots of fruits, vegetables, and grains.

As Daynard well knew, advertising claims that are literally true, but misleading when viewed in a real-world context, can violate state consumer-protection laws. In some states, like California, plaintiffs can force companies to disgorge all profits attributable to advertising that employs such statements, and the plaintiff can win without having to prove that even a single individual was actually tricked by the statement.

The idea of bringing such suits against the

(Cont.)

food industry is not unprecedented. In 1983, for instance, the California supreme court greenlighted a suit brought by an advocacy group against General Foods over the way such breakfast cereals as Sugar Crisp and Cocoa Pebbles—which contain 38% to 50% sugar by weight—were being marketed to children. The plaintiffs argued that "although promoted and labeled as 'cereals,'" the products "are in fact more accurately described as sugar products, or candies." The court suggested that ads even implicitly claiming that such products were nutritious or healthful were plausible lawsuit targets. (After the ruling, the case settled.)

Last July, Daynard attended an informal meeting of lawyers and public-health advocates in Banzhaf's office in Washington. "The first question at John's meeting was, 'Is there a there there?'" Daynard recalls. "What persuaded us was, in a sense, the media. This thing is so radioactive in terms of media attention that cases will bring in other lawyers and bring in other cases."

Later that month a lawyer who'd never heard of Banzhaf or Daynard crashed their party. Sam Hirsch, who runs his own small practice in New York City, had become interested in food issues after an overweight associate referred to a burger as a "fat bomb." Though Hirsch, 54, had never brought a class action, he now filed two, one in Brooklyn and another in the Bronx. The suits, brought on behalf of classes of obese people, named McDonald's, Burger King, KFC, and Wendy's as defendants.

The press loved the story. The industry response was ferocious. The Coalition for Consumer Freedom, a trade group of restaurants and food and beverage suppliers (McDonald's is not a member), promptly took out aggressive full-page ads in newsmagazines. One showed a man's bloated, bare gut spilling over a belted waistline. The copy read: "Did you hear the one about the fat guy suing the restaurants? It's no joke."

For plaintiffs lawyers and nutrition activists, the Hirsch suit was a mixed blessing. Some worried that it was such a laughingstock that it might strengthen the forces pushing for tort reform. As a tool of public education, on the other hand, the Hirsch suit was a landmark. Even if the industry was winning the talk-show shout-fests, its arguments about personal responsibility sent a double-edged message, according to Daynard. "'If you're stupid enough to use our products, you deserve to get the diseases our products cause.' That's what it means if you deconstruct it," he says. "This sort of discussion is not good for the lawsuit, but it's very good for public health."

In August, Banzhaf invited Hirsch to the second meeting of his group. Afterward Hirsch decided not to pursue his two lawsuits, which had been filed on behalf of adults, and to bring instead a new class-action suit on behalf of obese children. He focused this suit on McDonald's alone. One prospective class member, 400-pound, 15-year-old Gregory Rhymes, who suffers from type 2 diabetes, stated in an affidavit that he has eaten at McDonald's "nearly every day" since he was 6. Neal Barnard, a doctor who heads a vegetarian advocacy group, submitted a declaration asserting that "the consumption of McDonald's products has significantly contributed to the development of [Rhymes's] obesity and diabetes."

McDonald's has mounted a spirited defense. "Every reasonable person understands what is in products such as hamburgers and fries," McDonald's lawyers argue in their papers, "as well as the consequences to one's waistline, and potentially to one's health, of excessively eating those foods over a prolonged period." The lawyers also warn that the plaintiffs' theories, if accepted, would usher in "an uncontrollable avalanche of litigation against other restaurants and food providers, as well as other industries (such as the pizza, ice cream, cheese, and cookie industries)." In a statement to FORTUNE, McDonald's said that it has long made nutritional information available to customers upon request. "Nutrition professionals say that McDonald's food can be and is a part of a healthy diet based on the sound nutrition principles of balance, variety, and moderation," the statement continues. McDonald's has asked a federal court in Manhattan to take the case away from the state court and then to dismiss it. The court has not yet ruled.

Targeting kids is the food industry's Achilles' heel, says plaintiffs lawyer John Coale, a veteran of tobacco and gun litigation. Fast food, snack food, and soft drink companies focus their marketing on children and adolescents through Saturday morning TV commercials; through cuddly characters like Ronald McDonald (the second most recognized figure among children after Santa Claus); through contracts to advertise and serve soft drinks and fast food in schools; and through ever-changing toys included in Happy Meals.

If misleading advertising can be linked to childhood disease, Coale says, "you've got yourself not only a lawsuit but a movement." Food industry insiders have already come forward to speak to Coale about disturbing marketing practices, he claims. "We're not bringing down the fastfood industry next Tuesday," he says, "but there are legitimate legal issues here."

HIRSCH'S CASE, SAY MANY PLAINTIFFS lawyers, is like the earliest tobacco and asbestos cases, which failed because the damning evidence had not yet come out. But once cases progress into the discovery stage, smoking-gun documents may begin to emerge, showing that the companies knew more than the general public about the impact that their products and advertising were having on children's health. Tort reform advocate Schwartz does not doubt this. "As discovery goes forward," Schwartz explains, "plaintiffs lawyers will be finding documents that, if held up in isolation, make it look like the industry had something to hide. That gives the case heft." Schwartz predicts that it will take about five years to reach that point.

Not everyone on the defense side is as fatalistic as Schwartz. Thomas Bezanson of New York's Chadbourne & Parke, who has defended tobacco, alcohol, and pharmaceutical companies, thinks that what happened to the tobacco industry was unique. "You had a very powerful attack made by the plaintiffs bar, the press, the politicians, and the state attorneys general," he says. "That only works if you are able to use all of those in a coordinated way to persuade society that the object of attack is some kind of pariah. I doubt that kind of attack can be lodged against food companies."

There is another important difference between tobacco and food. The tobacco industry "can't make a safe cigarette," says Banzhaf, "but fast-food companies can do almost everything we want without going broke. They can issue warnings, they can post fat and calorie content on menu boards, they can put more nutritious things on their menus. In fact, they already are." Last year, for instance, McDonald's reduced trans fatty acids in its fried foods and introduced low-fat yogurt and fruit roll-up desserts. A press release touts the yogurt as a "good source of calcium" and says that the fruit desserts provide 25% of the daily recommended value of vitamin C. "As a mom and registered dietician," a McDonald's staffer says in the release, "I know the importance of having this type of nutrient value in a snack food that kids enjoy."

Such gestures are themselves fraught with legal peril, however. Daynard mocks the McDonald's press release on its new healthy desserts, for instance: "We're talking about *desserts* to have *after their Happy Meals!*" protests Daynard. "The suggestion is that a really good mother would order *four* of them, right?"

If companies that produce high-calorie and high-fat foods are worried about future lawsuits, they aren't saying. PepsiCo, Cadbury Schweppes, and Kraft all declined to comment. Their trade group was less shy. "We advocate getting good messages to par-

(Cont.)

ents to help children develop good eating and exercise habits," says a spokesperson for the Grocery Manufacturers of America. "What we think is counterproductive is finger-pointing, reckless accusations, and lawsuits that won't make anyone any thinner." All the same, prudent food companies might do well to start scrutinizing their advertising and packaging, tweaking product lines, and, yes, squirreling away some reserves for potential judgments.

For at least one industry, though, the new spotlight on fat may be a glimmer of unaccustomed good news. Anecdotally, we've heard that smoking has helped a lot of people lose weight.

"Is Fat the Next Tobacco?" *Fortune,* February 3, 2003, pp. 50–54.

Prospecting

As Latinos Fan Out Across America, Businesses Follow

Two Partners Find an Enclave In Charleston, S.C., Set Up Spanish-Language TV

An Ad Makes the Evening News

By Eduardo Porter

CHARLESTON, S.C. — Phyllis Bancroft and Jose Luis Villegas dreamed of owning their own TV station. So three years ago, after quitting their jobs working on the evening news at Spanish-language TV network Telemundo in Hartford, Conn., they sold their possessions and set out to find an untapped Latino market they could mine.

"We wanted a place where Latinos weren't served yet," says Ms. Bancroft, 44 years old.

"We looked in Anchorage, in Honolulu, in Flagstaff, Arizona," adds Mr. Villegas, 39.

Nothing seemed to work, until they happened upon a TV station for sale in, of all places, Charleston, S.C., where they found an unlikely Hispanic hub emerging among ancient oaks draped with Spanish moss. They looked at census data and asked around, and they discovered that the local Latino population had been surging for years. Ms. Bancroft now estimates the local Latino population served by the TV station at 45,000 people.

Last May, Ms. Bancroft and Mr. Villegas took their station to the airwaves as an affiliate of Telefutura, the new Spanish-language network of Los Angeles-based Univision Communications Inc. Theirs was the first Spanish-language station in a TV market ranked 131st in the nation in terms of number of Hispanic viewers.

The two friends and business partners are part of a growing number of businesses and entrepreneurs pursuing Hispanic consumers as they fan out across America from such established enclaves as California, Texas and New York. More and more immigrants from Latin America are pursuing plentiful jobs in meatpacking plants in Nebraska, poultry farms in Arkansas, fish-processing factories in Alaska and in construction and agriculture in South Carolina and many other states.

As their numbers grow in these budding enclaves, so does their spending. Latino disposable income nationwide has grown 160% since 1990, to $580 billion, according to a study by the Selig Center for Economic Growth at the University of Georgia. In Tennessee, by contrast, it swelled sevenfold to $3.2 billion in the same period. In Iowa, the amount quintupled to $1.5 billion, and in Delaware, it quadrupled to $700 million.

Lured by these numbers, businesses and entrepreneurs are rushing in. Overcoming language barriers and other hurdles, many are thriving. In Torrington, Wyo., local radio stations broadcast Spanish-language shows. In Idaho, readers can pick up Idaho Unido, an English-Spanish newspaper published every two weeks. In Fort Smith, Ark., Tortilleria Puebla sells nearly all of its tortillas to Hispanics. And in Tennesssee, pork producers have formed a cooperative aimed at selling pig carcasses to Hispanic meat markets across the state.

"We get two or three calls a week from people looking for bilingual people," says Ed Gumucio, a Bolivian immigrant who in March 2000 launched a service in Smyrna, Tenn., to train staff at local hospitals, banks and other companies to communicate with Spanish-speaking workers and customers. Business, he says, is thriving.

South Carolina's job market has been pulling in Hispanic laborers for more than a decade, some arriving from other U.S. states and others directly from Latin America. Mainly of Mexican origin, they have evolved from a migrant farm-worker group that swelled during the harvest season to a more permanent community with families and children in school.

Purchasing Power

Based on census data, the number of Hispanics in South Carolina more than tripled between 1990 and 2000, to about 95,000, or 2.4% of the state's total population. The Selig Center, extrapolating from 1990 census data on income, estimates that Hispanic purchasing power in the state has sextupled over the past 12 years, reaching $2.2 billion this year.

The state's Latino population continues to surge, though, as Ms. Bancroft and Mr. Villegas found in Charleston, precise numbers are hard to come by. To get an idea, they contacted the local chamber of commerce and visited nuns at a community outreach center. They asked the local police about Latino arrests. Ms. Bancroft had an "off the record" chat with a Census Bureau officer who, she says, admitted that Hispanics were undercounted because many illegal immigrants weren't tallied. Her estimate of 45,000 Latinos in the TV station's coverage area is about three times the number the Census Bureau counted two years ago.

Hispanics are in evidence throughout Charleston's suburbs—from the Spanish chatter heard in the trailer camps behind Ashley Phosphate Road to the workers on the suburban golf courses of Mount Pleasant to the tomato pickers on nearby John's Island. Sunday Mass in Spanish at Saint Thomas the Apostle Catholic Church is standing-room only. Men in cowboy boots and hats and sporting colossal belt buckles flock to the International Discotec to dance to the polka-like tunes of Los Terribles from Mexico and Grupo Misterio from nearby Myrtle Beach, S.C.

All this activity speaks to a flourishing Hispanic economy. Alberto Moreno, an immigrant from Mexico's northern state of Jalisco, makes a killing dispensing tacos from a trailer parked by the Amoco station off Ashley Phosphate Road. He says he paid off his trailer in four months, netting $2,500 to $3,000 per weekend, and he's itching to buy another.

A few blocks up Ashley Phosphate is Los Puentes, a Hispanic market where local Latinos can send money home, buy airline tickets and phone cards, and stock up on bull testicles, lard and statues of the Virgin of Guadalupe. Norma Jimenez, an Argentine immigrant who opened the store in early 2001, says sales reached $90,000 a month by the end of the first year. She says she executes 2,500 to 3,000 money transfers a month. Since launching the Charleston store, she has opened three more, in John's Island, Columbia and Rock Hill.

Some Anglo businesses in town are catching on. A formerly "oldies" AM radio station was flipped into Spanish a year and a half ago. Randy Withers, who owns a business that manufactures plantation shutters, last year launched Charleston's first Spanish-language newspaper, Vida Latina (Latino Life), after noticing that most of his work force was from Mexico and Guatemala. About a year ago, retailer Piggly Wiggly Carolina Co. began stocking Mexican products in its local grocery stores, including Jarritos soda pop and Maizena corn-flour drink mix. Last summer, the Charleston Battery soccer club tried to attract Mexicans by hosting a friendly match against the Mexican first division team Puebla.

Even a local politician made a play for Hispanic support. Charlie Smith, a real-estate agent who earlier this month sought a seat in the state legislature, actively courted the Latino vote with a TV ad inviting local Latinos, in broken Spanish, to a lunch of chicken, rice and beans. (He lost.)

Auto makers, food companies and other big national advertisers don't have to seek out pockets like the one in Charleston. They buy time on a nationwide network such as Telefutura, and when a local affiliate begins broadcasting, their ads reach the intended audience. And they are interested in reaching new audiences. In fact, it was through General Motors Corp. that Charleston's local McElveen GM dealership got the idea to take a stab at Hispanic advertising earlier this year.

"GM urged us to look at our local Hispanic market," says Doug McElveen. It translated one of its regular TV spots into Spanish and ran it for 90 days on the English-language CBS affiliate. The locals were so startled when that ad first appeared that the effort was at the top of the evening news. "They're getting a good response—from curious English-speaking customers," said an amused reporter.

For all the promise, it's still a struggle for mainstream Charleston businesses to sell to the budding Hispanic market. "It would take a big population to justify advertising on TV," says Robert Masche, vice president of retail operations for Piggly Wiggly Carolina. "I'm not sure there's enough yet to warrant that expenditure, though we've got to keep a tab on that."

Language Barrier

Some businesses ignore Charleston's emerging market, arguing that Latinos have little money and send much of what they do have back home to Latin America. Others haven't courted Latinos because they lack the staff to deal with customers who don't speak English. "We've been trying for months to get a bilingual sales person," says Richard Cooper of Charleston's local Ford dealership, Jones Ford. "We're not set up to handle these people."

Language is considered such a barrier that, to draw advertisers, the new Spanish-language AM station aired a job-mart program to recruit Spanish-speaking staff for potential advertisers. "Last week we found a person for a mobile home dealer," says Cliff Fletcher, who runs the station. "Many people want to tap the Hispanic market but don't know how."

After arriving in town two years ago, Mr. Villegas and Ms. Bancroft faced skeptical local financiers who doubted that a Latino audience could provide for a sound business plan. Eleven banks turned them down, including Bank of America. "I told the manager, 'You have the 'creemos en ti' [we believe in you] program to attract Hispanic consumers,'" says Ms. Bancroft, referring to a nationwide Bank of America campaign earlier this year to attract Hispanic customers. "But it was probably news to him."

Despite the many obstacles, South Coast Community Bank was eventually willing to finance Ms. Bancroft and Mr. Villegas in their TV venture. The chief lending officer was inclined to approve the loan because he had some experience with the Hispanic market. Among other things, he says, his son supervises Hispanic gardeners at a local golf course and he once financed a Dominican chiropractor.

Ever since WJEA Telefutura went on the air on May 6, Ms. Bancroft and Mr. Villegas have been pitching the story about Hispanics' growing purchasing power to local companies. They are also producing a Latino concert in December that they hope will boost their station's profile.

They are getting used to delivering primers on Hispanic marketing. One overcast afternoon last month, the message was pared down to the basics as they made their pitch to Derek Sharrer, general manager of the local baseball team, the Riverdogs. "In Mexico, it's more soccer. But Caribbean people like baseball," Mr. Villegas explained to Mr. Sharrer in the Riverdogs' stadium. "Colombians from the Coast, Venezuelans, Dominicans, they love it."

Mr. Sharrer was sympathetic. He once promoted a mariachi concert, he said, and has childhood memories of a morning show that featured the Puerto Rican boy band Menudo. Ultimately, he said, the Riverdogs would love to develop a Hispanic fan base to watch their games.

Mr. Sharrer rejected WJEA's initial proposal: a package to sponsor both the news and a family show that would feature an English lesson tentatively titled "R Is for Riverdog." But he liked the idea of promoting a "Cinco de Mayo" concert around the Mexican holiday. A second concert-plus-ballgame combo around Independence Day could stress a patriotic theme, with an immigration lawyer giving advice to fans about legal residence and citizenship.

In the end, Ms. Bancroft and Mr. Villegas came away with a small commitment to sponsor the December concert. Mr. Sharrer, for his part, was excited by the prospects for a Hispanic alter ego to the Riverdogs' mascot: "We could call Charlie the Riverdog, Carlos the Riverdog!"

Brand Builders

Cutting edge. (Gillette's Mach3 and Venus razors reach top of category)

By Christine Bittar

Gillette's Mach3 triple blade razor, introduced in 1998, was the category's biggest news in years. The company had spent six years in stealth-like research and development, and nearly $1 billion bringing the product to market. Despite initial sticker shock of $8 for the razor and nearly $2 per refill blade, Mach3 became the top-selling men's razor in its first year. Logically the next step for the brand was a women's version.

"Wall Street analysts and trade partners were asking us when it was coming," said Mary Ann Pesce, vp of new products-razors/blades at Gillette, Boston.

Launching a new razor for women presented its own set of challenges. Whereas shaving for most men is "life affirming and masculine," said Pesce, most women don't talk about the act openly and there's no gratification in the process.

Enter Venus. Launched in early 2001, the product lived up to its goddess-inspired name, designed in a feminine ocean blue color with an unusual-looking T-shaped handle for comfort. Its only obvious connection to the Mach3 was its triple blade. The cartridges had evolved from a square to a rounded shape with rubbery oval cushions meant to stretch and smooth the skin. The razor was packaged in a convenient shower dispenser, with individually packed and sealed blades to protect them from moisture.

Priced about the same as Mach3, Venus likewise shot up to the No. 1 non-disposable razor slot in less than a year with sales of $45 million through Oct. 7, per Information Resources Inc. Its refill blade sales of $35 million far exceeded those of its biggest competitor, Pfizer's Schick Silk Effects Plus, with $19 million in refill sales for a full 52 weeks. Initial Venus sales surpassed other Gillette female brands as well as competitors', including Schick. "We sold more than 11,000 pieces in six months, compared to about 6,000 refills of [Schick] Silk Effects," said a beauty aids buyer at one drug chain.

Retailers generally were pleased with Venus' eye-catching POP displays and wide media support. Gillette put $150 million into global advertising for the launch, almost $40 million in the U.S. Marketers timed the introduction to the arrival of spring and summer, when more women go bare-legged in skirts and bathing suits.

Despite Gillette's overall disappointing sales in other categories the last two years, demand for its premium razor brands has remained strong. The company's fourth-quarter sales fell 3% to $2.7 billion, but solid performance of its Mach3 and Venus razors led Gillette to its highest share of the U.S. shaving market—over 80% in both blades and handles—in 40 years.

"It wasn't about shaving. We were looking for an image of beauty and power."—Al Merrin, BBDO

To counter the notion of Venus as a male version of Mach3, marketers even spoofed the brand's own TV ads during a video presentation to the sales team. The Mach3 spots had featured jets, so the video showed a woman flying a pink fighter jet ("Machette") with her scarf blowing in her face. In the end, she gets approval from a male pilot who says, "Super shave fly girl."

"For a moment, no one knew what to make of it. Then one person started laughing and suddenly the whole room was laughing uproariously," Pesce recalled.

When Gillette launched Sensor for Women back in 1992, its product and ads were meant to be pretty. Venus, on the other hand, was seen as promoting skincare. That "aha" moment came during a briefing session with BBDO, said Pesce. "When the first round of story boards didn't cut it, I casually said, 'Guys, this is not just about shaving, it's skincare', and they quickly realized that was it."

The baton was then tossed to Al Merrin, vice chairman and executive creative director at BBDO, New York. "[Gillette] wanted a big idea immediately, and that gave us a big advantage creatively," Merrin said. "We knew from the start shaving is an afterthought and we wanted to elevate it. So that led to a name with a broader appeal."

Gillette marketers also looked for a campaign with a universal and emotional appeal. TV spots showed a cadre of suntanned women laying on the beach with legs crossed and their backs to the camera, tapping their toes to Bananarama's lively version of the song "Venus." The tagline: "Reveal the goddess in you."

Print ads, meanwhile, ran in women's beauty and fashion magazines, including *Cosmopolitan* and *Glamour.* Creative involved closeup product shots and copy

(Cont.)

highlighting core attributes: a longer lasting shave, three blades, protective cushions, the pivoting head and individually sealed blade refills. "Changing blades, made easy," one ad declared. "Now in one stroke, your skin stays smoother, longer," claimed another.

Marketers wanted the campaign to steer clear of images of primping females or a woman getting ready for a date. "It wasn't about shaving:" said Merrin. "We were looking for an image of beauty and power."

THE ENVIRONMENT WAS RIPE FOR ABUSE

Enron's unrelenting stress on growth and its absence of controls helped push execs into unethical behavior

At Enron Corp., they called her "the Weather Babe." Lynda R. Clemmons, a French and history major from Southern Methodist University, was supposed to be emblematic of the rebels in Enron's freewheeling culture. In 1997, as a 27-year-old gas-and-power trader, she launched an esoteric enterprise in weather derivatives. Within two years, her startup had written $1 billion in weather hedges to protect companies against short-term spikes in the price of power during heat waves and cold snaps.

Clemmons' story made the rounds, from a favorable Harvard Business School case study to *The New York Times* business section, where she was pictured in black leather on a Harley-Davidson. She was, after all, a product of what Enron's culture was supposed to be all about: smart, sassy, creative, and risk-taking. And Enron made the most of her business, trumpeting weather derivatives as yet another high-potential deregulated market.

Like other Enron initiatives, this one never lived up to the hype. "It was such a flaky business," says John Olson, an analyst at Sanders Harris Morris in Houston. "They got more mileage out of the public relations than they actually made in earnings." Not exactly the way Enron's "cultural revolution" was supposed to play out. But as everyone knows, with Enron, nothing was quite as it appeared.

For most of the 1990s, CEOs at Old Economy companies struggled to turn slow-moving organizations into nimbler, more flexible outfits. Failure cost chieftains their jobs at General Motors, Eastman Kodak, Westinghouse, and a host of other behemoths. Truth is, real transformations are the exception rather than the rule. Changing the core values, the attitudes, the fundamental relationships of a vast organization is overwhelmingly difficult. General Electric Co.'s John F. Welch and IBM's Louis V. Gerstner Jr. have been lionized for having led two of the very few successful makeovers.

That's why an army of academics and consultants descended on Enron in the late 1990s and held it up as a paragon of management virtue. Enron seemed to have transformed itself from a stodgy regulated utility to a fast-moving enterprise where performance was paramount. The Harvard case study put it simply enough: "Enron's transformation: From gas pipelines to New Economy powerhouse."

SKILLING Many say the CEO was encouraging all the risk-taking at Enron

If only that were true. Many of the same academics are now scurrying to distill the cultural and leadership lessons from the debacle. Their conclusion so far: Enron didn't fail just because of improper accounting or alleged corruption at the top. It also failed because of its entrepreneurial culture—the very reason Enron attracted so much attention and acclaim. The unrelenting emphasis on earnings growth and individual initiative, coupled with a shocking absence of the usual corporate checks and balances, tipped the culture from one that rewarded aggressive strategy to one that increasingly relied on unethical corner-cutting. In the end, too much leeway was given to young, inexperienced managers without the necessary controls to minimize failures. This was a company that simply placed a lot of bad bets on businesses that weren't so promising to begin with.

Before 1990, Enron was a sleepy, regulated natural-gas company dominated by engineers and hard assets. But that year, Enron Chairman Kenneth L. Lay hired McKinsey & Co. partner Jeffrey K. Skilling, who had been advising Lay as a consultant. Skilling's mandate was to build Enron Finance Corp. into an asset-light laboratory for financially linked products and services. Skilling expanded the unit into a model of what all of Enron would become. Its success led to his promotion to president in 1997 and to CEO in early 2001.

Skilling's recipe for changing the company was right out of the New Economy playbook. Layers of management were wiped out. Hundreds of outsiders were recruited and encouraged to bring new thinking to a tradition-bound business. The company abolished seniority-based salaries in favor of more highly leveraged compensation that offered huge cash bonuses and stock option grants to top performers. Young people, many just out of undergraduate or MBA programs, were handed extraordinary authority, able to make $5 million decisions without higher approval.

In the new culture, success or failure came remarkably fast. "One potential flaw in the model was that Enron managers tended to move relatively quickly, not within businesses but between businesses," says Jay Conger, a management professor at London

How a New Economy Corporate Culture Went Awry

TYPE OF CULTURE	EMPLOYEE EXPECTATIONS	REWARDS	LEADERSHIP
Old Economy	Security	Salary	Top-down
New Economy	Personal growth	Stock options	Inspirational
The Enron Twist	Personal wealth	A stake in the business	Know-it-all arrogant

Business School who studied Enron. "If you move young people fast in senior-level positions without industry experience and then allow them to make large trading decisions, that is a risky strategy."

It was not unusual for execs to change jobs two or three times in as many years. Indeed, turnover from promotions alone was almost 20%. Clemmons, for example, went from analyst, to associate, to manager, then director, and finally to vice-president running her own business, all in seven years.

"In larger companies like IBM and GE, even though there is a movement toward youth, there are still enough older people around to mentor them," says James O'Toole, professor at the Center for Effective Organizations at the University of Southern California. "At Enron, you had a bunch of kids running loose without adult supervision."

FASTOW Did he exploit performance reviews to get back at those who opposed him?

In theory, of course, the kids were closely supervised. Skilling often described the new culture as "loose and tight," one of the eight attributes of the successful companies profiled by McKinsey consultants Thomas J. Peters and Robert H. Waterman Jr. in their best-selling book, **In Search of Excellence.** The idea is to combine tight controls with maximum individual authority to allow entrepreneurship to flourish without the culture edging into chaos.

At Enron, however, the pressure to make the numbers often overwhelmed the pretext of "tight" controls. "The environment was ripe for abuse," says a former manager in Enron's energy services unit. "Nobody at corporate was asking the right questions. It was completely hands-off management. A situation like that requires tight controls. Instead, it was a runaway train."

The train was supposed to be kept on the tracks partly by an internal risk-management group with a staff of 180 employees to screen proposals and review deals. Many of the unit's employees were MBAs with little perspective and every reason to sign off on deals: Their own performance reviews were partially done by the people whose deals they were approving. The process made honest evaluations virtually impossible. "If your boss was [fudging], and you have never worked anywhere else, you just assume that everybody fudges earnings," says one young Enron control person. "Once you get there and you realized how it was, do you stand up and lose your job? It was scary. It was easy to get into 'Well, everybody else is doing it, so maybe it isn't so bad.'"

It didn't help that Enron's Risk Assessment & Control group was answerable not to the board of directors but to Skilling, who was encouraging all the risk-taking. Another essential "check and balance" in the culture—Enron's in-house legal staff—was also compromised because of its reporting relationships. Instead of being centralized at headquarters, it was spread throughout the business units, where it could more easily be co-opted by hard-driving executives. "The business people didn't want to slow down for much," says one former inhouse lawyer.

Central to forging a new Enron culture was an unusual performance review system that Skilling adapted from his days at McKinsey. Under this peer-review process, a select group of 20 people were named to a performance review committee (PRC) to rank more than 400 vice-presidents, then all the directors, and finally all of Enron's managers. The stakes were high because all the rewards were linked to ranking decisions by the PRC which had to unanimously agree on each person.

LAY The chairman hired Skilling in 1990 with a mandate to build Enron Finance Corp. into an asset-light laboratory for financially linked products and services

Managers judged "superior"—the top 5%—got bonuses 66% higher than those who got an "excellent" rating, the next 30%. They also got much larger stock option grants.

Although Skilling told Harvard researchers that the system "stopped most of the game playing since it was impossible to kiss 20 asses," other Enron managers say it had the opposite effect. In practice, the system bred a culture in which people were afraid to get crossways with someone who could screw up their reviews. How did managers ensure they passed muster? "You don't object to anything," says one former Enron executive. "The whole culture at the vice-president level and above just became a yes-man culture."

Several former and current Enron execs say that Andrew S. Fastow, the ex-chief financial officer who is at the center of Enron's partnership controversy, had a reputation for exploiting the review system to get back at people who expressed disagreement or criticism. "Andy was such a cutthroat bastard that he would use it against you in the PRC," says one manager. He could filibuster and hold up the group for days, the exec adds, because every decision had to be unanimous. A spokesman for Fastow declined comment.

CLEMMONS Her weather biz epitomized Enron pizzazz

Although managers were supposed to be graded on teamwork, Enron was actually far more reflective of a survival-of-the-fittest mind-set. The culture was heavily built around star players, such as Clemmons, with little value attached to team-building. The upshot: The organization rewarded highly competitive people who were less likely to share power, authority, or information.

Indeed, some believe the extreme focus on individual ambition undermined any teamwork or institutional commitment. At other companies, by contrast, an emphasis on individual achievement is balanced by a strong focus on process and metrics or a set of guiding values. "In the Enron culture, there was no significant counterbalance," says Jon R. Katzenbach, a consultant and former McKinsey colleague of Skilling who has studied the company. "The lesson is you cannot rely solely on individual achievement to drive your performance over time. Companies with only that one path overemphasize it and run into trouble, switching over to vanity and greed."

That emphasis on the individual instead of the enterprise may have pushed many to cross the line into unethical behavior. The flaw only grew more pronounced as Enron struggled to meet the wildly optimistic expectations for growth it had set for itself. "You've got someone at the top saying the stock price is the most important thing, which is driven by earnings," says one insider. "Whoever could provide earnings quickly would be promoted."

The employee adds that anyone who questioned suspect deals quickly learned to accept assurances of outside lawyers and accountants. She says there was little scrutiny of whether the earnings were real or how they were booked. The more people pushed

ORGANIZATION	CORPORATE GOAL	BOARD	APPROACH TO REGS
Hierarchy	Steady growth	Rubber stamp	Aim to meet regulations
Network	Fast growth	Independent	Push the limits
Individual fiefdoms	Appearing to grow fast	Rubber stamp	Circumvent the rules

(Cont.)

the envelope with aggressive accounting, she says, the harder they would have to push the next year. "It's like being a heroin junkie," she says. "How do you go cold turkey?"

The problem is, you can't. "For almost every model or system, there are certain limits," says USC's O'Toole. "It's harder to keep the growth growing and to keep coming up with new ideas. That kind of culture has a subtle encouragement to cut corners and to cheat. You can see everyone else moving forward, and you have to keep up."

Clemmons, who left Enron in March of 2000, isn't so sure. "It's quite clear that there were some accounting issues and bad decisions that had nothing to do with the trading side of the business," she says. "To distill it all down to the culture is utter bulls—."

As academics do their revisionist thing, they're not likely to agree.

By John A. Byrne, with Mike France, in New York and with Wendy Zellner in Dallas

Buying Behavior

Economic Inequality Grew in 90's Boom, Fed Reports

By EDMUND L. ANDREWS

WASHINGTON, Jan. 22 — Economic inequality increased markedly as the boom of the 1990's fizzled, even as incomes increased at almost every level, according to a detailed new survey by the Federal Reserve released today.

Conducted at the end of 2001, when the economy was in a recession, the survey compared wealth and income with levels of 1998. It suggests that the benefits of the economic boom were widespread but extremely uneven.

The wealth of those in the top 10 percent of incomes surged much more than the wealth of those in any other group. The net worth of families in the top 10 percent jumped 69 percent, to $833,600, in 2001 from $492,400 in 1998. By contrast, the net worth of families in the lowest fifth of income earners rose 24 percent, to $7,900.

The median accumulated wealth for families at the top was about 12 times that of lower-middle-income families through much of the 1990's. But in 2001, the median net worth of the top earners was about 22 times as great.

While income in the top 10 percent of households surged 19.3 percent from 1998 to 2001, income for the bottom fifth of households increased 14.4 percent.

The survey is compiled every three years and is based on interviews with more than 4,000 families. Its results come as President Bush proposes a plan to cut taxes $674 billion over 10 years. Opponents of the plan, which has as its centerpiece a proposal to eliminate most taxes on stock dividends, say most of the benefits would be showered on the richest taxpayers.

Administration officials respond that a large percentage of ordinary Americans now own stocks and would benefit from both tax-free dividends and any lift in market prices.

The survey provides some ammunition for both sides. It shows that wealth became more concentrated, but it also confirms that more than half of all families own stocks, either directly or through their mutual funds and pension plans.

A controversial element of the survey may be the part that deals with household debt.

American consumers provided much of the backbone for economic growth, but economists have long been worried that consumers ran up too much debt in the process.

The Fed's report contends that household debt is more benign than it seems. It noted that Americans did in fact borrow more in 2001 than in 1998 but said that their net worth rose even faster.

As a share of total family income, the Fed said, the aggregate debt burden of families in fact decreased to 12.5 percent in 2001 from 14 percent through most of the 1990's.

Even accounting for stock market declines after the survey was conducted, the Fed said, household wealth was still higher in 2001 than in 1998.

"Rising aggregate debt levels alone do not necessarily imply that conditions deteriorated at the level of individual families," the report said.

But at least some outside economists disputed that conclusion on several grounds.

They noted that in addition to a further stock market decline, unemployment rose after the survey was finished in December 2001. They also said that the survey understated signs of trouble that were already apparent.

Mark Zandi of Economy.com in West Chester, Pa., noted that the percentage of low-income households more than 60 days past due on a debt increased to 13.4 percent in 2001 from 12.9 percent in 1998.

Mr. Zandi said an abundance of newer data provided stronger evidence that lower-income households were under much more stress than before: personal bankruptcies, automobile repossessions, mortgage foreclosures and other indicators of bad debt all reached records in 2002.

The Fed calculations "clearly misrepresent the debt load as it existed in 2001 and even more clearly misrepresent the debt load as it exists now," Mr. Zandi said. "This is a problem that is going to get worse."

To be sure, the Fed survey also shows that even middle- and lower-income families benefited from the economic boom. Home ownership increased, even though

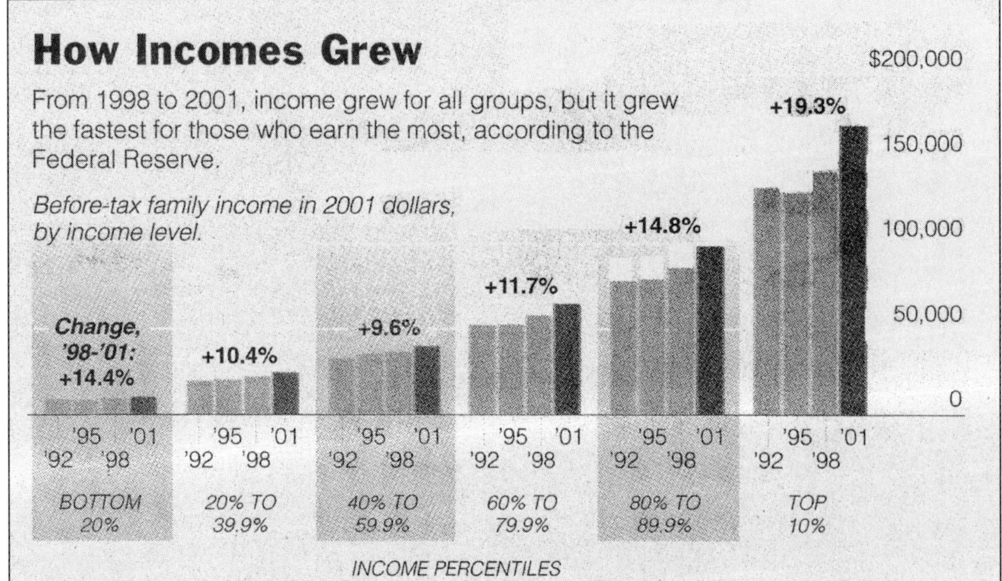

(Cont.)

A Look at Family Finances

Families' net worth rose, and more people owned stocks in 2001, compared with previous years. But more people in the lowest income level had credit card debt and trouble paying bills.

OVER ALL

	1992	1995	1998	**2001**
Median family net worth*	$61,300	$66,400	$78,000	**$86,100**
Share of families with stock holdings, *direct or indirect*	36.7%	40.4%	48.9%	**51.9%**
Median value of stock holdings, *of those with holdings**	$13,000	$16,900	$27,200	**$34,300**
Debt as a percentage of total family assets	14.5%	14.6%	14.3%	**12.1%**

BY INCOME LEVELS

Share of families with credit card balances

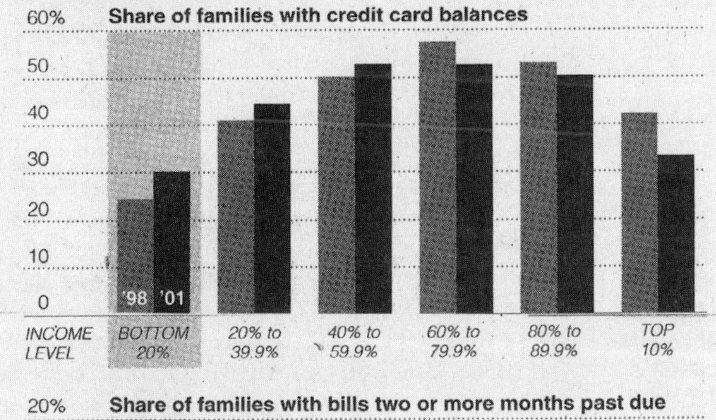

Share of families with bills two or more months past due

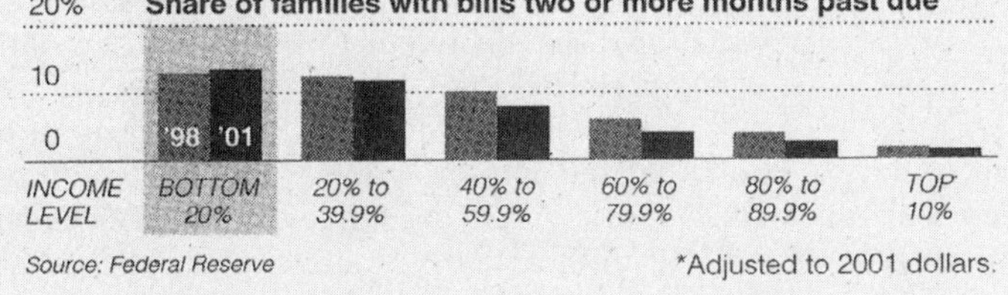

Source: Federal Reserve

*Adjusted to 2001 dollars.

housing prices climbed 25 percent. Stock ownership reached 51 percent of all households.

The average income of African-American families surged 20 percent from 1998 to 2000. But for reasons that Fed officials had difficulty explaining today, the average income for all nonwhite and Hispanic families barely increased.

"I am alarmed and disheartened by the growth in inequality in this report," said Jared Bernstein, senior economist at the Economic Policy Institute, a liberal research group based in Washington. "I am especially mindful of this problem, given the administration's tax proposals. I hope policy makers take this data into consideration."

Living alone in America

Singleness not the same as not settled; Divorce, late marriages and longevity figure in

By Craig Wilson
USA Today

ATLANTA—Years ago, Kris Osborn's father, a psychiatrist, gave him a bit of advice:

"If you go and chase after women, you'll never meet quality women. You only find quality women if you excel in your own life."

At 32, Osborn is working hard at excelling in his own life. One of the newest faces at CNN Headline News here, he became a general-assignment anchor back in July. He's still single, however. Can a quality woman be far behind? Well, there's a new love interest in Boston, but it's too early to tell.

At the moment, Osborn is leading the single man's good life in trendy Buckhead, his treadmill in front of the TV for those Sunday afternoons of football, nothing but bottled water in the fridge. He shares the apartment that faces west over the treetops—a requirement he gave his real estate agent—with a shelter cat named Byron.

While he lives alone, Osborn is not alone. The 2000 Census shows that more than 27 million Americans live by themselves, about one-fourth of all households, nearly 10% of the population. For the first time, one-person households outnumber married couples with children (fewer than 25 million).

"With the increase in the divorce rate, the increase in the age at which people first get married, and with our increasing longevity, the experience of being single is now one of the most widely shared experiences of adulthood," says Bella DePaulo, visiting professor of psychology at the University of California-Santa Barbara.

And when you add in the single people who are living together but not married—everyone from college kids in dorms to young singles sharing apartments to unmarried couples—the number of singles in America soars. Their ranks increased from 38 million in 1970 to 82 million in 2000. Single people now account for more than 40% of the adult population, up from 28% of all adults in the USA three decades ago, according to DePaulo, who cites Census statistics.

"These findings are not surprising. They reflect a 30-year trend in America to marry later in life, divorce or never get married at all," says Xavier Amador, co-author of *Being Single in a Couples' World: How to be Happily Single While Looking for Love* and director of psychology at New York State Psychiatric Institute in New York. "Being single is no longer synonymous with being immature, unsettled in life and irresponsible. Questions such as 'When are you going to get married and settle down?' belong to the past, not the reality of America today."

Zoe Woodland, a 27-year-old computer network manager at Hill Air Force Base near Salt Lake City, has heard the question before. Her response?

"Oh, when I'm 55. That's my standard answer," she says. "Actually, I imagine myself still single at 88. Playing bridge. And riding my mountain bike."

San Francisco retiree Harry Rudnick is 88 and agrees that single life suits him just fine. "If I go out with a lady friend, I take her to dinner and that satisfies me," he says.

According to the American Association for Single People (AASP), an "unmarried majority" has emerged in most major cities, as well as six states, facts the association disseminated on Capitol Hill last month during National Singles Week.

"And within a few years, the majority of households in the nation will be headed by unmarried adults," says AASP executive director Tom Coleman.

Up until a few years ago when the AASP was formed, virtually all singles groups were for dating and matchmaking, focused on social and recreational activities for lonely hearts. But singles today are looking for more, much healthier in their outlook on life. As Woodland says, "I think I'm different only because I'm told I am."

Now, more and more groups are formed for support, even political reasons.

"As single people begin to wake up and realize that we are being cheated—sometimes to the tune of thousands of dollars per year in higher taxes, higher insurance rates, fewer employee benefits and smaller Social Security benefits—more of their attention and support will shift toward organizations fighting for legal and economic reform," Coleman says.

Conservative groups have expressed concern

(Cont.)

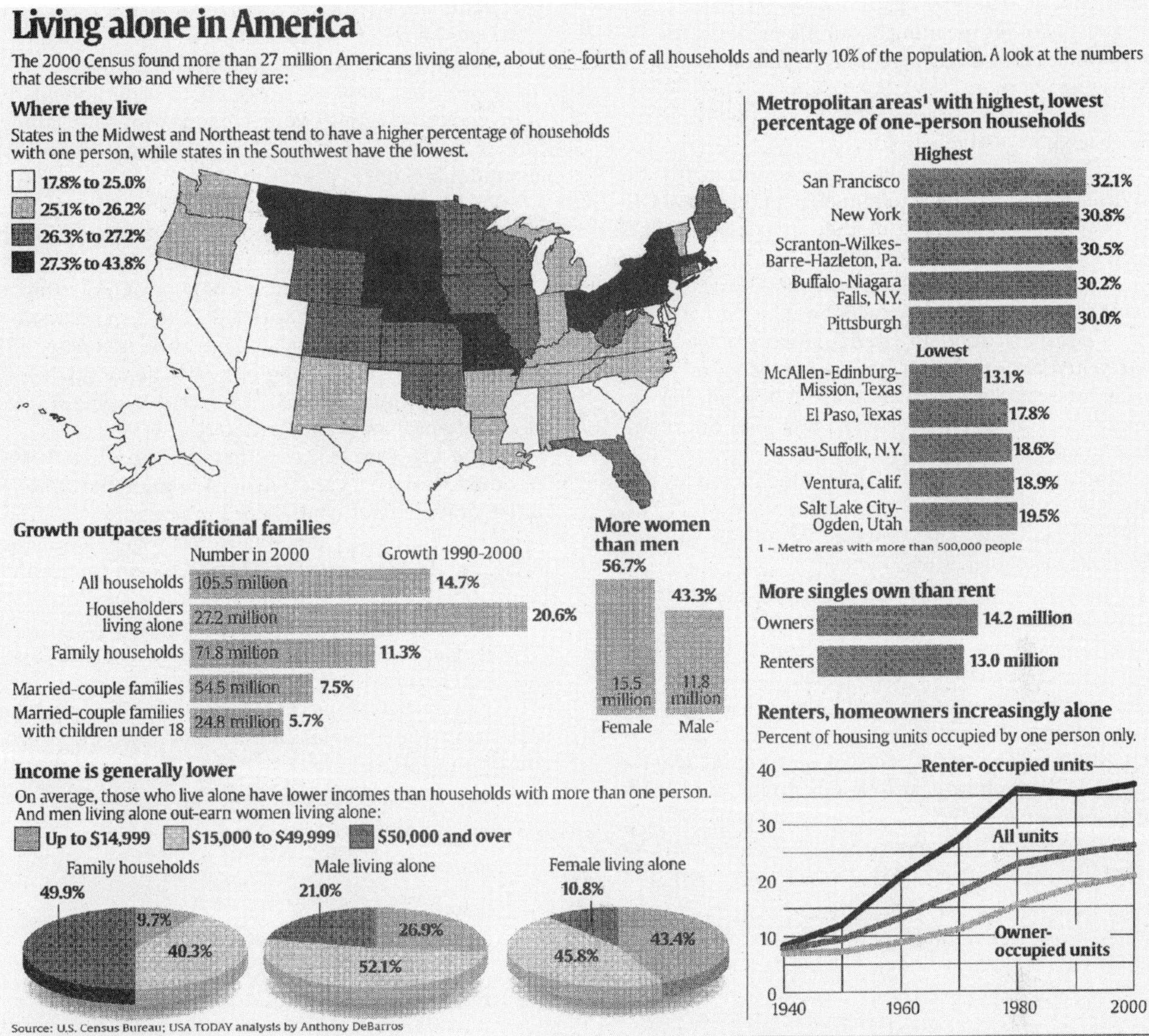

over the "single and alone" trend, calling it a troubling indicator of deeper societal problems. But demographers say what the trend truly reveals is that adults just prefer their own company, living near their families, but not with them. In fact, it's very American.

"Americans are individualists, and unless we're married and raising children, we tend to want to live alone, rather than impose on relatives," says Andrew Cherlin, a Johns Hopkins University sociology professor. "Plus, we like our privacy. So, those of us with more money tend to use it to live alone."

Cherlin says some people are worried that it makes for "a more detached society, but most people who live alone live near friends and family. Americans want intimacy at a distance. That's the highest good."

Demographers, however, point out that the "single" trend will have a profound effect on American institutions. With fewer households having children, for example, public schools will face a more difficult time gathering support for building programs and educational programs.

It also could have a negative effect on Americans' health. Linda Waite, a University of Chicago sociologist and author of *The Case for Marriage*, says several studies show that married people tend to live healthier and happier lives.

"There's evidence that our systems work better when there's someone around that we care about, and

(Cont.)

care about us. The stress goes down," she says. "Also, we get a lot of the meaning of our life by doing for others, taking care of other people. So if you live alone, that's just not there."

The recent terrorist attacks are sending some singles back into relationships.

"One of my girlfriends broke up with her boyfriend but went back to him on Sept. 11," says Gloria Olson, a single grandmother in Bismarck, N.D. "She said she realized life was too short."

Maybe, but the troubling times and health studies aren't scaring CNN's Osborn to the altar. With a swimmer's body and model-material looks, Osborn could marry just about anyone he wanted. Many a young woman has noticed his arrival at CNN headquarters, more than a few volunteering to help him out in any way he might need.

But at the moment, like many single men his age, he's devoted to his profession. "A huge amount of my time is my job now," he confesses. "Mainly because it's new and I like it so much."

Osborn is typical of many young bachelors in America today. He drives a nice car (a black Lincoln Town Car), wears designer suits from Calvin Klein, eats out more than in.

"If I fit any stereotype, it's that of the bachelor," he says. "Interior decorating is not my thing."

Although Osborn says he has dated often over the years—he had a four-year relationship in California—his professional life keeps getting in the way.

"I went to 10 different countries for Channel One News," he says. "I'm afraid that kind of travel schedule isn't compatible with a serious relationship."

Does he mind still being single?

"No, I like it," he says without hesitation.

"You don't have to worry about commitments to your career (affecting) your commitment to a family. I'm not ruling out marriage. I'm just being very specific about doing it once. There's no rush."

Woodland isn't in any rush, either, playing the field by her own rules, saying she's not obsessed with finding the right guy.

"I don't think that way. It's not one of those things that's necessary for my happiness. The men I date find out quickly that I don't need them as an accessory. If I like them, I'll let them hang out with me for a while."

Being in family-friendly Utah makes some singles more defiant than even Woodland.

"The pressure to marry here is incredible," says Woodland's pal Megan Walsh, 24, a graduate student at the University of Utah. "But I'm not going to settle. I don't care if I'm 65 and single. Yes, it gets old being alone, but there's a difference between being alone and being lonely. I have made the decision to be alone."

Stan Charnofsky, author of *Surfing the Single Life: A Memoir for Women and Men Making It Alone,* thinks all these singles are doing it right.

"Not everybody is paired off or familied up," he says. "Some are singles living marvelous, bountiful, contributory lives."

Contributing: Anthony DeBarros

New Beverage From Snapple Seeks to Avoid Stigma of Dieting

By SHERRI DAY

Trying to take some of the public embarrassment out of dieting, Snapple yesterday announced a new meal-replacement product that it hopes looks less like a weight-loss aid and more like, well, a Snapple.

Snapple-a-Day, a fortified juice smoothie that will be on store shelves next month, is the beverage company's entry into the $1-billion-a-year meal-replacement business, which is dominated by Slim-Fast from **Unilever** and includes products like Ensure and protein-laden powder drinks associated with the Atkins diet. Snapple-a-Day has 210 calories—10 fewer than Slim-Fast—as well as vitamins and minerals including calcium, zinc, potassium and folic acid.

Snapple's drink may also represent the first wave of new products from soda companies that are aimed at consumers, particularly women ages 22 to 44, who worry as much about their waistlines as about flavor. The **Coca-Cola** Company is working on a whey-based drink called BeginIt and **PepsiCo** is exploring the category as well, according to company spokesmen. Snapple is a unit of **Cadbury Schweppes.**

Snapple's edge, according to Jack Belsito, the company's chief executive, is that the product will not be marketed as a diet aid. By packaging Snapple-a-Day in 11.5 ounce plastic bottles swathed in bright red, yellow and peach labeling and promising a brighter, more Snapple-like taste, the company hopes to remove the stigma associated with drinking frothy meal-replacement drinks from stubby metal cans.

"Very rarely do you actually see people drinking this product," Mr. Belsito said, referring to Slim-Fast. "It's usually consumed in some type of shroud of mystery. I don't want to be asked questions about am I on a diet? Or how many pounds did I lose? It's not a conversation that I want to have at work."

Like many of its beverage counterparts, Snapple's juice business has registered steady returns but extremely slow growth, analysts said. To stem declining market share for carbonated soft drinks and other core brands, beverage companies have been looking for new products.

"To continue growing, they have to extend their product offerings," said John D. Sicher, the editor and publisher of Beverage Digest. "We've certainly seen that in the last few years with bottled water. Five or six years ago, neither Coke nor Pepsi sold bottled water in the U.S. Now they have the leading bottled water brands. That model will be duplicated in other beverage categories in the years to come."

But Snapple did not want to duplicate the chalky taste of some diet products. That challenge fell to the company's research scientists in the Flavor Lab, a suite of four laboratories deep in the bowels of the company's headquarters in White Plains.

The lab, which smells like a combination of apple, strawberry and citrus, is run by Smita Patel, the vice president for research and development and Snapple's most trusted palate. Ms. Patel, who has worked as a food scientist for 20 years on products like French's Dijon mustard and Cadbury Schweppes' cranberry ginger ale, took nearly a year to create Snapple-a-Day.

To avoid the appearance of simply copying Slim-Fast, Ms. Patel decided early against using a chocolate or vanilla base for its new drink. Snapple's food scientists tried using whey, but abandoned it soon after they discovered that it had a pungent odor that was difficult to mask. They also decided against soy milk because it tasted like soy beans, and ruled out skim milk powder, which when mixed with flavors smelled acrid and overcooked. After two months, Ms. Patel chose soy protein for its ability to maintain a relatively neutral taste. The company also decided to add some carbohydrates and soluble fiber that would help to make consumers feel full.

But with so many minerals then packed into the drink, the biggest difficulty, according to Ms. Patel, was finding the right flavors to counteract the "liquid vitamins" taste of the early prototypes. The peach-flavored drink and its tropical-blend counterparts proved fairly easy to formulate but the strawberry-banana version was particularly challenging. Ms. Patel said her team mixed at least 180 combinations to create just the right mix so that the product both smelled and tasted like strawberries mixed with bananas.

"We have to identify the right levels; it's 0.02 percent or 0.01 percent in each bottle," said Ms. Patel, who is credited with some of Snapple's best-selling products, including peach iced tea, apple juice and WhipperSnapple. "If you overdo it, it's perfumey and can cause a burn. If you don't have enough flavor, then you wonder what's in the product."

On Monday, even as mass quantities were already being produced in factories, the scientists were still mixing new concoctions.

"It's just constant monitoring, week to week, day to day, especially if it's a new product," Ms. Patel said. "We kind of baby it to check to make sure nothing is going off."

Once the base and flavors were settled upon, Ms. Patel's team conducted stability tests to see how the product would hold up in a variety of storage conditions. To simulate a beverage warehouse on a hot summer day in Georgia, the scientists put their new beverages into an oven. They also checked Snapple-a-Day's performance over six-month periods at room temperatures and in refrigerators. The final test, however, occurred when Ms. Patel poured herself a glass of Snapple-a-Day on ice.

Snapple-a-Day will sell for $1.59 a serving, more expensive than Slim-Fast, but unlike a lot of diet products it will be available in single servings in corner stores. Mr. Belsito said the company expected to have 10 percent of the sales in the category within the next two years. Slim-Fast has about 38 percent of the market and recorded $396 million in beverage sales last year, according to Information Resources.

"For them to be a home run they don't have to be as big as Slim-Fast," said Michael Bellas, the chief executive of Beverage Marketing. "They will be able to leverage the Snapple direct store distribution to put that in venues where you don't see Slim-Fast. They're in single-serve. They're in the immediate-consumption channel. It's a perfect place. It fits with the convenience-on-the-go lifestyle that we have today."

But some nutritionists warn that consumers looking to lose weight or eat healthier foods should be wary of any meal substitute.

"This is a vitamin-supplemented soft drink," said Marion Nestle, the chairwoman of the department of food studies at New York University and the author of "Food Politics: How the Food Industry Influences Nutrition and Health" (University of California Press, 2002). "It's the equivalent of a candy bar. It's got an ounce of sugars in it. You bet it's not for dieters. It's got 200 calories of which most of them come from sugars. If I were going to advise someone to diet, the first thing I would do would be to tell them to cut out stuff like this."

Will Soft Touches Mean Softer Sales for the Mighty F-150?

By DANNY HAKIM

DEARBORN, Mich. — THE 2004 F-150 pickup truck from the **Ford Motor** Company will not even go on sale until this summer, but the debate over its design, which Ford has unsuccessfully tried to keep a secret, has been raging for months. At Web sites like F150online.com and Ford-trucks.com, message board postings burst with spy photographs and taut emotion: love, devotion, outrage.

"The F-150 is a truck," wrote a man who identified himself as Matthew from Stillwater, Okla., "not a freaking glorified car."

Matthew was particularly dismayed by the presence of what will surely be the new truck's most controversial feature. For the first time on an American full-size truck, some of the high-end F-150's will have an automatic gearshift positioned between the seats instead of on the steering column.

Like a car's.

This is welcome news to some people. "If the new F-150's are gonna look like that," wrote Arturo from Miami, "I'm just gonna go ahead and put my name on the waiting list now!"

But it is heresy to others. "It might go over O.K. with women," said Shawn Crowe, 24, a Ford enthusiast from Lawrenceburg, Ky., in an interview about the gearshift, "but most men will throw an absolute fit."

The redesigned F-150 is the American auto industry's most important vehicle introduction in years. It will be unveiled to the news media tomorrow at the North American International Auto Show in Detroit; some models are shown for the first time in the official photographs accompanying this article.

Ford's F-Series trucks, dominated by the F-150, have been the most popular vehicle line in America for two decades. To Ford, they are at least as important as sport utility vehicles like the Explorer, the best-selling S.U.V. and the third-best-selling vehicle of any kind after the F-Series and the Chevrolet Silverado pickups.

But competition is mounting on all sides, and Ford has little margin for error. Not only will the new F-150 have to contend with other full-size trucks from Chevrolet, GMC, Dodge and Toyota, but for the first time this year Nissan will try to steal some of Ford's market share with its own full-size pickup.

Of even more concern to many analysts are the production costs of the truck, which was lavishly developed during the bull market. In a penny-pinching industry, the new F-150 will actually cost more to make than the current one, a problem that Ford executives have pledged to fix after production begins.

"Can they get the cost down to leave sufficient profit?" said David E. Cole, the president of the Center for Automotive Research, an industry consulting and research firm. "It's a tough hurdle. Everything I've seen and heard about it says it's a well-executed truck. The real question is: Can it be as profitable as it has been historically? And the answer is probably no because of the added competition and the added cost."

Both Ford and **Nissan Motor** will give official first looks at their new big pickups at the auto show, which opens to the public on Saturday.

As the migration of the shift lever indicates, Ford is trying to fend off competitors by making the F-150 a truck for every taste and driver, from the Marlboro man to the soccer mom. In all, there will be more than a dozen major configurations of the pickup, compared with the current eight, which range in price from $18,500 to $37,000.

The top-end versions of the new trucks, which Ford has not yet priced, even accomplish the modest feat of looking better inside than most American-made luxury cars.

Can one truck line be all things to all people? Can it appeal to desk jockeys and, at the same time, to construction workers who want pickups they can wash out with a hose? A true reading of public reaction is not possible from the spy photographs, which generally show snippets from only one of many versions of the truck. The formal debut at the auto show will offer a better indication of customer sentiment.

What is clear is that Ford, which turns 100 in June, can ill afford to lose ground with the F-150. The company has rarely been more beleaguered. After a staggering $5.5 billion loss in 2001, it rebounded with a slim profit last year. But overall sales fell 8.8 percent in 2002, Ford reported on Friday. That will only add to Wall Street's skepti-

Jeffrey Sauger for The New York Times

Julie Kurcz, a vehicle engineering manager at Ford, with a model of a new F-150 FX4. She said she tried to bring her personal perspective, as a 5-foot-2 woman, to the design.

cism about the pace of Ford's year-old corporate turnaround plan.

Ford's bonds are hovering near junk status, and its stock fell 40.8 percent in 2002. Its market share has been plunging as foreign automakers open plants in the United States and continue to flood the market with cars and trucks. Even **General Motors,** long moribund, has had small gains in market share for two years in a row.

"We take every launch seriously, but the F-150 is our flagship," said James J. Padilla, Ford's chief of North American operations. The truck, he added, "means a lot to our bottom line, and it means a lot to our dealers."

"Nearly a quarter of our North American sales comes from F-Series alone," he added.

In fact, the F-Series probably put Ford into the black last year, all by itself. Gary R. Lapidus, an auto analyst at Goldman, Sachs, estimated that the F-Series generated $2.6 billion in pretax income for Ford in 2002, $1 billion more than his projection for the entire company.

Ford executives have said they expect the F-Series to remain as profitable as it is now. Most analysts, though, say that will be difficult to achieve because of the cost of upgrading the trucks and because the F-150 will have a new competitor in Nissan.

Ronald A. Tadross, an analyst at Banc of America Securities, called the truck's high costs a holdover of the Jacques Nasser era. Mr. Nasser was Ford's chief executive until William Clay Ford Jr., the Ford family scion and chairman, forced him out in October 2001 and took over as chief executive himself.

Mr. Nasser was heavily criticized for not paying attention to the basics of the industry—what Ford spends to build each vehicle, for example. Last summer, Mr. Ford installed David W. Thursfield, who also heads international operations, as the head of purchasing. Mr. Thursfield is a veteran cost cutter, but analysts say major changes can take years to show results.

Reducing costs is "really hard to do in an existing model," Mr. Tadross said.

"Where you have your best opportunities is when you're developing new models," he added, and cost savings can be designed and engineered from the ground up. Going back, he said, is considerably more complicated.

The F-150 "was designed on the old regime's watch, which means it has a lot of new content, a little higher cost structure than the old one and probably a little more complexity," he said.

Mr. Lapidus said he doubted that "the next-generation F-Series in aggregate will be as profitable as the last generation."

"No matter what they do," he added, "it will be very difficult to hit that objective."

Already, the F-Series' share of the full-size pickup market has slid. It was 38 percent last year, compared with nearly 43 percent in 1998, according to the Autodata Corporation, a research firm. The top competitor is

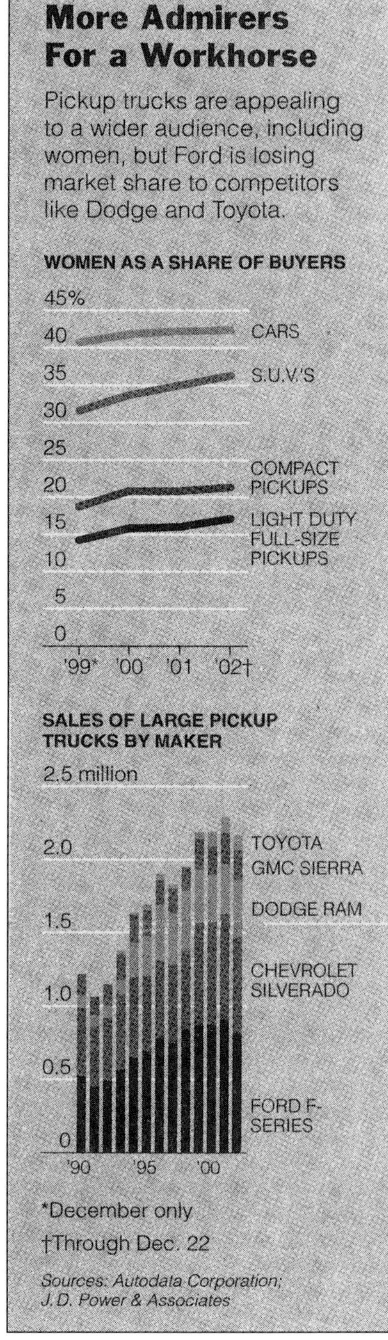

General Motors, which has about 30 percent of the market with its Chevrolet Silverado, the second-best-selling vehicle in the country, and an additional 9 percent with the GMC Sierra. But **Toyota Motor** has perhaps the most to do with the F-Series' recent share slide.

Toyota's first full-size pickup, the T100, fizzled in the mid-1990's, but the company has gained traction with a new full-size pickup, the Tundra, since it was introduced in 1999. In 2001, at the peak of full-size pickup sales, Toyota sold more than 100,000 Tundras, versus sales of more than 900,000 F-Series trucks by Ford and 700,000 Silverados.

For years, the pantheon of the American pickup truck was an uncomplicated place. Mostly men drove trucks, slogans were blunt ("like a rock" or "built Ford tough") and the music in commercials was left to the likes of Bob Seger, Chevy's former pickup pitchman known for his blue-collar anthems.

Lately, though, confusion has set in. Light trucks in general—a government classification that includes pickups, S.U.V.'s and minivans—now outsell passenger cars. Luxury car makers are increasingly making their money from trucks—BMW, Toyota's Lexus brand and Mercedes have all introduced S.U.V.'s—because many customers are willing to pay more for bigger vehicles.

In recent years, pickups have also become more luxurious. This trend reached an apotheosis in 2001, when Cadillac, of all unlikely brands, started selling a pickup. At a time when passenger-car sales are limping, manufacturers say pickups can offer much the same appeal that S.U.V.'s do: an aura of toughness with the trappings of comfort.

The growing popularity of light trucks has caused the fuel economy of the average American automobile to plummet to a 20-year low, despite many advances in technology. And light trucks pose dangers both to their own drivers, because of their increased risk of rollovers, and to car occupants because of the greater damage they inflict.

The new F-150 will have five major classes—varying mostly in interior glitziness—compared with just three now. In order, from no frills to fancy, are the XL, STX, XLT, FX4 and Lariat. Customers can order three different cab sizes: a regular cab has two seats, while the SuperCab and the jumbo SuperCrew have two rows of seats. The pickup bed is available in different lengths, and the sides of the truck can be ordered curvy ("flareside") or straight ("styleside"). Ford is also likely to continue offering limited-edition F-150's, like the upscale King Ranch and a model produced with **Harley-Davidson.**

Like many other American trucks and S.U.V.'s, the F-150 is getting bigger, with several inches added to its basic pickup bed and to the passenger compartment. The biggest version will cross the four-ton threshold for the first time. The grille is more imposing, and the oval Ford emblem at the back will almost double to nine inches in width.

The basic truck, the XL, is geared to the working man and has rubber floors in the passenger compartment that allow for hosing

(Cont.)

it out. At the top of the line, the Lariat is "geared toward buyers who view their trucks as a reward for achievement," according to the press kit.

The Lariat's interior comes in colors including "medium pebble" and has plenty of chrome, brushed steel and wood grains. It is not intended to be hosed out, nor is the FX4, which with its black leather seats looks more suited to a goateed bachelor—or, to the dismay of some male pickup enthusiasts, a woman.

Women now buy 18 percent of all pickups, up from 15 percent in 1999, according to J. D. Power & Associates, which monitors sales data from more than 5,900 dealer franchises nationwide. Even the basic F-150 has features tailored to nonconstruction workers, like a tailgate that is half as heavy to lift as the current version.

"I wanted it to be comfortable and smooth, a quiet and smooth ride free of shakes and head tossing," said Julie Kurcz, the highest-ranking female engineer on the F-150 project.

"I like to think that that's something I can bring to the part, my perspective; I'm 5-2 without high heels," said Ms. Kurcz, a baby boomer who declined to give her age. She and her husband are rebuilding a home with the help of her 2002 F-150.

Among the pickup's other options are heated seats and a selection of modular overhead storage areas that accommodate things like DVD players and Palm Pilots. (The F-150 already offers adjustable foot pedals for smaller people.) And, of course, there is the shift lever.

Mr. Padilla said he thought such features would help Ford attract a wider range of customers for the F-150. "I'll bet some of them are soccer moms," he said.

One of the F-150's most potent competitors last year was the Dodge Ram, whose surging sales were bolstered by the seven-year, 100,000-mile powertrain warranty offered by its parent company, **DaimlerChrysler.** (Ford offers a three-year, 36-month bumper-to-bumper warranty.) Dodge's advertising cranks up the machismo. The guy who drives the Ram in the company's television commercials looks as if he were chiseled from granite, and the Ram's grille has become cartoonishly muscle-bound. But this has an appeal.

"I see the Ram as the strongest competition from my standpoint, personally," said Roger Lemere, an F-150 driver in Sacramento, Calif., who sells aftermarket parts for Fords. "I describe it as bold and a man's-looking truck," he said. "I do like it."

But for many people, including Mr. Lemere, buying anything but Ford is unthinkable. He worships his black 1997 F-150, which he outfitted with a custom tweed interior; the truck "doesn't see rain and it's a big money pit," he said.

Mr. Lapidus of Goldman, Sachs, who has seen the new F-150's in the flesh, said their exteriors would hold up well and were "manly, like a truck should be."

He also said the transformation of pickups into luxury vehicles meant a fundamental change in how they are marketed and designed.

"I don't think they're ever going to replace the S-Class," he said, referring to the fancy Mercedes sedan, "but this is consistent with what we see all over the light-truck category."

"They're turning them into fashion-oriented private-use vehicles, and they do require more of the accouterments. The trouble is, they are more of a fashion item and will require more frequent upgrades and replacements. You're going to have to be constantly reinventing them to keep them fresh."

How Much Is Your Time Worth?

New Research Explores Actual Cost of Performing Household Tasks; the Economics of Garlic

BY JANE SPENCER;

Sarah Kalliney doesn't have time to do her laundry, visit her parents or change the cat's litter box. She eats out six nights a week, uses a personal shopper and gets her groceries delivered to her doorstep.

But the time-starved Manhattan executive, who bills at roughly $200 an hour, recently spent nearly 10 hours battling her cellphone company, Sprint PCS, over $9 in late fees.

Is it possible that was worth her time? It is a question economists are finally beginning to tackle. After decades of using time-value formulas to help companies maximize productivity, researchers and even the U.S. government are looking at how those concepts apply to the home front.

In an economy of convenience, where time can be purchased in everything from bags of prewashed lettuce and dog-walking services, these studies aim to help answer dozens of questions Americans wrestle with daily: Who can afford a babysitter? A lawn service? A personal shopper? "The household is a little firm," says Daniel Hamermesh, an economics professor the University of Texas. "It employs labor, it buys technology, it makes decisions about what services to outsource."

But it is a firm that could use some management consultants. Americans often make drastic miscalculations about the value of their time, taking a do-it-yourself approach to tasks that might be less costly in time and money to hire out. A simple oil change, for example, costs $24.99 at some Jiffy Lube locations. But the supplies to do it yourself can run about $21. Yet about 43 million U.S. residents say they change their own oil.

In the past, economists looked strictly at your income to put a price on your leisure hours. Now, the study of off-the-clock time—or "household production," as it is formally known—is getting a fresh look, even beginning to take into account intangible factors such as satisfaction and pleasure. In January, the Bureau of Labor Statistics launched its first study of household time use in an effort to provide reliable data for the emerging field. The monthly survey will ask people to report how much time they spend doing such things as practicing yoga and dropping off their kids.

A flood of academic papers, such as "Taking Household Production Seriously" and "Time Crunch or Yuppie Kvetch?" are also circulating. Other work has looked at the impact of time-saving technology from microwaves to washing machines.

This body of scholarship is gaining new relevance now that pinched budgets are forcing some to work longer hours, putting a higher premium on cost-effective use of free time.

Economists say one of the most common miscalculations is "outsourcing" child-care needs to free both parents to contribute to the household income. While plenty of parents choose to stay in the labor force because they enjoy their jobs, others stay because they think they can't afford not to. Sometimes the math proves otherwise, as Steve and Jan Lira recently discovered. She works three days a week as a tax analyst, bringing their combined income to more than $120,000 a year.

They recently looked at what her job was

Whose Chore Is It, Anyway?

With the help of an outside economist, we put together a framework for helping you decide whether it make sense to outsource a job or to do it yourself.

What Is Your Real Time Wage?

1. What is your two week take home pay, after taxes? .... $
2. How many hours do you typically work in a two week period? .... hours
3. Divide 1 by 2. This is your **real time wage** .... $

Does It Make Financial Sense For You to Outsource?

4. How much would it cost you to hire someone to do this task? .... $
5. How much time would you save, in hours, by hiring someone else to do this job? .... $
6. What are the costs associated with doing this job yourself? (e.g., buying supplies, ingredients etc.) .... $
7. Multiply 3 by 5 .... $
8. Add 6 and 7. This is the **total cost of doing the task yourself** .... $

OUTCOME: If 8 is less than 4, there is a strong financial case for doing the job yourself
If 8 is more than 4, there is a strong financial case for hiring someone else to do the work

Now, Consider the Psychological Costs and Benefits — Strongly Disagree 1 2 3 4 5 Strongly Agree

1. **Psychological Benefits:** I enjoy doing this task myself 1 2 3 4 5
2. **Skill Premium:** I could do this task as well as the person I would hire 1 2 3 4 5
3. **Opportunity Costs:** If I do this task myself, I will not miss out on other activities that are important to me 1 2 3 4 5
4. **Indirect Rewards:** If I do this task myself, I will get other benefits like exercise or self-confidence 1 2 3 4 5
5. **SCORING:** Add up your points ....

Point System

4-8 Points: The psychological costs are high, outsource the task if you can afford to.

9-12 Points: Let the financial calculations in the first part of this chart dictate your actions.

13-20 Points: The psychological benefits are great; do the job yourself even if you can easily hire it out.

actually costing them—from the $18,500 they will spend on daycare to the $14,000 they lose in tax credits. By the time they threw in her work-associated costs (office parking, dry cleaning, the restaurant meals they were consuming because they were both too exhausted to cook), they determined that if she left her job, the couple would lose only a few hundred dollars a month.

But economists recognize that for many families the numbers are just a starting point. You can temper the equations with what economists call "psychic variables." Some divide household activities into two categories: consumption (things you enjoy) and production (anything that feels like work). Love gardening? It is consumption. Hate gardening? That is production—increasing the argument in favor of hiring someone else to do it.

"It's not just about the money," says Dr. Hamermesh. "I get pleasure from listening to the symphony, other people get pleasure from harassing the airlines."

That is how Sarah Kalliney justifies her epic battle with Sprint: It was worth it for the satisfaction. "These people are jerks, and they're taking money that's not theirs," says Ms. Kalliney. "If they're going to ruin my day, I'm going to ruin theirs." She finally won—but only after she tracked down the phone number for the president of the company. Sprint PCS says it has since taken steps to improve its customer service.

The traditional approach, which valued a leisure time based on your after-tax hourly wage, was published by Nobel-prize winning economist Gary Becker in 1965. The idea was that any time that went toward leisure could be reinvested in work. But income-based formulas have obvious limitations. For instance, many people on a fixed salary don't have the option of getting extra pay if they work another hour. In addition, some people's work is keeping a house running, which doesn't come with a salary.

HOME ECONOMICS

Here's a list of tasks and the annual income at which it makes sense to hire someone to do them for you.

Task	Income
Doing your Taxes	**$13,900,000**
Chopping Garlic	**$ 10,000**
Organizing Messy Desk	**$ 570,000**
Paying Bills	**$ 196,000**
Mowing the Lawn	**$ 44,000**

Still, in figuring out how to maximize your time, salary is a logical jumping-off point. Economists suggest you begin by calculating what an hour of your time is worth, based on your salary after taxes. Using that figure, you can then compare the cost of doing the job yourself vs. outsourcing it. If you do it yourself, you have to add in the price of any materials; if you hire someone else, of course, you have to factor in the time it takes to hire and manage them.

Then, you are ready to tackle the other half of the calculation, which looks at the nonfinancial costs and benefits. Among the factors to consider: how much you enjoy doing the job yourself, and what you're giving up. All told, these conclusions will steer you in one direction or the other.

To see how this formula works in the real world, we outsourced tasks from lawnmowing to our tax returns—and then redid the jobs ourselves to compare. Buying a jar of prechopped garlic, for example, saved us 22 minutes of slicing and dicing. According to the formula, anybody who makes more than $10,000 a year can technically afford it. Emotional downside: fresh garlic tastes better.

Investing in technology—even a good garlic press—can change the dynamics of these calculations. That is what we found when we did our taxes. Visiting a walk-in tax preparer was a mere two minutes faster than the software program we used, factoring in our travel time to his office, but he cost $139 more. Under this particular scenario, you would need to make almost $14 million a year to justify hiring someone.

Then there was our messy desk. A $85-an-hour professional organizer whipped half of it into shape. The other half we tackled ourselves. The threshold income for hiring the pro? More than half-a-million dollars—partly because we had to hang around to help her navigate our piles of papers. But she did throw in a feng shui analysis of our bedroom.

Many hard-core do-it-yourselfers are grappling with these same variables. Mark Berg, a financial planner in Wheaton, Ill., changes his own oil and once rented a 70-pound jackhammer to rip out his concrete basement floor.

But the garage sale he held last summer challenged his view. After hours of planning and a long day in the June sun, he netted a nasty sunburn and a wage of $3.56 an hour—somewhat short of the $150 an hour he charges at the office.

"We will never do another garage sale," he says.

Safe at home and all plugged in

Electronics grow more elaborate as we embrace 'local area nesting'

By Mike Snider
USA Today

For Todd Skelton, there's no place like home.

The 37-year-old automotive executive has gone to extremes in outfitting his Palm Beach, Fla., home with a full complement of entertainment gadgets, including an automation and security system, and a theater with three rows of seats for him and his wife, relatives and friends to watch DVD movies on a 12-foot screen.

Although the work was finished in July, Skelton says, the home theater has been a particular source of comfort for his family—including stepchildren and their kids—since the Sept. 11 attacks. "It seems to me that there's a big shift toward spending more time at home and families' homes," he says.

Some trend spotters call it "cocooning," others call it "nesting." But the movement toward spending more time at home—and feathering our nests with more elaborate and entertaining diversions—may be more than a fad.

That, at least, is the hope of the makers and sellers of digital entertainment gadgets. Even though overall electronics sales dipped slightly in 2001, according to numbers to be released today at the annual Consumer Electronics Show in Las Vegas, sales of DVD players, digital TVs and home theater packages spiked significantly—and are predicted to continue their rise this year.

Consumers "want to stay in contact with loved ones. They want to be entertained. They want to have an escape, a diversion through home entertainment," says Jeff Joseph of the Consumer Electronics Association, which runs the CES show, expected to draw about 100,000 industry and media representatives.

The terrorist attacks may not have started the trend toward cocooning, but the events of the past few months have given it added momentum. "People were looking to balance their lives more coming out of the late '90s into the new century as the dot-com economy started to crash," says Cary Silvers of consumer research firm RoperASW. "People were starting to spend more time with family, usually at home."

But since the attacks, people "are keeping to their safe havens," Silvers says. Roper even has coined a term for the trend: "local area nesting."

A Roper phone survey over the weekend found that nearly one in four people intend to spend more on entertainment for the home this year—"a significant number," says Silvers, "and it has already been on an upward trend." More than 25% intend to rent more movies.

About 30% say they'll spend more on technology to keep them connected to family and friends. And in other surveys since Sept. 11, 29% of people said they were more likely to spend even more time at home and 27% were more likely to attend church or synagogue. That suggests nesting doesn't mean simply hunkering down and shunning the world.

"People are rediscovering their local community," Silvers says. "But the home becomes the center, almost like nuclei. . . . The home is the comfort zone."

Family therapist Evan Imber-Black isn't convinced cocooning will become instilled as long-term behavior. "At the beginning, people were staying put and investing in things they could do at home," says Imber-Black, of the Ackerman Institute for the Family in New York. "But it seems that was a more temporary thing. People are out again."

On the other hand, Imber-Black and her husband did buy a DVD player over the holidays—and a second one for their son. "We were looking into that way before 9/11 and just decided this year's Christmas was the time to get it."

As for "local area nesting," she says, "I think it remains to be seen. We are very early in the process. What we have seen in many families is a desire to connect with extended family to do work to repair certain relationships."

However, at Scottsdale, Ariz.-based market research firm Cahners In-Stat, tech analyst Neil Strother thinks the plugged-in nest may prove to have staying power. Consumers have decided to "stay home a little more and are doing more low-end purchases, maybe getting a (Nintendo) GameCube or (Microsoft) Xbox instead of a PC," he says. "Watching a movie or playing a game together is maybe more important than running off to Europe or taking vacations."

And after several years of increased importance

for personal computers and home information, "the television is becoming more important in the home again," says Dave Arland of Thomson Consumer Electronics, which makes RCA products. "People are spending more time in front of the tube."

That may or may not be a healthy development, says Shirley Glass, a Baltimore-area psychologist and marital therapist. "If people are buying more equipment for home entertainment, does that result in family time, or is it creating something where each person is more in their own hives within the cocoon?"

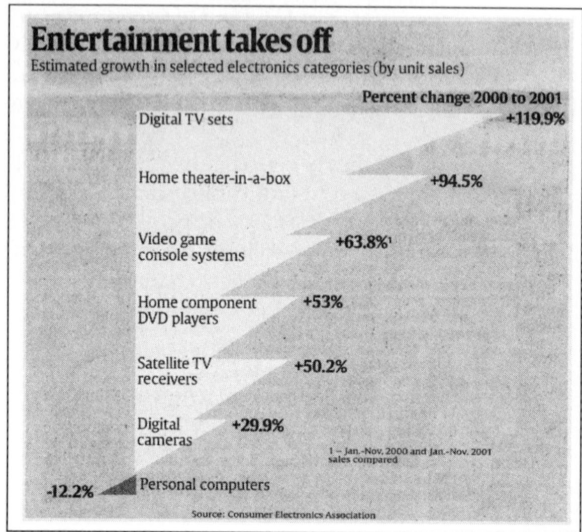

She has childhood memories of a neighbor who had the first TV on the block, who hooked the set to an extension cord and put it on the lawn. Neighbors brought out chairs and watched a Joe Louis boxing match. "Maybe this is the 21st-century version," she says. "People who have huge home entertainment systems often share them with friends and neighbors. Then it becomes a very nice social thing."

For much of the past decade, home PCs and other information appliances helped propel sales of electronics. But in 2001, PC sales dropped about 13% and are expected to decline again this year, according to factory sales figures to be released today at the show.

"Entertainment was the winner in 2001," Strother says.

Holiday sales at Denver-based Ultimate Electronics suggest that buyers are still focusing on the home. "People are a little more selective about their purchases, and I think we are in favor with the consumers now," says Dave Workman, president of the 36-store chain.

The low-priced DVD players that appeared over the holidays—some selling for less than $100—helped fuel consumer interest. DVD movies not only deliver video twice the quality of VHS, but also CD-quality surround sound.

Entry-level home theater surround-sound packages dropped to as little as $300, while systems complete with DVD players are being introduced at the show for as little as $350. Big-screen digital TVs, including sets that can display the high-definition broadcasts slowly being rolled out by the networks, have slid from $3,000-plus to less than $1,800.

"Three or four years ago, home theater was thought of as something rich people went out and bought. Now more people look at it as a way to expand on their television," Workman says.

With more than 25 million DVD players sold in less than five years, the product has become the most successful consumer electronics product ever, adopted more quickly than TVs, CD players or satellite TV systems. "That is obviously having a spillover effect to better televisions and better sound systems."

The industry would like to reach a similar critical mass soon in digital TV. Already about 225 broadcast stations are transmitting DTV signals, some in the high-definition format that offers far more clarity than current broadcasts, in a cinema-like widescreen format. Satellite TV services DirecTV and the Dish Network also offer high-definition movies and programming. But copy-protection issues in Hollywood and compatibility battles with the cable TV industry have slowed the rollout.

Nonetheless, consumers are moving to the new high-tech sets in anticipation of the future. Sales of regular, non-digital TV sets have decreased for two years in a row, while sales of digital sets nearly doubled last year. (Sales of non-digital sets still outnumber sales of digital models 15 to 1.) And digital sets are designed to improve the viewing of DVD movies and standard broadcasts.

The promise of a better picture recently drew Larry Baker, 66, of Rancho Palos Verdes, Calif., to invest in a high-definition TV set. "Prices have started to come down, and we're getting a few broadcasts," says Baker, who is retired.

As a result, he is considering buying a second digital TV to replace the 60-inch projection model in his den. "I certainly go to the theater a lot less. I wait for movies to come out on DVD," he says.

Installers of custom home theaters, security and other electronics systems are getting similar signals. In a survey to be released today, installers say they expect

(Cont.)

business to increase 25% to 30% next year, compared with the 15% to 20% increase that has been standard over the past five years, according to the Custom Electronics Design & Installation Association.

After the Sept. 11 attacks, there was an immediate uptick in custom installation requests, says CEDIA president Jeff Hoover, president of the West Palm Beach, Fla., firm Audio Advisors, which installed Todd Skelton's system.

"A large number of people had been putting off their (projects) and decided it was time to go ahead," he says. "People are designing their homes so they don't really need to leave all that often."

That's certainly true at Skelton's home, where his next project involves remodeling the kitchen and adding to the master bedroom. "There's a certain level of comfort in your home," he says. "It's always been difficult to get me out of the house, but I used to feel like I needed to get out of the house. Now, I want to do everything to avoid getting out of the house."

Exchanges

Making It Work

Meet Aaron Gillum: the face of one online exchange

By Peter Loftus

If you think customer-service work for a retail Web site sounds tough, imagine being responsible for a $10 million order for car-axle assemblies.

That's the kind of high-octane duty Aaron Gillum is charged with every day. He's what's known as an auction engineer for **Covisint** LLC, a business-to-business online exchange created jointly in February 2000 by the Big Three auto makers, **DaimlerChrysler** AG, **Ford Motor** Co., Dearborn, Mich., and Detroit-based **General Motors** Corp., in order to move more parts purchasing online to save costs and speed up buying cycles. Other companies that have since bought smaller stakes in the venture are Japan's **Nissan Motor** Co., French auto makers **Renault SA** and **PSA Peugeot Citroen,** and software makers **Oracle** Corp., Redwood Shores, Calif., and **Commerce One** Inc., Pleasanton, Calif. The Big Three are both owners and customers of Covisint, which gets a percentage of the value of all auctions. A total of 11 auto makers worldwide are Covisint customers. And some 5,000 suppliers are registered to participate in Covisint auctions.

Auction engineers set up auctions after purchasing managers at auto makers contact them with parts orders. A group of auction engineers works full-time on behalf of a certain auto maker. For instance, Mr. Gillum, who joined Covisint in October 2000, and a dozen others work exclusively with DaimlerChrysler. Auction engineers helped Covisint handle more than $50 billion in auto-parts orders last year. In its biggest auction ever, the Southfield, Mich., company conducted a four-day auction last May in which DaimlerChrysler purchased about $2.6 billion in auto parts. Compare that with eBay Inc., the top consumer auction Web site, which reported fourth-quarter gross merchandise sales of almost $2.4 billion.

"These auctions are for millions of dollars," says Mr. Gillum, 24 years old. "We're not messing around here with $10 at a time. You're not buying a digital camera or something like that."

Key to making such megadeals run more efficiently—and faster—is the Internet. In the old days, when fax machines were at the cutting edge of communications, auto-supply auctions could take several days or weeks. An auto maker would invite several suppliers to bid for a product order. The suppliers would mail or fax in their bids, with no way of knowing what others were bidding. Purchasing managers at the auto maker would sometimes ask for a new round of bidding in an effort to get a lower price. Or the purchasing manager would call a supplier and ask for a lower bid, but wouldn't say exactly how low.

Now, an auction can be wrapped up in as little as 10 minutes online—Covisint schedules auctions to run at least that long but the average auction lasts about 45 minutes. Once the auction starts, suppliers can place their bids and instantly see what others are bidding so they know how much to adjust their own price.

Prep Work

To DaimlerChrysler and many of its suppliers, Mr. Gillum is the face of Covisint. A DaimlerChrysler purchasing manager usually gives Mr. Gillum at least two weeks to set up an auction. When first notified, he asks the buyer for important details: date and time of the auction, parts numbers, a "quick-and-dirty" description of the parts needed, volume of parts and the opening price or the maximum amount the buyer is willing to pay.

Then the buyer must give Mr. Gillum a list of specific suppliers to invite to bid at the auction. Covisint recommends that the buyer invite at least three suppliers in order to get competitive bids. Some auctions end up with as many as 20 suppliers, Mr. Gillum says. Suppliers range in size from $50 million in annual revenue to more than $1 billion. Only the buyer and the invited suppliers can gain access to the online auction using a secret password on the Covisint Web site.

After getting the basics from the buyer, Mr. Gillum notifies the suppliers that they've been invited, and he provides details of what the auto maker wants to buy. The suppliers also can find this information on Covisint's Web site.

A few days before a scheduled auction, Mr. Gillum runs a trial auction with the suppliers to ensure that suppliers know what to expect and what to do. He types in "Part X" and enters an opening bid of $3 million and the suppliers enter their dummy bids. During the trial and real auctions, he can communicate with the suppliers by an instant-messaging system to answer questions and give live updates.

When auction day rolls around, he likes to visit the DaimlerChrysler purchasing manager's office to watch the auction unfold, especially if the manager is new to online parts auctions.

Others engineers also like to be with the buyers during auctions because a lot of money is riding on the outcomes, says auction engineer Aaron Parsons. In mid-January, he helped Covisint conduct a 13-hour auction for DaimlerChrysler. For some items, Chrysler saved 40% of the opening price, he says. And an engineer was with the buyer at that event.

"Because it's real time, there's not a lot of margin for error," Mr. Parsons says. But he isn't overwhelmed by all those zeros behind the dollar signs. "We're putting the same effort into a hundred-million-dollar event as we put into a small event."

When there is a problem, Mr. Gillum and the other auction engineers are the ones both sides turn to. If a supplier is having technical difficulties placing a bid online, he calls Mr. Gillum.

"Some people ask if they can make bids from home," Mr. Gillum says. "I say, 'You can do it from home, but you shouldn't. You probably want to do it from a place with a high-speed Internet connection.'" He says the problem is that some suppliers merely shell out $1,000 for a personal computer and use a dial-up Internet connection, which can have access problems, to participate in Covisint auctions.

If a DaimlerChrysler purchasing manager doesn't know how to run an online auction, Mr. Gillum drives 15 miles north to the auto maker's North American headquarters in Auburn Hills, Mich.

One morning late last year, he was about to run a DaimlerChrysler auction with a half-dozen suppliers. (Because of Covisint's confidentiality policy, Mr. Gillum says he can't disclose details about the suppliers or the Chrysler parts being ordered.) At the last minute, a supplier called Mr. Gillum to say a storm had knocked out his power supply, so he couldn't gain access to the online auction. The supplier was calling on his cellphone.

Mr. Gillum immediately notified DaimlerChrysler and the other suppliers that the auction would be postponed until the afternoon, hoping power would be restored by then. As a backup plan, if power was still out, he arranged for the supplier to phone in a bid to Covisint technicians, who would then enter the bid on the supplier's behalf.

"About 10 minutes before the auction started, the power came back on and the guy's computer came back on," Mr. Gillum says.

Luckily, most glitches aren't that complicated. "The biggest problem is [that suppliers have] lost their password," he says. When some suppliers worry that everyone in the industry will be able to see how much they're bidding, Mr. Gillum tells them that only the auction participants can see bids, and even then, the Covisint Web site only lists the lead bids and doesn't identify who made them.

Be Prepared

Most important, Mr. Gillum tells suppliers to know what their lowest possible bid will be before an auction. Some auctions are over in 10 minutes, which is hardly enough time to crunch the numbers if the prep work hasn't been done.

If a bidder places a bid within the last minute of the auction, it goes into "overtime"

(Cont.)

and is extended three minutes. During those three minutes, if a new low bid is placed, the auction's extended for another three minutes, and so on.

"Even if you get beat, at least you have a parameter for market pricing," Mr. Gillum says. "You always know what the lead bid is. You always have a chance to counter the lead bid."

Mr. Loftus is a special writer for Dow Jones Newswires in New York.

Silicon Valley techies suit up Army with sleeker gear

Engineers retool clunky gadgets quickly, cheaply

By Edward Iwata
USA TODAY

On a pitch-black night last fall, 40 Army Rangers parachuted into the forests at Fort Polk, La., simulating combat against an Eastern Bloc enemy.

They were outfitted with the "Land Warrior," a computer system full of high-tech firearms and communications gear.

On the ground, the troops used Land Warrior's satellite-mapping device and found each other in 30 minutes. It can take two or three hours using flashlights and paper maps.

One Ranger, peering through a heat-sensing thermal sight on his M-4 rifle, spotted "enemy" snipers in the dark 300 meters away and opened fire, "killing" them. The Rangers finished their mission twice as fast as a typical platoon.

"It's powerful technology," says Army Ranger Sgt. Chris Augustine. "We were apprehensive at first, but now we're begging for it."

That's a stunning turnaround from three years ago, when soldiers hated the clunky Land Warrior system and ripped it off their backs. The $2 billion project was on its deathbed after defense contractor Raytheon built a prototype called the "turtle shell" that was blasted by the General Accounting Office. Since then, the Land Warrior has been resurrected by a team of Silicon Valley engineers who retooled it in six months.

The firms—Pacific Consultants, Exponent, Pemstar and Computer Sciences—ignored rigid Army specifications and brainstormed ideas. They lightened the Land Warrior computer harness, wrote new software and worked closely with soldiers.

Today, the new Land Warrior is earning rave reviews from troops testing it. "A dramatic improvement," says Army Lt. Col. Scott Crizer. Military officials say 48,000 Land Warrior outfits may roll out by 2004 to be used by Army troops in training and combat. Even the Navy has tested the Land Warrior.

The tech firms hail the revised Land Warrior as a victory of their fast-track, entrepreneurial business model over the costlier defense industry model followed by the military for decades. They also tout their use of commercial products, such as Microsoft software and Intel computer chips, instead of pricier technology made by the government or large defense contractors. While corporate behemoths, such as Lockheed Martin and General Dynamics, rule the defense world, the small tech firms say their Land Warrior success has caught the attention of military brass and defense companies.

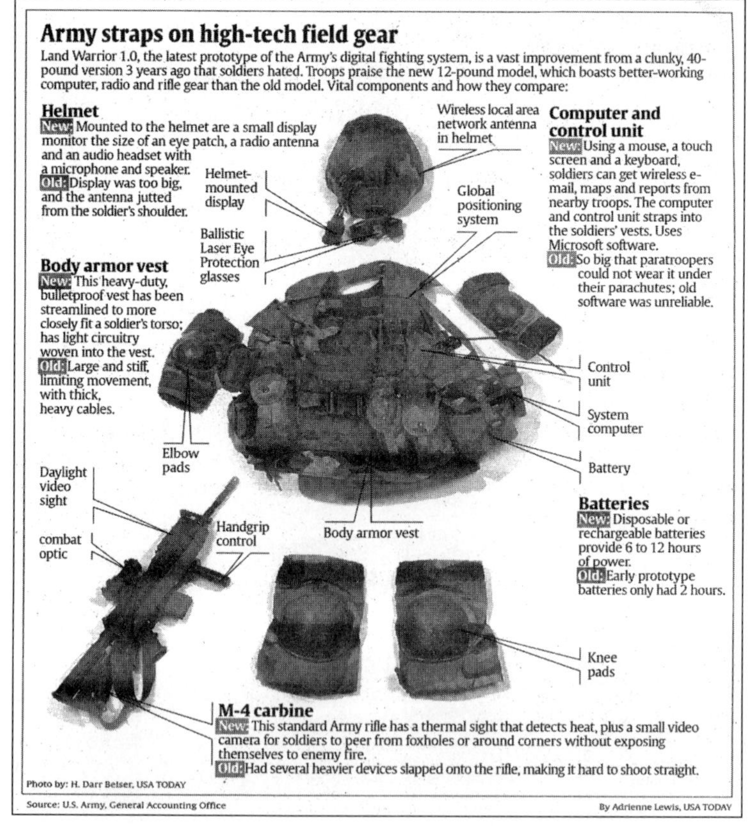

(Cont.)

"We made it the classic Silicon Valley way: quicker, cheaper and better," says Hugh Duffy, a former Pacific Consultants executive. "It's an uphill battle, but we think we can transform the old model."

Six years ago, the Army hoped the Land Warrior would revolutionize combat by creating the world's first digital soldier. Part of the Pentagon's sweeping $21 billion drive to create a digital battlefield, the Land Warrior would give the Army the same dominance on the ground that the Air Force enjoys in the skies.

In theory, the early Land Warrior would be an awesome fighting machine. Infantrymen would use a computer and radio harness, voice communication and wireless e-mail, a satellite-mapping system and other high-tech gear.

"The idea was to make our soldiers invincible," says Justus Decher, executive director of business development at Pemstar.

After intense bidding, the contract to develop Land Warrior was awarded to Raytheon, maker of the Tomahawk cruise missile and the world's No. 3 defense contractor, with $17 billion in revenue.

Troubled times

But the first prototype by Raytheon was a 40-pound monstrosity, according to GAO reports, Army officials and defense industry experts. During testing, soldiers who rolled on the ground got stuck on their backs like tortoises. The helmet was so heavy, troops who were crawling couldn't lift their heads to fire rifles. A thick helmet cable got snagged in bushes so often that soldiers ripped it out.

The early Land Warrior software rarely worked, and batteries for computers and radios lasted far less than the desired 12 hours. The system failed water tests, leaking badly. During jump exercises, the bulky computer packs wouldn't fit under soldiers' parachutes.

"It was a classic example of guys sitting around a table, wishing they had this and that," says retired Army Lt. Col. Tim Eads, an analyst at the Center for Strategic & International Studies. "You ended up with a 50-pound piece of metal that soldiers hated dragging around."

Raytheon declined to talk about problems raised in the GAO report but said the company laid the foundation for the Land Warrior concept. "We believe our efforts were invaluable to (the success of) the Land Warrior," says Raytheon executive David Martin.

Meanwhile, the cost of developing the Land Warrior units had soared to $2.1 billion from $1.4 billion, according to the GAO. Congress was threatening to cut off funding, and Army officials were under pressure to kill the program.

An intense Army colonel named Bruce Jette revived the Land Warrior system, according to military and defense industry insiders. Jette, a no-nonsense engineer with a doctorate in physics from the Massachusetts Institute of Technology, has a personal stake in the project's success: His son is studying at West Point.

To troubleshoot, in early 1999 Jette brought in high-tech consultants Exponent, a Silicon Valley firm that studies engineering and structural failures and accidents.

The firm felt that Raytheon had followed Army specs for the project too closely. The old prototype had to be trashed and a new computer and radio system built.

Raytheon strongly objected, say military and defense industry sources. The company had spent four years and millions of dollars developing the Land Warrior. It needed more work, but not a complete overhaul, they felt.

"We fulfilled our contractual obligations and designed what the government requested," says Raytheon's Martin.

In tense meetings and phone calls, Army officials asked Raytheon several times to work with the Silicon Valley engineers to change the Land Warrior. Raytheon refused, according to military and defense industry experts.

"Raytheon had a lot of ego and technical talent invested in the project," says Dan Causey, the Army's chief of technical management for the Land Warrior program. "They felt they were at the top of their game, and we hadn't convinced them. It was a real impasse."

The Silicon Valley engineers felt Raytheon could build missile systems but couldn't make cheap, reliable computer setups the way they could. Over beers at nearby bars, the engineers clashed over everything from software standards to computer chip speeds.

The budding partnership crumbled when Exponent refused to sign a subcontractor agreement with lead contractor Raytheon. Frustrated Army officials told Exponent to charge ahead anyway and design a new Land Warrior.

Going off the shelf

The Silicon Valley engineers slapped together a crude model in three months. They went to retailers Best Buy and Fry's Electronics and bought several cheap, off-the-shelf products, including Microsoft Windows CE software and a wireless card to allow Land Warrior computers to send data.

The most critical technical step: They wrote the software in common programming language used by most software engineers, rather than using old government programming language, as Raytheon had.

The Army sped up the months-long military procurement process by staging a Silicon Valley-style "bake-off" in late 1999 in Menlo Park, Calif. The bidders—Pacific Consultants, Raytheon and Motorola—demonstrated their proposed Land Warrior computer and software designs before a roomful of Army engineers.

"It was like the gunfight at the OK Corral," Duffy says.

Pacific Consultants said it could finish its prototype in six months for $2 million—more quickly and cheaply than the other bidders. The price tag for Pacific Consultant's prototype was $30,000 a unit, while Raytheon's version would have cost more than $60,000, say defense contractors and Army officials.

The Army decided in one day, choosing Pacific Consultants to design the Land Warrior's hardware, software and radio systems. The next year, Pacific Consultants led a consortium that won a $35 million contract to make the prototypes. In coming years, the military might dole out up to $18 billion to contractors to manufacture and repair Land Warrior units.

Soldiers say the newest Land Warrior is the best version yet. At 12 pounds, the vest and body armor fit snugly around a soldier's torso. Its Microsoft Windows 2000 software still has bugs but is nearing the project goal of 10 days of use without breaking down.

Soldiers who've grown up with computers love the Land Warriors, says Army Ranger Sgt. Don Boyle, who notes that a Delta Force Land Warrior video game is used during training at West Point.

Mindful that billions of dollars have been spent on ill-fated defense projects over the decades, the military hopes to buy more commercial technology. Even the Navy Seals have bought commercial speedboats and reinforced them to withstand gunfire.

"The Army may have led the world in solid-state electronics in the 1960s, but today, our technology expenditures aren't even one high-tech company's R&D budget," says Jette. "We have to use technologies in the commercial sector to our advantage."

Analysts say it's unclear, though, whether the Army's success with the Land Warrior will persuade the military and defense industry to change its ways. Too much is at stake, such as the $200 billion, 10-year contract won recently by Lockheed Martin to build the Joint Strike Fighter, a state-of-the-art jetfighter. Conservative military brass fear change. Politicians still want to funnel defense dollars into their districts.

"The forces arrayed against change are pretty formidable," says analyst Christopher Hellman at the Center for Defense Information.

Many of the large defense contractors have decades-old political ties to the Pentagon, Congress and the White House. Unless small tech firms own superior technology, they stand little chance of competing against the big guns.

Yet, the Silicon Valley model might be winning converts. Military experts say two new Army projects to modernize military vehicles and soldiers' communications systems will use commercial technology.

"That's a good sign," says Exponent executive John Geddes. "It means we've been successful."

Getting Information for Marketing Decisions

Corporate Intelligence

I-Spy

Getting the lowdown on your competition is just a few clicks away

By Susan Warren

Staff reporter of The Wall Street Journal

Pssst! Wanna Get the skinny on a business rival?

The explosion of company Web sites, chat rooms and e-commerce has produced a gold mine of information just waiting to be unearthed by resourceful businesspeople eager for the scoop on a competitor. With time, patience and a few quick keystrokes, you can comb the Web for loads of facts and figures your competitors would rather you didn't know. While you're at it, you might want to check out what people are saying about you.

"The good news is your competition's kimono is more open than ever," says Larry Chase, publisher of Web Digest for Marketers, an online newsletter. "The bad news is, so is yours."

In corporate-speak, it's called gathering competitive intelligence. But let's not mince words. We're talking about good old-fashioned spying with a big plus: You never have to leave your desk.

Ethnical Concerns

Sound shifty? Actually, business-ethics experts agree there's nothing wrong with learning what you can about your competitors from the wealth of public information available on the Web. Where you cross the line is if you anonymously coax proprietary information from an unsuspecting competitor, says W. Michael Hoffman, executive director of the Center for Business Ethics at Bentley College in Waltham, Mass.

Stephen Miller, a spokesman for the Society of Competitive Intelligence Professionals, says that his organization's ethical guidelines dictate that you should never misrepresent yourself when gathering information. But not misrepresenting yourself doesn't necessarily mean you have to identify yourself, he adds. Dropping anonymously into a competitors' Web site, Mr. Miller says, is akin to the time-honored business practice of wandering into a rival's store to look over his merchandise, how he's priced it, how he's advertised it and how he's displayed it.

"I'd be silly if I didn't try to find out—in an ethical way—about my competitor's product," Mr. Hoffman says.

Within these parameters, there are lots of ways to gather tons of useful information using the Web. A multitude of companies have sprung up that will do your searching, sifting and sorting for a fee. But if you're more budget-conscious, or simply want to get a feel for the kind of stuff that's available, there's lots of basic information you can collect yourself. Get ready to spend some time at it, though.

One of Mr. Chase's favorite tricks is to use a standard search site to look up all of the Web pages a business has open on the Internet. For example, at Altavista.com, a list of such pages can be had by typing in the address of the company you're investigating in the following format: url://companyname.com.

Sometimes Mr. Chase has even come across pages that the company meant to keep confidential, but neglected to make secure. "I've uncovered new business presentations that way. People put them up and think nobody will find them," says Mr. Chase.

You can also judge your competitors by the company they keep. At Altavista, the search string link://www.companyname.com will reveal who has Web sites that are linked to those of your rivals. (Also check link://companyname.com—some companies are catalogued with the three w's, and some aren't.) That list will give you an idea of how well-connected your competitor is in the Internet community. It may give you the chance to figure out why some sites are linked to your competitor, and not to your own company's site.

Don't Neglect the Obvious

Before you get too fancy with your searches, though, start with the basics: Check out your competitor's corporate Web site. This seems obvious, but a keen eye and a little reading between the lines can reveal some less-than-obvious insights, spying aficionados say.

Start broadly. Evaluating the design and layout of the Web site can give you clues to the company's sophistication and the image the firm is trying to project. Company profiles can reveal partnerships and general business goals.

For a publicly traded company, comb through the investor-relations site, which lays out the company's financial details, including quarterly reports on profits, losses and unusual expenses. All this is required by law to be public, but it's nice to have it compiled in one place. There are often other useful features, such as management profiles that will tell you the background and experience of the people running the rival firm, and copies of business presentations and speeches laying out corporate strategies and outlooks.

Make sure to review any press releases posted, which can provide information about new products and ventures, or signal trouble with announcements of layoffs or restructuring plans.

Even a company's listing of employment

Keeping Tabs

Want to keep an eye on your competitors? Here are some Web sites and searches that will give you useful information.

Altavista.com ■ Looking for advanced details of your competitor's Web operation? Try the following searches at the Altavista search engine:

■ Type in the search blank: url://yourcompetitor'sname.com for a list of all the individual Web pages on your competitor's site.

■ Type in the search blank: link://yourcompetitor'sname.com or link://www. yourcompetitor'sname.com for a list of Web pages that link to your competitor's Web site.

Google.com ■ You can get the tidbits listed above, and some others, at this search engine. Typing in your competitor's Website address yields this list of information you can retrieve:

■ Google's "cache" of your competitor's Web site. Many search engines store a copy of popular Web pages in what's called a cache. Why? When one of these pages turns up in a search, and you click on the link, the page doesn't take as long to load. But if those pages get updated, they often aren't cached immediately. So Google's cache provides a snapshot of your competitor's site that hasn't been updated and thus might reveal information deleted in a recent updating.

■ Web pages that contain the term "yourcompetitor'sname.com"

Anonymizer.com ■ When you visit a Web site, whoever runs the site can see the Internet address you came from—so, for example, if you visited "mycompetitor.com," your competitor would see that the site got a visit from "yourcompany.com." Anonymizer cloaks your home address so the Web sites you visit can't see it.

Epinions.com ■ Here you can check out consumer reviews to see how your products stack up against your competitors'.

Netsol.com ■ This site lets you plug your competitor's name into a search engine and gives you a list of Web domain names the competitor has reserved.

uspto.gov ■ The U.S. Patent and Trademark Office's site lets you conduct a search of patents or trademarks registered by your competitor.

Note: Some sites are for-profit, and supported by ads, and some ask for personal information. Read privacy policies carefully on each site's home page.

opportunities can provide fertile hunting grounds, says Curtis Cook, vice president of business intelligence for Global Trade Solutions, an Ottawa, Ontario, partnership that specializes in corporate intelligence gathering.

For example, does Brand X have a lot of openings for product engineers? "Then it would be a safe guess that they're ramping up to put a lot of research and development into a new product line," says Mr. Cook. Or maybe the company is seeking to beef up its sales force, signaling that it has finished the development part, and is getting ready to launch a new product that will need heavy marketing.

Realizing that they've been revealing more than is wise, many companies have begun scaling back the amount of detail they provide on their Web sites, including job postings and product prices. But with persistence, you can sometimes pick up the trail by searching through some of the Web sites that specialize in employment, such as Monster.com or Headhunter.net. There you might find listings that tell you not only what kind of jobs your rival is trying to fill, but how much the company is paying.

Working the Chat Rooms

While you're surfing, drop in on a few message boards and chat rooms dedicated to the company or business you're interested in. There's a lot of frivolous garbage to wade through, but with persistence, you can glean some valuable tidbits from exchanges between employees and between industry experts who also frequent the sites.

For instance, sniping and griping about a boss or policy can reveal chinks in a company's armor. More significantly, you might pick up talk of a new product or process that hasn't made it to the public eye yet.

"Oftentimes employees don't know that what they're talking about is confidential and proprietary," says Global Trade's Mr. Cook. "They're excited about what they're working on and the prospect of being on the cutting edge. So they share those types of things."

If you don't see anything interesting, toss out your own question, suggests Mr. Cook. You never know when you'll find someone eager to talk.

This is an area fraught with ethical concerns, however. Mr. Hoffman, the head of the Center for Business Ethics, views chat-room reconnaissance as ethically acceptable.

"A Toyota salesman can walk into a Honda dealership and ask questions [about nonproprietary information] like 'How do you make your gas tank? How do you sell your radio and CD combo?'" Mr. Hoffman says. This kind of information might be given to any inquisitive person who walked into a dealership. "I don't think I'm unethical in not saying, 'Oh, by the way, I'm with Toyota,'" Mr. Hoffman says.

If the person you're conversing with asks who you are, however, then without question you should reply truthfully. And if a rival should volunteer proprietary information to you during a chat-room conversation or anywhere else, Mr. Hoffman says, you have an obligation to immediately identify yourself.

Know Thyself, Too

Finally, sometimes the most useful information can be what you learn about yourself. It's a good idea to monitor those chat rooms and message boards for what's being said about your own company, too. Or check out the consumer reviews offered on sites like Epinion.com to find out how you stack up against your competitors in the customer's eye.

It all sounds relatively easy. But Internet spying has some big pitfalls, the experts warn. The biggest challenge is simply finding the time to wade through all the information you'll be bringing in. The more specific your intelligence goal (do you want to know more about your competitor's manufacturing processes? financial strength? marketing strategy?), the more focused your search can be. But even finely tailored research, when culling from the six billion pages indexed by the largest search engines, can bring in truckloads of information.

Sorting through your harvest can be a monumental task. And there's no guarantee that what you find is going to be current or accurate, so careful evaluation and analysis is important.

Otherwise, "before you know it, a day has gone by and you've found all kinds of interesting stuff, but none of it may actually be very valuable to you," cautions Mr. Cook.

Professional Help

Firms specializing in corporate intelligence combine their analysis and expertise with sophisticated technology to narrow searches and produce more useful information. One example is **Compete** Inc., Boston, which has developed software that can track Internet users around the Web, observing their shopping and buying habits.

"It's almost like watching shoppers move through Wal-Mart," says Man Jit Singh, Compete's chief executive, "watching which aisles they walk down, which products they pause to ponder, and what they finally buy."

For example, when Internet retailer BarnesandNoble.com put up three new product category tabs for shoppers on its home page, rival Amazon.com asked Compete to evaluate whether shoppers were using the tabs, and whether it was worth creating similar categories on its own site. By reviewing weeks of data from Internet provider firms, which showed what pages were visited and gave basic gender, age and income information, Compete was able to report back to Amazon that only one of the BarnesandNoble tabs was proving popular with shoppers. (BarnesandNoble declined to comment for this article.)

By reviewing user habits, Compete has also been able to guide banks on how to design their Web sites to attract the clientele they desire—young and malleable, or older and affluent, for example. Analyzing user data geographically allows the company to advise a car manufacturer to ship white cars to California and blue cars to Florida. By discovering which cars are proving most popular on a competitor's site, that same car manufacturer might find out that offering buying incentives on a similar car in its fleet could draw more buyers away from the rival.

Companies big and small benefit from corporate intelligence. **Cyveillance** Inc., based in Arlington Va., caters to larger companies with big brand names. Much of its business involves evaluating how a company's brands rank with customers and distributors, and how they're being used or abused. Information provided by Cyveillance has helped companies track down trademark and copyright violators, for instance, says Richard Moore, vice president of marketing.

Since the Sept. 11 terrorists attacks, Cyveillance's services have been sought by companies—and even some government agencies—concerned about security. The same kind of spying techniques used to cull intelligence on competitors can also pick up possibly threatening comments or behavior that might bear closer investigation in today's more security-conscious environment, says Mr. Moore.

Ms. Warren is a staff reporter in The Wall Street Journal's Dallas bureau.

WINGING INTO WIRELESS

It's cheaper and easier to install—and more companies are finding that it pays off big

Three years ago, U.S. Fleet Services considered building a wireless network for its drivers, but soon decided against it. Customizing mobile devices and developing software was too hard, and the company didn't have computer systems robust enough to make it worth the hassle. Then, last year, U.S. Fleet revisited the technology—and this time it put the pedal to the metal.

The reason? These days, wireless is cheaper and easier to deploy—and it's already paying off. In September, U.S. Fleet, which refuels vehicles for customers such as Coca-Cola and Nabisco, began equipping its 200 trucks with mobile devices and wireless connections to its corporate intranet. The price: $1.5 million, a quarter of what it would have cost three years earlier. Now, managers can check drivers' locations online, letting them rearrange routes on the fly—and increase the average number of daily deliveries per truck from six to seven. As soon as drivers fill a client's vehicle, the information is scanned into their handheld computers and zapped off to the network. That lets customers check deliveries immediately on U.S. Fleet's Web site, two days faster than before the system was installed. Wireless "makes good business sense and doesn't cost an arm and a leg," says Saul Cohen, vice-president of information technology at U.S. Fleet.

Once written off as overhyped and underperforming, wireless is enjoying a resurgence in Corporate America. Thanks to plunging equipment prices, new standards for radio links, and increased cellular coverage, even small companies can afford wireless systems once available only to deep-pocketed giants such as United Parcel Service Inc. "During the past 18 months, companies staggered around, not quite sure whether to touch wireless," says Martin Dunsby, a partner at Deloitte Consulting. "Now the interest is accelerating."

What's fueling the growth? Device makers, ranging from well-known names such as Palm Inc. to industry stalwarts like Symbol Industries are churning out smarter and smaller handhelds. Symbol's standard machine, for example, has gotten a tenfold boost in performance since 1999, while its price and weight have fallen by a third. That makes it cheaper for companies to equip workers and has cut the price of wireless projects in half over the past two years, says researcher IDC Corp. That, in turn, will help double the number of field reps with wireless devices, to 11 million, this year, says Yankee Group Research Inc. And in hospitals, offices, and factories, a standard called WiFi (a.k.a. 802.11b) that connects devices to wireless networks is simplifying installations. This year, employees using WiFi networks are expected to more than double, to 12 million, according to Gartner Inc. Another boost: Tiny radios can now track parts in warehouses or alert techies when machines are on the blink.

Still, lingering design and technical issues need to be ironed out. Some companies are waiting for the higher-speed wireless networks that phone companies such as Verizon Wireless and Sprint PCS Group are promising this year. Without those networks in place, companies fear their wireless initiatives won't have sufficient reach to make them pay. For instance, coffee distributor Millstone Coffee gave handheld computers to 400 field reps last fall but has delayed wirelessly linking them until connection speeds and coverage improve. And security holes uncovered last year in WiFi technology have sparked concerns about hackers intercepting corporate data.

Where the Wireless Web Works

Businesses flocked to wireless projects as their cost fell by more than 50% in the past two years. Here's what companies are doing:

	PROBLEM	PROJECT	PAYOFF
Workers on the move: The rollout of data networks helps companies improve customer service by getting info to reps more quickly.	**Pepsi Bottling Group's 700 technicians phoned in to get service-call data—and faxed back billing info.**	Now a wireless network sends details to the service rep's handheld. The device zips billing data to the office.	**Service response time cut by 20%. Errors from the old fax system gone. Correct parts ready for pickup.**
Wireless workplaces: Offices are setting up systems that transmit data from the Web or a company's intranet to employees moving about the workplace.	**Staff at St. Luke's Episcopal Hospital in Houston spent too much time on administrative tasks. Handwritten records had potential for errors.**	A wireless network for three of the hospital's floors lets staff check charts, lab results, and patient data, wiping out handwriting errors.	**Staff on the networked floor cut time spent on data entry 30%. The respiratory therapy group cut staff by 20%, saving $1.5 million a year.**
Smart machines: Wireless devices in plants and warehouses can automatically collect data from other computers around them, speeding up work flow and eliminating paperwork.	**Office Depot's 2,000 drivers sorted through info from 40-plus deliveries daily. This led to data-entry errors and slowed inventory tracking.**	Drivers' handheld devices automatically transfer customer data to the company's Web site when they return each evening.	**No more handwritten bills, which reduced customer complaints about missed deliveries by more than 10% last year.**

Data: Gartner Inc., International Planning & Research, Cahners In-Stat Group, Venture Development Corp.

(Cont.)

The biggest action is in reaching out to field personnel. In years past, Pepsi Bottling Group Inc.'s 700 soda fountain technicians spent too much time on the phone instead of time fixing the company's 1.3 million vending and fountain machines. Customers called in problems, then a call-center employee paged a technician, who would ring for details about the job. At the end of the day, repair workers would fax in forms detailing their visits—with results not available on Pepsi's intranet until five days later.

That system is on its way to the trash heap. Pepsi's technicians now have off-the-shelf handheld devices from Armonk (N.Y.) based Melard Technologies Inc. Dispatchers today retrieve from Pepsi's intranet everything the technicians need to know about a job and zap it off to the paperback-sized handheld. When the job's done, the technician sends an electronic bill to headquarters. At the same time, the handheld automatically tells the stockroom which parts were used, so when the technician stops in for supplies, replacements are waiting for pick-up.

The payoff? Pepsi answers calls 20% faster than it used to and has saved $7 million—meaning the project will pay for itself in just two years. And parts replenishment requests are now nearly 100% accurate, vs. 85% in the past, when legibility was a big issue. "We sell soda," says Gary K. Wandschneider, senior vice-president for operations of Pepsi Bottling Group. "When we tried to figure out why customers switched to our competitors, part of the answer was customer service and equipment failure."

Field workers aren't the only ones going wireless. In warehouses, offices, and hospitals, wireless technology gives mobile workers instant access to data. St. Luke's Episcopal Hospital in Houston spent $2.5 million on computers and a WiFi network for three of its 22 floors. Nurses and doctors bring laptops on their rounds, entering treatment info and zapping it to the hospital's intranet. Staff in the departments with wireless have cut data-entry time by 30%, says Gene Gretzer, the hospital's wireless project leader. The respiratory therapy group alone was able to shave staff by 20%, saving $1.5 million while handling 13% more patients.

Increasingly, companies are using wireless devices that talk to each other, cutting out humans entirely. Thermo King Corp., which makes cooling units for trucks and shipping containers, is selling self-monitoring equipment. When a truck returns from a delivery, a radio connected to the Net contacts sensors on the vehicle that track the performance of the cooling machinery. If there's a problem, an alert is sent to a Web site monitored by technicians. That can mean savings of up to $1,000 per truck annually by reducing spoilage and cutting maintenance staff.

Sure, the wireless Web hasn't lived up to expectations for consumers. For businesses though, the mobility of wireless combined with the wealth of data on the Internet are creating a one-two punch.

By Heather Green

The New Science of Focus Groups

by Alison Stein Wellner

Last fall, 15 million students headed off to college, many moving into that mysterious world known as the dorm. These first-time dorm denizens, along with their other college peers, spent an estimated $210 billion in 2002 on everything from microwave ovens to shower loofahs, representing a tantalizing marketing opportunity.

Yet how can retail-product designers, well beyond their college years, know what their young customers do not: what life in a dorm is like today? How can they help young adults away from home for the first time figure out how to navigate communal bathrooms as well as the intricacies of the clothes washer and dryer?

These are questions that intrigued *Target,* the Minneapolis-based discount retailer, primed to launch a product line aimed at the college segment. In search of qualitative research that would elicit deep insights, emotions and motivations from college students, Target hired San Mateo, Calif.-based research firm *Jump Associates.* What Jump delivered was a different spin on the traditional focus group, exemplifying the type of creative, eclectic approach to qualitative research that's becoming increasingly popular. The research enabled Target to hear firsthand from college-bound students about their concerns when shopping for their dorm rooms and to get a sense from college students of what life in a dorm is like.

"We were fascinated with the underlying social dynamic of going to college," says Dev Patnaik, managing associate at Jump. So the firm sponsored a series of "game nights" at high school grads' homes, inviting incoming college freshman as well as students with a year of dorm living under their belts. [Each was paid an incentive, similar to a focus group participant.] To get teens talking about dorm life, Jump devised a board game that involved issues associated with going to college. The game naturally led to informal conversations—and questions—about college life. Jump researchers were on the sidelines to observe, while a video camera recorded the proceedings.

The research paid off. Last year, Target launched the Todd Oldham Dorm Room product line designed for college freshman. Among the new offerings: Kitchen in a Box, which provides basic accoutrements for a budding college cook; Bath in a Box, which includes an extra-large bath towel to preserve modesty on the trek to and from the shower; and a laundry bag with instructions on how to actually do the laundry printed on the bag. Thanks in part to the Dorm Room line, Target held its own during the back-to-school season. In the third quarter of 2002, when most of the year's back-to-school shopping for college students was done, revenues at Target stores increased 12 percent over the third quarter of 2001, to $8.4 billion, while comparable store sales increased by only 1 percent.

Patnaik calls the game night "the antidote to the traditional focus group," a process he views as "a customer terrarium, with people behind glass," much the same way plants and lizards are taken out of their natural surroundings and observed for scientific purposes. In Patnaik's view, traditional focus groups often make it impossible for market researchers to learn the truth about what customers are feeling. Still, many companies rely on focus groups, in which 8-to-12 people are gathered in a room that has a two-way mirror, to make their marketing decisions. But according to Patnaik, "Focus groups are the crack cocaine of market research. You get hooked on them, and you're afraid to make a move without them."

Whether or not focus groups are addictive, marketers are certainly heavy users. In 2001, companies spent $1.1 billion on qualitative research, most of this for focus groups, says Larry Gold, editor and publisher of *Inside Research,* a monthly publication based in Barrington, Ill., that tracks the market research industry. But in an era of rising expectations, qualitative research, especially focus groups, is increasingly under the gun. In fact, despite the proliferation of focus groups that are held prior to product launches, an astonishing 80 percent of all new products or services fail within six months or fall significantly short of projections, points out Harvard marketing professor Gerald Zaltman, in his new book, *How Customers Think: Essential Insights into the Mind of the Market* [Harvard Business School Press, 2003].

Of course, it's not reasonable to place the blame for these product failures squarely on the shoulders of traditional focus groups—but even those who conduct them admit that the method has room for improvement. Today, the field of qualitative research is changing, not only in response to its critics, but also to benefit from advancing technology and research methodology. Some are turning

(Cont.)

to cutting-edge segmentation science to ensure that they're studying the right group of respondents. Still others are taking a page from ethnographic research, creating focus group experiences that are less clinical and a lot more like real life. And as research from the 1990s, dubbed the decade of the brain, wends its way into the business world, cutting-edge qualitative researchers are opting for one-on-one interviews and borrowing cognitive science techniques, such as response latency and neuroimaging, to access emotions and feelings that consumers don't even know they're having. Qualitative researchers predict that such creative and effective approaches may ultimately leave the traditional construct of focus groups far behind.

THE SCIENCE OF RECRUITING

The heart of qualitative research is still the interview: A market researcher talking to consumers in a group of 12, in smaller groups of two or three, or even one-on-one. Of course, the people recruited to participate are critical to the success of the focus group. "The way you screen for the respondents separates a successful group from a non-successful group," says Marie Joan Cohen, president of Marketing Insights, a Summit, N.J.-based qualitative research firm, whose clients include AT&T and Crayola. While researchers using traditional focus group often divide consumers into groups according to standard demographic breaks and with product usage history as a guideline [i.e., women ages 35 to 44 who have used toothpaste in the past year], a growing number of researchers recruit groups based on psychographics also. "We're looking beyond simple demographic differences," explains Trenton Haack, director of qualitative services at the research firm Burke, Inc., in Cincinnati.

In looking beyond demographics and product usage history, some qualitative researchers are tapping into the expertise gained over the past few decades by segmentation scientists, who divide consumer markets according to demographic and psychographic characteristics. For example, over the past 30 years the research powerhouse RoperASW in New York City has studied a consumer segment it calls "The Influentials"—the one American in every 10 who has significant word-of-mouth clout. Drawing on a database of more than 10,000 questions, and interviews with more than 50,000 Influentials and 500,000 other Americans, RoperASW uses its knowledge of this segment to help its clients recruit candidates for qualitative research, says RoperASW CEO Ed Keller.

"Influentials are two to five years ahead of the curve in their involvement with new trends and new products and lifestyle choices. They have this bellwether nature to them," he explains. Recruiting Influentials is particularly useful when a marketer is trying to determine how to launch a new product or how a product's use is changing over time, he says. "We'd never say that this is a panacea for every eventuality, but to the extent that you're looking for people knowledgeable, informed and open-minded, and ahead of the curve, Influentials are very appropriate

Whither *online* Focus Groups?

Back in the heady dotcom days, it seemed as though online polling was poised to make a clean sweep of market research—revolutionizing the way companies conducted quantitative and qualitative research. But although the Internet is firmly ingrained on the quantitative side, the qualitative side has not faired as well. From 2000 to 2001 alone, spending on online survey research, increased by 53 percent to $400 million, according to Larry Gold of Inside Research, while spending on online qualitative remains negligible.

The problem seems to be tied to the dotcom bust. In gauging respondents' emotional reaction to a product or an advertising campaign—one of the key goals of qualitative research—focus groups that were assembled online were never as effective as those that met in person. However, online groups were particularly well suited to examining Web-based business. Two years ago, for example, when Ruth Stevens was senior vice president of marketing at NatWest Bank's now-defunct CyBuy division [she's currently president of eMarketing Strategy in New York City], she found great value in online focus groups. "We were a launch business, so we literally only had a handful of people using our service. But we really wanted to understand what their experience was like. The fact that we could get them to log in from their homes and offices, all over the country, made it possible for us to fill up the virtual room," Stevens says. Now that the bumper crop of dotcom companies has shriveled, the market for online qualitative research is smaller.

Still, the ability to pull consumers together from all over the country to get quick, gut-level reactions, is not without its fans. Companies are finding that online bulletin boards, where a moderator posts a question and consumers respond when they want—and thus are able to give their responses more thought—are useful, says Gerry Katz, executive vice president of Applied Marketing Science, in Waltham, Mass. Although spending on this type of online research is still negligible today, over time, these bulletin boards are likely to become more popular.

(Cont.)

to study in qualitative research," adds Keller.

Naturally, there seems to be an infinite number of ways to segment the U.S. population, and qualitative researchers are also taking advantage of advances in geodemographics to improve their recruiting pool. As it happens, segmentation science is advancing to the point where psychographic and demographic characteristics, as well as media usage and purchasing behavior, can be overlaid, down to the neighborhood level—and now down to the household level. "Knowing exactly who you're going to get in a focus group is a way of eliminating respondent bias. It gives you a more accurate and more efficient method of identifying intended targets for focus groups, and of learning more about their lifestyle and media preferences even before they come in the door," says Josh Herman, product manager for segmentation at research firm Acxiom, in Little Rock, Ark.

Last Spring, Acxiom began to offer a database called Personicx, a system which assigns to each U.S. household a specific segment based on life stage, purchasing behavior and attitudes. While databases like this have long been available at the neighborhood level, the ability to target households within a neighborhood is a more specific form of segmentation that should be particularly useful to focus group researchers, says Herman. [The database is updated monthly.]

A case in point: Though the United States Department of Agricultures [USDA] isn't necessarily the first entity you'd think of as being on the cutting-edge of marketing, it relied on Personicx last year. The agency wanted to get a food-safety message out to households who were most at risk of improperly cooking burgers or mishandling salmon. The system enabled the USDA to recruit focus groups from households it believed fit a target demographic and psychographic profile, and it was also able to use its knowledge of the segments to help analyze the results.

DIGGING DEEPER

Once the respondents are recruited, focus group researchers plan their strategy for getting at what consumers really think and feel. It's a task that has always been a challenge for qualitative researchers—one that has depended on the skill of the moderator, says Kirk Ward, formerly director of new-product development at Hershey and now president of Innovation Focus Research in Lancaster, Pa. Phil Johnston, senior vice president at Cleveland-based ad agency Marcus Thomas, LLC, whose clients include the Cleveland Indians and Alcoa, agrees, saying that as Americans are sampled more frequently, they become more research-savvy.

"As people are exposed to more research, they begin to understand what's expected of them," he says. Frequently, consumers will simply parrot back marketing or advertising messages, which offers little to companies seeking consumer insights.

To help consumers relax and thereby elicit more authentic responses, qualitative researchers have been turning to approaches proven effective in ethnographic research. For one thing, they might downplay the marketing agenda of the research experience. "What will increasingly happen is moderators will acknowledge the importance of environment," says Insights' Cohen. "I've always been a big believer in using environments that are much more comfortable and that are more adaptive to the product," she says. She finds it more effective, for example, to speak to women about female health products in a living room setting rather than at a conference table, and to speak to children in a room arranged like a play area. Some companies are starting to offer researchers this flexibility, she says. INGather Research in Denver, Colo., offers facilities where focus groups can be held that look just like a living room, a kitchen, a playroom, a bar and even a courtroom—and all are equipped with large two-way mirrors along one wall.

Other qualitative researchers are breaking through people's defenses by resorting to subtle trickery. Rather than simply holding up print advertisements in a focus group and asking for reactions—which is not the way that consumers would encounter the ads in the real world—the Marcus Thomas firm inserted the print ads for a campaign it was testing into magazine mock-ups. "We then had the moderator, before leaving the room, tell the respondents that in addition to the task at hand, we were evaluating certain publications, and to take a few minutes to flip through the magazines," says Johnston, senior vice president at Marcus Thomas. As a result, the firm was able to observe the focus group recruits interacting with the advertising in a more authentic manner.

> Some qualitative researchers are turning away from focus groups entirely, believing that one-on-one interviews are more valuable then group interviews in obtaining fresh insights.

(Cont.)

JUST YOU AND I

Some qualitative researchers are turning away from groups entirely. Gerry Katz, executive vice president of Applied Marketing Science, in Waltham, Mass., says that for new-product development, one-on-one interviews are more valuable than group interviews in obtaining fresh insights. Katz says that when a company conducts "voice of the customer" research for new product development, searching for wants and needs not yet met in the marketplace, the goal is to hear something new—and group dynamics can often make that difficult. [He points to a 1993 study by Abbie Griffin and John Hauser, published in the journal *Marketing Science,* that compared focus groups to one-on-one interviews. Griffin and Hauser found that, hour for hour, individual interviews elicited more useful comments.]

Zaltman, at Harvard, is also a fan of the one-on-one interview. He believes that one-on-one interviews are better poised to take advantage of the cutting edge of cognitive science. He's highly skeptical about consumers' ability to report on their decision-making process accurately—or on the true state of their emotions. Zaltman argues that consumers rarely are rational when making decisions, that they rely far more on emotions than on rational thinking when they decide what to buy. Further, he maintains that consumers can't really describe their decision-making process because they "have far less access to their mental activities than marketers give them credit for—95 percent of thinking takes place in the unconscious mind." [For more on Zaltman's approach, see "The Power of Images" in *American Demographics,* Nov. 2001.] In his view, self-reported descriptions of a decision-making process may provide next to no insight into what actually motivated that person to behave in a certain way.

Zaltman believes that smart companies will start to exploit the advances made in the 1990s in physiological and psychological research. Market researchers can now study the movements of subjects' pupils, for example, to gain a window into unconscious emotions, and can measure the lag time in responses to questions, known as "latency response," to gain useful insights. On the frontier is the use of neuroimaging in market research. By hooking people up to a magnetic resonance imaging machine [MRI] and showing them advertisements, researchers could visually track bloodflow to the parts of the brain associated with positive or negative emotions, or the parts of the brain associated with memory, and get a more accurate read on how the participants are feeling and whether they will remember an advertisement.

This doesn't mean that scientific advances and whizbang technology will put focus groups out of business. Even Zaltman concedes that "there are circumstances where I think focus groups are warranted." For example, he says that if you want to learn the vocabulary a group of consumers uses to describe an experience or if you want to know about how word-of-mouth operates, focus groups are appropriate. "But you shouldn't use focus group to get in-depth insights," he says. Since focus groups typically run two hours and involve 10 people, he argues that each person gets only 12 minutes of time. "You can't get very far—you can't get very much depth—in 12 minutes with any one individual," Zaltman says. And since depth is the goal, the group approach that has been a fixture in marketing research for the past six decades may go the way of the dinosaur.

Mystery Shoppers Going High-Tech

They 'Spy' On Retailers

Small digital cameras and laptop computers now tools of the trade

By Stephanie Wilkinson
Investor's Business Daily

The man sits in his car in a Krispy Kreme parking lot, but he's not eating doughnuts.

He's tapping into his laptop computer. He stops and opens the box of doughnuts on the seat next to him. He cuts open a jelly-filled morsel, looks at it and places it on the box top. He reaches into his briefcase and takes out a small, pen-shaped camera. Then he snaps digital photos of the cut-open doughnut.

He clicks the camera into a cradle attached to his laptop to transfer the photos to the computer. He uses a cable to link his cell phone to his laptop, log onto the Internet and then e-mail the photos to headquarters.

Doughnut fanatic? No, this man is one of the new breed of high-tech mystery shoppers.

In the old days, individuals armed with nothing more than a paper questionnaire would make unscheduled visits to stores to check up on product quality and customer service. Their paper reports took days to process, creating a crucial lag between the time of the visit and the time when corporate decision-makers got the full report.

In some cases, companies found, certain mystery shoppers weren't bothering to go to the target stores at all. They made up answers. Mystery shopping got a few black eyes.

Today, thanks to such things as digital photography, camera miniaturization and the Internet, mystery shopping has been rejuvenated. One company bringing technology to the mystery-shopper/quality-control field is Pacific Research Group Inc. of Costa Mesa, Calif.

Steve Anderson, customer experience manager at Krispy Kreme Doughnuts Corp., based in Winston-Salem, N.C., says his company switched to PRG 18 months ago to conduct its ongoing mystery shopper program. Its previous mystery shopping company relied on paper, film-based photography and other low-tech methods.

"We made the shift because of PRG's use of newer technologies," he said. "We used to have to wait five weeks to see a report. Now we see them within 48 hours (of a mystery shopper's visit). If a store is inspected on Saturday and you get the report on Monday, you're much more likely to see problems get fixed."

PRG contracts with thousands of freelance shoppers around the country to perform surprise visits to fast-food outlets, gas stations, airlines and a host of other kinds of businesses.

PRG Likes PenCam

In total, PRG shoppers average 12,000 store visits a month, he says.

To qualify as a mystery shopper, candidates are required to have a Windows-based laptop and a minidigital camera. PRG has a link at its Web site to that of the PenCam, a tiny $59 digital camera made by Aiptek Inc. of Irvine, Calif. But mystery shoppers can use any such camera that works. For laptops, the PRG Web site includes links to the Dell Computer Corp. and Compaq Computer Corp. Web sites.

Before shoppers are given an assignment, they must take an online tutorial tailored to the specific client company and pass a test. "With digital photography, we can include photos in the tutorials to let the trainees know exactly what they should be looking for," said Darren Magot, vice president of sales at PRG. "We can show them exactly what constitutes a clean bathroom, or what a perfectly filled doughnut looks like."

The retail client company works with PRG to create an electronic questionnaire. Typically a mystery shopper looks at such things as trash in the parking lot, friendliness of the store's staff and the serving temperature of the food.

> "We use to have to wait five weeks to see a report. Now we see them within 48 hours."
>
> **Steve Anderson,** *Krispy Kreme Doughnuts*

Armed with minidigital camera and laptop, the shopper visits the store, makes a purchase and discreetly takes photographs.

Usually, shoppers retreat to their cars to fill out the questionnaire on the computer. Then they choose which photos to include. The reports are e-mailed to PRG editors, and then go to the customer's headquarters or store managers. The photos provide a lot of detail and remove much subjectivity, says Magot. "There's less opinion and more fact," he said. "It's hard to argue with photos."

The reports, though, serve many purposes, say Magot and Anderson. "They're not just used as a whipping stick," said Magot. "Many positive incentives are tied to the results of these stores."

Krispy Kreme franchisees, for instance, can earn trips to national conferences by doing well in these random spot checks. Each of the company's 215 stores is visited by a mystery shopper once a month.

New Camera Focus

Key to the evolution of the mystery shopper is the advent of cheap, small digital cameras. As the prices of digital cameras continue to fall and their resolution improves, other business uses of these small cameras will surface, says Michelle Slaughter, an analyst at InfoTrends Research Group Inc. in Boston.

That will be good news for the makers of these products. The market for sub-$100 digital cameras has actually declined, Slaughter says, from $136 million in revenue in 2000 to $46 million in 2001.

Several factors contributed to the big decline. For one, market leader Polaroid Corp. filed for bankruptcy reorganization. It's discontinuing its line of digital cameras. Slaughter says other makers also closed down or stopped making the cameras.

"Until recently, small cameras have been perceived as mere novelties, with manufacturers coming and going in the market rapidly," she said.

Companies made the mistake of targeting these small cameras to kids, who turned out not so interested in digital photography, she says.

"But as performance of sub-$100 cameras gets better and the learning curve eases, corporate consumers ought to help

(Cont.)

the market bounce back," Slaughter said. "Many industries such as real estate, insurance and construction already are taking advantage of digital photography."

"Mystery Shoppers Going High Tech," *Investor's Business Daily,* May 3, 2002.

FACING UP TO CRM

That pricey new technology promises to track your customers' every move. But will it help your bottom line?

By: Brian Caulfield

True story. One of the Big Three Detroit automakers put together a customer relationship management (CRM) system that helped it decide which cars to manufacture based on what was going out of dealers' lots. It worked great.

Well, except for one catch. According to Eric Almquist, VP at Mercer Management Consulting, the company's marketing team had just created sales incentives to get rid of a lot of lime-green cars, which no one wanted. As consumers snapped up the special deals on the cars, the CRM software noticed the surge of sales in lime-green cars and instructed the factory to produce more. The automaker lost millions of dollars before it caught the error.

No one doubts that CRM software is powerful stuff. It can slash call center costs, make a sales force dramatically more productive, and glue together offline and online sales efforts. Everyone knows stories like the one Stephen Pratt, global practice leader for Deloitte Consulting's CRM efforts, likes to tell about the telecommunications equipment manufacturer that used CRM software to coordinate its Web and offline technical-support teams. Tech support began running so smoothly that within six months, happy customers signed up for an additional $15 million in contracts.

But CRM can also go terribly wrong, causing interdepartmental chaos or never taking hold among key employees. The nightmare scenarios are all too common. Based on interviews with thousands of clients, Gartner Inc. projects that in the next five years, 55 percent of all CRM projects will fail to meet objectives. That failure rate represents a big financial risk, considering that CRM systems cost an average of $35,000 per call-center agent to deploy and that setup and maintenance of CRM sales software typically costs $28,000 to $40,000 per salesperson (over three years). How can you avoid ending up on the CRM casualty list? Head off the most common mistakes before they happen.

EXTEND THE OLIVE BRANCH.

CRM projects usually involve different departments, which means skilled diplomacy is in order. "Traditionally sales, marketing, and service have been enemies," Pratt says. "Marketing would blame sales for not closing leads, sales would blame marketing for not generating enough leads, and service would blame them both for too-high expectations. Asking them to work together goes against their DNA."

The trick is to find leadership that can cajole or force various fiefdoms to do the right thing. Rob Schauble, director of technology for Hewlett-Packard's (*HWP*) customer support division, gathered managers from marketing, production, sales, and customer service in order to get the cooperation he needed to install CRM software from Motive Communications on all the computers HP sells. The package would let HP technical support more quickly diagnose and fix a customer's problem. Rather than going over anyone's head, Schauble invited everyone with a stake in the project to help map out a strategy from the start. His initiative paid off; more than a year after the project's completion, he estimates that the software saves HP millions of dollars by reducing the time it takes to identify problems.

> ***CUSTOMER RELATIONSHIP MANAGEMENT SYSTEM:***
>
> Enterprise software that helps a company track customers and their interactions with the company. Frequently used by customer-support, sales, and marketing staffs, CRM systems allow employees to quickly call up the past sales and service records of a customer, as well as outstanding orders or unresolved problems.

EXPLAIN, EXPLAIN, EXPLAIN.

No amount of high-level cooperation will protect a CRM project from rank-and-file employees who hate it. Lisa Harris, CIO at HR-services firm Staff-Leasing, based in Bradenton, Fla., faced rebellion from the staff when she installed Oracle (*ORCL*) CRM software that helped solve some customers' problems online—without the help of a live operator. Call-center employees felt that the software

(Cont.)

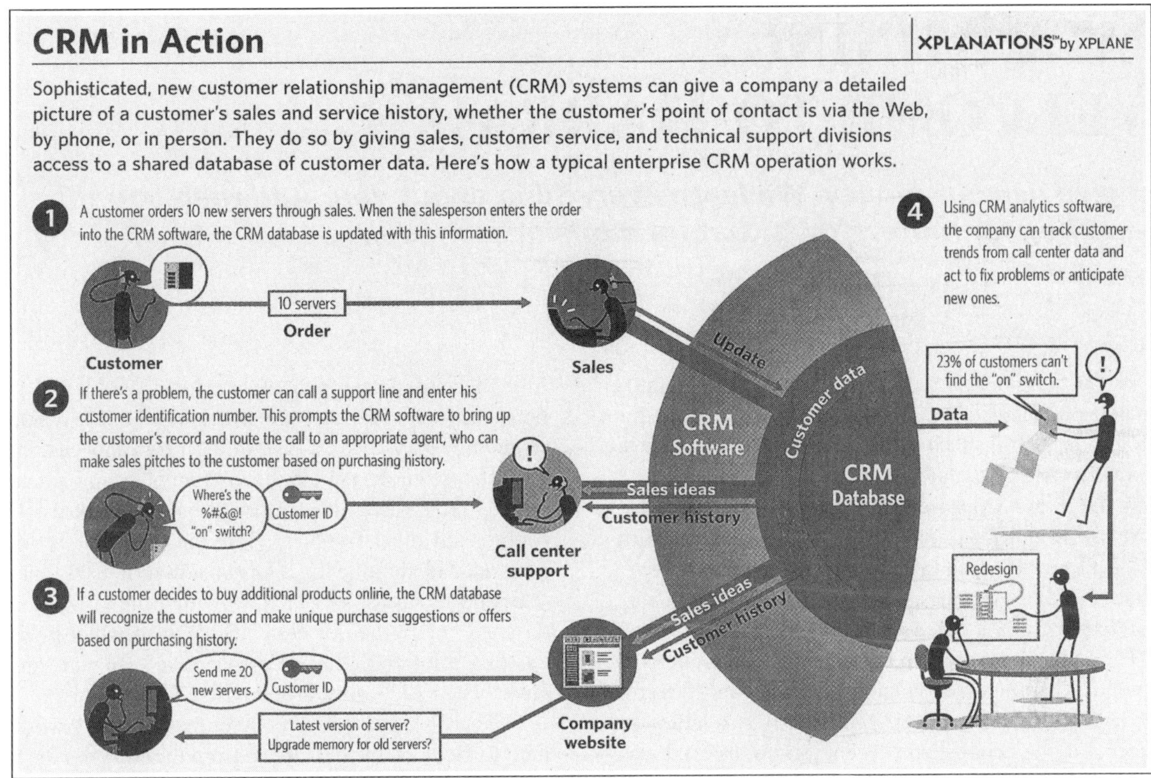

threatened their jobs, so they quietly discouraged customers from using it. "Our operators would say, 'Wouldn't you rather call up? I'll take care of everything you need,'" Harris says. She stuck with the online CRM, but also began talking to employees about the software. She changed their work routines to include more customer hand-holding and less data entry, which was increasingly done online.

SHOP AND INSTALL WITH CARE.

CRM software is complex to install because it often touches many different legacy systems. Four years ago, Staff-Leasing's Harris says she spent millions of dollars integrating a CRM application for a previous employer. But when she was finished, it took operators too long to get data on screen. She had bogged down the performance of the new CRM implementation by trying to integrate too many complicated systems. The project ended up a total bust.

> ***CALL CENTER:***
>
> A company department or a contractor that handles telephone duties such as sales or tech call support. There are 82,000 call centers in North America.

Harris says new products that link related applications into suites, like the one she's using from Oracle, typically work well together. But analysts say such suites, a relatively new trend, are still immature. The technology is further complicated by the fact that CRM firms are making the leap from client-server forms of CRM to Web-enabled ones. For example, early versions of Oracle's Net-enabled CRM suite, introduced early last year, tried to do too much too soon, which resulted in client problems, according to Wendy Close, CRM research director for Gartner Inc. Close adds that the Net-based systems, such as PeopleSoft's (*PSFT*) latest offering, have fewer features than client-server versions.

Finally, make sure that the system your techies build is really what the company needs. Many problems arise from lack of planning and communication, says Larry Senn, of Senn-Delaney Leadership Consulting Group. "There is a blind spot here, and the more technical the organization, the bigger the blind spot," he says. "Engineers tend to think if something makes sense, people will do it—but that's not how people operate."

"Facing Up to CRM," *Business 2.0,* August/September 2001, pp. 149–150.

DATA MINING: WELCOME TO HARRAH'S

You give us your money. We learn everything about you. And then you thank us and beg for more. How's that for a business model?

By: Joe Ashbrook Nickell, **April 2002 Issue**

If you ever want to witness, close up, the unheralded magic of the modern gaming business, just wander down any aisle full of chirping, chiming slot machines and watch the folks clutching the plastic buckets and pulling the levers. One afternoon last May at the Rio Resort in Las Vegas, I did just that—and plopped down in front of a 25-cent video poker machine to experience it all firsthand. For 10 minutes or so, I dolefully fed quarters into my Bally's "Deuces Wild" until I'd dropped $20. Then I moved on to a handful of other machines—a "Monopoly" slot game, video blackjack, and several more varieties of video poker. After nearly two hours on the floor, I'd notched just one decent jackpot ($40), I was out $350, and I wanted to leave.

Not exactly a magical experience for me. But for Harrah's Entertainment (HET), the parent company of the Rio and two dozen other casinos around the country, even brief slot binges like mine are worth far more today than their weight in quarters. As I moved from machine to machine, a tangle of computers in a Harrah's office in Memphis, Tenn., was collecting the biggest prize of all—an astonishingly detailed account of each second I spent at the Rio. Harrah's took note of how many different machines I had played on (nine), how many separate wagers I placed (637), my average bet (25 cents), and, of course, the total amount of money—called "coin-in"—I'd deposited in the machines. By the time I left the Rio, Harrah's had compiled enough information about me to build a detailed profile of my gambling habits, a plan for luring me back to the casino, even an individual profit-and-loss projection by which the company would gauge its future marketing investment in me. If traditional slot machines are one-armed bandits, these things are one-armed diabolical geniuses in the Dr. No/Goldfinger class.

And for all that information, Harrah's has an innocuous little piece of plastic to thank: a colorful card with a magnetic stripe that Harrah's slot players insert into machines while they play. Twenty-five million Harrah's customers, in fact, use these personalized frequent-gambler cards, called Total Rewards, to earn free trips, meals, hotel rooms, and other freebies while they test the decidedly long odds of slot playing. Harrah's, in turn, uses that data to refine its customer database, which now includes 90 targeted demographic segments, each of which receives custom-tailored direct-mail incentives to visit any of Harrah's 25 properties around the United States.

There's a reason, of course, that Harrah's works so hard to glean all the data it can from the slot crowds. Slots and other electronic gaming machines account for the majority of Harrah's $3.7 billion in revenue, and more than 80 percent of the company's operating profit. Largely on the strength of its new tracking and data-mining system for slot players, Harrah's—once an also-ran chain of casinos—has emerged in recent years as the second-largest operator in the United States (behind MGM Entertainment) with the highest three-year investment return in the industry.

> **HARRAH'S NATIONWIDE SLOT-TRACKING SYSTEM DOES WHAT EVEN ITS BEST CUSTOMERS CAN'T: MAKE GOOD BETS.**

If you believe the man who built that system for Harrah's—former Harvard business professor Gary Loveman, now the company's chief operating officer—the company's recent prosperity has little or nothing to do with cultivating his customers' impulses to gamble. It has everything to do, he says, with simply getting to know them so well through data profiling that he can give them the perfect reasons—a steak here, a free hotel room there—not to spend money at other casinos, where the odds, after all, aren't any better. "This is a whole new world that we couldn't get our hands around before," Loveman says. "All we used to know was how much money we made on each machine, but we couldn't connect what kind of customer used them. Now," he says, "I can get on the

(Cont.)

Who Gets the Free Steak?

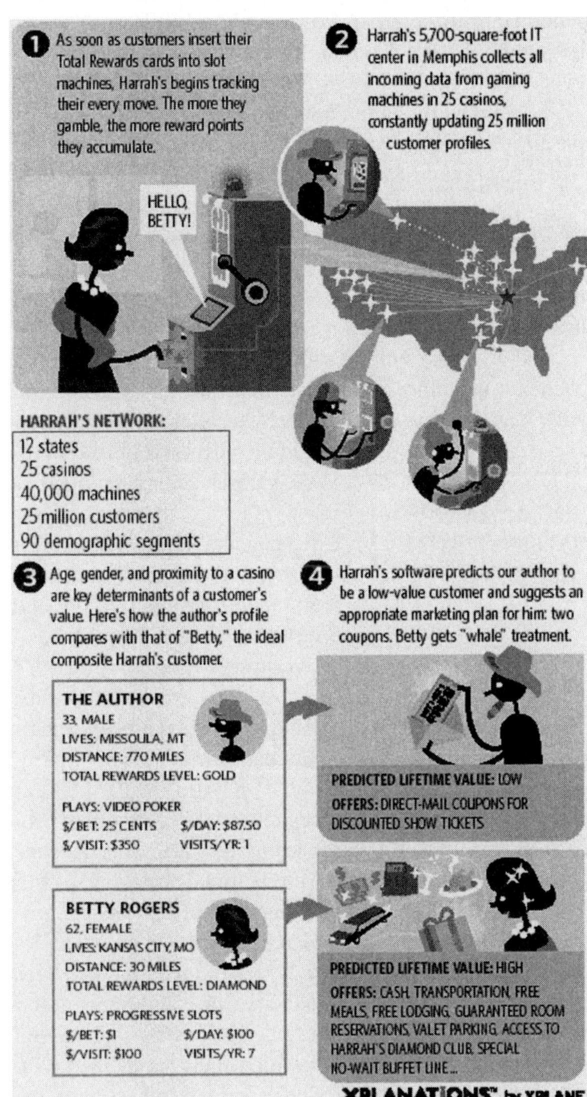

system and say, 'Where are all the 60-or-older females from North Carolina playing?' Boom, I'll know. This is the replacement of intuition and hunch with science."

How Loveman's system led to a turnaround of sorts for Harrah's underlines how painfully slow one of America's biggest service industries has been in getting to know its customers. In the first slot-machine "players clubs" introduced in the 1980s, the best slot customers were given punch cards, which attendants notched whenever customers hit jackpots; once the cards had enough notches, customers redeemed them for meals or other incentives. Archaic as they might seem now, the clubs proliferated and triggered an important shift in the industry: By the end of the 1980s, machines surpassed table games as the major casinos' biggest source of income.

Customer service, however, remained stuck in the 1970s. Casino managers who had long recognized the importance of building relationships with their most profitable clientele reserved star treatment for so-called whales, the big spenders that Las Vegas traditionally coveted, but only an occasional free drink for the folks toting plastic buckets.

All of that began to change in the early 1990s, when casinos began installing computerized systems that kept records on individual players. Using the magnetic strips on plastic cards, they allowed casinos to build records for an unlimited number of customers, and offer "comps" and other incentives based on the amount of money inserted into machines, not the amount won. At about the same time, state and federal laws changed to legalize gambling on riverboats and Indian reservations, and operators raced to open their doors in new markets. Between 1990 and 1997, Harrah's alone tripled the number of casinos it operated.

But as new markets grew more competitive, the business reached the point of diminishing return: Harrah's often found its early arrival usurped by grander, more extravagant casinos that opened next door. Making matters worse, each Harrah's casino operated and marketed itself separately from the others—"a system of feudal fiefdoms," says John Boushy, Harrah's chief information officer. "While management at each of our properties had been thinking, 'This is my customer,' customers had been wondering why they didn't get the same treatment at different Harrah's properties," Boushy says.

By 1997, Boushy and CEO Phil Satre understood that devising the means to keep their 25 million slot players loyal to Harrah's was the key not only to capturing the biggest share of their wallets, but also to staying a step ahead of competing chains. They began to consider the idea of electronically linking all of Harrah's players clubs—so that when Harrah's riverboat gamblers in Mississippi flew to Vegas, they could redeem their reward points for free Harrah's meals, rooms, or shows.

Enter Loveman, then a 37-year-old associate professor of business administration at Harvard who had never, he says, set foot in a casino. But occasionally he taught special classes on the service industry to Harrah's executives. The classes, as well as Loveman's research, focused on the profitability-through-customer-loyalty equation that intrigued Satre.

As he got to know the company and the gaming business, Loveman saw an opportunity to stress-test his theories. After trading notes with Satre, he outlined his idea to turn card data from each casino over to a central marketing brain for the company. Loveman soon found himself in Vegas, sitting in on executive strategy meetings and building support for his plan. In 1998, Satre gave Loveman the post of chief operating officer and a mandate to launch the system.

Today, Harrah's network links more than 40,000 gaming machines in 12 states, and operates on the belief that customers will, given the right inducements, become "brand-loyal" to Harrah's. In just the first two years of the Total Rewards program, the company saw a $100 million increase in revenue from customers who gambled at more than one Harrah's casino. "We were getting 36 cents of every dollar that our customers spent in casinos," Loveman says. "We realized that if we could just get to 40 cents, that would be monstrous." Harrah's current "wallet share" now stands at 42 percent. "If you increase that number ever so slightly," he adds, "the benefit to income statement and shareholder value is astronomical." He has a point: Since 1998, each percentage-point increase in Harrah's share of its customers' overall gambling budgets has coincided with an additional $125 million in shareholder value.

I KNEW I WASN'T COMING BACK AS SOON AS I FINISHED MY FIRST ROLL OF QUARTERS. SOMEHOW, HARRAH'S KNEW THAT TOO.

The central feature (and perhaps the greatest irony) of Loveman's system is its ability to do what its 25 million customers cannot—that is, consistently make good bets. Before I even sat down for my round of video poker at the Rio, for example, Harrah's had a pretty good hunch that I wouldn't be financing its next round of employee bonuses. It suspected that from the moment I signed up for my Total Rewards card in the casino lobby and filled in my name, address, date of birth, and driver's license number. Since I was a 32-year-old man from the distant state of Montana, Harrah's predicted that my long-term potential was already low. I was at the Rio three nights, yet I spent a total of just four hours and 40 minutes gambling. As Loveman explains, "It's important to know when to pull away from an investment in a customer [who] is not going to return." He attributes $20 million in annual cost reductions to the Total Rewards program.

Starting with four key pieces of information—your gender, your age, where you live, and what you play—Harrah's software predicts which customers are most likely to become big spenders. Then it designs appropriate marketing strategies—direct-mail offers are the most common—to lure those customers back. "Most companies look at it on a product-by-product basis: 'I want to generate this much revenue on a particular product,'" says Rich Mirman, a veteran of consulting firm Booz Allen Hamilton, whom Loveman hired as Harrah's marketing chief. "We flip that around: We want to maximize every relationship."

To make his point, Mirman sketches out the example of a Las Vegas vacationer who spends a week at the Mirage, blowing $1,000 a day in the casino. If that person wanders into the Rio, she may spend only $300 in its casino—yet she is exactly the kind of customer the Rio wants to draw. If the Rio doesn't match or beat the direct-marketing offers from the Mirage, "it doesn't take a lot of brains to realize she's not coming back," he says.

That's why Harrah's decided early on to approach each new customer as a long-term acquaintance. The company began sifting through gigabytes of customer data collected by player-tracking systems at the various Harrah's properties during the previous five years. Loveman and Mirman found that the 30 percent of their customers who spent between $100 and $500 per visit to a Harrah's casino accounted for 80 percent of company revenues—and almost 100 percent of profits. That's because those gamblers were typically locals who—unlike me—visited regional Harrah's properties frequently.

Loveman eventually began to reverse-engineer profiles of the ideal Harrah's customer. "Age and distance from the casino are critical predictors of frequency, coupled with the kind of game you play and how many coins you play per game," Loveman explains. He paints a picture of the perfect player: a 62-year-old woman who lives within 30 minutes of Kansas City, Mo., and plays dollar video poker. Such customers typically have substantial disposable cash, plenty of time on their hands, and easy access to a Harrah's riverboat casino (in this case, on the Missouri River in North Kansas City). "If we only observe her once in a quarter, it's likely that's because she's playing three or four times a quarter at our competitors," Loveman says. "So we're going to make an educated guess and market to her as if she were a more frequent visitor, and we'll let her confirm or disconfirm that. Then we'll update the profile based on what she does."

Once the Harrah's system identifies high-value customers, it places them into corresponding demographic segments. (Harrah's maintains 90 such segments.) Customers who live far away from Harrah's properties typically receive direct-mail discounts or comps on hotel rooms or transportation, while drive-in customers get

(Cont.)

UNDER THE HOOD

The main tech components of Harrah's nationwide customer-tracking network.

- **Magnetic card readers:** Harrah's Total Rewards card readers are installed on all of the company's 40,000-plus gaming machines. The readers capture a customer ID number from each card, and a small LCD screen flashes a personalized greeting along with the customer's current tally of reward points.
- **Electronic gaming machines:** The ratcheting levers and spinning reels on slots are nothing more than anachronistic eye candy. All gaming machines are computerized and networked. Each machine captures transaction data and relays it to Harrah's mainframe computers.
- **Onsite transaction systems:** IBM-based transaction systems are located at each casino property; they store all casino, hotel, and dining transaction data.
- **National data warehouse:** A Unix-based data center in downtown Memphis links all of the casinos' mainframe systems and customer data. Customer history and reward-point tallies are passed down from this database to the onsite mainframe systems—which, in turn, relay the data to card readers.
- **Predictive analysis software:** Developed by Harrah's and software firm SAS, these programs produce nearly instantaneous customer profiles that allow the company to design and track marketing initiatives and their results.

food, entertainment, or cash incentives. Most offers are time-sensitive, with tight expiration dates, in order to encourage visitors to either return sooner or switch a visit from a competitor to a Harrah's property. For each direct-marketing pitch, the company tracks response rates and return on investment, and adjusts its future campaigns according to the results—all of which is recorded at the company's central database in Memphis. "When I meet with our marketers," Loveman says, "anything we've done new, I ask, did we test it first? And if I find out that we just whole-hogged, went after something without testing it, I'll kill 'em. No matter how clever they think it is, we test it."

As bulletproof as Harrah's system appears to be, it's utterly invisible to customers who, while they might understand the long odds of slot playing, know little or nothing about the betting Harrah's does behind the scenes on every scrap of information they provide. Mirman brushes off suggestions that the program is deceptive. "If they don't want their play tracked, they don't have to use the card," he says. He acknowledges that certain practices—such as using face-recognition cameras to identify customers—would likely backfire. But, Mirman says, customers needn't worry about the most common privacy affront: Harrah's, he says, will never sell its customer lists to anyone.

Nor would Harrah's—God forbid—ever dream of getting people to actually increase their overall gambling. When asked about this, Loveman parries deftly with rhetoric worthy of a tobacco lobbyist. "It's all about customers bringing their existing gaming business to us," he says. "It's rarely about more gambling. It's a lady who lives in Philadelphia, comes to Atlantic City 10 times a year, visits Harrah's three times, but now she's got a reason to come to Harrah's six times." But it doesn't take a cynic to realize that, by offering credits toward comps based on the amount of "coin-in" (the ratio is approximately one reward credit per $10 gambled), and by promoting tiered programs such as Total Platinum, Harrah's and other casinos are giving customers more reason than ever to justify more gambling.

Ethical nuances aside, the cold logic behind Loveman's tracking methods has proved to be good medicine for Harrah's. The company's record earnings of $3.7 billion in 2001 were up 11 percent from 2000. And more than half of the revenue at Harrah's three Las Vegas casinos now comes from players the company already knows from its casinos outside Nevada.

As for me, well, I already knew I wasn't coming back to Harrah's as soon as I'd finished off that first roll of quarters. Somehow, Harrah's knew that too, despite my having generously dropped $350 in one of its casinos in just a few hours. But as Mirman explained before I left, "You live in Montana, you're relatively young, you're playing in Las Vegas, and I would guess that your bankroll is not sufficient to push you into the high-value group." He was right: Since my visit, I've received a single piece of mail from Harrah's: a foldout flier offering discount admission to shows at the Rio, which I promptly tossed. "We would probably predict you'd be unresponsive to the kinds of offers you would qualify for," Mirman said, "so you probably won't hear much from us. But don't worry," he added. "It's just a segmentation, not a personal evaluation."

"Data Mining: Welcome to Harrah's," *Business 2.0,* April 2002, pp. 48–54.

Ratings Agency Says It Erred In Measuring Web Site Use

BY SAUL HANSELL

ComScore Media Metrix, one of the leading companies that measure Web site audiences, has discovered flaws in the methodology that it introduced in October, and it has restated its measurements for the last three months of 2002.

Web ratings services have faced questions about accuracy since they began trying to estimate audiences by projecting the behavior of a panel of presumably representative users. Despite their limits, ComScore's ratings, and those of its main competitor, Nielsen/NetRatings, are widely used by advertisers, investors, journalists and the Web sites themselves.

The biggest differences in ComScore's ratings, announced last week, come in its estimates of Web use at the workplace, always the most difficult to measure. Big companies in particular do not want employees to install the software that the ratings companies use to track Web site usage. When ComScore adjusted its formulas to account for the underrepresentation at big companies, its audience projections increased, in some cases sharply.

For instance, ComScore now estimates that **Primedia's** sites, mainly those run by about.com, had 56 million users in the United States in December, rather than the 44 million counted under its previous formula, a 25 percent increase. **EBay's** audience was increased 19 percent, to 54 million. The estimate for Terra Lycos was increased 21 percent, to 51.6 million users. That change moved Terra Lycos to the sixth-most-visited site in December, from seventh under the previous numbers, putting it in front of Google.

As with any ranking, being placed at No. 1 is an invitation to gloat. WeatherBug, a fast-growing service of **AWS Convergence Technology,** has noted in news releases that it is "the No. 1 source for weather information on the Web, according to ComScore Media Metrix."

ComScore's restated data, however, shows WeatherBug second to Weather.com, the site run by the Weather channel, owned by **Landmark Communications.**

"There was some bragging rights associated with being No. 1," said Andy Jedynak, the general manager of WeatherBug. "To the extent we have lost those, we are disappointed."

WeatherBug's bragging, of course, did not go down so easily at Weather.com, which was still listed as the No. 1 weather site by Nielsen.

"It was annoying," the chief executive of Weather.com, Deborah Wilson, said, "I can't say that it undermined our sales efforts, but to have obviously bad data floating around was a nuisance."

The restatements result from the financial collapse last June of Jupiter Media Metrix, a company that combined Web audience measurement with Internet prognostication. As Jupiter was disassembled, it sold the Media Metrix business and its panel of Web users to ComScore, an upstart with a different technology that was created mainly to monitor products that Web users bought online.

However, the software program that Media Metrix had used to track Web audiences was not sold to ComScore but to Nielsen, ending a patent dispute between the two companies.

ComScore very quickly had to start using its own monitoring technology. It also expanded the size of the Media Metrix panel of users at work, introducing in October what it called Media Metrix 2.0.

In response to complaints by its clients, the company has discovered some flaws in its new system. It decided to publish restated data for last fall rather than change its formulas from now on.

"We could have made these changes on a forward basis," Peter Daboll, president of ComScore's Media Metrix division, said. "We felt it was the right thing to do to make the changes to provide an accurate trend."

Marketers and adverting experts agreed that ComScore's approach ultimately improves the quality of the data available.

"It's kind of embarrassing to have to admit this," said Rex Briggs, the principal of Marketing Evolution, an online advertising research firm. "I applaud them for trying to make their measurements better."

The impact of a restatement, even of this magnitude, Mr. Briggs added, is less now than it would have been a few years ago, when billion-dollar deals were made on the basis of Media Metrix ratings.

"Stock prices are no longer tied to the number of unique visitors you have," Mr. Briggs said. "Now investors have this little idea of being profitable."

Furthermore, these audience measures are not used to set Internet advertising rates, as they are in radio and television. Since broadcasters have no way to tell how many people are watching a given program, they must use Nielsen's television ratings to determine how much to charge advertisers. On the Internet, Web sites charge to display an advertisement a certain number of times.

Still, some industry executives worry that

Web Recount

Having discovered problems with its Web audience measuring methods, ComScore Media Metrix has restated its ratings for the fourth quarter of 2002. Here is a look at the original and revised data for one category: top Internet "properties," which refers to groups sites under a single corporate owner.

Unique visitors, 4th quarter (in millions)

Rank Before Restated Results		Initial Results	Restated results	Change
1	AOL Time Warner network	107.8	110.7	3%
3	MSN (Microsoft sites)	100.6	107.9	7
2	Yahoo sites	101.9	107.3	5
5	About/Primedia	44.5	55.6	25
4	eBay	45.3	53.9	19
7	Terra Lycos	42.6	51.6	21
6	Google sites	43.2	48.7	13
8	Amazon sites	37.9	46.2	22
9	Gator networks	28.1	36.0	28
	Total Internet	**144.8**	**144.9**	0

Source: Comscore Media Metrix

(Cont.)

the restatement will add further doubt about the online medium, which is still trying to establish its credibility with marketers.

"They have some explaining to do," said Geoffrey Ramsey, an analyst with eMarketer, a research firm that uses data from ComScore, Nielsen and other sources.

This uncertainty and potential undercounting of daytime audiences is especially problematic for news and information sites, which are used mostly by people at work.

"Daytime is prime time on the Internet," said Michael Zimbalist, executive director of the Online Publishers Association, a trade group. "The at-work numbers of the ratings companies are notoriously bad."

Estimating Internet use in the workplace is a challenge.

The biggest changes that ComScore made involved how it estimated work audiences. But there were other issues as well. For example, after the acquisition, ComScore changed its method for calculating how much time users spend on each site, in some cases cutting the numbers by far more than half.

Some publishers that boasted that their users spent an hour a month on their site, an unusually high amount of time, found the new system giving them credit for only 15 minutes. ComScore discovered that it had been allocating some of the time that users spend on some Web pages to the sites of advertisers rather than the Web publisher. Its revised system changes that.

Not surprisingly ComScore and Nielsen each insist that their methods are more statistically rigorous. ComScore says that its sample of people at work has 30,000 people, far more than the 7,000 claimed by Nielsen.

Nielsen, by contrast, says its work panel is chosen by placing phone calls to random telephone numbers, an expensive but methodologically superior method. ComScore uses various other methods to recruit its work panel, like sending e-mail messages to random names on lists it buys.

It does not help that Nielsen and ComScore are vastly different in their estimates of most sites' audiences. ComScore, for example, now says Yahoo had 107 million users in the United States in December. Nielsen counted only 81 million.

Some of that difference is because ComScore measures usage on college campuses and Nielsen does not. But the difference in the estimates of Yahoo's audience, 26 million users, far exceeds the total American dormitory population.

ComScore claims that its numbers are far closer to the internal counts generated by Web site operators. But William Pulver, chief executive of **NetRatings** Inc., the company that publishes the Nielsen/NetRatings measurements, argues that there are good reasons that a measurement service will count fewer people than a site's own computers.

"Just because numbers are higher doesn't mean they are more accurate," he said.

Many advertisers and publishers, however, say they are tired of such claims and counterclaims and want both rating services to submit to the sort of independent audits that are regularly conducted of the services that measure traditional media. Both ratings services have so far refused, saying the audits are expensive and apply standards that are not realistic for the Internet.

"There is no consistency over time or common guidelines applied to either of these services," Mr. Zimbalist said. "They need to be audited just like radio and television ratings."

Like, What's a Spin Cycle?

Trying to Get GenY Psyched About Appliances, Whirlpool Tests Sleek, Portable Wares

BY ELLIOT SPAGAT

When **Whirlpool Corp.** started studying how it could sell appliances to the 18-to-24-year-old crowd, it dared to watch how young people do their laundry.

The Benton Harbor, Mich., company put cameras in dorm rooms and apartments. It interviewed young adults. And a few things came out in the wash.

Sometimes, doing the laundry meant rinsing jeans in the sink and leaving them to drip. Sometimes, it meant spraying a shirt with deodorant. Unlike those over 30, who often own houses and have families, 20-somethings couldn't care less about spin cycles and water temperatures, said Charles Jones, Whirlpool's vice president of global consumer design. Their ideal machine would have just a single push button.

"If you talk to a Gen-Y'er about laundry and washing and drying clothes, their eyes glaze over and you immediately lose them," he said.

With its traditional market saturated and sales slowing, Whirlpool is looking for ways to reach a relatively untapped group who has been ignored for good reasons: young adults, who rarely have much money, floor space or interest in appliances. The nation's largest appliance maker is hoping to appeal to young buyers with well-designed products.

The company is testing a sleek and small silver refrigerator, as well as a microwave oven and an air purifier with orange-colored accents, in Best Buy stores in Dallas, Chicago and Los Angeles. It has other items on the drawing board, including a microwave dryer just big enough for a pair or two of jeans. Whirlpool declines to comment on sales; Best Buy, the only retailer where the appliances are being tested, says it is angling to get young customers interested in appliances. Meantime, a **General Electric** Co. spokesman says GE also is developing appliances targeting Gen Y, but wouldn't elaborate.

The efforts comes as the Association of Home Appliance Manufacturers estimates that shipments of stoves and ovens will slide 4.3% this year, the first decline since 1995, and shipments of refrigerators will slip 2.6%, only the third drop in 12 years. Shipments of microwave ovens are expected to fall 5.2%.

People under 30 were the least likely to own laundry equipment and full-size refrigerators among any age group tracked last year by the Washington, D.C., industry association.

"These are people who don't have a set lifestyle," says Marise Kumar, Whirlpool's vice president of developing categories. "They move from place to place. They'd like to put all their appliances and household goods in the back of a truck and move to the next location."

Whirlpool studied the group by watching students last year at the University of Illinois at Chicago and the University of Notre Dame in Indiana. In other cities, it doled out disposable cameras to people under 30 and asked them to photograph likes and dislikes.

In addition to discovering that washing clothes is rare, it learned that leftover pizza is a real problem to store.

So an orange refrigerator in the works for the "Pla" (as in "play") line features special internal handles to hold a large pizza box and wheels to make the fridge more portable. The prototype dryer, also orange and shaped like bowling pin tipped on its side, is small enough to sit on a dresser, hold a couple of pairs of jeans, and do the job in 12 minutes. In choosing orange, the company borrowed a page from Apple Computer Inc., which is known for its sleek and coloful designs. The color "makes a statement," says Ms. Kumar.

Whirlpool's efforts began in 2000 when it exhibited funky microwave ovens and cookware, dubbed "Macrowave," at European museums and trade shows. A lightweight, battery-operated oven featured a pop-up top resembling a portable compact disc player and a strap to carry it over your shoulder, just like a purse or knapsack. Another oven had clear panels, so you could watch your frozen dinner turn to a boil. Macrowave ovens were experimental designs and never intended for store shelves.

It followed up with an unusual line of prototype washers and dryers—named "Project F," as in fabric—which made its debut at a Berlin trade show in February. A silver floor-to-ceiling "personal cleaning" box combined separate compartments for a shower, sink, washer and dryer. An environmentally correct washing machine had six small tubs separated by water hyacinth plants that absorb phosphorous from detergent.

Apartment-dwellers say Whirlpool faces a tough sell with its new commercial line. In many parts of the country, apartments come equipped with basic appliances. Lauren Bloxom, a 24-year-old saleswoman for Guess jeans in Dallas, said the sleek wares would have worked in her dorm room but the three-bedroom pad she shares with two roommates includes a full-size refrigerator, microwave oven, washer and dryer.

In high-rent areas, by contrast, apartments may be too small for even the smallest appliances. Gabe Banner, 24, wouldn't mind a few, but the two-bedroom rental he shares with a roommate in Manhattan's East Village is too small even for that, he says. Shelves are stacked high on his walls, and he stashes out-of-season clothes under his bed. To make room for an appliance, he might have to get rid of stereo equipment, an unthinkable trade-off.

And Whirlpool isn't promising any savings. Prices are similar to traditional models, with the minirefrigerator going for $220, the air purifier for $190 and the microwave for $100. Adam Mitchell, a 25-year-old retirement home worker who rents a one-bedroom in Dallas, said he would rather spend spare cash on a TV, a stereo, beer, or on throwing a party.

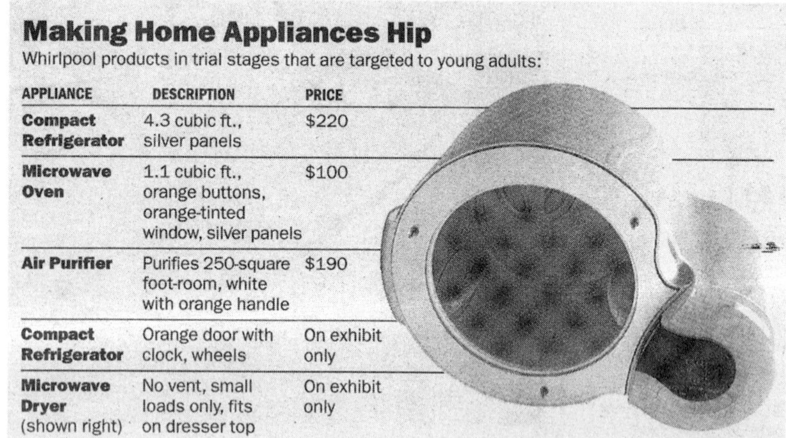

Making Home Appliances Hip

Whirlpool products in trial stages that are targeted to young adults:

APPLIANCE	DESCRIPTION	PRICE
Compact Refrigerator	4.3 cubic ft., silver panels	$220
Microwave Oven	1.1 cubic ft., orange buttons, orange-tinted window, silver panels	$100
Air Purifier	Purifies 250-square foot-room, white with orange handle	$190
Compact Refrigerator	Orange door with clock, wheels	On exhibit only
Microwave Dryer (shown right)	No vent, small loads only, fits on dresser top	On exhibit only

Product

Shoe Fetish

New Balance has no celebrity endorsers, does minimal advertising, and yet in the past five years has gained more customer loyalty than any other athletic shoe brand.

By: John Gaffney

Michael Jordan, Tiger Woods, and Mia Hamm hold court for Nike (*NKE*). NBA MVP Allen Iverson spins his hip-hop, straight-from-the-playground style for Reebok (*RBK*). And Jordan's air-apparent, L.A. Lakers wonderkid Kobe Bryant, dunks for Adidas. All told, athletic footwear makers spent more than $5.9 billion on advertising and celebrity endorsements last year, and guess which company commands the most brand loyalty?

None of the above, yo.

The highest levels of customer devotion in one of the most volatile and hotly contested product categories on the planet belong to a small New England company that is proudly endorsed by . . . no one. According to market research firm Brand Keys, Boston-based New Balance Athletic Shoes hasn't simply replaced Nike as the footwear brand with the most loyal customers. It is also the only athletic shoe brand in the Brand Keys index's top 20, and during the past five years, its high-performance shoes have gained more loyalty than any other competitive brand.

More remarkable, New Balance has accomplished all of this in a period during which brand loyalty in general has been eroding faster than Ken Lay's credibility. Just ask Robert Passikoff, Brand Keys president and a professor at New York University. To create the Brand Keys brand loyalty index, he surveys 16,000 consumers twice a year about their level of satisfaction with nearly 150 U.S. companies. Since the index began in 1997, Passikoff has seen significant erosion not just in athletic footwear but also in financial services, telecommunications, and airlines, among other categories. He attributes this to the sheer volume of products on the market. Today there are nearly 10,000 athletic shoe models, filling every niche from $15 Keds to $200 Nike Air Jordan XVII basketball shoes.

Measured by market share, New Balance is number four in this standing-room-only category, behind Nike, Adidas, and Reebok, but it has been gaining rapidly. Between 1999 and 2001, its domestic share climbed from 3.7 to 11 percent, while revenues jumped from $550 million to $813 million. What's more, the growth came on just $13 million in national advertising last year. Nike, by comparison, spent $155 million and Reebok $49 million, according to Competitive Media Reporting.

How does New Balance do it? To start with the most basic reason, the company gives customers a truly unique product: athletic shoes in varying widths. No other athletic footwear manufacturer makes shoes for wide or narrow feet, while New Balance covers all sizes from AA to extra-wide 6E. "I can't tell you how many people tell me that we make the only shoes they can wear," says Paul Heffernan, New Balance vice president for global marketing.

The company backs up its product with a marketing strategy that emphasizes consistency and subtlety and targets serious athletes between the ages of 25 and 45. These customers spend less on sports shoes than teens do—$2.3 billion compared with $3.5 billion—but according to Heffernan, they are far easier to hold on to. "Our customers are upwardly mobile, settled, very intense people," says New Balance marketing services manager John Donovan. "They're serious about fitness and their desire to achieve. Let me put

(Cont.)

it this way: Our customers don't really think they can win the Boston Marathon. But they believe they can beat last year's time."

New Balance ads feature unknown athletes and run in niche magazines like *Outside, New England Runner,* and *Prevention* and on cable-TV channels favored by older viewers such as CNN, the Golf Channel, and A&E. New Balance's low-key slogan is "Achieve New Balance." It hasn't changed for five years. Even its ad tag lines go right after the Gen X and boomer mind-set: "Life sucks, go for a run." Or "Turn off your phone and fax . . . achieve New Balance."

The company's advertising didn't always play it so quiet. In fact, New Balance was the first athletic footwear company to offer a multimillion-dollar endorsement deal, to L.A. Lakers star James Worthy, in the mid-1980s. But after sales of its basketball shoes got no juice from Big Game James, New Balance pulled the plug on celebrity deals and has shied away from mass-market advertising ever since. "I don't have a poster of Michael Jordan in my bedroom anymore," Heffernan says, "and neither do our customers."

New Balance's low-key approach has worked well with brand extensions into kids' shoes and apparel, Donovan says, since both were designed to appeal to its core customers. Promotions for the kids' line, for example, aim at parents who wear New Balance sneakers themselves. Print ads tout shoe widths and urge parents to "nurture and care for kids" and their feet.

New Balance is also cautiously edging back into the youth market, from which it had retreated after the failure of the James Worthy basketball shoe. One strategy is built around PF Flyers, a casual-shoe label popular in the 1980s, which New Balance acquired in 2001 and plans to relaunch in 2003. The reasoning behind the sub-brand, Donovan says, is that PF Flyers will be positioned too far from the mother brand to fit under its wing. "PF Flyers is more about fashion and flash, and it will have some low price points," he says. "It's not a good brand extension for New Balance."

The brand's other bid for the youth market—to apply the New Balance "N" to a new line of basketball shoes—is far riskier. It will bring New Balance toe-to-toe with the likes of Nike, Adidas, and Reebok in a hyper-competitive category. Why not use another sub-brand? Donovan says the company decided that the shoes belonged under the New Balance umbrella because the focus will be on high performance, not high fashion, and the target audience will be serious athletes—albeit in the fickle 15-to-21 age range.

To promote the shoes, New Balance plans an uncharacteristically edgy campaign. A Hoop Troop featuring hotshot amateur ballplayers will visit street courts in 10 cities to talk up the basketball shoes and even give away a few pairs for free. Simultaneously, New Balance will roll out a $7 million TV and print ad campaign. Heffernan admits that the campaign is a stretch for the traditionally low-profile company but says it's what's needed to compete in the youth market. He does promise that one thing won't change: You won't see any NBA superstars. "We go about things our own way," he says. "We've become a celebrity brand by avoiding celebrities."

"Shoe Fetish," *Business 2.0,* March 2002, pp. 98–99.

TYSON: IS THERE LIFE OUTSIDE THE CHICKEN COOP?

It's mounting a risky bid to sell brand-name pork and beef

Think of it as a giant game of chicken. Springdale (Ark.)-based Tyson Foods Inc. is betting big that its name can become as dominant in beef and pork as it is in poultry. With almost a quarter of the market for chicken, Tyson has already pulled off the improbable feat of convincing consumers that choosing the right brand matters in what's essentially a commodity purchase. Now it wants the Tyson name to rule the roost at the meat counter as well.

Tyson's grand ambitions stem from its contentious $4.6 billion merger in late 2001 with beef and pork giant IBP Inc., which tripled Tyson's sales to $23 billion. But IBP, which is the leader in beef and No. 2 in pork, has nowhere near Tyson's name recognition. Instead of a single brand, IBP depends mostly on a mishmash of regional labels. That's a problem for Tyson, which supplies national giants such as Wal-Mart Stores Inc. and Albertson's Inc. Besides, it needs the marketing efficiencies and the higher margins of a strong brand.

Tyson's solution? It's scrapping all but the strongest IBP brands and slapping its own name on the rest. To make sure consumers understand that Tyson now stands for more than just chicken, the company is shelling out a cool $100 million in ads and consumer promotions.

A lot is at stake. The company risks confusing customers. But more important, the "new" Tyson brand is the linchpin in the company's long march to move beyond low-margin commodity cuts. In chicken, Tyson has already proved that consumers will pay extra for breaded, marinated, or ready-to-microwave items that can be prepared in nothing flat. Such value-added products now account for about half of Tyson's $7 billion in yearly chicken sales and carry margins four or five times that of fresh meat. Tyson hopes to apply the same recipe to its beef and pork business.

Deciding which products would carry the Tyson name required careful research. Tyson discovered that many retailers see red meat as a signature item. They want fresh beef cut to their specs and packaged under their labels to give consumers the sense that they're getting fresh-from-the-butcher goods. Besides, while Tyson raises its own chicken, it buys beef from hundreds of suppliers, making it harder to ensure consistent quality. The upshot: Only some specialty cuts will carry the Tyson name.

To drive home its message, Tyson is marshaling $40 million in TV, radio, and print ads created by agency DDB Chicago that portray sentimental family scenes, such as a daughter's first dance, to reinforce its tag line: "Tyson. It's what your family deserves." The ads will also introduce a crop of products, including an array of deli meats and a line of beef and pork roasts that can be microwaved in minutes. It'll spend another $60 million on coupons, samples, and other promotions.

The campaign comes at a trying time for Tyson. In 2001, it tried to back out of the IBP deal, citing concerns about IBP's finances. But a federal judge ruled that Tyson had simply gotten cold feet and forced it to complete the deal. Now, a glut of meat, a sluggish economy, a weak export market, and higher grain costs have put Tyson's earnings under pressure. It reported a 69% drop in first-quarter profits, to $39 million, on flat sales of $5.8 billion. That has clobbered the stock, which is down more than 25% over the past year, to $9.36 recently. Meanwhile, Tyson is making headlines as it goes to trial on federal charges of smuggling illegal immigrants to work in its chicken plants, allegations it vehemently denies.

It's not a great time to throw big money at the Tyson name. But execs say they're building for the long term. "The time you ought to be spending is when things aren't going as good as you want," says Bob Corscadden, chief marketing officer. Tyson faces tough rivals, including Smithfield Foods, Hormel Foods, and ConAgra Foods, in the bid to sell products that let mom fix a home-cooked meal in under 20 minutes. If it can use the brand it built in chicken to sell steaks and pork chops, Tyson could have something to crow about.

By Wendy Zellner in Dallas, with Pallavi Gogoi in Chicago

HERE'S THE BEEF

How poultry king Tyson is using its IBP acquisition to build a brand in beef and pork:

REPLACING IBP's Thomas E. Wilson brand with the Tyson name on 14 heat-and-eat beef and pork roasts and other products

ROLLING OUT a line of 31 prepackaged beef, ham, and other meats to be sold next to the deli counter

SPENDING $40 million on TV, radio, and print advertising

SPENDING $60 million on coupons, online marketing on food-related Web sites, in-store demonstrations, and other promotions

Data: Tyson Foods Inc.

China's Power Brands Eye Global Expansion

Haier, others aim to become U.S. household names

By: Normandy Madden

[HONG KONG] Global marketers like Procter & Gamble Co., General Motors Corp. and Coca-Cola Co. see China's one billion-plus population as the world's biggest market, but the country is also home to a new generation of companies eager to enter the world stage themselves. Among them: local players Legend, Haier, TCL and dozens of others itching to become household names in the U.S. within the next decade.

"Rising quality standards and heavy ad spending by local companies have created a handful of powerful Chinese brands," said T.B. Song, chairman of WPP Group's Ogilvy & Mather, Greater China, in Shanghai.

While there are still stumbling blocks, Chinese companies are waking up to marketing. They are also turning out products that compete on price and, increasingly, on quality, following in the footsteps of cheap and once-shoddy Korean imports turned global brands like Samsung, Kia, Hyundai and LG. Samsung, for example, now commands a $400 million global ad budget, with Interpublic Group of Cos.' Foote Cone & Belding Worldwide as lead agency.

When, Not If

"It is a matter of when, not if, Chinese brands go beyond the borders of Greater China," said Chris Walton, CEO of WPP's MindShare, China, in Shanghai.

The standouts, like Haier and TV marketer TCL, are progressive. They benefit from sheer sale, cheap labor, and a Confucian can-do attitude.

Haier has been transformed by savvy management from the near-bankrupt Qingdao Refrigerator Plant to a $19 billion group that cracked the Middle East market with an air conditioner developed exclusively for the desert. Haier also found a home for its compact refrigerators in U.S. college dorms.

"I fully expect companies in the categories of automobiles, airlines, real estate, finance, insurance and food to quickly join the likes of Haier and Legend over the next five to ten years," Mr. Walton said.

In November 2002, Haier named Grey Global Group to develop a national marketing communications platform in mainland China, the first step towards turning it into a global brand.

Presence

Haier already sells well in the U.S. from its own factory in Camden, S.C. In 2002, Haier sold almost $500 million in air conditioners, refrigerators, freezers and wine cabinets through chains like Wal-Mart, Home Depot and Target. The company hopes to double U.S. sales by 2005 and is likely to seek a U.S. stock exchange listing. "Haier has a vision that we are eager to translate into an umbrella positioning and branding platform to establish the company as a world-class player," said Viveca Chan, Grey's chairman-CEO, Hong Kong & China.

China's top-selling computer brand, Legend, started in 1984 as a distributor for giants like IBM Corp. and Hewlett-Packard Co. Legend combined its knowledge with its own local language capability and access to cheap labor to make its own computers, gaining more than one-third of China's computer market. Known more for low prices than quality, Legend is beefing up R&D and branching into other areas such as digital cameras, printers and audio players.

Another example is Tsingtao Brewery Co. A staple in Chinese restaurants around the world, Tsingtao forged a strategic alliance in 2002 with Anheuser-Busch Cos. to get its brand into overseas supermarkets, in return for giving A-B a strategic foothold in China, the world's second-largest beer market.

On another front, the 999 pharmaceutical division of the SanJiu Enterprise Group distributes Chinese medicines all over the world, such as Gan Da tablets to treat hepatitis, and 999 Gingko leaf tablets for high blood pressure and heart disease. So far, 999 has only dabbled in advertising aimed at overseas Chinese communities, but these traditional remedies complement a growing interest in natural medicine in the U.S.

Different Approach

Taking a promotional approach, the Li-Ning Sports Goods Co., China's largest sporting goods brand, is sponsoring teams in countries like France and Russia, even

(Cont.)

though the company doesn't do any international advertising yet. But the sponsorships help build brand exposure and relevance, said Dennis Wong, CEO, Hong Kong & China of Publicis troupe's Leo Burnett Worldwide, Hong Kong. "Li-Ning wants to become a major player in international sports brands in the next five to 10 years."

So far, the battle between Chinese companies and foreign rivals has been on Chinese turf. Since joining the World Trade Organization, many of China's tariffs and other trade barriers have been reduced. Chinese companies have fought back, with better distribution and lower pricing but now are discovering the bonus of branding.

Two years ago, local companies "contributed nothing" to J. Walter Thompson Co.'s Chinese revenues, said Tom Doctoroff, the WPP agency's area director, Northeast Asia and CEO, China, based in Shanghai. But in 2002, clients like TV marketer TCL, 999 and ginseng king Wenji accounted for 28% of JWT's mainland Chinese revenues. "Nimble local competitors are appearing in every corner of the competitive battlefield."

Globally, multinationals still have several advantages over Chinese competitors, which so far have had little brand equity among consumers. Haier refrigerators, for example, sell across America on price, not branding. "At this moment, Haier is perhaps more established [than other Chinese brands] in their international sales network, but they still need a lot of work to get to global brand status," said Grey's Ms. Chan.

POP QUIZ

Chinese brand ambitions for the U.S. still have a way to go. Can you match the company to the brand?

BRAND	CATEGORY
1. Legend	**a.** home appliances
2. Tsingtao	**b.** computers
3. 999	**c.** TVs
4. TCL	**d.** pharmaceuticals
5. Haier	**e.** beer

Answers: 1b, 2e, 3d, 4c, 5a

Government Influence

Also, many large state-run companies are heavily influenced by China's Communist party, even in the rare case of a CEO who is not a party member. Staying tuned to both the market and the party line can result in decision-making chaos.

Among mainland companies that are tomorrow's brand leaders, Janice Chan, M&C Saatchi's Hong Kong-based managing director, Greater China, said many still lack know-how and "need a deeper understanding of buyers and consumers in foreign countries, better marketing skills and more respect for rules of the game played by the rest of the world."

But they are learning fast. Multinationals probably have just a few years to shield themselves from the Chinese threat, said JWT's Mr. Doctoroff. "In some industries, the tidal wave is already approaching the shore."

Salad in Sealed Bags Isn't So Simple, It Seems

By AMANDA HESSER

YUMA, Ariz. — For millions of Americans, preparing a mixed green salad is as easy as opening a sealed plastic bag. But here in the land of lettuce, complexity is a given, and time is the enemy.

There is a reason bagged lettuce costs more than twice as much as a head of iceberg. It is not easy getting those perfectly formed leaves, washed and still fresh, from the soil to the table. The process requires speed, technology, secrecy about that technology and plain-old farmers' ingenuity.

Bagged salad sales in the United States have soared in the past decade, exceeding $2 billion last year, according to ACNielsen, the market research company. And while iceberg may still be king, accounting for 73 percent of all lettuce grown in this country, that is a decline from 84 percent in 1992. Consumption of romaine and leaf lettuces like green leaf and red oak has more than doubled since the early 1990's.

"We have a department working on lettuce breeding," said Peggy Miars, a spokeswoman for Earthbound Farm, a grower here whose annual sales have grown an average of 55 percent since 1995. "You don't want a bagful of lettuces that are all flat. That is the main reason we have the frisee in there—for texture. They are also breeding for better colors. Deeper reds are desirable."

Whatever the color, speed is of the essence. The moment the plants are shaved from the ground, the clock starts ticking. Six days is allowed for washing and bagging the lettuce and transporting it around the country, and about a week more to sell it. After that, the leaves turn slimy.

And slimy lettuce can be disastrous. As Bill Zinke, vice president for marketing at Ready Pac Produce of Irwindale, Calif., which processes bagged salads, said, "It's constantly a business of staying up to and ahead of what fields you will be harvesting, not just today and this week but weeks and months in advance."

Earthbound said it was the first company to package lettuce in bags, starting in 1986. And by packaging whole baby leaves instead of mature heads cut into bite-size pieces, it can move lettuce to market without giving it the "nitrogen flush" that bags of cut-up romaine or iceberg lettuce need to keep the cut edges from browning.

But baby greens have to be harvested in just a few days, before they grow too big. Each bag of what the company calls its "mixed baby greens" has at least eight varieties of specialty lettuce, nearly all of which had to be ready for harvest the same day.

For Earthbound Farm, the country's largest producer of organic salads, it all begins in fields here. More than 90 percent of all lettuce in the United States is grown in Arizona and in California, mostly from two regions—Yuma in the winter, and the Salinas Valley in the summer.

The places where the greens are sorted look like a Rube Goldberg drawing. Bins of freshly cut leaves are rushed from nearby farms to the packing plant in refrigerated trucks. Then the bins are lifted into a vacuum tube the diameter of a subway tunnel.

In 20 minutes, the vacuum brings the temperature of the lettuce down to 36 degrees, and it goes into cold storage. Maintaining that temperature until it reaches the grocery will keep it fresh for about 15 days.

Inside, the packing plant is cold and wet, and loud as a jackhammer, as enormous production lines ferry the tiny greens from bin to bag. First, they are upended onto conveyors, passing a row of inspectors and sweeping down a flume into the world's largest salad spinners. Then up conveyors they go, to giant scales and bagging machines. More than 14,000 pounds of lettuce can be processed every hour.

This is where the secrets are kept. The way the flume swishes the lettuce and how harshly the spinners treat it affect how much it is damaged and how nearly perfect and dry the leaves are in the bag. A photographer sent to capture the process was not permitted to take close-ups of the newest machines. Pen and paper were heavily discouraged.

"It is a very competitive environment," Drew Goodman, the president of Earthbound Farm, said. "At most, you get six months" before new ideas are picked up by rivals.

"With the different service providers and maintenance people," he added, "most any new development is going to be—*available*, let's say, to others."

Mr. Zinke would not discuss Ready Pac's salad washing or drying process. "It's a very slim-margin business," he said. "So you hang closely on your points of difference that give you a competitive edge."

Almost none of the technology now used in the industry existed 15 years ago. Mr. Goodman and his wife, Myra Goodman, the founders of Earthbound Farm, started growing lettuce in their backyard in the 1980's. Last year the business, which specializes in baby organic lettuce, had sales of more than $200 million.

The Goodmans developed much of their machinery out of necessity—a salad spinner, for example, that dries smaller batches of lettuce at lower speeds, causing less damage to the leaves. Machines like it are now widely used in the industry.

In Earthbound's new 115,000-square-foot plant in Yuma, the water flumes have swirling jets to keep the delicate leaves from clumping. The temperature throughout the plant is controlled by a master computer. Charles Sweat, the chief operating officer, travels by company jet between here and the summer plant in San Juan Bautista, Calif., and he can adjust the temperatures by remote control on his laptop.

Once the lettuce is bagged, it is sent off in refrigerated semitrailers to stores around the country. Company officials can only hope that the cooling units on the trucks work well and that the markets store the salad in a cool place.

Fresh Express, which deals mostly in head lettuce that is cut and put into bags, has processing plants around the country, so its workers can cut the heads into bite-size pieces closer to their destination, increasing shelf life. Other companies, including Ready Pac, simply have to hurry to get lettuce on the road.

One of the most important advances in keeping baby and cut lettuce crisp from the time it is packed on the West Coast until it arrives on the East Coast was the development of a new bag to pack it in.

"We had a breakthrough in 1989 that allowed us to take it national," said Robin Sprague, a spokeswoman for Fresh Express, one of the companies that began using the process. The packaging, a plastic film that her company calls "modified atmosphere packaging," gives the cut lettuce a longer shelf life by slowing the rate of decay.

At nearly the same time, Ready Pac came up with two more innovations: a system for washing the lettuce three times and a "pillow pack," a bag that is inflated with extra nitrogen to protect the leaves from bruising during shipping.

Organic lettuce is still just about 4 percent, of a giant industry whose change and growth is rippling through other businesses. "What we're talking about," said Ken Hodge, the communications director for the International Fresh-cut Produce Association, "is a phenomenon that has cut across the whole produce industry." Freshly cut fruits are expected to be the next big thing.

Still, salad makers are fighting to take their industry to a new level. They are busy reducing the amount of salad that clumps in the machine. They are improving the tatsoi's texture, and the time it takes lettuce to go from the Arizona field to a dinner table in Bangor, Me.

"This business is really about performing every day," said Mr. Goodman of Earthbound Farm. "So that means having the best quality every day and innovating every day. So hopefully, we're on to our next innovation while our competition is figuring out our last one."

Cannibalize Your Own Products? If You Don't, Someone Else Will

Author: MIKE ANGELL
Investor's Business Daily

It's not an appetizing subject for many companies. But when should a new product cannibalize sales of an older product?

Cannibalization—when a company's new product takes sales from an older one—gets a bad rap. Marketing texts say it's bad, says Rajesh Chandy, assistant professor of marketing at the University of Minnesota's Carlton School of Management.

But he calls it "an important part of business. The whole reason is to create a larger revenue stream. The revenue impact of a new product should be greater than the loss of the older product."

Yet the downside is worrisome.

Home Depot successfully cannibalized older stores with new ones for years. Clustering stores built barriers to entry for rivals.

But Home Depot cut the number of new stores in 2001 because they steal sales from older ones. Analysts figure they stripped 6% to 8% from same-store sales.

Old For New

In 2001, Home Depot opened 204 stores vs. 225 planned. It now sees about 200 new stores a year over the next three years.

Retailers don't lend themselves to cannibalization, says Chris Conley, an assistant professor of product design at the Illinois Institute of Technology. "Stores tend to run into limited geographies."

But cannibalization is needed in technology, consumer products and autos. All of these products enjoy a period of strong growth followed by flat sales.

"It's very important to have a new product that can make the curve go back up," said Conley. "The best companies continuously manage product portfolios."

Before decline sets in, Conley says, a company at least should have a new product on the drawing board. Too many expect their products to have long shelf lives.

"I don't know if it's denial or just raw determination to keep selling a product," Conley said.

Question Is When

But how does a company know when sales of a product might decline before the fact? Answer: good market research.

Outside research firms or units within a company can do the job.

"That requires spending time with customers, or even the customers of your customers, since many products are sold to other businesses rather than consumers," Conley said.

EMC Corp. rode a decade-long wave of spending on large, very expensive storage computers. But that market cooled.

Clients needed smaller, less expensive storage computers that were coming from companies like Sun Microsystems, Dell Computer and Network Appliance. It wasn't until 2000 that EMC offered a less expensive system.

"Incumbent firms have a hard time cannibalizing because they have so much interest in existing investments," Conley said.

How a firm is organized can promote cannibalization, Chandy says. Internal units competing for resources are more likely to have instances where products cannibalize each other.

In the 1980s, Hewlett-Packard's printer unit mostly focused on laser-jet printers. They were faster and more durable than ink-jets.

But another HP unit sought to improve ink-jet technology, with the company's blessing.

Greg Wallace, marketing manager for HP's printer business, says the employees at the laser-jet unit weren't happy.

"There was a concern that ink jet would cannibalize sales from laser jet," Wallace said. "We had a lot of worries and a lot of angst over the decision. But we had the courage to attack ourselves."

At HP, product managers led the drive to improve ink jets. Conley says product managers are the best people to know when a product should be cannibalized. They're most familiar with what the current product does and what it should do in the future.

Salespeople should be involved in the process, but shouldn't lead it, Conley says. They're often too focused on short-term gains.

"Salespeople can't tolerate ambiguity and risk with a new product," Conley said. "In some cases, there's confusion in the marketplace because customers ask what product do we use."

At HP, the laser-jet people were up in arms about the ink-jet unit's plan to use the line "laser quality" in marketing. So the ink-jet crew eventually had to find other ways to tout quality in ads.

"There was some initial confusion about marketing," Wallace said. "But it resolved itself."

Other firms take a different tack. Gillette only advertises newer razors, not older ones, says spokeswoman Michele Szynal.

It expects the new razor, in this case the Mach3 Turbo, to take sales from the existing Mach3 line as well as older ones. The more expensive Mach3 Turbo is expected to more than make up for lost sales.

But there is a risk if the one product makes up too great a portion of a company's sales.

"If existing products are the primary source of revenue, it's very risky to move," Chandy said.

"Cannibalize Your Own Products? If You Don't, Someone Else Will," *Investor's Business Daily*, January 16, 2002, p. A1. Reprinted by permission.

When Hybrid Cars Collide

Several Gas-Electric Systems Jockey to Become a Standard; Echoes of VHS vs. Betamax?

BY NORIHIKO SHIROUZU

Detroit — As auto makers gear up to bring hybrid gas-electric vehicles into the mainstream, they could be headed for another VHS vs. Betamax technology war.

A battle for control over the future of hybrid technology is taking shape, echoing the bruising format collision from home video's early days. Companies are placing bets on which technology they think will become a market standard—and which could end up as costly experiments.

U.S. sales of the first generation of hybrid cars are growing steadily. **Toyota Motor** Corp. has sold more than 40,000 Prius hybrids in the U.S. since 2000, with sales up 29% in 2002. **Honda Motor** Co. has sold more than 20,000 of its hybrid cars, the two-seater Insight, launched in the U.S. in 2000, and the Civic hybrid, launched in 2002. Meanwhile, **Ford Motor** Co. plans to have what would be the first hybrid sport-utility vehicle, a gas-electric version of the Escape, on the market by early 2004. **General Motors** Corp. plans to launch a hybrid SUV, the Saturn Vue, in 2005.

Hybrids, in addition to their regular gasoline engines, have one or more electric motors to propel the vehicle at low speeds and assist the gas engine at higher speeds. The electric motors run off a battery that gets charged every time the car brakes. For now, each auto maker is putting its own spin on this basic hybrid technology. But Toyota and GM are aggressively jockeying for strategic positions, each one marketing its propulsion system to rivals in hopes of breaking away from the industry pack.

The differences between the GM and Toyota powertrains are subtle. Toyota's Prius has a big electric motor to propel the vehicle and a smaller one for charging the battery and assisting the bigger one. In the Saturn Vue, both electric motors do both jobs.

Another critical difference is in the transmission: The Saturn Vue will have what GM describes as an "automatically shifted manual transmission," which a spokesman says gives the vehicle better fuel economy on the highway. Toyota's Prius has a more complex electrically controlled transmission system that shifts gears smoothly even as the vehicle switches between electric drive and the gasoline engine.

The biggest difference, however, is in the software controlling the powertrain. GM's system is geared toward driving patterns in the U.S., where some 60% of driving is on freeways. The Prius was designed for Japan's urban driving, although Toyota executives say it has been fine-tuned to suit the U.S. market.

For consumers, the stakes aren't quite so stark as they were in the case of Betamax vs. VHS, when some people were stuck with VCRs that couldn't play tapes in the winning VHS format. In contrast, all hybrid cars run on the same gasoline. Buyers who buy a hybrid in a format that goes on to lose will still be able to drive the car, although parts may become scarce.

Car makers, however, want to realize potentially huge cost advantages from driving high-volume sales to a single standard.

Gas-electric vehicle systems cost more than their conventional counterparts, in part because hybrid powertrain components are produced in low volumes. The cost premium varies but is generally estimated at about $5,000 or more per vehicle. Toyota's gas-electric Prius compact car costs $20,000; a similar-size, conventional-engine Toyota Corolla is priced from $14,000 to $15,500. For buyers, tax incentives can offset some of the difference.

Toyota executives had hoped GM would back its system. In 1999, the two auto companies formed a five-year partnership to develop hybrid and fuel-cell vehicles. But instead of accepting Toyota's technology, GM is working to make its own hybrid propulsion system the industry standard.

Larry Burns, GM vice president of research and development, says he is well aware of the risks of a format war. He commissioned a study of the tactical moves Sony Corp. and Matsushita Electric Industrial Co. made in the 1970s that determined the outcome of the Betamax-VHS war. Matsushita made VHS the home-video standard by rallying support from other electronics companies.

Mr. Burns says the lesson is that sitting

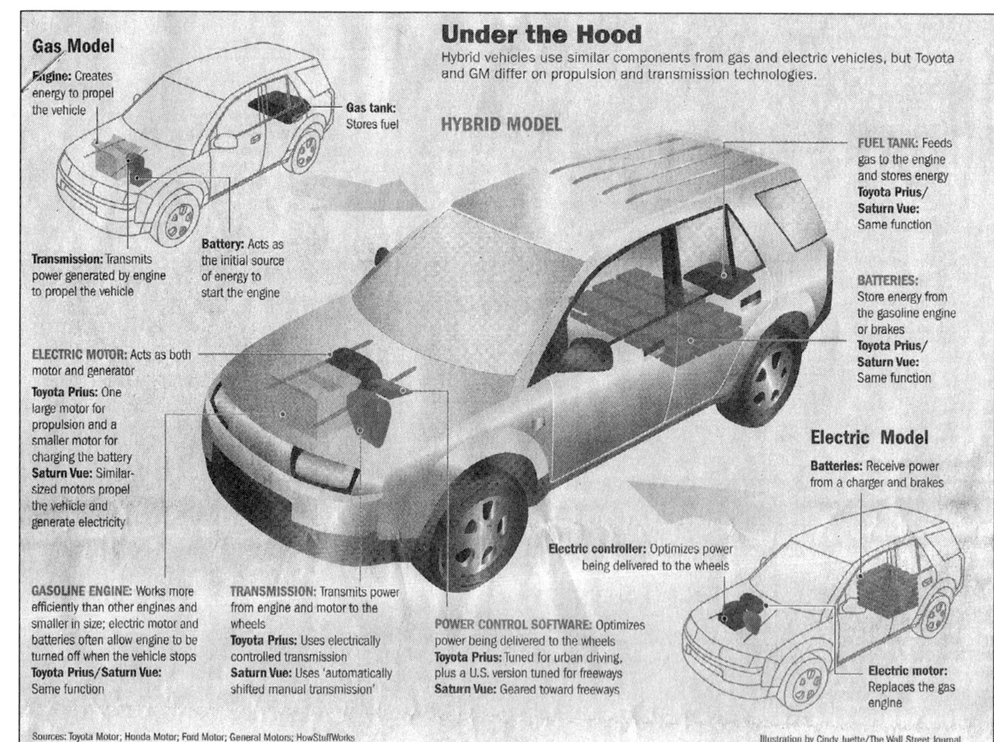

(Cont.)

Toyota and GM each are aggressively marketing their propulsion systems to rivals, hoping to break away from the industry pack.

on the sidelines is risky. "If [hybrids] are going to be mainstream, we intend to be the industry leader," he says. "It would be a very risky position for General Motors to relinquish that knowledge and rely on another auto company."

Now, the race is on to win over other auto makers. Mr. Burns says GM is willing to share its technology with another maker or enter into a joint development program. He says GM is talking with a number of companies.

Toyota says it has had an "open system" for several years. "We'll open our technology to whoever knocks on our door," says Akihiko Saito, executive vice president of technology. "It's only natural that different makers will have different approaches. But eventually the best system will prevail." Next year, Toyota plans to launch a hybrid version of the redesigned Lexus RX SUV and may offer hybrid systems as an option for the Toyota Highlander SUV. President Fujio Cho has said Toyota hopes to sell 300,000 hybrids a year around the world by mid-decade, mostly in the U.S.

Ford and Honda could emerge as swing votes in the technology race. Honda isn't leaning toward either Toyota or GM, relying instead on its own system. Koichi Amemiya, Honda's No. 2 executive, says it's too early to bet big on hybrids.

Ford's Escape hybrid uses Ford's own technology, although Ford will buy some components from a Toyota supplier. "It's absolutely clear in our mind we must have control of our own hybrid electric technology," says Richard Parry-Jones, Ford group vice president for global product development. "It is too important to become totally reliant on another company."

Tuning into HDTV

Coming into Focus

By Kenneth Hein

What's held back HDTV? For years, consumers didn't know what it was and marketers couldn't explain it. But now that prices have dropped and the programs are here, just how big will HDTV be?

Last month, during the busiest shopping period for consumer electronics, I set out to find an informed salesperson who could explain exactly why I should invest in a high definition television (HDTV) set. And, assuming I would, tell me which brand I should buy.

At P.C. Richard and Son, a bargain retailer in the New York tri-state area, the floor was packed with HDTVs, flat-screen monitors and those sleek wafer-thin plasma TVs that wealthy people hang like art on their living room walls. Yet, only one Panasonic set was actually receiving a high definition signal, of a football game. The rest were running a DVD loop of the first *Lord of the Rings* movie in varying degrees of muddiness.

"If I buy an HDTV set with a tuner already installed, do I need to put an antenna on my roof to receive the signal?" I ask.

"I don't know," responds salesperson No. 1. "Hold on."

As he disappears, I check out the store's array of oversized monitors, which all look identical except for the brand names: Samsung, Sony, Sharp, Panasonic, Philips.

Sales guy No. 2 emerges with a jargon-filled explanation I couldn't possibly decipher, raising new questions about "HDTV-ready" versus "upgradable" sets, converters/decoders, pixel counts and DirecTV compatibility. I ask him how I should choose one brand over another. He notes that the Philips unit comes with free wall brackets, "which are like $400 right there."

At which point I find myself listening to yet another salesperson, who says that I can simpy use an old "rabbit ears" antenna on my new $3,999 TV purchase and $999 tuner. (Sounds improbable, but I discover later it does work.) When I inquire which brands are the best, he mumbles, "The pictures are all the same."

Welcome to the circuitous land of HDTV.

Despite all the hype about its extraordinary picture and sound quality—which, by all accounts, is true—a combination of factors has kept HDTV from penetrating the ordinary American household. Chief among them has been the technology's prohibitive price tag. A 34-inch Sony HDTV introduced in the U.S. in 1998, for example, cost $9,000.

Tuning In The Finer Points: AN HDTV PRIMER

WHAT IS DIGITAL TV? Simply put, "digital" TVs can receive and display digital images, which can carry 10 times the number of pixels of traditional analog signals. Digital TV encompasses both standard definition television (SDTV) and high definition television (HDTV), plus potential data broadcasting capabilities. SDTV delivers approximately the same resolution as regular analog TV, but without the annoying snow and ghosting, so the actual picture quality is higher. Digital TV also provides broadcasters with the capability of multiple channels of digital surround sound.

WHAT'S THE DIFFERENCE BETWEEN WIDE-SCREEN, FLAT-SCREEN, PLASMA, DIGITAL TV, DIRECTV AND HDTV? All HDTVs are configured in a movie-style wide-screen format, which explains why DVDs displayed on them do not have those black bars running across the top and bottom. Plasma refers to an "emissive" display technology, either in TVs or computers. Not all flat-screens are plasma displays. Flat-screen TVs simply have a flat screen, so they don't have the edge distortions of a conventional curved monitor. DirecTV is a satellite broadcasting company that now beams three HD channels: HBO, Showtime and the sports channel HDNet.

WHAT DO I NEED TO RECEIVE DIGITAL SIGNALS? HDTV units require a "tuner" or "converter" to plug into the sets to decode the signals. HDTV-ready sets come with tuners installed, but also require a separate set-top box from a cable company or special oval dish from a satellite provider. Under the recent "push and play" agreement between the Consumer Electronics Assn. and the National Cable and Telecommunications Assn., cable-ready HDTVs introduced in the next few years will no longer need the separate box to receive digital broadcasts.

IF I BUY AN HDTV SET, WHAT CAN I WATCH? Cable companies are not required to broadcast high-definition programming, but most of the nation's top 10 providers have started adding HD channels to their digital-cable lineups. Each cable operator has to complete a separate deal with the networks to determine which shows will be aired. What's available depends on one's local market. Right now, for example, Time Warner in New York has a deal with CBS, NBC, HBO, PBS and Showtime to carry their HD programming, but not with Fox or ABC, even though ABC now offers nearly all of its national prime-time shows in high definition.

Years after manufacturers began boldly predicting a revolution in the television industry, many consumers still don't know what HDTV is or why they should want it. TV stations, meanwhile, have been reluctant to spend the money necessary to broadcast programs in high definition. So, even for the few who've owned one, there has been little they could watch.

But, the picture is changing. Starting in early 2002, prices on HDTVs began to plunge, to as little as $1,000-1,500 for the smallest sets. Although that price doesn't include the cost of tuners, nor guarantee that viewers can receive the required digital, vs. analog, signal.

As the audience for high definition programs grows, so too does the amount of available programming. Currently, CBS and ABC offer much of their prime time lineups in HDTV. NBC, which had lagged behind, stepped up last year with the Olympics and has added several entertainment shows in the format this season. (Fox has been relying on the lesser "enhanced definition" wide-screen digital format.) On Jan. 26, ABC will air Super Bowl XXXVII from San Diego in high definition, and will follow for the first time with an HDTV broadcast of the Academy Awards in March. Disney's ABC/ESPN tandem networks also plan HDTV coverage of the National Basketball Association and Stanley Cup finals later this spring.

All the while, sales of HDTV monitors have risen steadily, to an estimated 2.5 million in 2002, up from 1.4 million in 2001 and 648,000 in 2000, per the Consumer Electronics Association in Arlington, Va. For comparison's sake, sales of traditional TVs remained flat last year at 25 million.

The question is, what does the future now hold for HDTV?

"We expect the market to come close to doubling again in 2003, with about 4.1 million sets sold," said Michelle Abraham, senior analyst at Instat/MDR, a technology consultancy based in Scottsdale, Ariz.

Some observers are predicting that the long-awaited explosion in HDTV sales is finally ready to materialize. But, many steps must still take place before that actually happens:

- The nation's cable operators must upgrade their systems in order to transmit digital signals. Federal regulations call for an end to analog broadcasting in 2006, or when 85% of households can receive digital signals. Many cable operators and satellite providers have resisted the moves due to high costs.
- TV manufacturers, who've been delaying for the same reason, need to step up their efforts to incorporate HDTV-capable tuners. The Federal Communications Commission has mandated the transition by 2007.
- HDTV set prices must drop further to within realistic levels for mass audiences, with most estimates falling below the critical $1,000 mark.
- TV buyers must be willing to replace their sets more often than in the past (typically, once every 10 years).

Some analysts submit to all of the above. According to the Boston-based Yankee Group, U.S. household penetration of HDTV, at a mere 2% in 2002, is forecast to reach 30% between 2006-07. During that time, "there will be three or four forces coming together to cause an enormous boom," said Yankee Group analyst Ryan Jones. "Content will be available from cable and satellite providers, prices will come within reach of the majority of consumers and there will be a momentum change in [the culture]. People will feel compelled to get a fancy, flat TV because the neighbors have done so."

All of which may mean a flurry of activity for marketers in the home entertainment/electronics categories, who now find themselves grappling with a number of branding challenges arising from HDTV's complex technology.

To begin with, how does one convey the benefits of vastly improved picture/sound quality through an ad? Zenith, Samsung, Philips, Pioneer, Toshiba, Hitachi and RCA have all been running print ads touting their digital televisions. Problem is, they are all virtually identical, involving people depicted as being blown away by the razor-sharp images. Hitachi uses a shot of the space shuttle taking off. Zenith is currently promoting its wide-screen 34-inch HDTV with an image of a snowboarder jumping down a mountain while being tagged by a helicopter against a clear blue sky.

Observers question whether such efforts will actually drive consumers into stores. Unless people see HDTV in person, the argument goes, they won't truly appreciate what they're missing.

For the time being, no HDTV manufacturer appears to have established itself as an authority in the category. At this point, "brands are trying to put a stake in the ground," said Robert Passikoff, president of New York-based Brand Keys, a consultancy specializing in brand loyalty. "There truly may be some meaningful electronic differences [between manufacturers], but no one's really been able to distinguish what they are. Most people aren't interested."

For now, consumers may be drawn to the names they already know. "Some people are probably driven by brand. They want a Sony or a Panasonic," said Steve Spiwak, an economist with the Columbus, Ohio-based consultancy Retail Forward. "[However, others,] especially with new technologies, are a bit more open minded and want to see them side by side, and see which picture delivers in their view."

Still, some companies like Zenith have gone further in terms of marketing their HDTVs to consumers. This past fall, the company included TV spots in its $30 million marketing campaign, attempting to capture the HDTV experience in one futuristic commercial involving a family flying a spaceship and doing battle with aliens. Suddenly, the sequence breaks to a living room with enthralled kids watching. "I told you this thing was awesome," says the dad, followed by a voiceover: "The world's first 60-inch plasma HDTV, from Zenith. An epic experience, just four inches deep."

Not everyone is gung-ho on the media strategy, however. As Ed Wolff, vp-merchandising for the Secaucus, N.J.-based Panasonic Display Group, conceded: "It's very hard to show [the benefits of HDTV] in TV commercials that show the picture. You can say 'We're cutting edge, digital, flat' . . . Those messages get them interested and have them come to the store."

How can consumer electronics marketers get TV viewers hooked on the medium? "That's the most important question in the industry," said analyst Jones. "For wealthier consumers, they can stress styling," he suggested. "For the mass market, that doesn't work. They have to stress quality enhancements, which is an uphill battle."

But opportunities do exist to target the technology to specific consumer groups. Other than placing ads in magazines like *Sports Illustrated,* for example, marketers have yet to aggressively court sports fans, who are a natural audience for HDTV.

Catering To The In-Crowd: A swanky HDTV floor display is a focal point at high-end retailer Bang & Olufsen.

With the sports market, the benefits—and potential sales—are huge. Because of HDTV's wide-screen format (16 x 9), viewers can see an entire basketball court, as opposed to the half court they're accustomed to. In football, both the entire offensive and defensive teams are in full view, not just a portion of the playing field. Tennis fans could go so far as to hear the echoes emanating from the cavernous Arthur Ashe Stadium—and discern the texture of the strings on Pete Sampras' racquet—when CBS aired a high definition broadcast of the 2002 U.S. Open from Flushing Meadow, N.Y.

"This spring, ESPN is planning to start an HDTV simulcast network in which it will air 100 telecasts of baseball, NBA and NHL games," said John Consoli, who covers the emerging HDTV market for *Mediaweek.* "Once people sample that, I believe, it is going to spur sports fans to go out and start buying HDTV sets."

A Clearer (Retail) Picture

Unlike a Walkman or a CD player, there is a steep educational curve required to make an informed purchase of an HDTV set. Until the technology reaches critical mass, retailers will be called upon to aid marketers in developing an effective sales pitch.

So far, it's been a bumpy road. Even at electronics-heavy chains like Best Buy and Circuit City, sales staff must follow the same learning curve as shoppers. Plus, stores have encountered difficulty receiving the digital signals for their HDTV displays.

Many retailers are now enlisting their employees in training sessions. Best Buy, for example, conducts in-store training and sends out information about new products through its *Retail Weekly* internal publication, while also posting news on its intranet. What consumers can expect in terms of expertise varies from store to store. A P.C. Richard outlet in Paramus, N.J., for example, has made strides with its training program, which includes mandatory seminars for all employees.

Noted Dave Zapfel, product manager for the high-end electronics equipment maker Bang & Olufsen, "We have training sessions regionally. We take about half a day to discuss the concept of what [HDTV] is, what's different about it." For the launch of its BeoVision 5 plasma-screen TV at the end of last year, B&O hosted in-store viewing parties featuring movie clips, even serving customers wine and cheese.

Specialty retailers, such as the Good Guys chain, will be key to speeding adoption of the new technology. "Specialty retailers have been going out of their way [to demonstrate HDTVs], creating living room type settings, complete with a couch and coffee table, so people can watch them," said Spiwak. "I'm not sure how successful those efforts have been, since price plays a big role. If people can get a better price at Wal-Mart [which recently began offering HDTVs], they'll go to Wal-Mart. Although I have my doubts about them right now."

Still, Spiwak warned, as big discounters get into the game, it poses a serious threat to smaller chains' position. "Ultimate Electronics and Tweeter have been reporting abysmal sales, with people cutting back on purchase of HDTVs," he said. "The Wal-Mart factor might be playing a role. I was surprised to see Wal-Mart pick up on it so soon."

Toshiba's distribution strategy has been to position its top-of-the-line digital items at smaller stores that have the personnel to explain HDTV's benefits, leaving more everyday items to mass-market players.

"Our Cinema Series [HDTV] line is more complicated," said Scott Ramirez, vp-marketing for Toshiba America Consumer Electronics, Irvine, Calif. "It has more features, and those features need explaining. Our standard sets have wider distribution."

Manufacturers often stress they are assisting in the educational process by guiding retailers through manuals and devoting special HDTV links on their Web sites.

To get consumers to bite, Philips has also been dangling zero-percent financing, free Blockbuster movie rentals and a free Digital Home Theater System. Such perks are "a very important tie-breaker at retail," said Mike Keel, director of advertising for Philips. "True innovators and earlier adopters want and need to be first on their block. These are primarily males who want to have the newest gadgets. We're all chasing their wallets."

Looking to cash in on a sports tie-in with its retailers, Samsung recently partnered with Sears, CBS and Echostar for "Game Day," a promotion during which shoppers could come to Sears on a Saturday between September and December to see a live NCAA basketball or football game.

"We want the consumer to come in and see what a live college sport event looks like on [high definition]," said Steve Panosian, senior marketing manager for Samsung Electronics America, based in Ridgefield Park, N.J. Samsung offers extended financing, while Sears separately offered a free DVD player or stand with purchase. Other retailer incentives have included free delivery, a gift with purchase (e.g., TiVo) and rebates on consumers' first year of high definition cable service.

Some industry observers aren't sure the enticements will work. "A consumer purchasing an expensive HDTV, even if you throw in a little goody, is still going to balk if the price is too high," said Spiwak, particularly in the current economic climate, which has discouraged discretionary spending.

That bottom-line thinking, most analysts agree, will continue to motivate buyers and ultimately determine the future of this still-unproven category.

"Price has to come down so dramatically that the value is there," said Tom Edwards, an analyst with The NPD Group in Port Washington, N.Y. "Look at [what's happened] with products like DVD players. I've seen toasters that are higher priced."

Indeed, consumers may think they have witnessed this pattern before. Quickly becoming a commodity, DVD units plummeted from an average of $550 in 1997 to $190 last year, and are now available for as little at $60, per The Yankee Group.

For HDTV makers, the question is: How long will average buyers sit on the sidelines while their neighbors take the plunge?

"While more people are willing to buy larger-screen TVs . . . they are probably still not educated enough about the benefits of high definition to be willing to pay significantly more for a TV with a smaller screen," offered Mediaweek's Consoli. "Many people are willing to pay $800 or $900 for a 36- or 42-inch analog TV, but unless they have actually seen a high definition telecast, most are probably not ready to spend $1,700 and up on an HDTV with only a 30-inch screen."

They may not have to. At Tweeter Home Entertainment Group, a 170-unit chain based in Canton, Mass., prices continue to fall. A top-of-the-line Pioneer Pro1000HD Plasma TV, for example, has dropped from $20,000 to $12,000. "There are price drops every month on all models," said Noah Herschman, vp-video merchandising. The digital TV business has been so brisk for Tweeter that "we don't really carry anything that's analog anymore," he said.

More and more, it looks like the pieces of the HDTV puzzle are starting to fall into place. Just last week, eight more TV stations announced they have begun transmitting digitally, bringing the total to 700, more than half in the U.S. Soon, purchasers will be able to receive high definition programming as easily as they now can with their analog set, as the new HDTV-ready units will no longer need a separate box to receive digital broadcasts.

To check all this out, I head down to a local Circuit City, where an eager salesperson spots me eyeing the new HDTVs. I rattle off a list of questions and he shakes his head. "You don't need an antenna or tuner," he said. "They're just making it complicated so you buy more stuff. Just buy the TV."

"Tuning into HDTV: Coming into Focus," *Brandweek*, January 13, 2003, pp. 20–24.

Twilight Of the CD? Not if It Can Be Reinvented

BY LAURA M. HOLSON

Tonight in Manhattan, rock stars, divas and rappers will descend en masse on Madison Square Garden, arriving at the Grammy ceremonies in a parade of glamour and attitude. But the excitement they create will only mask the growing anxiety in the recording industry about the future of its fundamental product, the CD, which is threatened with the same obsolescence that it long ago foisted on the LP and then the tape cassette.

Introduced in the United States 20 years ago, the CD is losing its allure. From 2001 to 2002, some 62.5 million fewer of them were sold—a decline of 9 percent to 649.5 million, according to Nielsen SoundScan. Online swapping of songs is growing at a crippling rate, forcing almost every corner of the music industry to try to divine exactly what role, if any, the CD will play in a future dominated by Internet delivery and competition from popular new technologies like the DVD.

Most analysts and industry executives agree that selling music online is the future. But they say it will take at least two years for companies to devise a business plan for it that makes financial sense. In the meantime, the CD will remain the biggest source of revenue for both music retailers and recording companies, who will try to squeeze as much profit as they can out of each and every sale.

As a result, the CD is being rethought, repackaged and, in some cases, repriced.

Experiments to resuscitate this ailing product are growing. In January, Bon Jovi created a compact disc, with eight previously unreleased songs, exclusively for **Target** stores. Priced at $6.99, it was intended to help bolster sales of other Bon Jovi albums, including the newest, "Bounce."

Best Buy, the No. 1 electronics chain in the country, is selling prepaid cards good for 10 downloads that allow consumers to create compilations to play either on discs or on computers. And last year, the Interscope recording label gave a DVD to the first million buyers of "The Eminem Show" as an incentive to buy the CD.

All this is happening as the economic underpinnings of the CD continue to deterioriate, endangering the music business altogether. With the rising popularity of online music, much of it available free, technology-wise teenagers, the industry's most voracious buyers, can easily use CD-burning technology to make bootleg copies and sell them at school for as little as $1.

Companies are showing signs of cracking. Two industry veterans have recently lost their jobs: Thomas D. Mottola, the head of **Sony Music Entertainment,** which lost more than $132 million last year; and Jay Boberg, president of **MCA Records.** The music retailer **Wherehouse Entertainment** announced in January that it was filing for bankruptcy protection, partly because of lackluster sales. And the **EMI Group,** based in London, the only major music company that is not a part of a media conglomerate, is struggling with debt and is believed by analysts to be considering merger prospects.

"Large companies tend to wait until they feel pain to act," said Dan Hart, chief executive of Echo, a recently formed consortium of retailers that hope to sell music online. "Now they feel pain."

Doug Morris, chief executive of the Universal Music Group, said: "We are definitely in the middle of a transition. It was always a packaged-goods business, but that is changing. We are slowly moving forward."

Compact disc sales have slipped for several reasons, not all of them related to piracy or online music swapping. Critics complain that there is a dearth of blockbuster acts these days and that those with hits, like Britney Spears, often have short-lived careers. And with the average price of a compact disc at $14.21, they contend that music is simply too expensive for frequent purchases.

But Hilary B. Rosen, chief executive of the Recording Industry Association of America, countered that a recent study by the association found that only 3 percent of the consumers polled said they were buying less music because prices were too high.

Still, there is no question that other activities are taking up listeners' time, thanks to the growth of electronic games and multichannel cable and satellite television. Perhaps most threatening is the popularity of the DVD, which emerged in the mid-1990's. By 1999, DVD players had gained mass-market appeal, and they now cost as little as $50, about the same price as a portable boom box. In some retail stores, DVD sales have surpassed those of CD's.

"The DVD is moving into the bedrooms of the next generation of young kids," said Gary L. Arnold, senior vice president for entertainment at Best Buy, which announced in January that it was closing 107 stores. The next generation of young people has no affinity for the compact disc. For them, he said, "it's about gaming and PlayStation."

To thwart online swapping, several music companies, including Sony and Universal, have experimented with copy-protected compact discs, much to the ire of paying consumers, who complain that they cannot listen to some of those discs on their computers.

(Cont.)

The industry does not use a standard copy-protected format, so consumers do not know what kind of disc they are buying. Fearing a consumer backlash, the industry has slowed down those copy-protection efforts.

Software makers are trying to come up with alternatives that address the needs of both consumers and recording companies. At a recent music conference in Cannes, France, **Microsoft** said it had developed technology to allow music companies to record two sets of identical songs on a compact disc, one that could be played on a home or car stereo and the other, called second session, that could be copied to a personal computer. The second-session songs would have limitations, perhaps barring consumers from sharing files or copying songs onto another disc.

Recording companies probably placed too much hope on super audio CD's, which are said to have superior sound compared with regular CD's. The technology, introduced two years ago, has not taken off because super audio CD's cost nearly four times as much to buy as regular CD's—and they require a special machine to experience the full impact.

And super audios, championed by Sony and **Philips,** are not alone in offering sound quality that surpasses that of the typical CD: a dueling new technology in DVD audio, supported by **Panasonic** and **Pioneer,** is setting up a battle reminiscent of the VHS-Betamax wars.

Until all these new technologies are sorted out, recording companies and retailers are betting on promotions and marketing deals to increase sales. Bruce Kirkland, a member of Bon Jovi's management team, said the album that Bon Jovi put together for Target had also increased sales of the "Bounce" album in its stores. In the first week of the promotion, Target's share of the market for "Bounce" for all retail stores jumped to 26.1 percent from 15.9 percent, he said.

"I think the onus is on the retailers to take care of this because the recording companies always shoot themselves in the foot," Mr. Kirkland said.

Mr. Arnold of Best Buy said he believed that DVD's could well replace the CD in the future because they play not only music but also video images. In the last 12 months, sales of DVD's have surpassed those of compact discs at Best Buy, he said.

But before they can become a new industry standard, he added, they will have to more adeptly meld music and video.

Music distributors and retailers, battered by the slump in compact disc sales, are embarking on their own efforts to give consumers more and easily accessible music. Last month, six music retailers, including major outlets like Best Buy, Wherehouse and **Tower Records,** said they would form the Echo consortium to sell music on the Internet through their retail Web sites. As recently as a year ago, that would have been unthinkable, as retailers and music companies were at odds about how best to tackle online distribution.

The compact disk could join the LP in the dustbin of technology.

In another joint effort, **Anderson Merchandisers,** one of the largest magazine and music distributors in the United States, bought technology from **Liquid Audio,** an online music pioneer that distributes 350,000 songs through retailers, in the hope of exploiting the growth in digital music.

"It has not been the norm that retailers should be the ones helping us rethink our business," said John Esposito, president of United States distribution for the Warner Music Group. "But retailers are telling us the current model does not work."

Best Buy has been one of the most active retailers in this regard. It recently began testing a program in 30 stores that allowed consumers to buy a card with a preset value that could be used to buy downloads to a computer or disc. Scott Young, vice president for digital distribution at Best Buy, said the experiment had had limited success and was under review.

Mr. Hart of Echo said retailers would primarily seek to sell downloads over their Web sites that consumers could call up from their homes. But as well as selling digital downloads, partners of Echo are likely to explore several options, including the use of store kiosks where consumers can make personalized compact discs.

Such a venture, like any in the digital music world, is fraught with risk. In 1999, Sony Music Entertainment tried a similar strategy but consumers did not respond, analysts said.

There are, of course, other problems facing distributors and retailers, most notably acquiring the rights to distribute whole catalogs of music online. The music companies faced that issue early on, when starting their own Web sites. Competing companies declined to offer all their music on both PressPlay, a joint venture of Sony Music and Universal Music, and MusicNet, which was formed by Warner Music, EMI and **BMG.** It took months for them to begin sharing music, leaving consumers disillusioned and frustrated.

For all of these ventures, companies will still have to grapple with why consumers would pay for music they can easily get free. One major retailer, according to a music executive, has suggested to several recording companies that it might put a cap on the price of any compact disc it sold in its stores. Only a store like **Wal-Mart** would have the strength the pull that off, he added.

"I think the biggest problem is, the industry doesn't know how to get started and take steps where you get an incremental gain," said Phil Leigh, a digital media analyst at Raymond James & Associates in Tampa, Fla. "If compact disc sales continue to drop and there is no increase in online sales, then artists will be mad and your bosses are mad, too. There is an old expression that pioneers are the ones with arrows in their backs. The one thing executives don't get paid for is rocking the boat."

Hello, tech designers? This stuff is too small

Fingers fumble with tiny buttons, eyes squint at minuscule screens

By Jefferson Graham
USA Today

PALO ALTO, Calif. — We've gotten used to phones with tiny buttons and screens, digital cameras the dimensions of an Altoids tin and smaller, and music players the size of our two middle fingers.

Projects still in the lab promise even more minuscule products: cellphones worn like rings, digital cameras hanging from our neck like a pendant.

But how will we operate such marvels? We struggle with what we own today. Our fingers are already too thick and clumsy to stab the buttons on our gadgets, and, as our eyes age, we squint even harder to see the shrinking screens on our stuff.

"I carry my cellphone with me everywhere I go, which is a convenience," says Bill Kircher, 56, a lawyer in Irvine, Calif. "The downside is I can't see the damn thing to dial, or look up a number at night, even with back lighting. After a few attempts with my digital camera, I gave up. I would've had to have a pair of reading glasses to operate it, and it wasn't worth the trouble. What are these people thinking?"

Ask tech designers, the folks who dream up these things, in the Bay Area where many of these devices are spawned. They say it's easy to criticize one product; that's why different models are available.

"There's no such thing as 'one size fits all,' " Sony designer Andy Proehl says.

Ever-smaller cellphones, for example, are "what people desire," product designer Dennis Boyle says. He works for Ideo, a premier design lab responsible for everything from the first consumer computer mouse to the Palm V PDA.

The ring-phone concept is his creation—a receiver on one finger, a speaker on another and a wireless transmitter on the belt. "Technologically, something like this is capable now. You don't have to carry it in your pocket, and it would always be with you," he says. In general, "thin and small is the Holy Grail, because now there are no impediments for taking it everywhere. Where's the limit? No one knows."

In one hand he holds an 8-inch black mobile phone from 1988—complete with a coil that attached to a separate in-car receiver. In the other, he has a new flip phone at a hair under 4 inches. "Look at how far we've come," Boyle says. "Things getting this small may seem ridiculous at first, but people have an amazing ability to adapt."

Perhaps. But as the gadget-buying population of the USA grays and the rush to miniaturization accelerates, the disconnect sometimes seems to be widening between what designers believe we want and what we find we can comfortably use.

Take the Palm PDA, which later this year will appear on the screen of a Fossil watch. The $199 time tool will push the limits of the human eye. People who may have strained to check appointments, addresses and directions on a standard 2-inch square Palm display will face a 1-inch screen.

Focus on fashion:
A necklace camera has an eye on portability.

'The rest of us are irrelevant'

The concept "shows total contempt for the majority of consumers," says usability guru Jakob Nielsen of the consulting firm Nielsen Norman Group. "They have these young, hotshot engineers and designers; they don't have vision problems and don't believe anyone does. To them, all that matters is cool teenagers, and the rest of us are irrelevant."

Nielsen says people believe that the vision problem lies with them. "The fact is, everybody, like clockwork, when they reach 40, gets this way. We have to demand that technology adapt to human biology, not the other way around."

Technology, of course, has some answers.

Jeff Parrish, the manager of user experience at Palmsource, the software arm of Palm Computing,

(Cont.)

says that, because he's 49, "I'm sensitive to this issue." He says screens are about to get a great deal easier to see, thanks to a technology known as organic light emitting diodes, or OLEDs.

Unlike LCD screens, which can lack clarity and are tough to see from some angles, OLEDs are brighter, have higher contrast and are viewable from any angle.

"They are expensive, and there are power issues, but OLEDs are the next step," says Tim Parsey of cellphone maker Motorola. The screens offer "a richer, deeper color."

For the time being, Parrish points out, anyone who squints at Palm screens can call on many tools to make it easier. An $11 program called Teal Magnify enlarges the type; a $30 magnifying glass available in stores from Officeonthego clips onto Palm units.

> **Wee watch:**
> The Wrist PDA with Palm OS has an illuminated touch screen with a stylus integrated into the band. The screen is 1-inch square.

BIGGER, CLEARER SELLS BETTER

Of course, a bigger screen to start would help. Sony's Proehl and his team recently designed the new top-of-the-line $800 Clie PDA that has been winning raves here for taking a different approach to PDAs. Beyond the standard organizer functions, the device has an MP3 music player, a photo viewer, a keyboard and a digital camera.

But notably, the unit has the largest screen of any Palm device—3 by 2 inches, in color, compared with Sony's $129 entry-level model with a 2-inch-square black-and-white screen.

Sony's PDA customers have said clarity and color matter most to them. Manufacturers had a dismal year, with PDA sales falling 9%. No. 1-ranked Palm was down 10.4%, and No. 3 Hewlett-Packard/Compaq dropped 45%. But sales at No. 2 Sony, known for its brighter displays, more than quadrupled, says analyst Todd Kort of research firm GartnerG2.

"Palm is losing the upgrade market to Sony," he says. "When you walk into a Best Buy and see the PDAs lined up, Sony has these beautiful displays. If you watch, people all migrate to the products with the better color."

Though Sony has profited by emphasizing vision in PDAs, it has just gone in the opposite direction for digital photography with what appears to be one of the smallest cameras ever, about the width and height of a business card.

Some mini-cameras eliminate the viewing screen, but Sony's U-20 hits a new low with a 1-inch viewing area, a third smaller than the norm. "I don't see how anyone could compose a shot without using a microscope," sniffs Jon Sienkiewicz of competitor Minolta.

Kodak and Kyocera are going in the other direction: Both announced models this week with 2½-inch viewing screens.

'ALL THUMBS' KEYBOARD TAPPING

Our fingers also are getting a readjustment on ultra-miniature keyboards. The Handspring Treo, a combination phone and PDA, was first designed without a keyboard. But Handspring founder Jeff Hawkins said the letters and numbers were vital to its operation, so he included a tiny qwerty keyboard. He says it takes getting used to, "but once people start using them, they can't imagine going back."

Research in Motion's popular Blackberry e-mail pager has proven just that, even though its Lilliputian keyboard sits under an equally tiny screen. "When that came out, people laughed," says Boyle, who teaches product design at Stanford University. "No way anyone could type on something that small. But now nearly 500,000 people use it, and I assure you no one's laughing."

The process, also used on the Clie and the Treo, is called thumb typing. You hold the unit with both hands and use both thumbs to hunt and peck a quick response.

This form of typing is hugely popular in Asia and Europe, where short message service communication—tapping out instant messages on the tiny buttons of cellphones—is as common as instant messaging in the USA. "Something similar will take off here as people get more used to it," Proehl says.

> **Talk to the hand:**
> When you get a call on the Penta Phone, your pinkie finger ring vibrates, and the thumb ring beams the sound toward your ear.

"It took me all of two hours to master it," says Blackberry fan Alex Pournelle of Pasadena, Calif., who works in the special-events industry and has his device attached to his belt. "It's won the 'cold dead fingers' award for me. That's the only way anyone will be able to take it away from me."

The idea of typing on the fly is so popular, Hawkins says, that in coming years "half of all phones

(Cont.)

will have keyboards. For e-mail and messaging, you really need it."

Other phone makers are experimenting with ditching buttons entirely. Samsung's new $500 phone/PDA gives users a larger screen, with a virtual dial pad that appears when you need to make a call. Or you can dial by just saying the numbers into the phone or by tapping names in the address book.

Unlike Boyle, Motorola's Parsey believes cell-phones probably won't get much smaller, only slimmer. "Small for the sake of small has run out," he says. "The opportunity now is (to) understand that miniaturization means working with thickness, (not) width or height."

Then again, Boyle's and Parsey's teams dream up "concept" devices that may one day reach stores. Besides ring phones and necklace cameras, they've unveiled such possibilities as toe rings with global positioning circuitry (presumably to point your feet in the right direction) and hooded sweatshirts with built-in speakers for music.

"All trends point to us wearing our computers and communication," Boyle says. "That's coming closer to reality every day."

Of course, then we'll have problems fitting into our gadgets.

Nokia's Hit Factory

The cell-phone giant's unorthodox research-and-development machine has cranked out innovation after innovation, thanks to an eccentric leader known as Mr. Advice.

By Paul Kaihla

Yrjö Neuvo's name is tricky to pronounce, even for fellow Finns, so let's just call him Mr. Advice. That's a literal translation of his surname, and slyly fitting for a former university professor. On a recent Sunday at a remote farmhouse on Finland's south coast, Mr. Advice's face is flushed and sweaty. Clad in Kevlar overalls, he has just chainsawed down an ash tree the size of a telephone pole. His wife is feeding branches into a bonfire. Mr. Advice begins enthusing about his hobby of collecting farm tractors. He proudly shows off a 13-horsepower Chinese job. Without explanation, he fires up a second model, a green beast with a hinged body that looks like a giant insect. He talks a reluctant visitor into taking the controls. "Turn here!" he commands with a wave.

The term "nutty professor" may be coming to mind about now. But there is a lot more going on at this little house on the tundra than at first meets the eye. Neuvo is always trying to figure out how to get people to try something new, anything new. It could be getting a stranger to ride a tractor. Or it could be getting greenhorn engineers to ponder wild avenues of thought that lead to revolutionary cell-phone innovations—which, as it happens, Mr. Advice has done, repeatedly. Neuvo is the humble, if eccentric, technologist who heads research and development at Nokia (NOK), arguably the best product-driven R&D organization in the world.

Nokia's R&D apparatus is unlike anything in multinational corporate history. Most large-scale R&D operations are centralized, hierarchical, no-nonsense—science as brute force. Nokia's 18,000 engineers, designers, and sociologists are scattered across the globe and form a kind of federation of rule-breaking, risk-taking hackers. Most of them answer not to countless layers of managers but to Neuvo, who considers it his missionary duty to break down his people's mental inhibitions, freeing their minds to roam toward the next big breakthrough. "We operate the way a great jazz band plays," Neuvo says. "There is a leader, and each member is playing the same piece, but they can improvise on the theme."

That approach has made some beautiful music for Nokia. Since Neuvo took over Nokia R&D, its engineers have churned out an unmatched string of technical firsts: the first mass-market cell phone with the antenna on the inside, the first one-chip phone, the first compact battery with long-lasting power. Breakthrough features mean hot phones, and no competitor has come close to equaling Nokia's record of monster product hits—it has had half a dozen models that sold as much as 50 times the company's own internal projections. That run has enabled Nokia to amass a 38 percent share of the cell-phone market, roughly equal to that of its four biggest competitors combined. A decade ago, Nokia was close to bankruptcy; now it's closing in on $30 billion in annual sales. It makes the vast majority of the profits generated by the entire mobile-phone industry.

The Big Winners

Phone model	Year released	Unit sales (in millions)
101	1992	12
2100	1994	20
5100	1998	100+
3200	1999	45*
8200	1999	35
3300	2000	70+

*Europe only. SOURCE: Industry estimates

Of course, that's not as big a deal as it once was. The cell-phone business has been hammered; Nokia's stock has fallen 70 percent during the past two years. And the company's freewheeling R&D approach has produced some duds. Still, Mr. Advice seems to have pulled off one of the trickiest balancing acts an R&D chief can achieve: unleashing the combined creative energy of thousands of engineers without being swamped by anarchy.

* * * * * * *

Nokia, headquartered just outside Finland's capital of Helsinki, has a storied history. The company was founded in 1865 as a forest products concern and went through many reinventions on its way to becoming a consumer electronics conglomerate. The most radical came in 1992,when Nokia decided to shed everything except a business that at the time represented only 10 percent of the company: mobile communications.

(Cont.)

When Neuvo came to Nokia in 1993 from the electrical engineering faculty at Finland's University of Tampere, Motorola (MOT) and Ericsson (ERICY) were the engineering heavyweights of the wireless world. Ericsson was outspending Nokia on R&D by a 5-to-1 ratio. Nokia was seen as an upstart that got by on thinly engineered fad phones. Neuvo seemed an unlikely choice to blast Nokia forward: He's a lanky, soft-spoken man, described even by friends as unprepossessing and vaguely odd. He still carries the same kind of briefcase he lugged around campus, a leather satchel that resembles a doctor's bag. It's crammed with gadgets like cell-phone speakers, as well as a tool kit he uses "to fix certain things if they are broken—somebody's eyeglasses or computer parts." A multimillionaire, he rides his bike to work every day, even in the fierce Finnish winter.

Nokia had already begun to disperse its R&D operations before Neuvo arrived. In the traditional corporate model, R&D is centralized and manufacturing is distributed. Siemens, for instance, directs most of its research out of a single huge complex in Munich. Nokia, by contrast, lets teams at 69 sites—from Boston to Bangalore, India—run their own projects. Nokia has far less R&D hierarchy than its competitors do, says Lauri Rosendahl, Deutsche Bank's Nokia analyst. "That's why freaky ideas from junior engineers can end up in a product rather quickly," he says.

The bare bones of Nokia's distributed R&D system may have existed when Neuvo arrived, but he put the meat on them. One of his first steps was to drastically accelerate the expansion of R&D sites, while keeping the teams within them small. His reasoning is simple: The smothering influence of the home office can lead to tunnel vision. "If you just have R&D campuses around headquarters, you might become what we call 'home blind,'" Neuvo says. "You need to have your finger in the wind in many places" to fuel the imagination. Colleagues say he used his international academic connections like an intelligence network to cherry-pick acquisitions ranging from hot startups to R&D sites that other companies had put on the block, as well as to identify rising young talent. In three to four years, Neuvo's division had tripled in size; today it's eight times bigger than when he started.

But Neuvo's crucial achievement was to infuse his burgeoning operation with a hacker spirit, to make his staff, as he puts it, "challenge and not shrink from making mistakes." Building that kind of a culture isn't easy. It helped that, in Finland, Neuvo is an engineering legend, an inspirational figure whose research in digital signal processing brought him international renown. He kept himself close to his engineers and waged daily warfare against hierarchy (in Nokia as a whole, there are only three layers of decision-making between the most junior engineer and the president of the company). Neuvo constantly prowls the far-flung R&D labs, prodding engineers to be audacious in pursuit of their scientific muse, and makes it clear that no idea is too harebrained to receive a hearing. Neuvo "is a techno-freak who is always crossing the line," says Erkki Kuisma, a veteran Nokia engineer. "He encourages people to do crazy things if they believe their crazy idea is right."

Kuisma knows this firsthand. In 1996 he came up with what at first seemed like a truly crazy idea: removing the antenna from the cell phone and hiding it inside the device. Kuisma, whose official assignment at the time was to conduct radio frequency research, had kicked around internal antenna specs with a couple of colleagues. He brought it up with Neuvo at the Helsinki airport while the two were on a business trip; Neuvo's eyes lit up. In no time, Kuisma was in his basement at home, cutting the aerial off an existing 1611 GSM phone and patching the

FIVE WAYS TO UNLEASH INNOVATION

1 DON'T LOCATE ALL YOUR R&D IN A SINGLE PLACE, ESPECIALLY IF IT'S NEAR THE SMOTHERING INFLUENCE OF HEADQUARTERS. DISPERSE IT AROUND THE GLOBE.

2 KEEP TEAMS SMALL—NO LARGER THAN 50 IF POSSIBLE—AND GIVE INDIVIDUAL ENGINEERS AND THEIR MANAGERS A LOT OF POWER AND AUTONOMY.

3 FLATTEN HIERARCHY AND STAY AS CLOSE AS POSSIBLE TO YOUR ENGINEERS. HIERARCHY DISSIPATES ENERGY.

4 ENCOURAGE ENGINEERS TO GENERATE CRAZY NEW IDEAS OUTSIDE THEIR OFFICIAL WORK ASSIGNMENTS BY CELEBRATING SECRET TINKERING AND SIDE PROJECTS—AND GET INNOVATIONS INTO PRODUCTION WITH ROCKET SPEED.

5 WELCOME MISTAKES. IF YOU'RE NOT MAKING THEM, YOU'RE NOT PUSHING THE ENVELOPE HARD ENOUGH.

(Cont.)

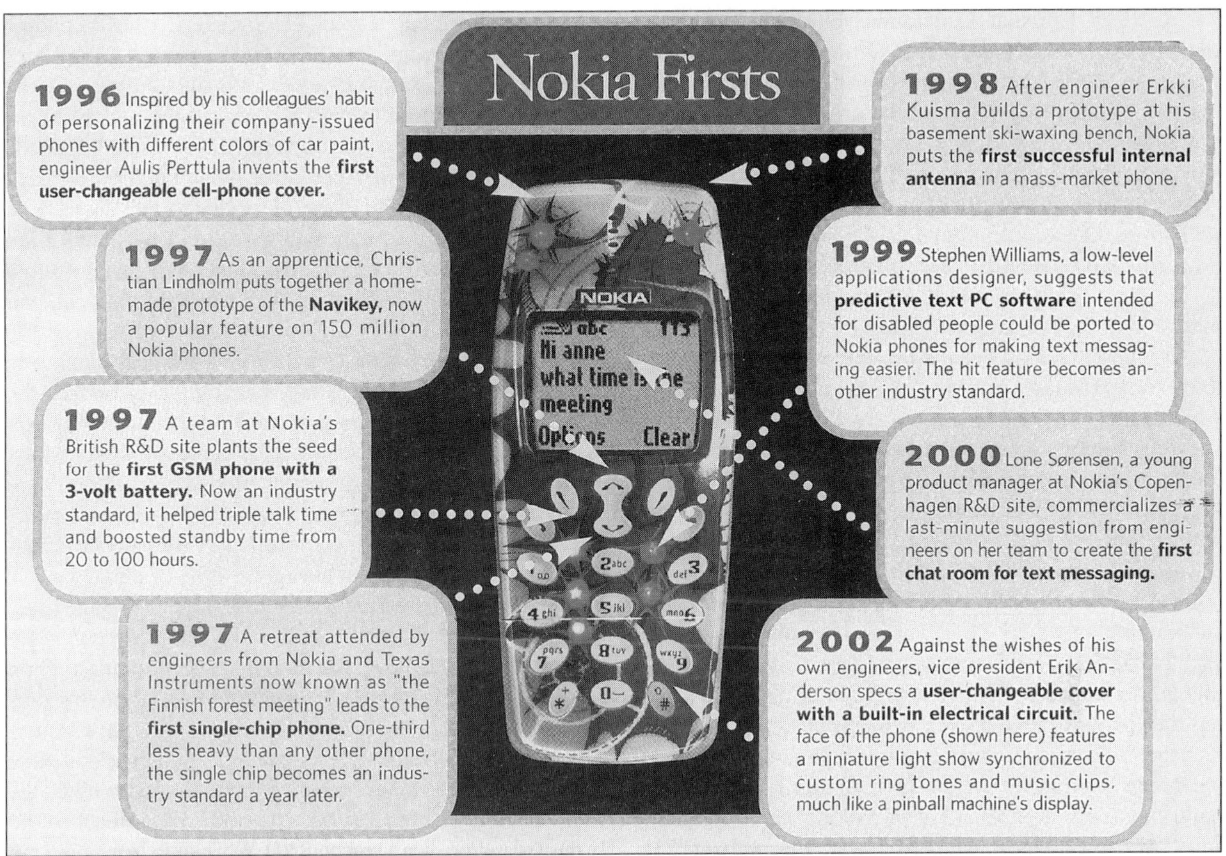

hole by remolding the plastic casing after melting it with a blow-dryer he uses for waxing cross-country skis. Kuisma fashioned an antenna from a square piece of copper tape and inserted it beneath the phone's back plate.

The idea immediately hit resistance. Some Nokia executives were afraid customers would assume that a phone without a visible antenna wouldn't be powerful enough. But Neuvo began showing Kuisma's prototype to top Nokia executives, pinning them in lobbies and meetings, putting his personal credibility on the line. That's what Neuvo does when he believes his engineers are on to something, and he has one advantage from his days as a professor. More than 100 of his former students work at Nokia—including the president of the mobile-phone division (Neuvo was his master's thesis adviser). If he finds an executive who needs more convincing, Neuvo lets the engineers do the talking. "What counts for a lot in this company is how committed the engineers themselves are," explains Erik Anderson, a close Neuvo colleague and head of two of Nokia's largest R&D sites. "We tell the engineer, 'Go sell this guy.' We pick the key people, and we aim the engineer like a missile."

In Kuisma's case, Neuvo put him through an exhaustive coaching session about how to make the pitch to doubters, like a thesis adviser would with a student doing an oral defense. Thus prepped, Kuisma won the day, and his internal antenna debuted in 1998 in Nokia's 8800 series "luxury phone," the model that was famously launched on haute couture runways rather than at wireless industry trade shows. It became one of the most profitable products in Nokia history, with gross margins of 70 to 80 percent. The internal antenna was quickly imitated by competitors—a point of great pride for Neuvo, and validation that Nokia had closed the engineering gap.

* * * * * * *

Many of the other pioneering features in Nokia phones similarly bubbled up from the culture of uninhibited dabbling Neuvo has fostered. Nokia's signature Navikey, the user interface that radically reduced the number of buttons above a phone's keypad by combining three of them into a single fat bar, is regarded as one of the great design innovations in cell-phone history. It was sketched out by a 28-year-old Nokia apprentice during his first few weeks on the job.

(Cont.)

In 1995, Christian Lindholm, who was still finishing his master's degree in economics and had never worked in telecom before, was assigned to a group studying user interfaces. He started tinkering on his own. "I was just talking to myself—'Let's get rid of some keys, and make the keypad more universally intuitive,'" he recalls. Lindholm and another young newcomer created 10 prototypes. One of them found its way to Neuvo; he wasn't particularly focused on user interfaces at the time, but he seized on Lindholm's idea. "It was a radical technical innovation," Neuvo says with relish.

Lindholm hadn't been at the company long enough to even meet Neuvo, but Mr. Advice immediately began working the corridors and company cafeteria, excitedly showing senior colleagues what Lindholm's interface could do, and improvising new ways to use it. Within a year, the Navikey was on the market, wowing consumers with its ease of use. Navikey-equipped models like the low-end 5100 and 6100 became huge blockbusters, making the Navikey one of the company's most important subbrands.

Nokia takes flat hierarchy and free-range engineering culture so seriously that some innovations have gotten into phones without even being approved by senior managers. For new features that involve modest risk and resources, product managers have authority to simply build them into a phone. One of Nokia's current rising stars is Lone Sørensen, who at the age of 24 was put in charge of Nokia's 3310, a phone that has sold more than 70 million units since its release two years ago. She slapped a program into a phone that allows users to send text messages to each other in a chat room—another mobile industry first. She cooked up the feature as a secret side project, and added it to the phone at the last minute without consulting her nominal boss, Anderson. "It just shows up," Anderson says with a shrug. "If you try to pay an organization to work full-time coming up with ideas like this, you won't get it. You need some jackass down in R&D who just says, 'Hey, let's do this.'"

* * * * * * *

Sometimes, though, a jackass is just a jackass. Neuvo's long leash means there's tremendous potential for some lightly supervised project to go off the rails. It seems to have happened with Nokia's 5510 MP3 phone, introduced last fall amid much trumpeting. The phone, which allows users to listen to FM radio and play MP3s, has proved too bulky and too expensive, and Nokia is quietly pulling it off the market. (Nokia officials concede that the phone is a disappointment but won't elaborate.)

Such screwups, most observers agree, have been relatively rare. But can that last? R&D hot streaks are like hot streaks in other fields: They often spring from a mysterious confluence of good timing, good talent, and good luck, and they can end suddenly. Sometimes the music just stops. At Nokia, keeping the hits coming is complicated by the swirling technological changes the company faces; phones that have dominated the market will soon be rendered obsolete by devices that will allow users to access the Internet at high speeds. There's no guarantee that Nokia—and not, say, Sony, Samsung, or even Microsoft—will come up with the R&D breakthroughs that define the new generation of phones.

Back at his seaside farmhouse, sipping sausage soup, Neuvo is calm about the future and Nokia's place in it. He notes that Nokia now spends roughly $3 billion a year on R&D. While rivals have been cutting R&D spending during the tech slump, Nokia increased R&D outlays 16 percent last year. Neuvo talks about an upcoming phone that will allow users to take a picture and send video clips. It's an advertisement for his distributed approach: The phone's software was written by Nokia engineers in Copenhagen, Dallas, Tokyo, and Finland. Colleagues in Britain designed crucial wireless protocols. The Hong Kong R&D unit came up with the cradles.

But always, Neuvo returns to his deep belief in innovation as art and his faith that if his engineers chase their muse, the breakthroughs will come. "When an artist is really excited and does a sculpture day and night, then he is energized by it, because it's in his hands and he owns it," Neuvo says. "This is how you get art. Our artists aren't just closing their eyes and waiting until the innovation comes. We are innovating all the time."

"Nokia's Hit Factory," *Business 2.0,* August 2002, pp. 66–70.

Place

Buyers seek hard-to-find Tostitos Gold

Ads don't rate highly, but chips fly off shelves

By Theresa Howard
USA TODAY

Tostitos Gold chips went on sale in supermarkets in late December, but many consumers have yet to see them. The new chips have proved so popular, Frito-Lay has had trouble keeping pace with demand.

"The No. 1 consumer complaint right now is that they can't find the product," says Frito spokeswoman, Lynn Markley. "We're running flat-out on making this product."

The chips—thicker, more dip-worthy versions of the Tostitos tortilla chip—are the latest addition to the $1 billion Tostitos brand line.

It's also the latest "innovation" from Frito-Lay, which relies on new products to drive its business. Such products don't mean only new customers for the PepsiCo division. They are often about adding perceived value that can command premium prices—getting existing customers to pay more.

Tostitos Gold represents the premium strategy that Frito-Lay will continue to try to exploit in the coming year. The company will introduce "better for you" organic products and Lays Stax to compete against Pringles.

Such products often require a negligible cost difference to produce—but can command a 40% higher price per pound at retail, according to Morgan Stanley research.

In keeping with the premium strategy, Tostitos Gold is packaged in 12-ounce bags with a suggested retail price of $3.49. Tostitos' regular Restaurant Style chips sell at the same price in 14-ounce bags. Consumers, though, don't seem to mind. Last week, short supplies of the product around the country cost Frito-Lay an estimated $500,000 in sales.

Fueling demand for the new Gold chips has been a pair of celebrity ads by BBDO, New York, which first aired New Year's week, starting with the Tostitos Fiesta Bowl national championship football game.

The ads show how serving the chip that's "extra thick for hearty dips" can inject life to otherwise boring situations.

In one ad, upbeat *Tonight Show* host Jay Leno replaces a ho-hum host at a house party, and the band Smash Mouth replaces a droning organ player.

In another ad, a Shakespeare play gets livelier for viewers when Little Richard appears on stage to sing Shout. Cindy Taylor, host of E's Wild On, appears in both ads.

"The ads appear to be extremely effective in driving consumer trial," says Tom Sebok, managing partner, BBDO, New York. "The ads make a big deal of the uniqueness of the chip and show an understanding of the brand with clear demonstration of product innovation that serves a specific need."

That need: the unbreakable chip.

Tostitos ads chip away at dullness

A weekly look at how much consumers like a major advertising campaign compared with other ads rated by this poll – and how effective they think the ads are in helping to sell the product.

Today's ad

Tostitos Gold

A boring party and dull Shakespearean play get a lift with some help from new Tostitos Gold chips, which are "extra thick for hearty dips." The band Smash Mouth replaces a droning keyboard player at a house party, and an upbeat *Tonight Show* host Jay Leno replaces a boring host who talks about fertilizers. A second ad shows viewers uninterested in an outdoor performance of the slaying of Caesar, but when Little Richard appears on stage with a piano to sing *Shout*, the third act becomes more interesting. Viewers turn their blankets into togas and sing along.

Banish boring: Ads for Tostitos Gold chips use Little Richard, Jay Leno and Smash Mouth to liven up a play and a party.

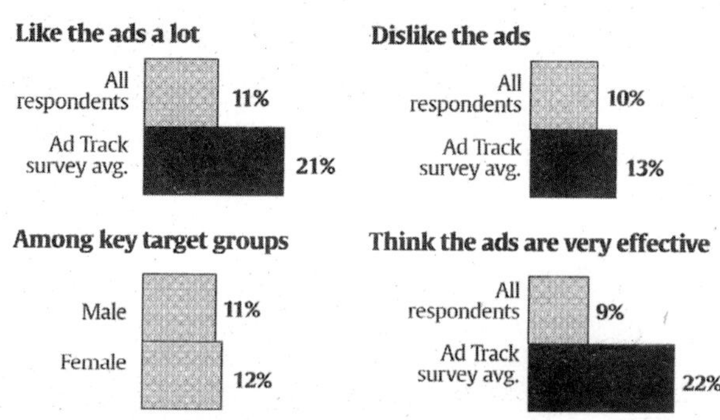

To subscribe to Harris Ad Track Research Service, contact David Krane of Harris Interactive at 212-539-9648. Based on a nationwide poll of 628 adults who had seen the Tostitos Gold ads. Poll was conducted Jan. 21-27; margin of error is ± 4 percentage points. Overall average based on 351 ads.

(Cont.)

Tostitos Gold claims to hold up from plunge to mouth, even when scooping up seven-layer dip.

The latest Tostitos variety continues the brand's quest to offer consumers a specialized chip for nearly every condiment occasion. Restaurant Style and Restaurant Style Hint of Lime offer traditionalists a typically shaped tortilla chip to dunk in their salsa.

The Scoops variety can be filled to make pretty party platters and is also useful where salsa drippage is an issue. Bite Size Rounds are for popping into your mouth.

For the calorie watchers and nutrition label readers, there are Baked Tostitos and Wow (fat substitute) varieties.

Though consumers seem to be going for the Gold, those surveyed by Ad Track, USA TODAY's weekly consumer poll, were less enthusiastic about the ads. Just 11% of those familiar with the campaign like the ads a lot. And only 9% rated the ads "very effective."

The numbers don't faze Frito. "We're seeing robust growth," Markley says. "We're burning on all cylinders. In a good way."

The division was a key driver in pushing PepsiCo's full year 2002 profit up 26% and fourth-quarter profit up 15% compared with the same periods a year ago, in results reported last week. Frito-Lay's sales accounted for 57% of North American revenue for PepsiCo.

PepsiCo also said, along with the earnings announcement, that it would create a "salty" division within Frito-Lay that would focus solely on core salty snack brands, such as Tostitos. It will be led by John Compton, Frito-Lay's former chief marketing officer.

It also said Frito-Lay would be making a major effort this year to further expand its offerings of "convenient foods"—ready-to-go single-serve snacks.

Deflated

How Goodyear Blew Its Chance To Capitalize on a Rival's Woes

Tire Maker Raised Its Prices And Mishandled Dealers—All Amid Firestone Fiasco

Ads Ask, 'Are We There Yet?'

BY TIMOTHY AEPPEL

At Topline Tire & Auto Center in Brooksville, Fla., owner John Wogan thought he'd hit the jackpot when Firestone announced its massive recall nearly three years ago. His store sold mostly Goodyear tires, and with consumers and car makers furiously seeking replacements for Firestone tires, he often placed weekly orders for 300 Goodyear tires to handle the onslaught.

But over and over, Goodyear Tire & Rubber Co. sent him fewer than half the tires he had requested. Mr. Wogan had a frustrating start with the company, which took months just to mount a Goodyear sign on his metal pole out front. Then the Wal-Mart across the street began selling some Goodyear tires for far less than he could afford to. Last year, fed up, he called Firestone. Its new sign was up within days.

At Goodyear, Mr. Wogan says, "they just seem to get caught up with their big-company bureaucracy."

His experience explains much about why one of the nation's oldest and most revered industrial brands is struggling to avoid a blowout. Earlier this month, Goodyear eliminated its dividend for the first time since the Great Depression. Its shares, which traded at \$75 in 1998, fell below \$4, the lowest level in at least four decades. In the days that followed, the century-old tire maker disclosed that it was renegotiating bank loans as it desperately tries to deal with a liquidity crisis that needs to be resolved to avoid bankruptcy proceedings.

What's startling about this mess is that Goodyear squandered an extraordinary opportunity. In the summer of 2000, its main North American rival, Bridgestone Corp.'s Firestone unit, nearly had a credibility meltdown when it had to recall 6.5 million tires linked to fatal accidents, mostly on Ford Explorers. As people scrambled for other brands, Goodyear, the largest tire maker in the U.S., ought to have benefited most. On top of that, Goodyear was selling into the greatest U.S. car-buying binge in recent history. Car sales boomed with the economy in the late 1990s, then were bolstered even in the downturn by cheap financing and big discounts.

But Goodyear misjudged its core customers. The Firestone recall briefly swamped Goodyear with more business than it could handle. It also convinced Goodyear executives that their brand carried a certain cachet and a reassurance of safety for which Americans would pay a premium price. Goodyear executives described the phenomenon as a "flight to quality." But once the Firestone recall fell out of the headlines, the public did what it has increasingly been doing: buying whatever was on sale.

Goodyear's sales deflated, particularly in North America, which accounts for half of Goodyear's roughly \$13.6 billion in revenue. Its North American market share fell last year to 28.4% from nearly 31% in 2001. Japan's Bridgestone Corp., whose market share slipped only about two percentage points to 21% as a consequence of the recall, managed to stem a further decline. It did this in part by launching a massive advertising campaign under the slogan "Making It Right." It also pushed the Bridgestone brand in place of the tainted Firestone name and injected \$1.3 billion in capital into Firestone to help it over the bump. Goodyear's other big overseas competitor, France's Michelin, has seen its 23% share of the North American market hold steady since the Firestone recall.

Robert J. Keegan, 55 years old, who became chief executive last month, denies that Goodyear lost touch with its market amid the Firestone recall. "We always insisted that we look at this as a windfall, that we could not take it for granted as a long-term change," he says. "We didn't have complacency."

He concedes that Goodyear did a poor job listening to its dealers, something he's now pledging to fix. He says there was too much direction flowing out of headquarters in Akron—telling dealers why they should be able to charge more for their tires, for instance—rather than listening to the problems the dealers were encountering on the ground.

Goodyear's biggest mistake appears to be its effort to capitalize on the Firestone recall by raising its prices. Starting in January 2001, Goodyear boosted prices on its passenger and light-truck tires up to 7%, and followed up with another hefty increase the following June. Partly, the company saw itself asserting its right to charge prices closer to those of Michelin, which generally had the highest in the market.

But in the eyes of many customers, Goodyear failed to justify the increases. To charge a premium, a tire maker has to offer some advantage, even if it's just an aura of quality—which Michelin has historically promoted. While it's difficult to measure, Michelin also has a reputation among consumers for safety. The U.S. government sets minimum standards for tire safety, but it doesn't rate the safety of specific brands.

Goodyear's huge \$60 million advertising campaign, launched in 2001, apparently didn't help. In the commercials, parents in different parts of the world—Russia, Tibet and Africa—are shown enduring children whining in their respective native tongues: "Are we there yet?"

"It didn't address the issue that's in the top of the mind of the retail consumer—some combination of price and value," says Tom Geiger Jr. of Capital Tire in Toledo, Ohio, a major Goodyear dealer and distributor for 56 years. "I didn't have people coming in and saying, 'I saw that cute commercial, let me see some of them tires.'"

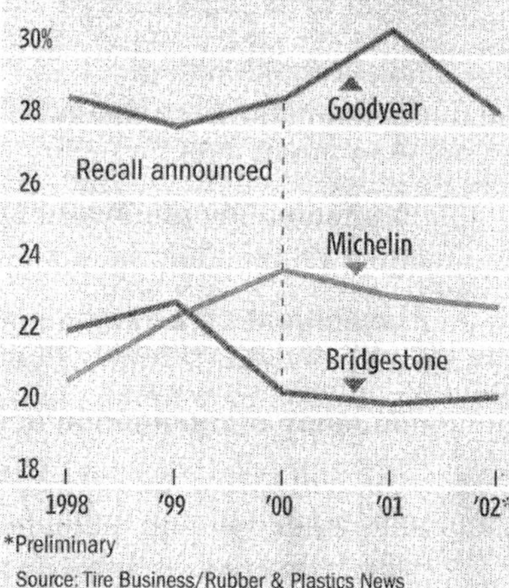

He adds, "Goodyear got this idea of a flight to quality, but when the economy goes south, the flight stops," he says.

In the tire industry, innovations are quickly copied, so it's hard to retain a genuine edge for long. But Goodyear has underspent its rivals on research and development. Goodyear spent \$376 million on R&D in 2001, while Bridgestone spent \$476 million and Michelin spent about \$645 million. In years past, Goodyear made up for that through muscular sales and marketing and a network of dealers that pushed its products with near-religious zeal.

(Cont.)

Michelin and Bridgestone also have advantages Goodyear doesn't. Both are dominant brands in their home markets of Japan and Europe, where price competition from imports is far less intense and where consumer prices overall have held up. Michelin also makes much of its money from commercial tires, which command higher premiums. Globally, Michelin sells its tires for an average of $73.17, while Bridgestone fetches $64.28, according to estimates by industry analyst Stephen Girsky of Morgan Stanley. Goodyear sells tires at an average price of $56.95. However, both of the Goodyear rivals have been able to use the high prices in their home markets to underwrite lower prices in the U.S. and lure cost-conscious Americans.

Goodyear's price changes came at a time when dealers were already in near-rebellion over a host of other complaints. Goodyear had become notorious for its poor "fill-rate," the percentage of times the tire maker actually delivered the number and types of tires a dealer ordered. This was in part a result of the Firestone recall and the car-selling boom: Goodyear was so busy shipping tires for replacements on Ford Explorers and for use on new cars that it didn't have enough to send to dealers. It was a problem that dogged the company before the recall and has lingered long after.

Frustrated, many dealers who had always sold Goodyear looked for other brands. "There were guys who had never thought of handling a Michelin or a Yokohama who got a taste and decided, 'Gee, this is pretty good,'" says Mr. Geiger, the Toledo dealer.

Even Goodyear's loyal dealers say they were disappointed. "I just can't imagine a company with the reputation it has and the assets it has performing so poorly," says Robert Purcell, president of Purcell Tire & Rubber Co. in Potosi, Mo., a Goodyear dealer with 70 stores in the Midwest and Western U.S.

This past August, Goodyear was forced to backpedal on the price increase, selectively reducing some lines of tires to restore their competitive position in the market. The company insists it corrected the problem and recently announced a price increase of 4% to 5% for the beginning of January, citing high raw-materials prices. Mr. Geiger, for his part, says his sales of Goodyear tires perked up again after the company scaled back prices.

Goodyear's management had other missteps. Chairman Samir G. Gibara took on nearly $1 billion in debt back in 1999 to buy the non-Japanese tire operations of Japan's Sumitomo Rubber Industries Ltd., a price which turned out to be far too rich. Many of the acquired plants were outmoded and required heavy investments to update. Mr. Gibara then announced plans to shut a factory in Gadsden, Ala., just as demand for tires in the U.S. was surging. The company later decided to keep part of the plant open.

Meantime, Goodyear pension funds are short some $2 billion and the company has $3.6 billion in debt. Without more cash rolling in, it's almost impossible for Goodyear to meet these obligations while also spending money on things needed to turn around, including the $100 million or more it costs to shut just one big tire plant.

Churning in the executive offices didn't help matters. In five years, the North American operations had four different top executives. "The company got so caught up dealing with its internal issues, it lost sight of its customers," says Lee Fiedler, the former president of Goodyear's Kelly tire division, who retired in 1999 and is now mayor of Cumberland, Md.

For years, Mr. Gibara, who had spent virtually his whole working life at Goodyear, focused heavily on Europe. That huge market played a key role in his plan, touted to investors in the late 1990s, to make Goodyear a $20 billion tire-making juggernaut by 2003. The acquisition of Sumitomo gave Goodyear the Dunlop tire brand, which is strong in Europe and which Mr. Gibara saw aiding the company in its fight to become a stronger challenger to Michelin in that region.

> In the tire industry, innovations are quickly copied by producers so it's hard to retain a genuine edge for long. But Goodyear has underspent rivals on research and development.

Stateside, Goodyear plants increasingly have been running below capacity as demand slipped, boosting costs. The company is trying to address that, and will likely shut down at least two or three of its 15 North American plants. Its unionized work force is typically among the best paid in the region where the plants are located.

The company told employees in January—shortly after announcing the elimination of 700 jobs, including many at its technical center in Akron—that it would need to shed 15% of its North American capacity this year. Plants considered possible targets for closure include an aging facility in Union City, Tenn., and a Dunlop plant in Huntsville, Ala., which Goodyear acquired when it bought Sumitomo.

Many Goodyear plants are relics of an earlier era. The company's sprawling tire factory on the outskirts of Danville, Va., for instance, has its own skeet-shooting range, ball fields, and a lush golf course used by both hourly employees and management, though in separate leagues. There's even a stocked fishing pond reserved for workers, with a fenced-off area along one muddy bank to shield anglers from stray golf balls.

Mr. Keegan, the new CEO, is taking steps to counteract Goodyear management's tendency to be insular. Shortly after he arrived in October 2000 to the company's sprawling headquarters, where executive offices are grouped in a long, dark-paneled corridor, he ordered the decorative stained-glass windows on his office to be pulled open. It was a symbolic message that he wanted the company to become outward-looking, he says.

Some investors say there is little Goodyear can do to avoid a longer-term liquidity crunch. Merrill Lynch & Co., which issued a "sell" rating on Goodyear two weeks ago, said that even if the tire giant matched its best-ever two-year performance, which was in 1993 and 1994, its cash from operations would still fall short of its obligations.

But the company has gotten some breathing room: A waiver from its banks until March 7 to pay $500 million into its pension plans and continued access to about $1.1 billion in two credit facilities. Goodyear said that as of the end of January it had more than $600 million in cash on hand and another $700 million in various lines of credit.

Mr. Keegan insists the company can be turned around. He says he must raise Goodyear's revenue and slash its costs, which will mean making unprecedented changes in the way the company produces tires. "This is not going to be without pain," he says, declining to elaborate on the revival plan, which will be presented to investors next month. As for the talks with the banks aimed at restructuring Goodyear's loans, he says, "suffice it to say we're doing the right thing to get it done."

THE NEW TEAMWORK

This generation of collaboration technologies is making it easier for companies to work with partners and deliver products in record time

Mark the time and place: Oct. 26, 2001, Lockheed Martin Aeronautics Co. in Fort Worth. On that day, the defense contractor won the first piece of the biggest manufacturing contract ever—$200 billion to build a new family of supersonic stealth fighter planes for the Defense Dept. That Friday also marks the kickoff of a new technology era, one that could transform the basic workings of every major corporation.

Lockheed's mega-win will require some intricate teamwork. More than 80 suppliers will be working at 187 locations to design and build components of the Joint Strike Fighter. It's up to the 75-member tech group at Lockheed's Aeronautics division to link them all together, as well as let the U.S. Air Force, Navy, and Marines, Britain's Defense Ministry, and eight other U.S. allies track progress and make changes midstream if necessary. All told, people sitting at more than 40,000 computers will be collaborating with each other to get the first plane in the air in just four years—the same amount of time it took to get the much simpler F-16 from contract to delivery in the 1970s.

A project this enormous requires a feat of computing to keep all its moving parts in sync. Lockheed and its partners will be using a system of 90 Web software tools to share designs, track the exchange of documents, and keep an eye on progress against goals. Major partners such as Northrop Grumman Corp. already are hooked up. In about six months, the rest will be on board. "We're getting the best people, applying the best designs, from wherever we need them," says Mark Peden, vice-president for information systems at Lockheed Martin Aeronautics. "It's the true virtual connection."

Management experts have long talked about the so-called virtual corporation: a company that focuses on what it does best and farms out the rest to specialists who can do it better. Now, a new generation of Net-collaboration technologies is making it easier for companies to work hand-in-hand with their partners to bring new products to the market in record time—and on penny-pinching budgets.

These jazzy new technologies could take the Web a step closer to delivering on its potential. Companies can reinvent entire business processes, such as product design, supply-chain management, and sales and distribution relationships. The Net allows people from different companies with incompatible computing systems to meet in the middle on Web sites that speak a common language. And, instead of simply sending data from PC to PC, these Web tools let people separated by oceans interact with one another as if there were not even a wall between them. They can talk via their computers while looking at shared documents, carry on e-mail chats, and use electronic white boards—where two or more people can draw pictures or charts, in real time, as the others watch and respond.

If this stuff takes off, the corporation as we know it could be turned inside out. Picture it: Companies that have done everything in the past from ordering parts to bolting them together to selling them could instead use the Web as a giant electronic Yellow Pages—to find experts to do many of these jobs and then to collaborate with them over the Net on a minute-by-minute basis. The same company could offer its expertise to other firms, assembling and disbanding teams as projects begin and end. Tighter relationships between companies also could spur innovation as they tap the best talent from anywhere in the world. Workers might end up identifying less with their company than with their cross-company team—and get bonuses based on the team's performance. Potentially more radical than reengineering, Web collaboration could reshape the traditional corporation, says George Colony, CEO of tech market researcher Forrester Research.

For now, most companies would be content with technologies that make them far more flexible and efficient. Previously, they mostly relied on a pricey older technology called electronic data interchange, or EDI, to trade basic information like purchase orders. Because of the limits of the technology and resistance to changing business processes, only about 10% of large

Expediting the Xbox

Working with manufacturing partner Flextronics, Microsoft Corp. used a Web collaboration system to bring its new Xbox video game console to market last Nov. 15. The system helped slice about two months off the original production schedule. In one case, Microsoft decided that a metal bracket for holding the disk drive in place was too heavy, so it replaced it with a plastic one that was several ounces lighter and stronger.

Step 1 Microsoft creates a 3-D design for the new part and, tapping into the system, tells Flextronics to make the change. The system automatically sends an e-mail alert to Flextronics' manufacturing and design teams.

Step 2 Flextronics engineers log on to the system, see the change order, and discuss it among themselves. They determine that the change doesn't cause any problems with manufacturing.

Step 3 Microsoft makes a prototype of the part and discovers the bracket isn't a perfect fit. It e-mails Flextronics with some proposed changes to the design.

Step 4 Flextronics logs on and approves the changes. An e-mail alert is sent to the Flextronics unit that makes the plastic part.

Step 5 The parts people see the e-mail, log on to the system, and approve the change. The manufacturer modifies its tooling machines and builds a new version in two weeks.

Step 6 Microsoft makes another prototype, tests it, and approves the part to go into full production.

(Cont.)

companies are collaborating with partners, according to Raymond E. Miles, professor at the Haas School of Business at the University of California at Berkeley. "People don't know yet how to do this, but they have to do it," says Miles. "You're not going to create wealth in the 21st century the way you did in the 20th."

The new tools are barely out of the box, but some early experiments are showing solid results. By using the Web to coordinate auto design by internal engineers and external suppliers, General Motors Corp. can get a car into production in 18 months, down from the 42 months it took in the mid-1990s. Land O'Lakes Inc. has saved $40,000 a month since September by using the Web to stuff butter and cheese into trucks it shares with companies such as Georgia-Pacific Corp. And Deloitte Consulting says it can bring a new team member up to speed on a project in a day or two, down from three weeks, by keeping everything they need to know on a Web site.

If this stuff delivers on its promise, it could help drive productivity growth for years. Yankee Group Research Inc. says that over the next five years, collaborating over the Net can save companies $223 billion by cutting transaction, production, and inventory costs. "There's an opportunity for a whole new level of business-performance improvements in the collaborative redesign of processes, using the Internet as the great enabler," says James A. Champy, chairman of consulting at Perot Systems Corp. and author of *X-Engineering the Corporation: Reinventing Your Business in the Digital Age*.

Still, Net collaboration is only in its toddler phase. Network connections aren't always reliable, so real-time collaboration sessions sometimes cut off suddenly in midstream. Technology novices tend to be flummoxed by logging on to Web sites and uploading documents. And even when the software works as advertised, it isn't always quickly adopted. Culture is the main hangup. Like squirrels burying nuts for winter, companies and their divisions have traditionally hoarded information—even from each other—as a competitive advantage. The challenge is to come up with ways to reward employees for working in new ways.

Tight technology budgets also have slowed adoption of new software. Many companies delayed collaboration projects in the second half of 2001. "They weren't going full-bore because they got burned before" by earlier Internet technologies that didn't deliver, says analyst Heather Bellini of Salomon Smith Barney. "Next year is when we'll move beyond initial deployments. We're still very much in the early adopter phase."

Being a collaboration pioneer has paid off big-time for Juniper Networks Inc. It farms out operations like manufacturing, logistics, and customer support so it can concentrate on what it does best: designing and selling networking equipment. Because the company is so efficient, even when revenue growth slowed to 32% in 2001 from a fivefold jump in 2000, it was able to increase research and development spending by 80%. "We were able to manage costs to protect strategic investment," says CEO Scott G. Kriens. "This has a lot to do with the outsourcing."

Juniper's network links its own operations with those of partners—setting off a digital chain reaction. Customers place an order via the Web, which relays the order to Juniper's core planning software, which spits out the details to every internal department that needs the info—from finance to supply chain and to outsiders like contract manufacturers. Juniper's production planning system automatically vets the manufacturer's inventory, raw materials, and production lead time—then coughs up a date when the product will be shipped directly to the customer. If a customer changes her order on short notice, a team of material planners and process engineers from Juniper and its contractor manufacturers are alerted by e-mail. They get together in a Web conference to figure out what needs to be done to deliver on time.

One of the most effective uses of the new collaboration technologies is in the area of product development—everything from designing cars to developing new prescription drugs. This kind of teamwork not only increases efficiency but boosts innovation—the holy grail of companies hoping to produce the Next Big Thing in their industry. General Motors, for one, has chalked up big wins since setting up a collaborative engineering system in 1999 that allows GM employees and external auto parts suppliers to share product design information. Previously, GM had no way of coordinating its complex designs across its 14 engineering sites scattered across the world, plus the dozens of partners who design subsystems.

Now, GM's collaboration system serves as a centralized clearinghouse for all the design data. More than 16,000 designers and other workers use the new Web system from Electronic Data Systems Corp. to share 3-D designs and keep track of parts and subassemblies. The system automatically updates the master design when changes are finalized so everyone is on the same page. The result: GM has slashed the time it takes to complete a full mock-up of a car from 12 weeks to two. The time saved by online collaboration frees up workers to think more creatively—mocking up three or four more alternative designs per car.

After products roll off the assembly line, Web collaboration software can help sell them. Companies with complex sales channels are turning to the Net to help sign up resellers and coordinate marketing. PTC, in

New Ways to Get Work Done

Web sites where workers can collaborate change the game for corporations by saving time and money on everything from product design to mergers

BUSINESS PROCESS	PAYOFF
Product Development: Companies are making products more cheaply and quickly by using the Web to synchronize the design process with suppliers.	Using a collaborative system at 11 General Motors Corp. factories, the company has cut the time it takes to finish a vehicle mock-up from 12 weeks to two weeks.
Supply Chain: Companies can use shared Web sites to work closely with contract manufacturers and suppliers—reducing inventories.	By purchasing food ingredients and other goods via an online service that allows it to interact with suppliers, H.J. Heinz Co. has cut its supplier costs by 10%.
Sales Channels: On Web sites, companies and their resellers share technical information, conduct employee training, and track sales leads.	Toshiba Canada Office Products Group has reduced by half the time it takes to process orders handled by its resellers and has cut printing and mailing costs.
Transportation: Logistics exchanges take the hassle out of delivering goods by offering quick price quotes, truck availability, and shared trucks.	Georgia-Pacific Corp. has saved $600,000, or 19%, since June on a single cross-country route that it shares with General Mills Inc.
Project Management: Law firms, consulting firms, and banks can use electronic bulletin boards to manage complex deals and projects.	Deloitte Consulting can bring a new team member up to speed on a project within a day or two rather than the three weeks it used to take.

Needham, Mass., which makes product-design software, is using Web-collaboration software to reach out to resellers it needs to expand to new markets not already served by its sales force. The software from ChannelWave Inc. automates the recruiting and certification process. It now takes a day to sign up a partner—down from a week. In a year, PTC has signed up about 170 partners. PTC expects to recoup the $22,000 a month it pays for ChannelWave with an improved rate of converting leads for resellers to sales—35%, vs. 20% in the old days. It will be able to use the Web site to hand off leads to specific resellers and track their attempts to land customers. If a reseller is having trouble, PTC can step in to help cement the deal.

Once a sale is made, the next step is delivering products. Collaboration technologies are saving money in warehouses and on 18-wheelers. A dozen companies including Land O'Lakes and Georgia-Pacific use a collaboration system devised by Nistevo Corp., a software company in Eden Prairie, Minn., to use the fewest trucks possible and keep them full by matching loads and routes. The companies submit all the details about their routes and contracts with truckers to the Nistevo Web site. The company matches up the participants' schedules and notifies potential partners by e-mail. Once the companies agree to terms, they log on to a Web site to place an order for a truck and track the shipments.

The rewards are starting to roll in. In just six months, Georgia-Pacific says it has saved $600,000 on one, six-legged route from Chicago to Maine and back again. And Fernando Palacios, vice-president for operations and supply chain at Land O'Lakes, says, based on initial results, the company expects to save a half-million dollars this year. Payoffs like that more than cover the average $250,000 annual cost for Nistevo and the $75,000 installation fee.

There's no matching Net collaboration when a crisis breaks out. Web sites can be set up in minutes. People are able to share data, schedule meetings, conduct forum discussions, and view up-to-date drafts of documents they're working on. Using a Web site provided by New York-based IntraLinks Inc., 80 people from seven consulting firms produced a report for the New York City Partnership on the economic impact of the September 11 attacks. It took just six weeks—rather than the normal six months or more. The timing was crucial since the city needed facts to back up its pleas for relief funds. The Web site made sharing information a snap. Every morning, Jenny Abramson, an associate with Boston Consulting Group, posted links to newspaper articles on the Web site—alerting her colleagues with e-mails. "We were able to spend more time on the content issues, and less on logistics," says Abramson.

Those are some of the best-case scenarios. In other cases, collaborative projects have yet to deliver the goods. Last spring, Baker & McKenzie, a Chicago law firm with 3,000 attorneys and 62 offices worldwide, was enthused about a new multimillion-dollar collaboration system from Lehi (Utah)-based Nextpage Inc. that would allow its lawyers to manage cases and corporate mergers with other parties over the Web. The company had an ambitious plan to roll out the service to 10 of its offices in the second quarter and get the other offices online by the end of the year.

It didn't happen. The firm underestimated the training costs and the difficulties of changing peoples' behavior, especially among workers who weren't computer-savvy. During an early training session, one older lawyer actually confused a Microsoft PowerPoint presentation they were using to train people for the collaboration service itself. "Getting people to practice in a different way is a very ambitious exercise," says Mark Swords, a partner heading the initiative. Now, Swords says, Baker & McKenzie plans to roll out the service in the second quarter, a year later than expected, and in only two offices instead of 10 or more. The firm remains committed to it because he believes it could help land new clients.

Changing old habits is only one of the roadblocks to smoother collaboration. Technology bugs and a competitive wariness are making people move gingerly. One tech manager at Boeing Co. complains that Microsoft Corp.'s NetMeeting software for online meetings "is terrible. . . . Everything freezes so people have to reconnect." Engineers fret about the time it takes to transfer bulky design files. And early users of a collaboration system made by Groove Networks Inc. in Cambridge, Mass., complain that they have to reformat Microsoft Word documents before they can share them in cyberspace. Software companies are scurrying to work out the bugs so their tools catch on faster.

One of the key early lessons is that for collaboration to work well, it has to be between people, not just machines. Management experts say digital workspaces can't completely replace more traditional interactions, especially in the creative process. In-person communication is important for training, building relationships, and riding herd on a difficult project. Nistevo addresses that by mixing tech wizardry with old-fashioned meetings. Palacios of Land O'Lakes says companies participating in Nistevo's trucking project build trust and sort out their problems by meeting face-to-face every quarter.

Lockheed won't have the luxury of waiting for in-person confabs to get over hurdles. Its suppliers span 26 states and three countries. But it's willing to put up with the glitches that are inherent in electronic collaboration. The Lockheed team is heading into the digital wilderness with no thought of turning tail. "This wasn't an accounting decision," says Lockheed's Peden. "It was a what-do-you-want-to-be-when-you-grow-up decision."

Other companies will face similar choices as these teamwork tools improve. For many outfits, finding a way to make collaboration work across corporate boundaries may be the surest path to reaching a ripe old age.

By Faith Keenan and Spencer E. Ante
Contributing: Ben Elgin and Steve Hamm

INSIDE CISCO'S $2 BILLION BLUNDER

How the world's most admired supply chain screwed up, and how CEO John Chambers plans to fix it.

By: Paul Kaihla

As corporate humiliations go, it had to be one of the worst. In May 2001, Cisco Systems (*CSCO*) announced the largest inventory write-down in history: $2.2 billion erased from its balance sheet for components it ordered but couldn't use. The gaffe was made all the more embarrassing by waves of prior publicity about Cisco's brilliant integration of its vast information systems. The network was so responsive, gushed Cisco CEO John Chambers, that the company could close its books in 24 hours, any day of the year. Yet the system wasn't responsive enough to stop building billions of dollars' worth of stuff nobody wanted.

Cisco blamed the fiasco on a plunge in technology spending that Chambers called as unforeseeable as "a 100-year flood." If company forecasters had only been able to see this coming, Cisco implied, the supply-chain system would have worked perfectly. But *Business 2.0* has learned that, in fact, flaws in the system contributed significantly to the breakdown. Cisco recognized many of these problems even before last year's inventory bubble, and ever since, an elite group of execs and engineers has been working on a top-secret remediation program called eHub. Here's the first inside look at how this ambitious, multimillion-dollar project could help avoid a repeat of last year's disaster . . . if it works as planned.

INFLATING THE BUBBLE

During the late 1990s, Cisco became famous for being the hardware maker that doesn't make hardware. Instead, Cisco farms out most of its routers and switches to electronics contract manufacturers. This arrangement has several advantages. For one, it allows Cisco to concentrate on marketing and product innovation. It also liberates Cisco from much of the hassle and expense of maintaining inventory, as Cisco's information systems make it possible to ship fully assembled machines directly from the factory to buyers, more or less on demand.

But the Great Inventory Wreck of 2001 highlighted some ugly bugs in the system. Cisco's supply chain is basically structured like a pyramid, with Cisco at the point. On the second tier reside a handful of contract manufacturers—including Celestica (*CLS*), Flextronics (*FLEX*), and Solectron (*SLR*)—responsible for final assembly. These manufacturers are fed by a larger sub-tier supplying components such as processor chips (Intel and Xilinx) and optical gear (JDS Uniphase and Corning). Those companies, in turn, draw on an even larger base of commodity suppliers scattered all over the globe.

Communication gaps between the tiers eventually got Cisco into trouble. To lock in supplies of scarce components during the boom, Cisco ordered large quantities well in advance, based on demand projections from the company's sales force. What the forecasters didn't notice, however, was that many of their projections were inflated artificially. With network gear hard to come by, many Cisco customers also ordered similar equipment from Cisco's competitors, knowing that they'd ultimately make just one purchase—from whoever could deliver the goods first.

The result was double and triple ordering, which bloated demand forecasts and put the squeeze on component supplies. A missing link in Cisco's supply-chain management system magnified this problem. Suppose Cisco projected sales of 10,000 units of a particular router. Each of the company's contract manufacturers would compete to fill the entire order, and to gain an edge, they often tried to lock up supplies of scarce components. Suppliers would be swamped with orders, but Cisco's supply-chain system couldn't show that the spike in demand represented overlapping orders. If, say, three manufacturers were competing to build those 10,000 routers, to chipmakers it looked like a sudden demand for 30,000 machines. Cisco became enmeshed in a vicious cycle of artificially inflated sales forecasts, artificially inflated demand for key components, higher costs, and bad communication throughout the supply chain. Eventually, the bubble burst.

BETTER LIVING THROUGH AUTOMATION

Cisco's inventory woes highlighted the shortcomings of a communication system that stopped only partway down the pyramid. That's where eHub comes in.

As it happens, work on eHub began in 2000, when the last thing on anyone's mind was a slump in demand.

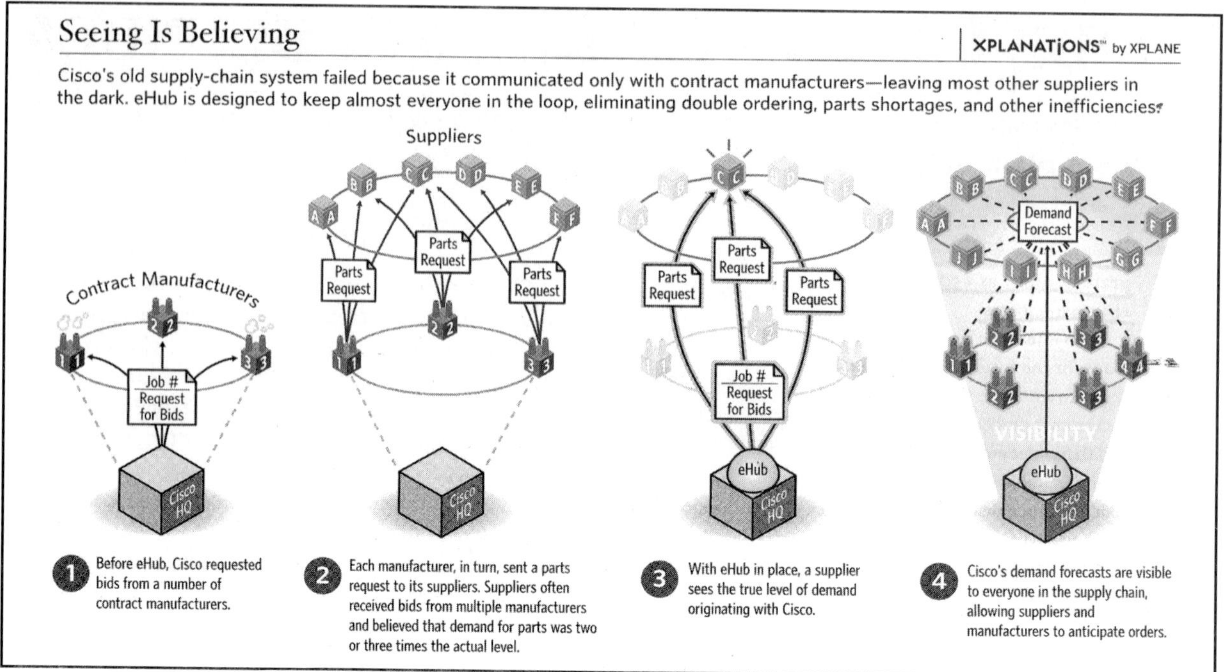

Instead, the project was intended to help eliminate bidding wars for then-scarce components. "It was created for scaling *upward*," says Carl Redfield, Cisco's head of worldwide manufacturing and logistics. "It was put in to ensure that enough material would always be on hand."

By the summer of 2000, Cisco had produced a 3-inch-thick specification binder that served as a blueprint for eHub. Its central nervous system would be run by Irvine, Calif., supply-chain integration firm Viacore, which would take Cisco's already advanced supply-chain engine to a new level.

Private exchanges that link members of a supply chain are nothing new. In the past, companies like Dell (*DELL*) and GM (*GM*) have created electronic hubs that feed supply-chain data to outsource manufacturers and suppliers, and vice versa. These exchanges typically provide a Web interface where vendors manually type in things like sales forecasts, purchase orders, and shipping schedules. The systems are not real-time, and they're plagued by data-entry errors.

eHub practically eliminates the need for human intervention. Instead, the system automates the flow of information between Cisco, its contract manufacturers, and its component suppliers. The key ingredient is an XML technology called Partner Interface Process, or PIP. eHub's dozen or so PIPs indicate whether a document requires a response—and if so, how quickly. For example, a PIP purchase order might stipulate that the recipient's system must send a confirmation two hours after receipt and a confirmed acceptance within 24 hours. If the recipient's system fails to meet these deadlines, the purchase order is considered null and void.

Under eHub, Cisco's production cycle begins when a demand forecast PIP is sent out, showing cumulative orders. That forecast goes not only to contract manufacturers but also to chipmakers like Philips Semiconductors and Altera Corp. (*ALTR*) "Before, if Celestica, Flextronics, and Solectron all came to Philips at the same time, and each said they wanted 10,000 of a certain chip, that was a total of 30,000 chips," says one senior engineer who worked on the eHub project. "Now, Philips can say, 'Hold on, I'm on eHub. I know that total aggregated demand is only 10,000.'" By requiring all the systems in the supply network to talk to each other, eHub ferrets out inventory shortfalls, production blackouts, and other screwups almost as fast as they occur.

Complexity and cost have put eHub a bit behind schedule. Cisco originally planned to connect 250 contractors and suppliers by the end of 2001. Instead it linked roughly 60, including Agilent Technologies (*A*), Hitachi, IBM (*IBM*), Intel (*INTC*), LSI Logic (*LSI*), Motorola (*MOT*), and Xilinx (*XLNX*). This year the number should rise to 150 or more, and Cisco's ultimate goal is to integrate as many as 650 supply-chain participants.

eHub is just the first stage of Cisco's plans for the future. Ultimately, Cisco hopes to automate the whole

(Cont.)

enchilada: A customer purchases a product online, and that order goes into both Cisco's financial database and supply-chain system simultaneously. For now, however, eHub will be plagued by a timeless software limitation—it's only as good as the data it receives. Garbage in, garbage out.

"If the inputs are wrong, the world's best supply chain can't save you," says Steve Kammen, an analyst who covers Cisco for CIBC World Markets. Nevertheless, when the next tech boom comes, Cisco expects eHub to provide the parts it needs; the next bust, eHub might keep it from getting stuck with so much unwanted stuff. Cisco isn't ready to boast about all of this—yet—but the buzz is building. "I walk into our customers today," marvels Viacore CEO Fadi Chehade. "They say, 'Oh, we heard that you are operating the Cisco eHub. Can you copy it for us?'"

"Inside Cisco's $2 Billion Blunder," *Business 2.0,* March 2002, pp. 88–90.

The Friction Economy

American business just got the bill for the terrorist attacks: $151 billion—a year.

■ *by Anna Bernasek*

It's a frigid early morning in January, and Michael DePasquale, or Rusty, as he prefers to be called, has finished loading his van with containers of milk, sugar, cups, and coffee-brewing equipment. Barreling into the front seat, the heavyset 33-year-old, a driver for national coffee distributor Filterfresh, begins his haul to downtown Boston, looking more like a bouncer than a deliveryman. Everything about Rusty, with the possible exception of his wild Fu Manchu mustache, calls out "no nonsense." He wants to cover his route, get the job done, then pick up his two kids from school. That's it. No messing around. But just 45 minutes after he leaves the company warehouse in Woburn, Mass., a mess is exactly what he gets. He used to be able to unload his freight and walk right in the building at 53 State Street, a 40-floor office tower that's home to many financial services firms. Not anymore.

Now there's a guard on duty at the loading dock who carefully inspects Rusty's paperwork and the brand-new ID badge he has to carry. The guard knows him—but still has to call upstairs and double-check. No one answers. The guard waits a few minutes and tries again. This time the receptionist is there to give the okay. "I hate this building," Rusty spits out. "A few weeks ago I came in the front door as I always do to clean the coffee machines—it's much faster than waiting for the freight elevator, which can take 15 minutes—and they wouldn't let me in because I wasn't on the list. Nothing worked, and I couldn't do my job."

Since Sept. 11, Rusty and his fellow Filterfresh drivers have at times felt as if they're fighting a new war, battling their way into office buildings. Vans are often searched inside and out at some buildings—and those are the few that still permit on-site parking. Such nuisances are minor, it would seem, but they add up. Indeed, they add up in a surprisingly large way. For Filterfresh's 250 drivers across the country, delays have tacked on an estimated full hour per day to each route.

Back at Filterfresh's head office in Westwood, Mass., CEO Daniel Cousineau is explaining what that extra hour means to the $300-million-a-year business. A sophisticated, clean-cut French Canadian, Cousineau speaks with soft precision as he leans forward in his chair. Five additional hours a week per delivery person, he says, equals an extra 1,250 hours a week. By that measure, Filterfresh needs 24 more delivery people to do the same work it did prior to Sept. 11. "That's a 10% increase in our labor costs just so we can hold our ground," Cousineau says.

Four months after the savage terrorist attacks, American business is back to normal in many ways. The headlines have shifted from the Afghan front to the homegrown blight of Enron. Fear and uncertainty, once pervasive, now mingle with resignation. Leading economic indicators, as measured by the Conference Board, have risen for the past three months, and even Fed Chairman Alan Greenspan seems to believe the recession has turned toward the exits. Yes, things are back to normal. What's remarkable, however, is how much "normal" has changed.

It wasn't so long ago that corporate chiefs and management gurus were boasting that godlike efficiency was within the reach of their businesses. The unrestrained flow of goods and capital—thrust forward by free trade, the borderless Internet, and deregulation—made the productivity marvel possible. Companies like Dell were fast shrinking the inventory they kept on their shelves, shipping off products as quickly as their virtual supply chains could package them. American companies connected with suppliers and customers halfway around the world, it seemed, almost as easily as with those in neighboring states. The effect was massive. Allen Sinai, chief economist at Decision Economics in New York City, estimates that the free flow of money and merchandise alone contributed at least three-quarters of a percentage point to annual U.S. growth from 1995 to 2000.

One can't help but feel nostalgic. Today, post-Sept. 11, the economy faces a subtle new reality: Call it friction. It's as if fine sand has been sprinkled into the gears of American business—the intricate productivity machine that had been so well oiled during the 1990s. From higher security costs to airport delays, from planning for supply-chain breaks that might arise to dealing with personnel problems that have already occurred, companies are staring at substantial new costs in their operating budgets. The bill this year may top $150 billion, a full 1.5% of U.S. domestic output. (More on that later, we promise.) And worse still, Wall Street's economic models—you know, the ones pointing to a full, if sluggish, recovery by midyear—don't appear to have factored these costs into their scenarios. The surprise could be nasty for CEOs and shareholders alike.

The already weak economy doesn't help. In an environment where price discounting is rampant and excess capacity abounds, even the smallest bump in expenses can do big damage to a company's bottom line. Indeed, if the trends continue, the U.S. could well see the reverse of what happened during the past decade.

Whether the squeeze will be proportional to the dramatic expansion of the '90s has yet to be seen. But consider where just some of that sandy friction is falling, and you realize that it's landing all around us: in the higher premiums companies are forced to shell out for property insurance, in the jacked-up rent on office buildings as new security measures are passed on to tenants, in increased IT spending to beef up Internet security, and in extensive new spending on backup computer operations. Longer waits at the border (to say nothing of office lobbies), higher shipping and air-freight costs, and less predictable mass transit are also grinding the gears. So are heavier inventories, mail delays, rising premiums on workers' compensation, and a raft of new government regulations.

How painful is the final bill? To come up with a fair estimate, we've added and subtracted, rounded off, eliminated double counting, and vetted the findings against a consortium's worth of economists. That left us with the staggering figure of $151 billion, not including the tip. What it does include is $18 billion of new costs related to workplace security, $15 billion for IT security and contingency operations, $65 billion for logistical changes to supply chains, $12 billion for employee travel, $35 billion for insurance and liability, and $6 billion for employee absenteeism. (See table for specifics.) Yes, there's plenty of guesswork here, but we've deliberately erred on the side of conservatism. Nor have we included the squishy costs—things like morale, psychology, fear, distraction from strategic goals—all of which exist but prove even more difficult to quantify.

(Cont.)

There's another rub, besides. Many of these friction costs are ongoing and must be figured into future company expenditures. A firm that hires ten new security guards, for instance, has to pay those ten salaries each year. That means the $151 billion tab facing corporate America could well be an annual one. As most of that cash is diverted to protective uses from productive ones (such as spending on research, product development, and more efficient technology), that $151 billion—while still a small part of GDP—can have a wallop on growth. Richard Berner, Morgan Stanley's chief U.S. economist, figures the cost over time to be a half-percentage-point reduction in annual growth in domestic output.

If all these projections seem too high in the ether of theoretical science, consider your monthly insurance bill. Business after Sept. 11 is simply a riskier proposition, and companies have little choice but to swallow the additional risk in the bitter form of surging premiums. It's happening right now. "We're seeing broad-based hikes," says Bill Yankus, a managing director at investment firm Fox-Pitt Kelton, which studies the insurance industry. "And it's of a magnitude we've never really seen before." Not only are property and life insurance premiums jumping by large percentages and even multiples of what they were a year ago, workers' compensation costs are rising between 30% and 50%, Yankus says. Wall Street analysts estimate a $35 billion rise in corporate insurance costs this year—which alone is likely to cause rumbles on the bottom line. Alice Cornish, an analyst at Prudential Securities in Boston, calculates that pretax profits for the companies in the S&P stock index could drop by an average of 2.5% in 2002 because of higher insurance premiums.

Airport delays are an equally obvious if potentially more costly friction point for businesses. If you thought your preflight wait was bad during the high-alert weeks just after the terrorist attacks, well, get ready to visit that airport bar. New baggage security rules imposed by the federal government on Jan. 18—mandating that every bag be screened or matched with a passenger—are likely to compound the wait. Some airlines are recommending that domestic passengers check their luggage not just two hours prior to departure, but three.

To be conservative, however, consider what only a single extra hour at the airport costs the economy. Economy.com, a West Chester, Pa., economic consulting group, has actually done the math. With 17 million business travelers flying each month, the loss in productivity neatly adds up to 17 million hours a month. At last year's output per worker of $40, Economy.com figures a loss in output of $680 million a month, or $8 billion a year.

STICKER SHOCK

Did someone say profit recovery? Last year FORTUNE 100 companies earned a total of $277 billion. Start subtracting . . .

Logistics — **$65** billion

David Closs, a professor of logistics at Michigan State University, has calculated a best-case and worst-case scenario for the increase in costs associated with supply chains, transportation, and inventory storage. The best-case scenario, he says, is a $50 billion rise. The worst case: $80 billion. After conferring with other logistics experts, we took the midpoint.

Insurance and liability — **$35** billion

Forecasts on Wall Street range from a $25 billion increase in insurance costs to a $50 billion hike. A credible if perhaps low-end figure may be $35 billion.

Workplace security — **$18** billion

Security consultants believe that business spending on security will increase 20%, or $24 billion, in 2002. Zurich Financial chief economist David Hale estimates a slightly lower increase in security costs of 10% to 15% in 2002. Spending would cover 300,000 new security guards, screening equipment, new ID systems, video surveillance, and other gear, he says. We went with Hale's conservative estimate of 15%, or $18 billion.

Information tech — **$15** billion

Experts say that as many as 10,000 companies will need disaster-recovery backup systems, and figure the average cost of such a system to be $1 million. That represents a total of $10 billion for backup IT systems alone. Including other security-enhancing IT, contingency sites, and backup operations, technology analysts say firms could easily spend $15 billion.

Travel and transportation — **$12** billion

Economy.com calculated the cost of an extra hour's wait at airports to be an annual $8 billion. We added an extra half-hour to that, for the latest baggage security procedures, to reach $12 billion. That still doesn't take into account extra costs associated with overnight hotel stays to ensure timely arrival at meetings, or delays in other areas, like customs and immigration at the 301 ports of entry into the U.S. Taking those delays into account, the cost could be much higher.

Employee costs — **$6** billion

In the year ending June 2001, the direct cost to business from unscheduled absenteeism was $755 per employee, according to the Society for Human Resource Management. The Bureau of National Affairs has reported a 20% rise in absenteeism due to the terrorist attacks, though several workplace consultants FORTUNE queried put the figure lower. With 100 million people in the work force, and assuming a modest 8% upswing in absenteeism, we figured a $6 billion tab. Estimate does not include tardiness and lost productivity.

TOTAL — $151 billion

(Cont.)

The effect, unfortunately, has been magnified at the Long Island headquarters of Audiovox, a major supplier of wireless products like cell phones. For CEO Phillip Christopher and his 50-member sales and engineering team, travel is a way of life. If they're not on the road showing off new products to telecom outfits like Qwest and Sprint, they're not doing their job. But more than four months after the initial shock of Sept. 11, flying remains something of a dirty word at the firm. "Most of our people are fearful and really reluctant to travel," says Christopher. "It has presented quite a challenge to us."

So the boss found a solution. His staff, he discovered, was more willing to fly if each person had a buddy so they could travel in pairs. While that has coaxed his sales and engineering team back into the air, it has meant a loss of productivity to the firm—a meeting that would normally involve one person now takes two.

Aggravating the situation, Audiovox's salespeople and engineers carry loads of electronic equipment, making the routine of airport security that much more arduous and time-consuming. The compounded delays have meant that Christopher now has to send his staff the night before to ensure that they're on time for morning meetings in distant cities. Thus, the one-day visits Christopher and his team used to make to a company like Sprint in Kansas City have turned into two-day affairs, requiring an overnight hotel stay. So far, Christopher calculates that all this has raised the firm's total operating costs by 1%. "Not huge," he says, "but in this economic environment, every dollar counts."

No kidding. And the fact is, higher airport security costs have already raised costs elsewhere in the economy. The annual $29 billion cost of air freight has risen 3% since Jan. 1, according to Jim Valentine, a transportation analyst at Morgan Stanley. UPS and FedEx have likewise increased their general shipping charges by 3% to 4% since the start of the year instead of the more typical 2.5% annual increase. Both firms say the higher costs reflect new inefficiencies caused by heightened security. On top of general charges, both FedEx and UPS have jacked up some other prices by 20%, including those for pickups and, naturally, the transport of hazardous materials.

Remember just-in-time inventory? Well just-in-time has morphed into "just in case." The change is having a significant impact on costs. It's not merely delays at American airports that are causing problems. Certain European hubs now require a 24- to 96-hour hold on cargo. At the same time, all border crossings into the U.S. are taking longer, though nowhere near the chaotic delays seen immediately after the September attacks. Many industrial companies have had to "buffer" their operations by stockpiling more parts, components, and materials at plants, says Joseph Martha, vice president of global supply-chain management at Mercer Management Consulting in Cleveland. But some firms, particularly those in the electronics, automotive, and high-tech industries, will have to go further, he says, by "looking carefully at their suppliers and deciding what should now be sourced domestically."

It's an issue Jim Commiskey doesn't need to be reminded of. Vice president of global services at Vector SCM in Michigan, he helps manage GM's $5.5-billion-a-year global logistics operations. Commiskey used to assume a one-hour lag for U.S. customs in his planning estimates when it came to GM parts arriving from Canadian plants. Now it's more like four. "Are we going to return to the days when going to Canada was like crossing from Michigan to Ohio?" he asks. "No. Those days are gone, and you have to build it into your supply chain."

The new frictions, in some capacity, affect virtually every company that moves its products around the country—but that's especially true if what's being moved could be turned into a weapon. Witness the recent experiences of Du Pont, the country's largest chemical company, where Jerry Donnelly, director of its $1.6-billion-a-year logistics operations, has had a trying couple of months. "I don't anticipate it's going to settle down much in the next year either," he says. "I'd like to get back to the business of shipping safely and saving money, but there are all these other things to deal with."

Like what happened on Oct. 7, 2001. That was the day the U.S. went to war in Afghanistan, but for Donnelly it marked the start of a focused period of contingency planning. That Sunday evening he got a frantic call from a colleague, informing him that Washington had stopped the shipment of hazardous materials by rail. Some 20% of the group's sales are from substances classified as hazardous, and he feared the worst. Du Pont normally keeps two to three days of feedstocks at its plants, and without those supplies they'd be forced to shut down.

On Monday morning Donnelly mobilized his team of 150 people at Du Pont's Wilmington headquarters, and they went to work—first figuring out inventory levels at 15 plants across the country, then coming up with alternative ways to move the chemicals. Donnelly felt they could probably ride out the crisis in all but one case—Du Pont's shipments of chlorine, a chemical used extensively to purify drinking water. The main obstacle: Chlorine, which is toxic if breathed into the lungs, can be transported only by rail. Checking inventories, Donnelly knew that after 72 hours several of its plants needing chlorine would sit idle. The problem "tied up our whole group for three days," says Donnelly. "We were running around with our heads off."

Luckily for Du Pont, the government called off the red alert by Wednesday afternoon. Yet for Donnelly the lesson was so clear that he's been planning for threats to the company's supply chain ever since. "Things that we thought would never happen have, and we need to adjust," he says. And that means considering shipping chemicals by trucks or barges—and in the case of chlorine, deciding whether to relocate the entire supply chain, a far more costly enterprise.

Uncertainty in and of itself is a frictional cost. And Donnelly is facing it from all sides, even from the government. For example, the Chemical Security Act, now being debated in Congress, would require companies to do everything from conducting more thorough inspections of chemical shipments, to providing detailed documentation of their production and delivery systems, to beefing up security at plants. The effect of new regulations for Du Pont will mean one thing, says Donnelly—adding operational cost. "We'll either have to use more equipment and have higher carrying costs, or we'll keep more inventory and that will increase our costs too," he says.

Smart logistics are the cornerstone of an efficient economy—indeed, many economists credit the relentless drive to lessen the costs of moving and storing goods as a key factor in the supercharged 1990s economy. Michigan State University logistics expert David Closs measures the progress this way: By 2001 the average large American business held 1.36 months of inventory, compared with an average of 1.57 months a decade earlier. Closs, unfortunately, thinks that progress is over—at least for a while. He expects the figure to rise to 1.43 this year as higher transportation costs and security measures lead companies to hold more just-in-case inventory. New logistics costs alone could add $50 billion to $80 billion to corporate America's bill in 2002, he estimates.

Security, you wonder? David Hale, chief economist at Zurich Financial Services in Chicago, estimates that the nation's businesses will cough up big money to hire 300,000 new security guards. John Santora, an executive vice president at real estate giant Cushman & Wakefield in New York City, believes that security costs at corporate headquarters will rise by an average $250,000 per year. The majority of firms don't have complete disaster-recovery or backup computer systems yet, according to several experts. They may have to add them—at a cost of $1 million for a typical software system. Throw in a few thousand background checks for new employees—at an average cost of $2,500 to

(Cont.)

$5,000 per person—and the security bill grows bigger still.

Few of those expenses are likely to be productive in terms of generating sales or improving operating margins. The new security measures divert scarce funds from R&D and technology that might improve a firm's operating efficiency—at a time when industry titans like Intel, General Motors, and Calpine have said they will slash their 2002 capital-spending budgets even further than previously announced. In a December survey of 3,200 CFOs by Financial Executives International and Duke University, a surprising 47% of companies said they will reduce cap-ex spending this year. Duke professor John Graham, who ran the survey, says that it's the largest number of firms making such cuts since the poll began in July 1996. "Before Sept. 11, cap-ex spending was flat," he says. "That really pushed it over the edge."

But the biggest costs may not be the nuts-and-bolts expenses associated with airport delays, insurance premiums, and Internet firewalls. They may instead be what we've called the squishy costs—the kind that are hardest to isolate, to quantify, and perhaps to avoid. Squishiest of all is the stuff of hundreds of management books and how-to seminars: thinking big. Whether you call them strategic initiatives or Big Hairy Aggressive Goals, the seeds of growth come from the mindset and often the sheer will of a management team—a commitment to invest in an uncertain future, to take risks.

That mindset seems to be a short-term casualty of the war on terror. Just ask Joe Forehand, managing director of global consulting group Accenture. Forehand has found that his biggest challenge since the terrorist attacks is boosting the morale of his 75,000 worldwide employees. "The loss of economic and personal security removed the anchor a lot of people had," he says.

The expense—in terms of the boss' time, at least—has been real. Forehand estimates he's budgeted an extra 20% of his hours to focus on employee issues. Rainmaking, to a minor extent, has given way to regular town meetings, which he conducts in Accenture offices around the world. "There's been a shift in my emphasis," he explains, "inwards—to our business and people—and away from business strategy." The candor is telling in itself. What modern-day CEO (a management consultant, no less!) admits to not being consumed with growth 24 hours a day?

The country's work force appears to be adjusting its priorities as well. Some people are focusing on family rather than career; others are suddenly shunning urban commutes and high-rise office towers. Morale, of course, is a messy thing to measure. But at least one recent survey, conducted by the Bureau of National Affairs in Washington, D.C., has tried. Out of 146 employers queried, a stunning 74% reported "fear and anxiety among employees" more than two months after the attacks. Some 27% said they'd seen a greater need among workers for counseling services, a quarter saw a decline in productivity, and a fifth claimed a drop in morale.

Some of that anxiety clearly comes from the nation's response to the terrorist attacks rather than the terror itself—for example, not being able to get into downtown office buildings. Which brings us back to Filterfresh and its 60-person sales team. The harder it is to get inside, the harder it is to generate new sales, a fact that plainly bothers CEO Cousineau. Before Sept. 11, the company's sales force would generate new accounts by walking from floor to floor in every office building, knocking on doors. Until recently the big worry for Cousineau's salespeople was whether they could get a meeting with an office manager to pitch their products.

Now they have a bigger concern—how to get in the door to set up the meeting in the first place. It's simply impossible now for the salespeople to enter most buildings without permission. And if you think Filterfresh is alone in this challenge, take a walk over to the photocopy machine. Companies like Xerox, snack-food groups like Hostess, and linen and bottled-water companies all generate sales by knocking on office doors.

Morgan Stanley's Berner calls these new economic drags a "terrorism tax" and adds pointedly that they're here to stay: "Even if we catch bin Laden, part of the way we'll continue to feel safe is by being prudent and cautious." What's more, the terrorism threat could have lasting global impact, retarding the advances made in the 1990s on macro issues like free trade and deregulation. "I'm worried we'll back away from our commitment to keep markets open and competitive," Berner says. Many executives in the trenches agree. "The ability to trust people has been a great strength of this economy," says Don Schneider, who presides over one of the world's biggest trucking companies. "When all of a sudden you have to check and double-check everything, it becomes embedded in our costs and makes us less efficient."

So the question becomes, Is there any way to shelter the already fragile American economy from all this falling sand? Some would answer with a resounding yes. A lesson that can be taken from the events of Sept. 11 is how economies adapt—and American business has proven in the past to be particularly resilient. The new frictions, say some economists, will offer a fresh incentive to improve efficiencies in other ways.

Paul Strassmann, a former head of IT at Xerox, General Foods, and Kraft, and now a productivity consultant, is one of those who predict a robust efficiency rebound. He contends that the new frictions will ultimately lead to savings as companies become smarter in dealing with them. Unnecessary business travel will be cut out, he says. Costly office space in metro areas will be shunned in favor of highly distributed office locations in less expensive areas. And firms will realize that the best defense is to be strategic about long-term security, not simply to throw money into lobby guards in the rush of panic. "It's an environment of using your head," says Strassmann, "not your muscle."

Optimists also point to the example of Israel. In the two years following the onset of the intifada in December 1987, productivity and business investment dived. But then both began to tick up as firms adjusted to the new environment. Richard Kasmin, head of research for Hotspot FX, a foreign-exchange trading firm in New Jersey, says Israel eventually built an economy that could function under the threat of terrorism. For the U.S., he says, the shock of domestic terror is going to diminish productivity, but firms will readily adjust.

In the meantime, however, anyone counting on a swift and strong recovery should think twice. And don't worry—you'll have plenty of time to think at the airport.

"The Friction Economy," *Fortune,* February 18, 2002, pp. 104–112.

E-Commerce Report

Some Web merchants fill a void, and make a profit, by selling coffins and other funeral supplies online.

BY BOB TEDESCHI

With so many consumer purchases proving popular online—whether books, concert tickets or prescription drugs—the question was eventually bound to arise. Why not coffins?

Funeral industry executives and analysts say that consumers are increasingly interested in being able to shop online for their funeral needs and that some Web merchants are stepping up to serve them.

"When you visit casket dealers online, you can look at something over and over again," said Jay Kravetz, editor of Death Care Business, a trade publication. "You're not pressured—you have time to look with relatives and friends. It's really easier online."

And it can be cheaper, given that some funeral directors mark up their coffins as much as 300 percent over wholesale, knowing that most consumers are reluctant to haggle or shop around.

On the Web, **Funeral Depot,** which sells funeral supplies both online and offline from its Hallandale Beach, Fla., store, is able to earn a profit of about 40 percent by charging double the wholesale price of its coffins—and still significantly beating funeral homes' prices. The average price of Funeral Depot coffins sold online is about $1,500.

"I'll offer the same coffin at a fraction of what a funeral home charges, deliver it overnight for free, and still make substantial profit and walk away the hero," said Dean Magliocca, president and owner of Funeral Depot.

Mr. Magliocca is among the more successful online merchants of funeral supplies, with projected revenue this year of $1.5 million—the bulk of it from his Web operation. It is a modest number, to be sure, but Mr. Magliocca is not complaining. "We're very pleased with our progress," he said. "It's taken us a little over three and a half years to get us where we're at, but we've finally perfected what we do, and we're starting to generate a lot of revenue with nice margins."

At the time he started the Web operation, Mr. Magliocca had been selling only monuments and grave markers from his storefront. "I started to hear from families that they didn't have enough money to spend on markers because the coffins were $5,000," he recalled. "I found out it wasn't necessarily because of the wholesale costs."

Mr. Magliocca, who started the online business "with about $400 worth of Web publishing software and a lot of elbow grease," offers nearly 300 different coffins, with prices ranging from $745 for an unsealed thin-metal box to $18,500 for a solid-bronze model that he says "looks like it belongs in space, not the ground."

FuneralDepot.com also sells "theme" coffins made by **White Light** Inc., which are painted in various motifs, including an auto racing theme. For the whimsical there is a coffin done up like a special-delivery package and stamped "Return to Sender."

Mr. Magliocca sells coffins from all leading manufacturers, like **Hillenbrand Industries'** Batesville Casket Company and **Matthews International's** York Group. But he has to buy them from third parties because he says that none of the major manufacturers will sell their coffins directly to him, or to any online coffin merchant, for that matter.

The problem, which has plagued manufacturers and online retailers in many industries, is referred to in business parlance as channel conflict. Manufacturers or their distributors either do not trust Net sellers to protect the image of their brands, or they do not want to upset their established resellers—in this case, funeral homes—by allowing online retailers to sell their wares at a discount.

To work around this problem, Mr. Magliocca has set up a nationwide network of about 45 independent funeral homes that are authorized to sell coffins from well-known manufacturers and have agreed to ship orders on Funeral Depot's behalf. These funeral homes earn a small percentage of each of these sales—business they would not have otherwise gotten—and many have received referrals from FuneralDepot.com customers who call or send e-mail messages to ask the company to suggest funeral homes in various cities.

Funeral Depot's arrangement with the independents has drawn legal fire from at least one manufacturer, Batesville, which says it has a lawsuit pending against Funeral Depot. While Batesville would not comment on the suit, a Funeral Depot lawyer said the case focused on whether the company could legally continue to use the Batesville name when offering Batesville coffins on FuneralDepot.com or link to images from the Batesville catalog that are shown on other Web sites.

Other online coffin sellers are coming up with their own work-arounds to secure brand-name merchandise. Kim Powers, president and founder of **Memorial Concepts Online,** which sells coffins and other funeral-related items on the Web, declined to say exactly where her company bought its coffins.

Ms. Powers, whose three-year-old company is based in Ponca City, Okla., said Memorial Concepts was now profitable, despite the fact that she could not sell in her home state. In Oklahoma, as in nearly a dozen other states, the law prohibits anyone without a funeral director's license from selling a coffin—critics say the policy is meant to protect the interests of funeral homes.

Last year, Ms. Powers sued the state, arguing that the law violates, among other things, her right to economic liberty under the United States Constitution's "Privileges or Immunities" clause.

In December, a Federal District Court in Oklahoma ruled against Ms. Powers, observing the longstanding practice of federal courts to defer to the judgment of state legislatures when the lawmakers regulate "nonfundamental rights," like those involving working conditions or the right to earn a living (as opposed to "fundamental rights," like the right to privacy). Ms. Powers and the organization that is representing her, the Institute for Justice, a libertarian advocacy group in Washington, are appealing the case to the United States Court of Appeals for the 10th Circuit in Denver.

A similar case brought by the Institute for Justice on behalf of a non-Internet coffin seller in Tennessee could help Ms. Powers's cause. In that case, in which the plaintiff is challenging a law that is nearly identical to Oklahoma's, a Federal District Court struck down the Tennessee regulation, saying it served "no legitimate governmental purpose." Tennessee's attorney general has yet to decide whether to appeal to the United States Supreme Court.

Even though the Oklahoma law prevents Ms. Powers from selling coffins in the state and has cost the company time and money, she said the publicity had been helpful. "Our business has always been very good in other areas, like markers and monuments," she said. "But since we brought this case, our coffin business has more than quadrupled."

While buying coffins online may be a way for consumers to save money, it may not necessarily be the best thing for the newly bereaved, according to Robert M. Fells, general counsel of the National Funeral Directors Association.

Mr. Fells, who said his group was "just fine" with allowing independent coffin sellers to operate online, said grief counseling experts advised people to visit funeral homes in person to help select coffins or urns as a way to ease the grieving process.

Yet, he said, "more and more, instead of going to the funeral home, people are saying, 'I don't need that—I'll e-mail you.'"

One Nation Under Wal-Mart

How retailing's superpower—and our biggest Most Admired company—is changing the rules for corporate America. ■ *by Jerry Useem*

Bentonville, Ark., does not come to the world. The world comes to Bentonville. Whether you're a media mogul or a toy tycoon or King Tut, you drive your rent-a-car north on Walton Boulevard, past Smokin' Joe's Ribhouse and the Lube N' Go, and into one of the parking spots marked SUPPLIER. Don't expect a welcoming party. You make your way into a packed waiting room that reminds you of the Department of Motor Vehicles and have a seat. Thirsty from your trip? Coke machine in the back. Coffee? Ten cents in the box, please. Change machine over there if you need it.

The young buyer who emerges to greet you has a paycheck that's far smaller than yours, a name that's far less celebrated, and a budget of about $1 billion. He ushers you into a seven-by-ten-foot blue roomlet—one fluorescent light, one table, one photo of Mr. Sam. So, says the buyer in his unfailingly polite manner, how can Disney help Wal-Mart?

If you are an executive from Walt Disney, you've been here before. Your company sells movies, Pooh merchandise, and many other items to Wal-Mart. But when the buyer wonders whether Disney could make a short video involving Wal-Mart and a Disney character—you know, something to get the store associates fired up or perhaps to play on Wal-Mart's in-store TV network—you have to say no: Disney characters aren't allowed to be so crassly commercial. Well, that's okay. Jeffrey Katzenberg was down here, and his team at DreamWorks made the nicest video of Shrek doing the Wal-Mart cheer ...

Not only was the *Shrek* video a huge hit, but Katzenberg has spent more time around Bentonville than anyone might suspect. "I've been there three times in the last 45 days," he confirmed recently. "I cannot tell you how much I respect and love the bare-essentials efficiency... I'm flattered by the opportunity they've offered." If this strikes you as unconvincing, you haven't seen Katzenberg do the Wal-Mart cheer.

That an important studio boss like Katzenberg would answer calls of "Give me a *W*." with fist raised might generate snickers among his peers. But nobody was laughing in 2001 when Wal-Mart—its stores bristling with displays of the green ogre—helped turn *Shrek* into the year's bestselling DVD. "Jeffrey figured out something his competitors didn't," says Warren Lieberfarb, the former Warner Home Video chief, who is known as the father of DVD. "Wal-Mart is the largest single revenue generator for Hollywood in the world."

And so, you see, there are two types of executives these days: those who have learned to play by Wal-Mart's rules, and those who still haven't learned the right answer to the cheer's closing question: "Who's No. 1?"

"The customer! Always! Whoomp!!!"

For most of Wal-Mart's 41 years, Corporate America refused to acknowledge the retailer as one of its own. Wal-Mart was Podunk, U.S.A., Jed Clampett, Uncle Jesse's pickup—and worse yet, a *discount store.* This year its transfiguration is complete. Wal-Mart is FORTUNE's most admired company, marking the first time the world's biggest corporation—yes, it replaced Exxon Mobil atop the FORTUNE 500 last year—is also its most respected. You might say that Wal-Mart finally belongs in corporate America. More accurately, you could say corporate America belongs to Wal-Mart.

To understand this astonishing development, you need to grasp the difference between a big company—what Wal-Mart was at the time of Sam Walton's death in 1992, when it was about one-fifth its present size—and a company that has created a whole new definition of bigness. If conventional metrics, like Wal-Mart's $240 billion-plus in sales or its 1.3 million "associates," don't do the trick, these may help:

► Wal-Mart's sales on one day last fall—$1.42 billion—were larger than the GDPs of 36 countries.

► It is the biggest employer in 21 states, with more people in uniform than the US. Army.

► It plans to grow this year by the equivalent of—take your pick—one Dow Chemical, one PepsiCo, one Microsoft, or one Lockheed Martin.

► If the estimated $2 billion it loses through theft each year were incorporated as a business, it would rank No. 694 on the FORTUNE 1,000.

What this means for Wal-Mart's lowprofile CEO, Lee Scott, is that he runs what is arguably the world's most powerful company. What it means for corporate America is a bit more bracing. It means, for one, that Wal-Mart is not just Disney's biggest customer but also Procter & Gamble's and Kraft's and Revlon's and Gillette's and Campbell Soup's and RJR's and on down the list of America's famous branded manufacturers. It means, further, that the nation's biggest seller of DVDs is also its biggest seller of groceries, toys, guns, diamonds, CDs, apparel, dog food, detergent, jewelry, sporting goods, videogames, socks, bedding, and toothpaste—not to mention its biggest film developer, optician, private truck-fleet operator, energy consumer, and real estate developer. It means, finally, that the real market clout in many industries

COMPANY	% OF ITS TOTAL SALES TO WAL-MART
Tandy Brands Accessories	39%
Clorox	23%
Revlon	20%
RJR Tobacco	20%
Procter & Gamble	17%

PRODUCT	WAL-MART'S U.S. MARKET SHARE*
Dog food	36%
Disposable diapers	32%
Photographic film	30%
Toothpaste	26%
Pain remedies	21%

*Percent of all sales through food, drug, and mass-merchandisers.

no longer resides in Hollywood or Cincinnati or New York City, but in the hills of northwestern Arkansas.

If this sounds fanciful, then you haven't visited Newell Rubbermaid's new Bentonville office, just a 60-second drive from Wal-Mart headquarters. One of 200 corporate embassies here that form a ring known as "Vendorville," it's home to the 50 members of Newell's Wal-Mart Division. "Everything in here is like Wal-Mart," says one manager, and he means it literally. The carpets mirror those in Wal-Mart headquarters. Same with the cheap cubicles. The first floor has an "exact replica of a Wal-Mart store" showing the placement of Newell glassware, Sharpie pens, trash cans, Levelor blinds, and so forth. Upstairs, Sam Walton's image and aphorisms hang on the walls, while even the Gregorian calendar has given way to "Wal-Mart time": Week 9 is understood to mean nine weeks into the company's fiscal year, starting Feb. 1. "You need to *be* your customer," explains my host.

Newell's reasoning comes down to one number: 15, the percentage of its merchandise that passes through Wal-Mart cash registers. That number helps explain why Newell CEO Joe Galli spends four weeks a year touring Wal-Mart stores, and why Newell seldom designs or launches a new product without Wal-Mart's involvement, and why division president Steven Scheyer gives every new employee a copy of Sam Walton's autobiography. (It also helps explain why there are no direct flights from New York City to Little Rock, but you can catch one of American Airlines' two daily nonstops from LaGuardia to Bentonville.) "We live and breathe with these guys," says Scheyer. "People are focusing on 'What's the right Sharpie for Wal-Mart, what's the right closet product for Wal-Mart, what's the right stroller?'" Little wonder that Stockholm Syndrome—the phenomenon in which hostages come to identify with their captors—has been a problem for some companies. "At first there's resistance, then they break down, then they go to the other side," says Steve Cleere, a consultant at TradeMarketing. "They're thinking like Wal-Mart people instead of brand people, and they need to be rotated out."

How Wal-Mart thinks has never been a big mystery: Buy stuff at the lowest cost possible, pass the gains on to the consumer through superlow prices, watch stuff fly off the shelves at insane velocity. (Critics who say Wal-Mart is obsessed with its bottom line have one thing wrong: Wal-Mart is obsessed with its top line, which it grows by focusing on the consumer's bottom line.) Suppliers are expected to offer their best price, period. "It's not even negotiated anymore," says Paul Kelly of Silvermine, a consulting company that helps manufacturers sell to big retailers. "No one would dare come in with a half-ass price." As for a supplier *raising* prices, good luck: In some cases Wal-Mart has been known simply to keep sending payment for the old amount. "The days of the price increase," Joe Galli has told his troops, "are over."

By systematically wresting "pricing power" from the manufacturer and handing it to the consumer, Wal-Mart has begun to generate an economy-wide Wal-Mart Effect. Economists now credit the company's Everyday Low Prices with contributing to Everyday Low Inflation, meaning that all Americans—even members of WhirlMart, a "ritual resistance" group that silently pushes empty carts through superstores—unknowingly benefit from the retailer's clout. A 2002 McKinsey study, moreover, found that more than one-eighth of US. productivity growth between 1995 and 1999 could be explained "by only two syllables: Wal-Mart." "You add it all up," says Warren Buffett, "and they have contributed to the financial well-being of the American public more than any institution I can think of." His own back-of-the-envelope calculation: $10 billion a year.

That, mind you, is Wal-Mart today. "As Wal-Mart grows," writes consultant Ira Kalish of Retail Forward, "it will transform its competitors, its suppliers, and the industries it dominates." In apparel, for instance, Wal-Mart is moving from staples into cheap-chic fashion, exemplified by its new George line, which offers career basics like skirts and blazers priced between $8.87 and $28.96. That in turn is pressuring everyone from Bloomingdale's to Banana Republic to compete on price as well as image. "Wal-Mart has caused the fashion industry to go topsy-turvy," says Marshal Cohen, co-president of NPDfashionworld.

In Hollywood, Wal-Mart's push for cheap DVDs (as low as $5.88) has exacerbated a schism between studios like Universal, which don't want to cannibalize the lucrative rental business, and those like Warner, which are pushing a high-volume, low-margin approach. Caught perilously in the middle is Viacom's Blockbuster. "We don't plan to participate in the below-cost DVD madness," says CEO John Antioco.

Convenience stores, meanwhile, are threatened by the 700 gas stations now in Wal-Mart parking lots, causing petroleum sellers to lobby vigorously for protective legislation. "We are seeing margins on fuel that we haven't seen this low in a decade or more," says Jeff Lenard, a spokesman for the National Association of Convenience Stores.

The battle of the brands, too, is increasingly played out on Wal-Mart turf. In batteries, perennial third-place Rayovac has used a low-cost "Wal-Mart *über Alles*" strategy to challenge Energizer and Gillette's Duracell. Tattered Levi Strauss, once too cool for discount stores, has bet its future on sub-$30 jeans to hit Wal-Mart racks this summer. And toy companies anxiously watch the fate—and try actively to boost the fortunes—of Toys 'R' Us, fearing a unipolar world. "If Toys 'R' Us goes under, and then Kmart too, are you selling 60% of your toys to Wal-Mart?" asks Alex Lintner, a retail expert at Boston Consulting Group.

Wal-Mart in 2003 is, in short, a lot like America in 2003: a sole superpower with a down-home twang. As with Uncle Sam, everyone's position in the world will largely be defined in relation to Mr. Sam. Is your company a "strategic competitor" like China or a "partner" like Britain? Is it a client state like Israel or a supplier to the opposition like Yemen? Is it France, benefiting from the superpower's reach while complaining the whole time? Or is it ... well, a Target? You can admire the superpower or resent it or—most likely—both. But you can't ignore it.

It is an odd fact that the public face of Wal-Mart continues, after all these years, to be the folksy visage of Sam Walton. Spend enough time inside the company-where nothing backs up a point better than a quotation from Walton scripture—and it's easy to get the impression that the founder is orchestrating his creation from beyond. The explosive growth of the past decade has, of course, actually occurred under the earthly apostleship of David Glass and, since 2000, 53-year-old Lee Scott.

Yet the best way to understand Wal-Mart is to talk to people like Shelly Chandler. Daughter of a Marine colonel, she started out sorting invoices for $4.65 an hour. As a $50,000-a-year apparel buyer in the mid-1990s, she controlled a budget of $1 billion. "Tough as I am—thank you, Sam—I got good deals," recalls Chandler, who still speaks of the company as "we" despite having left in 1996, when her child fell ill. "Sam taught us to be tough but fair. That's what makes Wal-Mart go round and round and round." Pressed on how it felt to control a thousand million dollars, Chandler paused. "I had the biggest pencil in the United States of America," she said, "and if someone didn't do what fit with our program, I could break my pencil, throw it on the table, and never come back."

Early power retailers like Sears and A&P started out with the upper hand. A 1930 FORTUNE article noted that "A&P's terms become, practically, Economic Law." (The magazine also marveled that "if every person in New York City were a hen laying regularly, there would not be enough eggs to fill the A&P demand.") It was the coming of television, plus laws that prevented stores from selling products below their listed price, that shifted the advantage to mass-marketers like P&G, Coke, and Revlon (which not only sponsored but owned the top-rated '50s TV show *The $64, 000 Question*). "What Wal-Mart has done," says Harvard's Tedlow, "is turn that on its head again. The store has a helluva lot of power."

How Wal-Mart chooses to wield this power is today's $244 Billion Question. Many assume that the company uses it crudely, cracking suppliers' heads and stealing their lunch money. But if that were the case, you'd expect to see manufacturers' margins shrinking. And? According to Value Line, operating margins of household product makers actually grew 48% between 1992 and 2001; food processors' went up 30%; soft drink makers' rose 14%. Though horror stories do circulate (some entrepreneurs have accused Wal-Mart of knocking off their product proposals), Wal-Mart also towered as the "best retailer with which to do business" in a Cannondale Associates survey of 122 manufacturers. "I think most would say that Wal-Mart is their most profitable account," says Silvermine's Paul Kelly.

How can that be? It begins to make sense if you consider the byzantine demands that most retailers impose on suppliers. Slotting fees. Display fees. Damage allowances. Handling charges. Late penalties. Special sales and rebates. Super Bowl tickets. Each is a small inefficiency that benefits the retailer at the supplier's expense and, ultimately—since the supplier builds those costs into its prices—the consumer's. Wal-Mart, by contrast, is famous for boiling everything down to a one-number negotiation. "It's very pure," says Newell Rubbermaid's Scheyer. "All the funny money—1% for this, 2% for that, 'I need a rebate ... I need a special fund for our annual golf event'—it isn't there. They'll negotiate hard to get the extra penny, but they'll pass it along to the customer."

While this part of the negotiation is strictly arm's-length (figuratively anyway, given the cubby-like dimensions of the blue rooms), Wal-Mart also operates in "partnering" mode, in which both sides swap information to streamline the flow of goods from raw materials to checkout counter. "They would rather extract fat from the process than extract their suppliers' profits," explains Ananth Raman, a Harvard Business School professor who studies supply chains. So while Newell Rubbermaid's "We ♥ Wal-Mart" strategy can seem the ultimate in corporate vassalage, consider what Newell gets out of the deal: not only huge volume but, thanks to Everyday Low Prices, *predictable* volume, which lets it keep its factories running full and steady. There are no advertising costs, no "funny money." And Wal-Mart will even back up its trucks to Newell's factories. Many suppliers, including P&G, like the model so much that they've pushed it on their other customers.

There's more. Newell gets product ideas from Wal-Mart. Hundreds of them. A store associate in Arizona mentions that Hispanic customers are looking for a kind of cookware called a *caldero*. Done. The hardware department sees an opportunity for "light industrial" cleaning products. Time to market: 90 days. Shoppers, in effect, get direct control of the nation's manufacturing facilities—reason to see Wal-Mart as the world's most finely articulated tool for turning customer wants into reality. A win-win-win.

Playing this game, however, requires constant hustle. Besides continually cutting your costs, you need to handle all that data pouring off RetailLink—the system that lets suppliers track their wares through Wal-Mart World—since you wouldn't want to annoy Wal-Mart with excess inventory or, worse yet, not enough. An electronic "vendor scorecard" will let you know how you're doing.

In the meantime, you should also be peppering Wal-Mart with "retail-tainment" ideas about how to make its stores more fun. If you're the maker of Power Rangers, that means creating the world's largest inflatable structure—a 5,000-square-foot moon—for a tour of Wal-Mart parking lots. If you're Coke, it means routing your L.A.-to-Atlanta Olympic Torch Run past every Wal-Mart possible. You may be "encouraged" to buy time on the instore TV network. And should you enjoy the privileged position of "category manager," you'll be expected to educate Wal-Mart on everything happening in the jelly or lingerie or Hulk Hands markets. Above all, you'd better start thinking like a retailer. "If you're focused on your shipments, you're screwed," says Dennis Bruce, a vice president with Newell Rubbermaid's Bentonville team. "You gotta be worried about what's moving through the registers."

The company of giants

Wal-Mart's share of the economy isn't the biggest ever, but it will be in four years if its recent growth rate continues.

YEAR	COMPANY	% OF GNP
1917	**US Steel**	**2.8%**
1932	**A&P**	**1.5%**
1955	**GM**	**3.0%**
1983	**Sears**	**1.0%**
1990	**IBM**	**1.2%**
2002	**Wal-Mart**	**2.3%***

*Estimate.

"Vendor offenders," as some Wal-Marters jokingly call them, don't last long. "People think they're wired in at the top of the company, but the relationship in itself means nothing if you don't perform," says Newell's Scheyer, whose father sold to Sam Walton in the 1960s.

Then, too, Bentonville isn't above dropping the occasional bomb. Procter & Gamble's storied partnership with Wal-Mart began on a 1987 canoe trip when Walton and a P&G boss agreed to start sharing information instead of hoarding it. Yet there was little warning when, in 2001, Wal-Mart unveiled its Sam's American Choice detergent at roughly half the price of P&G's family jewel, Tide. (The move "in no way strains our relationship," a P&G spokeswoman said at the time. Uh-huh. And we have no problem with a McDonald's" brand FORTUNE.) Now there are rumors—which Wal-Mart does not confirm—that the retailer is planning to introduce a second, even cheaper detergent under its Great Value label. "I'm not sure [P&G] didn't pay way too high a price to achieve that partnership," says TradeMarketing's Cleere. "They taught Wal-Mart about the laundry business."

Tide still commands about four times the shelf space of Sam's Choice, and Tom Coughlin, chief of Wal-Mart's US. stores, says manufacturers' brands will remain the company's cornerstone. But Wal-Mart's private-label assault has turned even its most trusted suppliers into its competitors. With little fanfare and no advertising, Wal-Mart's Ol' Roy dog food (named for Sam Walton's English Setter: 1970-81) has charged past Nestle's Purina as the world's top-selling brand. Great Value bleach outsells Clorox in some stores.

That raises a tricky question: What, exactly, is the brand here? As Wal-Mart flexes its muscle as a marketer and not just a merchandiser, it could accelerate the demise of weaker brands. Even P&G has refocused on just 12 powerhouses, like Crest and Pampers. Now manufacturers worry about losing their direct connection to the consumer. Two decades ago 65% of their ad budgets went to television and other mass media, while today 60% go to retailers for in-store promotions and the like. The worry, as a Forrester report predicts, is that "Wal-Mart will become the next Procter & Gamble." The nightmare: Wal-Mart becomes your company's new VP of marketing.

If the trip on Gulliver's coattails is no joyride, it sure beats being a Lilliputian underfoot. Over the years Wal-Mart has thundered its way up the retail food chain, first flattening mom-and-pop stores, then stepping on discounters like Ames, Bradlees, and Kmart, and finally sitting on specialty retailers like Toys "R" Us—threatening, in effect, to kill the category killer. Now no category seems safe.

Just ask your grocer. The quintessentially low-margin business had benefited from a decade of consolidation and cost cutting by giants like Kroger and Albertsons. Yet most of the gains dropped to the companies' bottom lines, not the consumers'. Now, feasting on fat margins in the presence of Wal-Mart is a bit like tucking into a juicy sirloin in the presence of a grizzly: Your dinner won't be there for long, and unless you start running, neither will you. Only ten years after launching its food business amid much guffawing, Wal-Mart is the world's biggest grocer, driving down prices an average of 13% in the markets it enters, according to a UBS Warburg study. The effect has been seismic: Kroger has gone on a cost-cutting drive to narrow the price gap, Albertsons has abandoned some markets entirely, and an army of consultants now advise grocers on how to grapple with the 800-pound gorilla. When Wal-Mart moves, it adheres to the Powell doctrine of overwhelming force.

Now imagine you're a Wal-Mart strategic planner on the prowl for other high-value targets. Where else are middlemen taking fat profits and stiffing consumers? Did someone say used cars? Of course! The last castle of medieval retailing. Visit the parking lots of several Houston Supercenters, and you'll find a dealer quietly testing a no-haggle approach under the name Price 1.

What else? Well, what about Microsoft? Its margins are—can this be right?—44%, and it's sitting on $38 billion in cash. Mr. Sam would not approve. Log on to walmart.com and you'll find $199 computers powered by a fledgling Windows competitor, Lindows.

Financial services! Regulators have twice thwarted Wal-Mart's attempts to buy a bank, but hey, you don't need a bank to offer wire transfers and money orders. And get this: Western Union charges $50 to wire $1,000 from Texas to Mexico. How about a flat $12.95 instead, and 46-cent money orders instead of the 90 cents charged by the U.S. Postal Service? Available at a store near you.

Wal-Mart vacations. Internet access. Flower delivery. Online DVD rentals à la Netflix. All happening.

Wal-Mart stresses that many of these experiments are just that: experiments. But the company has long excelled at using itself as a testing lab, tweaking and refining a concept until—boom!—it's everywhere. That's why even the looniest speculation—Wal-Mart partners with a Korean auto company to make a private-label car, WalMart acquires a drug chain, Wal-Mart becomes a wholesaler to other merchants—can't be dismissed. Just because you're paranoid doesn't mean Bentonville isn't out to get you.

Wal-Mart's zero-to-60 engine is driven by three powerful cylinders: scale, scope, and speed. The scale part is obvious. The scope part allows Wal-Mart to "flex" its toy section before the holidays and collapse it afterward, while Toys "R" Us is stuck selling toys year-round. (Scope also lets Wal-Mart use entire categories—gas, soft drinks, whatever—as loss leaders to pull people into the stores.) The speed part may be the most intimidating. Wal-Mart's turnover is so rapid that 70% of its merchandise is rung up at the register before the company has paid for it. Speed is why it routes ships from China through the Suez Canal and across the Atlantic, so that exactly 50% of imports end up on each coast—more expensive in the short run, but faster in the long. And while the interior of a Wal-Mart distribution center evokes the final scene of *Raiders of the Lost Ark*—42-foot-high corridors of toilet paper stretching toward a vanishing point—many items never hit the warehouse floor, moving directly from truck to truck along 24 miles of conveyor belts.

That leaves competitors with two options (surrender not one of them; Bentonville doesn't do acquisitions). Option No. 1 is to play Wal-Mart's game. Very risky. In the mid-1990s, Kmart proved it to be ritual suicide. On the other hand, companies already steeped in discounting—Costco, Family Dollar, grocery chain Publix—have more than held their own against Goliath. Option No. 1 should thus carry the warning found atop black-diamond ski runs: EXPERTS ONLY.

Option No. 2: Don't play Wal-Mart's game. Typically a better choice. Grocery folks regularly tromp through H-E-B, a Texas grocery chain that's held Wal-Mart at bay with such "destination products" as ice cream made from Poteet strawberries, a local favorite that H-E-B freezes in vast quantities. Not surprisingly, Wal-Mart is already thinking along similar lines, mining its mountains of data to tailor individual stores to local tastes.

The question on everyone's mind, of course, is, How much more dominant can Wal-Mart get? More than 70 million people already roam its aisles each week. Its truckers are trained to avoid deluded motorists who dream of a collision and a Wal-Mart-sized settlement. The U.S. Mint chose Wal-Mart, not banks, to introduce its Sacagawea gold dollar in 2000. Target had difficulty finding American flags on Sept. 12, 2001, because guess who had begun buying every flag it could the previous day. Hegemony, it would seem, doesn't get any more complete.

Yet a bit of fifth-grade math produces a startling result: If Wal-Mart maintains its annual growth rate of 15%, it will be twice as big in five years. "Could we be two times larger?" asks CEO Lee Scott. "Sure. Could we be three times larger? I think so."

Crazy talk? Maybe not. Roughly half of Wal-Mart's Supercenters (groceries plus general merchandise) are in the 11 states of the Old South, leaving plenty of room for expansion in California and the Northeast. And Bentonville is getting creative about overcoming the political and real estate hurdles there. In January it opened its first inner-city Supercenter in the Baldwin Hills neighborhood of Los Angeles, a three-story affair with special escalators for shopping carts. All told, Wal-Mart will open roughly a store a day this year.

As it expands outward, it's also filling in the gaps. "We've found that a smaller population than what we originally had thought can support a Supercenter," says Scott. "So you can put two Supercenters—Rogers (Ark.) and Fayetteville—roughly four miles apart. Same thing is true in Dallas, Houston, Atlanta." Within those four miles Wal-Mart is building new Neighborhood Markets, or "Small-Marts": smartly designed food/drug combos with conveniences like self-check-out, honor-system coffee and pastries, drive-through pharmacies, and halfhour film processing (this last based on a finding that 50% of women shoppers have an undeveloped roll of film in their purse). In Arkansas, Wal-Mart's even dabbling with stand-alone pharmacies. Throw in Sam's Club, with 46 million paid memberships, and walmart.com, with its mission of "easy access to more Wal-Mart," and you start to wonder: Is there any format Bentonville won't consider on its march to "saturation"? Well, yes, says Scott. "You're not going to see Wal-Mart casinos."

Which brings us to a final issue: Is someone going to decide that Wal-Mart has too much power? Doesn't the government break up companies that get this big? The short answer in this case is "not likely." Antitrust law is aimed at protecting consumers, not competitors. (In the US. anyway: A German judge last year ordered Wal-Mart to raise its prices.) Monopolists jack up prices. Wal-Mart lowers them—making it, in some instances, a more effective trustbuster than the trustbusters themselves.

Yet the company has grown self-conscious about its size. While Sears and Woolworth once announced their power by erecting the world's tallest skyscrapers, Wal-Mart strives to be everywhere and nowhere, hidden in plain sight—just your friendly hometown superpower. The reasons for that may be less calculated than cultural. Sam Walton used the language of service and democracy—customers, he said, "voted with their feet"—

(Cont.)

to build a republic of fervent consumer advocates. Today the company still sees itself that way—and seems confounded when the rest of the world does not. For lest we forget, America's most admired company has also been one of its most maligned, recently attracting headlines about class-action lawsuits alleging that associates were forced to work unpaid overtime. "In the past we were judged by our aspirations," says Scott. "Now we're going to be judged by our exceptions."

It's more than a little reminiscent of another fledgling republic that became a superpower and discovered to its shock that much of the world saw it as an imperial.

"One Nation Under Wal-Mart," *Fortune,* March 3, 2003, pp. 64–78.

Return of the Middleman

Remember how the Internet was supposed to kill resellers like CDW? Surprise—turns out, plenty of people don't want to buy direct.

By: Scott McMurray

The order you placed yesterday for 10 Belkin computer monitor cables arrives from CDW Computer Centers (CDWC), the largest reseller of computer gear in the country. You open the box, but you count only 9. You complain, and your CDW salesperson e-mails back a digital photograph of your order—automatically snapped just before the box was shipped. Sure enough, the 10th cable is right there in the bottom of the box. You feel sheepish, but you have to admit that photographing outgoing boxes is pretty impressive quality control. So you decide to order from CDW again, as most customers do. Congratulations, you've just helped bury one of the bubble era's defining myths.

A few years ago, tech industry pundits were convinced that companies like CDW were doomed. The beauty of the Internet was that it would eliminate the middleman, they said, particularly for IT goods. After all, why would people pay CDW's markup when they could buy directly from manufacturers with a few mouse clicks?

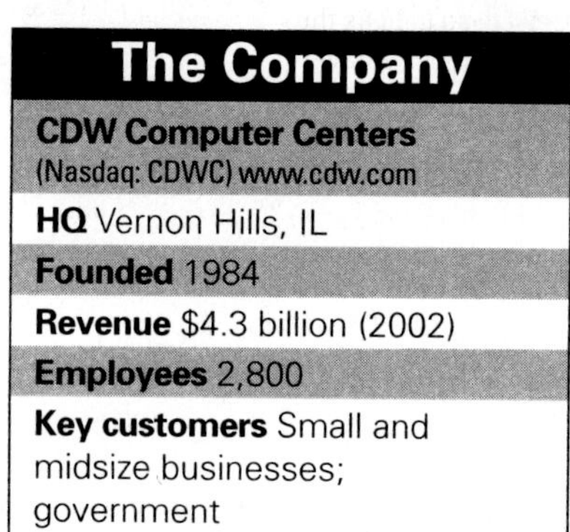

The Company

CDW Computer Centers
(Nasdaq: CDWC) www.cdw.com

HQ Vernon Hills, IL

Founded 1984

Revenue $4.3 billion (2002)

Employees 2,800

Key customers Small and midsize businesses; government

Once again, the pundits didn't have a clue. CDW has not only survived the collapse of the tech market but thrived. Revenues at the Vernon Hills, Ill., reseller hit a record of $4.3 billion last year, even as computer hardware sales flatlined industrywide. Profits stormed past Wall Street's expectations to $185 million, a 10 percent increase from the year before, and no one is happier than the tech companies that sell through CDW. When Hewlett-Packard (HPQ) wrested the title of No. 1 personal computer maker back from Dell Computer (DELL) in the fourth quarter, says Kevin Gilroy, vice president and general manager of HP's North American Commercial Channels, "CDW was a major reason we got there."

Like Dell, the epitome of the direct model, CDW had humble origins. Michael Krasny, a 29-year-old aspiring entrepreneur, launched the business by selling used computers out of his kitchen in the early '80s. By last year, CDW—at one time known as Computer Discount Warehouse—had risen to the top of the reseller industry, essentially as a modern-day catalog company.

> When it comes to reaching small businesses, says Cisco account manager Michael Mayes, "CDW is better than anybody else on the planet."

Two years ago Krasny handed over the wheel to a new chairman and CEO, John Edwardson, a former chief operating officer of United Airlines. Lanky and softspoken, the 53-year-old Edwardson favors jeans and an open-necked shirt around the office and looks fairly relaxed for a man whose business was supposedly doomed. "Despite all the bold statements by the dotcoms a few years ago," he says, "the personal touch still matters."

It's true that the Internet has lessened the need for some middlemen, notes Andrew McAfee, who teaches a course on managing information technology at Harvard Business School. Plenty of people now book airline tickets without a travel agent, for example. But as long as there has been trade, most customers have preferred to deal with someone they believe is working on their behalf. "Middlemen thrive on relationships," McAfee says.

And that's why CDW is in business. The bulk of its roughly 360,000 customers are small and midsize businesses. (Fewer than 3 percent are individual consumers.) Such outfits have modest IT departments at best, and they lack the volume to command much attention from equipment manufacturers. They need a relationship with a knowledgeable vendor, which is exactly the service CDW sells. Michael Mayes, a major account manager for Cisco Systems (CSCO), has seen CDW's sales of Cisco gear grow from $8 million to $130 million in four years. When it comes to reaching small and midsize businesses, he says, "CDW is better than anybody else on the planet."

One reason is its clockwork-like 450,000-square-foot distribution center in Vernon Hills, 30 miles northwest of

(Cont.)

What Works

Aided by data-mining software, CDW salespeople aim to anticipate customers' hardware needs.

Chicago, where CDW fills some 17,000 orders daily. An astonishing 99 percent of them are shipped out the day the order is received, so long as the product is in stock. Dell, by contrast, takes about five days to fill orders. Speed is especially important to small businesses, which tend not to have backup systems to tide them over during technology outages. To turn orders around quickly, CDW keeps some $130 million of inventory on hand. Inventory costs—particularly for IT hardware, which depreciates faster than "Super Bowl Champion" T-shirts in Oakland—were the reason middlemen supposedly couldn't compete. But CDW gets stuff out the door so quickly that the entire inventory turns over on average about every two weeks. Quality-assurance safeguards—like the cameras that record each hand-packed carton's contents—make sure that shipped stuff stays shipped.

The company also goes to great lengths to make small businesses feel that CDW understands them. Its 1,320-person sales force goes through some of the most extensive training in the business: Before they make a single phone call to a customer or prospect, staffers spend two months at an in-house "university" learning about the company's products and sales techniques. Once on the job, each salesperson becomes the single point of contact for his or her clients and is encouraged to act almost as an extension of their IT departments. The idea is that the salesperson should anticipate clients' needs, helped by CDW's proprietary data-mining software, rather than wait for them to ask. "They can ID customers who are ready to upgrade better than any reseller I've seen," Mayes says.

Still, CDW's is very much a sales culture, collegial but intense. One recent morning at the company's sales office overlooking the south branch of the Chicago River, the top producers from each sales team were racing each other around the central elevator banks on miniature bicycles. But then it was back to work. Signs on cubicle walls publicly announce everyone's individual sales goal. Top performers win prizes such as trips to Mexico. Underperformers leave: Turnover is about 25 percent a year.

A certain amount of intensity is in order for any company competing with Dell, which is pushing its low-cost direct-sales model beyond computers into printers, switches, and other gear sold by CDW. Luckily, CDW doesn't have to face the Texas giant alone; in response to Dell's expansion, competing manufacturers have pumped up rebates and sweetened financial terms to entice CDW to push their products more aggressively. In fact, on a visit to Dell headquarters last summer, Edwardson says, he thanked Michael Dell for driving so much business his way. "I guess you could say Michael thought I was a little brash," he recalls.

But brashness isn't a bad attribute to have right now. Edwardson says he's trying to sign up bigger clients and boost CDW's share of each customer's total "tech spend," which currently averages about 15 percent. (One recent win: Chicago publishing giant R.R. Donnelley (DNY), which chose CDW over Dell for a large order of desktops.) If CDW can do that—and continue to provide top-notch, specialized service—this particular middleman will still be thriving long after the pundits have logged off and gone home.

CDW's Three-Part Strategy

Service

CDW boasts that even the smallest business customer gets a dedicated salesperson—called an "account manager"—to handle orders and serve that client over time.

Choice

Customers say one big appeal of buying from CDW is that they don't get locked into buying one brand. CDW sells 80,000 products from hundreds of companies.

Speed

Ninety-nine percent of CDW's orders are sent out the day they're received, so long as the product is in stock. By comparison, Dell takes an average of five days to ship an order.

"CDW: Return of the Middleman," *Business 2.0*, March 2003, pp. 52–54.

Promotion

For Immediate Release!

Super Bowl Advertisers Use PR Firms to Generate News About Their TV Commercials

By Suzanne Vranica
and Vanessa O'Connell

Late last week, reporters and producers at 45 major media outlets across the country received mysterious blue tote bags. The contents: one plush toy squirrel, a plastic football, two pounds of chestnuts, two packs of Trident gum, and videotape with scenes from an as-yet-unaired television commercial.

Now, *there* were the makings of a hot story!—or so the LaForce & Stevens public-relations firm in New York hoped would be the reaction at "Late Show With David Letterman," "Late Night With Conan O'Brien" and other tote-bag recipients.

The bulletin: **Pfizer** Inc.'s Adams division is scheduled to introduce a new Trident commercial during the Super Bowl this Sunday. The spot will spoof Trident's familiar "four out of five dentists surveyed would recommend Trident" message by revealing the fate of the fifth dentist: A squirrel bites him.

Yes, the annual pre-Super Bowl hype by participating advertisers is in full swing—and more intense than ever. With so many flashy ads competing for viewers' attention, advertisers such as Pfizer are increasingly turning to PR firms to generate news that will have viewers anticipating a particular commercial.

General Motors Corp.'s Cadillac, **H&R Block** Inc., **Levi Strauss** & Co. and Monster, the online-recruiting concern owned by **TMP Worldwide** Inc., are using publicists to help pump up interest in their Super Bowl ads. A typical two-month pre-Super Bowl public-relations project can cost marketers about $150,000 to $200,000, on top of whatever they spend for the commercial airtime.

With the cost of securing Super Bowl commercial time reaching as much as $2.2 million for 30 seconds, or $73,333 per second, many companies believe it is no longer enough to simply advertise on television's most watched event. (Last year, the game reached more than 42.6 million homes, according to Nielsen Media Research.)

"You have to take your advertising and try to exploit it to the greatest degree possible," says Harris Diamond, chief executive officer of **Interpublic Group** of Cos.' Weber Shandwick Worldwide. The firm devised the publicity efforts of some companies advertising on this year's game, such as H&R Block and Monster.

Among the current PR campaigns:

- H&R Block has hired four full-time PR staffers to provide 600 hours of hyping for its Super Bowl ad tied to singer Willie Nelson's tax woes. The company is distributing 100 million entry cards for a "Tax Freedom for Life" sweepstakes tied to the ad.
- **Sara Lee** Corp.'s Hanes's press kit includes a T-shirt tied to an ad featuring basketball great Michael Jordan.
- **Reebok International** Ltd. mailed out coolers containing popcorn, pretzels, sunglasses and a football jersey.
- **PepsiCo** Inc. has posted its Super Bowl ad for Sierra Mist on the Web, where consumers can vote for their favorite ending.
- Pfizer's Trident, in addition to the tote-bag promotion, has hired two men who will dress up in fuzzy squirrel costumes and prance around outside the "Today" show studio sometime this week, hoping for some free TV time. A staple of the show, on **General Electric** Co.'s NBC, is panning the crowd outside. Trident is also sending letters to 45,000 dentists nationwide urging them to tune into the Super Bowl.
- Monster is using three full-time in-house PR professionals to trumpet its Super Bowl ad to the media and enlists seven full-time PR professions from Weber Shandwick. The outside team is likely to spend roughly 1,400 hours on Super Bowl tasks, which include arranging media interviews for Monster executives. The goal: Top the roughly $3 million in free press the company got last year.

Is it all worth the effort? Yes, if it generates enough pregame publicity. "It's more cost effective than buying prime time spot on 'E.R.,'"says David Byers, H&R Block's chief marketing officer, referring to the popular medical drama that airs on NBC. Confident that the extra media coverage would be valued at a minimum of $2.5 million in exposure, the company is hoping to top the 400 Super Bowl-related news stories it generated last year with a commercial directed by the Coen brothers, who are known for offbeat movies such as "Fargo" and "O Brother, Where Art Thou?"

Already, this year's Willie Nelson spot has received news coverage on **AOL Time Warner** Inc.'s CNN and in **Hearst** Corp.'s San Francisco Chronicle and **Dow Jones** & Co.'s Wall Street Journal. The syndicated TV show "Access Hollywood," is expected to do a full feature on H&R Block's Super Bowl plans in return for being the only TV outlet given permission to air the complete version of the Nelson ad.

Such publicity gambits often work because marketers are learning to stage them well in advance of game day, when the Super Bowl press corps is hungry for stories. Jeffrey Kuhlman, director of communications at GM's Cadillac, says he realized the company didn't reach out as much as it could have last year and vowed to "start earlier" this time. Today, the car maker has two PR firms working on behalf of its Super Bowl ad: **Publicis Groupe** SA's Hass MS&L and Bragman Nyman Cafarelli, a unit of Interpublic. One ploy: go-cart races featuring celebrities.

Quizno's Corp., the fast-food chain, is playing up a Super Bowl ad featuring Chef Jimmy, the company's founder. Quizno's is

Vying for Your Attention

Advertisers are hoping pregame buzz will help pump up interest in their Super Bowl spots. A sampling:

AD	AD DETAILS	QUARTERS
Anheuser-Busch	Singer Tim McGraw promotes responsible drinking	All
Gatorade	A present-day Michael Jordan plays a Chicago Bulls-era version of himself	1st
H&R Block	Willie Nelson promotes shaving cream after he learns he owes the IRS $30 million	1st
Quizno's	The company's founder becomes the fast-food chain's pitchman	1st
PepsiCo	A smart baboon promotes 'Sierra Mist,' among other spots	1st, 2nd, 3rd
Hanes	Jackie Chan attempts to remove annoying tag from T-shirt; Michael Jordan comments	2nd
Levi Strauss	Images of the Old West mix with modern images of young, hip people in jeans	2nd
Monster	An 18-wheeler missing a driver wreaks havoc on a small town	2nd
Trident gum	Trident spoofs its own 'four out of five dentists recommend Trident' message	2nd
AT&T Wireless	Viewers find out specifically what an 'mLife' is like	2nd, 3rd
Cadillac	A 1950s man daydreams about Cadillac's modern-day cars	3th
Hotjobs	Ordinary folks sing 'Rainbow Connection' at their jobs	3th
Reebok	Terrible Tate, an overzealous office worker, rights the wrongs of co-workers	3th
myfico.com	Families achieve a dream such as buying a new home	4th
Sony Electronics	A man liquidates his assets for his coming space trip	4th

(Cont.)

hoping for the the same attention it got last year after its public-relations firm pitched CNBC a story about how the company was risking the majority of its advertising budget on purchasing a Super Bowl time slot. The result: the cable channel did an entire segment on Quizno's.

For this year's Super Bowl commercial, Quizno's (along with General Motors) has scored with Gannett Co.'s USA Today. Headline: "Last year's rookies back for more; Quizno's shows a guy in his undies as Cadillac bets it all on 90 seconds."

The pregame hyping of Super Bowl ads is often traced to **Apple Computer** Inc., which almost 20 years ago chose the game as the venue to launch its "lemmings" spot. Before game day, Apple teased consumers and the media with a full-page newspaper ad warning: "If you go to the bathroom during the fourth quarter, you'll be sorry."

During the dot-com boom, advertisers became more ambitious. Upstarts such as Monster and Hotjob began providing reporters with copies of their Super Bowl commercials ahead of the game in order to get free publicity.

These days, PepsiCo releases its commercials about a week in advance of the game "to capitalize on the buzz surrounding Super Bowl," says Dave DeCecco, senior manager of public relations for Pepsi-Cola North America. The beverage and bottling concern got an estimated $10 million in free publicity for a 90-second Britney Spears performance it used to promote Pepsi soda last year.

Some, though, buck the trend. Contrarian **Anheuser-Busch** Cos., the world's largest brewery, traditionally keeps its Super Bowl ads under wraps until they run, a practice favored by some brand experts who say pregame publicity diminishes the impact of an ad.

Brand Builders

Up with Brown

By Dale Buss

The ubiquitous chocolate-brown delivery trucks and uniformed drivers of United Parcel Service qualify as genuine cultural icons, even playing cameo roles in movies such as *Charlie's Angels* and *Legally Blonde.* But early in its new "What can Brown do for you?" ad campaign, UPS kept its trucks and drivers on the fringes of TV spots that featured transportation managers and mailroom employees. The reason? The company did not want to distract from the main goal of the marketing effort to convince customers that UPS can do much more for their needs than simply deliver packages.

UPS still controls 80% of the $60 billion package delivery market, but its overall shipments were down about 2% in 2002 and the company has lost ground in the last two years to a rejuvenated FedEx. During that time, however, UPS has been able to mine new revenue streams by offering its business-to-business customers a range of related logistical services, including preparing and financing shipments, tracking deliveries and consulting on supply-chain management issues.

Throughout the protracted economic downturn, companies have curtailed expenses including shipping services, contributing to a stagnant package delivery market. The $3.2 trillion global logistics industry, meanwhile, continues to grow, boasting higher margins, fewer competitors and a distinct advantage for UPS: The ability to draw on its reputation and expertise in tracking and delivery.

UPS recorded $2.4 billion in non-package services revenue in 2001, up 42% from 2000, on total revenues of $31 billion. Through September 2002, non-package revenues were $1.93 billion, an increase of 35% from the prior year period, per company figures.

"They're getting some customer wins and awareness from the fact that UPS isn't just little brown boxes."
—Satish Jindel, SJ Consulting

Both company executives and industry observers say that Brown has accelerated UPS' diversification strategy. UPS credits the campaign with landing a series of major accounts in 2002, including a contract from Nikon outsourcing distribution of its entire digital camera business to UPS, and a deal with snap-and-button manufacturer Scovill Fasteners for services ranging from a revolving credit line to management of the company's distribution center in Laredo,Texas.

"We know there are companies six months or two years ago that would have called on long-distance trucking lines for some of these services who now are turning to UPS logistics," said Satish Jindel, president of SJ Consulting, a Pittsburgh-based transportation marketing firm. "They're getting some customer wins and awareness from the fact that UPS isn't just about little brown boxes."

Paul Meyer, group manager-brand communications for Atlanta-based UPS, said that Brown has "engaged people across the business landscape by giving them a new path for thinking about UPS and the role we could potentially play in their operations."

Take Ford, for example. Part of the logistical problem for automakers has been tracking vehicles once they leave the plant. Several billion dollars are tied up in vehicle inventories that sit on transport trucks, in holding lots or dealer showrooms. UPS says the new online tracking system it customized for Ford saved the automaker more than $1 billion in 2001, allowing the manufacturer to cut the number of vehicles it kept in distribution at any particular time.

UPS is finding such applications in widely diverging industries. In 1999, after signing a huge contract with Wal-Mart, breast feeding equipment maker Lansinoh Laboratories built a new warehouse at its headquarters in Alexandria,Va. But president Resheda Hagen said she felt more like an inventory manager than the new product developer who had built Lansinoh into a $10 million company.

After hearing from her UPS sales rep, Hagen soon turned over all of Lansinoh's inventory management to UPS,which she says significantly reduced her overhead. Hagen even contracted the importation of a proprietary line of breast pads to UPS, saving $2,000 per oceangoing freight container, or a total of about $6,000 per week.

UPS began moving toward diversification by investing in new technologies back in the 1980s, and now manages operations in customer service, warehousing, Internet retailing and overnight parts repair at its logistics hub in Louisville. CEO Michael Eskew, a 30-year UPS veteran who took the reins in January '02, is accelerating the strategy initiated by his two predecessors.

(Cont.)

"Because of the nature of our big brown trucks and drivers, people look at the company in a low-tech fashion," said Rick Radermacher, national ad manager for UPS. "But the company is as sophisticated as anyone in how we move 13 million packages a day, track them with almost constant visibility, flow that information to our customers ... All of that was below the surface; we never told anybody or showed anybody."

Its sponsorship of the Winter Olympics in Salt Lake City last February, and its Nascar tie-in starting in 2001 gave UPS the necessary marketing platform.

Tongue-in-cheek TV/radio ads trying to persuade Nascar driver Dale Jarrett to drive a brown UPS truck instead of his signature No. 88 Ford Taurus proved wildly popular with the sport's faithful. The spots, via Richmond,Va.-based The Martin Agency, stood out in the crazy-quilt world of Nascar marketing, say UPS execs.

Martin's research confirmed that many clients had no idea UPS could help them construct a system for ecommerce fulfillment, à la IBM or Oracle. Consumer surveys, meanwhile, kept turning up strong associations with the color brown. Drivers were called "Brownies" or "Brown" and positive references to the big brown trucks were nearly universal.

That came as somewhat of a surprise. "We thought 'Brown' conjured up 'small package' and 'ground' and that there was almost a negative connotation to that," said Radermacher. "But we found that [those attributes were] an acknowledgement of what we do best."

UPS spent $45 million in the first phase of the Brown campaign (it won't disclose subsequent outlays) in ads that debuted during the Olympics and the NCAA basketball tourney last March. Marketers continue to reach out to potential B2B clients with a nod to consumers. TV ad placements include shows such as *Friends* and *Frasier,* and various sports programs on Fox and ESPN.

Now, nearly every marketing message from UPS echoes Brown, including radio spots and print ads aimed at job recruits. "It's the right message," said Daniel McKinley, an analyst who follows UPS for McDonald Investments, a Nashville-based securities firm. "The challenge is to get it through to the right people."

That explains why several Brown ads are target specific. A logistics manager hails UPS for allowing her to communicate with suppliers online. "Other colors may be cute," she says, "but they don't call you back." Another spot involves a 50-ish CEO in wire-rim glasses who declares, "Brown's visibility helps me see my supply chain minute by minute." A herd of elephants traverses the screen in an allusion to trouble. "Brown shows me problems before they get bigger ... [but] never says to me, 'You can't do that.'" He pauses. "That's what lawyers are for."

UPS has also used Brown to try to boost its core shipping business. Its "One" ad, for example, keys on the fact that a single UPS driver can handle any type of pickup, an unspoken comparison with the implied inconvenience of FedEx, which has three different networks of drivers. UPS acknowledges that Brown hasn't yet noticeably lifted the company in package delivery where price and other variables dominate.

Still, Brown's momentum has begun to lead UPS in unanticipated directions. The company has launched a regional test rebranding of the Mailboxes Etc. chain of franchised packaging stores, which it acquired in 2000. The Nascar tie also built up speed when George Thorogood appeared in TV spots, begging Jarrett to drive the UPS truck while spoofing his own hit song "Bad to the Bone" as "Brown to the Bone."

The ads made great theater for UPS sales reps entertaining clients and even for potential customers watching at home. "Believe it or not," said Meyer, "the Nascar TV audience is a strong mixture of the kind of business decision makers we're trying to reach."

"Brand Builders: Up with Brown," *Brandweek,* January 27, 2003, pp. 16–18.

Direct Response Getting Respect

As OxiClean moves to stores, Clorox and P&G try infomercials

By: Jack Neff

When OxiClean pitchman Billy Mays met Procter & Gamble Co. Chairman-CEO A.G. Lafley last summer at a wedding, the encounter may not have been as unlikely as it seemed.

Mr. Mays and his direct-response industry have married into conventional consumer-products marketing in more ways than one. Increasingly, they're selling their wares in stores while still taking toll-free orders from consumers. Mass retailers are shedding reluctance to carry such direct-response staples as Orange Glo International's OxiClean. Some, such as drug-chain heavyweight Walgreens, devote entire front-of-store sections to "As Seen on TV" goods.

Old Dogs, New Tricks

But wait, there's more. Noting success of these upstart rivals, package-goods stalwarts whose brands have been "seen on TV" for years in 30-second ads increasingly are dabbling in longer-form direct-response ads. P&G's Swiffer WetJet motorized floor-cleaning gadget made its U.S. debut on Comcast's QVC home-shopping network in 2001. More recently, a flight of WetJet infomercials helped propel the brand past Clorox Co.'s rival Clorox Ready-Mop in four-week data from Information Resources Inc. in November for the first time since ReadyMop launched last January, according to Alliance Capital Management's Sanford C. Bernstein.

P&G's Dryel home dry-cleaning kit, on the market since 1999, recently tried a bare-bones direct-response ad in addition to its ongoing 30-second ads, both from Red, Cincinnati. As with Swiffer, the pitch was for consumers to call in for coupons rather than the products.

"Both the brands are doing well," said a P&G spokeswoman. "They're seeing an increase in sales, shipments and awareness. ... They attribute that to their overall communications mix, of which DRTV is a piece."

Clorox has been doing DRTV, too, including a two-minute ad to help launch ReadyMop last January. When Clorox launched OxiClean-rival Clorox Oxygen Action last summer, it turned to Encino, Calif. based direct-response shop Inter/Media Advertising to supplement conventional 30-second ads from Omnicom Group's DDB Worldwide, San Francisco.

Clorox is spending under 1% of its media budget on DRTV and is learning about the medium, a spokeswoman said, adding that the marketer is exploring how DRTV might help it develop alternative distribution channels for some products.

Joel Appel, president of Orange Glo, a Quaker Oats Co. marketing executive for Gatorade before leaving to join the business founded by his father, said, "We never could have put the kind of spending we've done behind our brands without direct response." Though industry insiders say brands can't turn a profit on DRTV ads once they have national retail distribution, direct sales still help pay the media freight.

Changing retail attitudes have opened the door for hybrid DRTV-to-retail rollouts, said A.J. Khubani, president of TeleBrands, marketer of such products as Amber Vision sunglasses and the Roll-A-Hose. "It used to take three to four years to get full retail distribution for DRTV products," he said. "Now, you see 'As Seen on TV' products in stores within a month of going on TV."

Other Advantages

The P&Gs of the world can afford big media budgets without those operators standing by. But direct-response offers other advantages. Brands such as Swiffer can develop a consumer database for direct-mail or e-mail offers aimed at building repeat sales of replacement supplies.

Mr. Khubani has no doubt OxiClean opened eyes of package-goods advertisers to direct-response. At a trade show last year, he said he met with P&G executives who quizzed him extensively about DRTV.

But the marriage isn't always a smooth blend. When Mr. Mays met Mr. Lafley, he says he needled him gently about informal complaints P&G had registered about OxiClean ads. Mr. Lafley's "a really nice guy," said Mr. Mays, though he referred questions to company lawyers.

On The Web, Word-Of-Mouth Marketing Can Become "Viral"

Firms reaching out to people who influence others' buying decisions

By Marilyn Alva
Investor's Business Daily

BigSoccer, PSXNation and XboxHardcore aren't your everyday Web sites. They're niche portals where hyped-up soccer and video game fans share information.

But a growing number of marketers see dollar signs there. They're trying to harness the passion they see on those sites to launch new products, services and ad messages.

Take Sony PlayStation 2's new "DragonballZ:Budokai" game. Early promotional videos, shown on targeted Web sites such as PSXNation, generated a buzz among core users. That helped rocket the game to the best-seller list soon after its launch in early December.

Why? Users of such sites "are the authorities on the subject," said Marc Schiller, chief executive of marketing firm ElectricArtists, which specializes in creating word-of-mouth ad campaigns. "They're living and breathing these brands."

Word of mouth is often called "viral marketing." It was popular during the Internet boom, but went into remission after the bubble broke.

But it's back with a fury. The concept is based on an age-old phenomenon: People will tell others about things that interest them.

Now a new wave of marketers is finding more precise and sometimes more scientific ways to get consumers behind new campaigns through word of mouth.

Passionate Taste-Makers

Video game companies are in the forefront of the movement to home in on target audiences. They understand, for instance, that an Xbox aficionado isn't interested in a Nintendo game.

The Web is an important avenue for finding passionate taste-makers who will carry a message forward.

"They have e-mail lists. They have their own networks. They understand how message boards work," said Schiller. "That means one individual can reach out to 30,000 to 40,000 targeted people—not just you and me."

Old-line consumer firms such as Procter & Gamble and PepsiCo are also turning to viral marketing.

The reason? Traditional advertising isn't as effective as it used to be, experts say. The net cast by TV advertising is so wide, it catches all kinds of fish, not just the ones marketers desire. That means a lot of dollars are wasted.

"It is so much more powerful hearing from your friends and neighbors about a brand than seeing it on a TV or magazine ad," said Laura Ries, president of Ries & Ries, a marketing strategy firm.

Experts call viral messengers by a few names: influentials, connectors, enthusiasts.

They have some things in common. They are opinionated, information-hungry, socially engaged and likely to spread information.

"They are about three to five years ahead of the average American in terms of new product adoption and lifestyle trends," said Ed Keller, chief of RoperASW, a market research firm.

One in 10 Americans have become trusted sources for their family, friends and co-workers, Keller says.

"You have to find a way to reach them and engage them in a dialogue," he said. "Their communities could be geographic, workplace or online."

Some marketers use squads of net-savvy "analysts" to comb through select message board threads to find users who seem to have the most influence over others. Those people are zapped offers and information on client products or services.

"It's not hopping into chat rooms and pretending to be a teen-ager," said Jonathan Carson, chief executive of BuzzMetrics. "We're pushing our clients to think of people on these Web sites as thought leaders who can really get their message out there."

Before any TV ads hit the air last year, PepsiCo used viral campaigns online and offline to generate buzz for the debut of its Code Red soft drink. The product became a surprise hit.

For instance, the online component included a "Mission: Code Red" game that gave players the chance to get free samples before the drink hit shelves.

Procter & Gamble even formed a viral marketing unit, Tremor Marketing Solutions. The division uses the Internet to find a core group of 200,000 teens around the U.S. to spread messages to other teens.

Cracking The Code

They were selected via random surveys on major Internet portals, usually as part of a promotional offer.

"We believe we've cracked the code to build word-of-mouth marketing programs for brands on a national scale," said Ted Woehrle, Tremor's general manager.

One viral campaign last year for Cover Girl didn't even involve a new product, and it happened offline. In one big metro market, Tremor mailed to selected teens a tin embossed with the Cover Girl logo. Inside were tips on ways to use foundation, mascara and lip color.

"We were able to create a viral story simply by giving the connectors provocative information on products that were currently on the market," Woehrle said. "Then we let them do what they like to do—share information."

The result? Sales for lipstick, mascara and foundation were nearly 10% higher among teens in that market than in others, Woehrle says.

JetBlue Airways, Starbucks and Krispy Kreme are good examples of brands that became successful because of positive word of mouth, says Seth Godin, author of "Unleashing the Idea Virus."

"It's about building a remarkable thing to begin with and letting the idea virus take over. Krispy Kreme is an idea virus even though it's a doughnut," Godin said.

For a "virus" to spread, it needs to be accepted by the host carriers. "The consumer decides when something is viral; the marketer does not," said Rudy Grahn, senior analyst at Jupiter Research.

Face-Off

An Unlikely Rival Challenges L'Oréal In Beauty Market

Procter & Gamble Draws On No-Nonsense Marketing To Battle Parisian Chic

Eureka in the Laundry Room

[1]Procter & Gamble purchased Clairol in 2001 [2]As of Dec. 1, 2002 Note: Figures exclude Wal-Mart, club stores
Source: Information Resources Inc.

What do women really want?

For two very different answers, step into the battle over the $90 billion beauty-products industry. For years one company, France's L'Oréal SA, has dominated the business by wooing women with Parisian chic, the promise of looking like its sexy spokeswomen, and the self-assured slogan, "Because I'm worth it."

What L'Oréal offers, says Chief Executive Lindsay Owen-Jones, is a "unique cultural heritage, which is Paris, which is beauty, which is fashion, which is an eye for things that are beautiful and that inspire consumers to spend more with the feeling of being special."

Now L'Oréal is feeling pressure from a rival with an entirely different approach to selling beauty. It's Procter & Gamble Co., wheeling out the no-nonsense comparative advertising that it's long used to sell soap and diapers, reciting statistics to show how its products are superior to "Brand X."

A current P&G promotion for Pantene conditioner offers a "10-day challenge," promising hair that is 60% healthier, 85% shinier, 80% less prone to breakage and 70% less frizzy. In another case, after using 60 different methods to measure the size of pores, length of wrinkles and the color and size of age spots, P&G researchers used results from one of the tests to proclaim in national ads that Olay Total Effects Night Firming Cream worked better than leading department-store brands. The ad featured a jar of Olay atop a stack of other products. The fine print listed the losers—among them, two products from L'Oréal's Lancôme.

P&G began the beauty wars in earnest in 2001, with its $5 billion takeover of Clairol—the biggest acquisition in the company's 165-year history. P&G thus leapfrogged L'Oréal's leading position in mass-market beauty, becoming the largest seller of cosmetics in supermarkets and club stores. P&G has the upper hand in skin cleansers, moisturizers and shampoos. L'Oréal, however, remains the world leader in beauty, and leads the U.S. market in color cosmetics and hair-color products.

Now the two are colliding more than ever. P&G is trying to penetrate the high-end market, where L'Oréal rules, while L'Oréal is trying to sell more shampoo and conquer Wal-Mart, P&G's biggest customer. And both P&G and L'Oréal have flirted with Beiersdorf AG, the German maker of Nivea skin cream, with P&G contemplating a $10 billion bid.

A.G. Lafley, P&G's chief executive, insists that his company can win by giving women an honest answer about how products stack up against competing brands. "Frankly, too much of beauty care has been promises unkept," he says.

Sitting in front of a row of L'Oréal products in his Paris office, Mr. Owen-Jones, a charismatic Briton who has run L'Oréal for the past 14 years, sniffs that L'Oréal ads don't "have the comparison of a T-shirt that's shrunk on one side and the one that hasn't on the other." In cosmetics, "you have to both inform, convince but also seduce consumers . . . and not just ram facts down their throats."

Mr. Owen-Jones adds, "You've got to decide whether something is beautiful, and by the way, even with the most sophisticated marketing methods, nobody is actually going to tell you whether this bottle is beautiful or not—you've got to shoot from the hip."

But today L'Oréal finds itself playing catch-up in some areas. After P&G launched Olay Total Effects anti-aging cream two years ago, L'Oréal quickly followed with a similar-sounding product called Visible Results, packaged in a bottle virtually identical to Total Effects'. "Imitation is the sincerest form of flattery," says Susan Arnold, P&G's president of personal beauty care, who started at P&G in 1980 as a brand assistant working on Dawn dish detergent. (L'Oréal says Visible Results is aimed at a different, younger demographic than P&G's product.) Total Effects, which has become the best-selling anti-aging cream in mass retailers in the U.S., retails for $19.99, one of P&G's most expensive products.

Keeping Up Appearance

P&G's interest in beauty is more than cosmetic. In the '90s the company's sales growth began to falter. Now many of its markets are mature, and profit margins for its core products, such as diapers and toilet paper, are under constant price pressure from generics and branded competitors. P&G has tried for years to relieve that pressure, and revive sales, by diversifying its product line.

Notably, Durk Jager, Mr. Lafley's predecessor as CEO, tried to move P&G heavily into the pharmaceuticals business—but his bid to purchase American Home Products Co. and Warner-Lambert Co., for more than $100 billion, fell through in January 2000. That March, P&G announced a steep earnings drop, sending its stock into a free-fall and capping a three-month stretch that saw the company lose nearly half its market value. Mr. Jager resigned that June.

When Mr. Lafley took over as CEO, he immediately set his sights on enhancing the beauty business. The company wasn't a complete stranger to the game: P&G made its first big foray into the field in 1985, when it picked up the Pantene and Olay brands with its acquisition of Richardson-Vicks. Until that point, the company's beauty revenue totaled just $1 billion, and its biggest beauty brand was Ivory soap, a product best known for its ability to float in bathwater.

Mr. Lafley, the company's first CEO

from the beauty division, dramatically increased the size of the beauty business, snapping up Clairol and pouring money into P&G's other beauty brands, while slashing costs and improving operating efficiency. He also joked about his short, spiky white hair, saying he was one of the only people left who didn't use dye.

In the first half of 2002, ad spending on Olay, Cover Girl, Clairol and Pantene accounted for about one-fifth of the $900 million P&G spent on advertising in the U.S., according to Competitive Media Reporting. Moreover, P&G, like L'Oréal, pours hundreds of millions of dollars a year into beauty research and development.

This attention has lifted P&G's beauty business and helped the company reverse its slide. Roughly $8 billion of the company's $40 billion in revenue now comes from beauty products, and under Mr. Lafley, P&G's stock has risen 51.74%. It ranked as the second-best-performing stock in the Dow Jones Industrial Average last year.

L'Oréal, meanwhile, has been in the beauty business since the early 1900s, when a chemist named Eugene Schueller started the company by peddling hair dyes to French beauty salons. A century later, L'Oréal has become the world's largest cosmetics company, with $14 billion in annual sales and a long record of double-digit profit growth. Investors have rewarded the performance by making L'Oréal France's second-most valuable company, with a market capitalization of $50.4 billion.

That impressive growth has made Liliane Bettencourt, Mr. Schueller's only child, Europe's richest person. In an unusual three-decade-old arrangement that was meant to protect the company from a takeover, the 80-year-old Mrs. Bettencourt controls L'Oréal in a partnership with giant Swiss food group Nestle SA. Mrs. Bettencourt, who has never taken an active role in managing L'Oréal, owns 51% of Gesparal, a holding company that owns 53.7% of L'Oréal. Nestle owns the other 49% of Gesparal, a stake it bought in 1974.

Crossing the Channel

L'Oréal owes much of its recent success to Mr. Owen-Jones, who joined the company in 1969 at age 23 as a product salesman. Steadily climbing the corporate rungs, he rose to the top job in 1988, becoming the first and only foreigner to head a big French company. Mr. Owen-Jones, now 56, cuts an unusual profile in the clubby Gallic business establishment: Born and reared outside of Liverpool, he bypassed the elite French schools that groom the country's CEOs. In his spare time, he likes to race cars.

Mr. Owen-Jones diversified L'Oréal's French portfolio by adding some American brands to reach a broader audience. The new additions, ranging from Ralph Lauren perfume to the Matrix hair-salon line, now represent 20% of L'Oréal's overall sales. And L'Oréal today derives a third of its revenue from North America, compared with just 14% from France.

The most successful addition by far has been Maybelline. Since acquiring the lipstick maker in 1996, L'Oréal has increased its sales nearly fivefold to $1.4 billion. Part of the makeover involved jazzing up Maybelline's offerings with some flashy new colors, such as lemon yellow and peppermint green in the Miami Chill line. To give the brand more cachet, L'Oréal also moved its offices from Memphis, Tenn., to Manhattan, and quickly changed the brand to "Maybelline New York."

Under Mr. Owen-Jones, L'Oréal's polished image has edged ever more toward glamour. One of his coups was to hire the model and actress Isabella Rossellini to endorse Lancome when he was head of L'Oréal's U.S. subsidiary in the early 1980s. That move helped turn the company's premium brand into a household name in the U.S. and popularized the use of celebrities in cosmetics advertising.

These days, L'Oréal employs what Mr. Owen-Jones has dubbed "the Dream Team"—a stable of dozens of models and actresses to plug its wares in billboard ads and on TV. The team currently includes supermodel Claudia Schiffer, Destiny's Child singer Beyonce Knowles and actresses Andie MacDowell, Heather Locklear and Catherine Deneuve.

P&G acknowledges that it can't compete with L'Oréal in trendiness. For the most part, the women who speak for P&G's beauty products are unknowns.

Mr. Lafley brought Domenico De Sole, chief executive of Italian fashion house Gucci, onto his board and recently sent a group of P&G product designers to visit him. Lecturing the P&G executives on the essence of beauty and luxury, Mr. De Sole held up his Gucci watch to illustrate the point that products that weigh more give the impression of higher quality. He also described how Gucci uses special tissue paper in its stores. Impressed, P&G responded to the advice by printing "Olay" on the inside of its moisturizer packages, a move calculated to give the product a more upscale look.

At L'Oréal, P&G's ambitions draw snickers. "They're mainly laundry-detergent makers," says Bruno Bernard, a biology Ph.D. who heads L'Oréal's research into hair follicles at a Paris lab. "Their vision of hair is of something you can wash like you would a piece of clothing."

P&G researchers don't dispute that idea. In fact, P&G's strategy to revive Clairol's hair-color business started in the company's laundry room. P&G turned to researchers at the company's fabric-care division, home of Tide laundry detergent, for new insights on how tapwater affects fibers. The P&G scientists found that there are a lot of similarities between a strand of hair and a string of fabric. The result: a new technology to block trace amounts of copper in tapwater, which diminishes the ability of hair-color molecules to penetrate hair follicles. "You've got to lift the natural melanin out of the hair and at the same time deposit new color," explains Wilbur Strickland, a P&G researcher who worked for three years to help develop the new technology. "With fabric-care products there is the same dynamic of taking things out [such as dirt] and putting something back in"—such as fragrance or fabric softeners.

The new ingredient will be added to Clairol's Nice 'n Easy hair color and is part of P&G's effort to stop a decades-long slide in Clairol's market position. Today, L'Oréal's two main brands, L'Oréal Paris and Garnier, control 47.9% of the U.S. hair-color market, according to Information Resources Inc. Clairol has 35%.

Now, both P&G and L'Oréal are looking to make big moves in each other's core markets. Mr. Lafley covets Beiersdorf, maker of

Brand Battle

Mass-Market Brands

	P&G	L'ORÉAL
Hair	Clairol's Nice 'n Easy Clairol Herbal Essences Pantene Head & Shoulders	L'Oréal Paris, Garnier SoftSheen-Carson
Cosmetics	Cover Girl, Max Factor	L'Oréal Paris Maybelline
Skin	Olay Noxzema	L'Oréal Paris
Fragrance	Old Spice	none

Prestige/Salon Brands

	P&G	L'ORÉAL
Hair	Miss Clairol Complements Textures & Tones	Mizani Matrix Essentials Redken, Kerastase
Cosmetics	Max Factor Gold (sold in Asia)	She Uemura Helena Rubenstein
Skin	SKII	Lancôme, Biotherm
Fragrance	Hugo Boss Joy by Jean Patou Giorgio Beverly Hills	Ralph Lauren Giorgio Armani Lancôme

(Cont.)

Nivea cream, the biggest skin-care brand in the world—an acquisition that would provide P&G with a strong foothold in Europe. Mr. Lafley declines to comment on discussions with Beiersdorf, saying only, "If you're not in the habit of being a hostile acquirer, the seller always controls the timing." L'Oréal took a look at Beiersdorf over the summer but has since backed away, according to people familiar with the matter.

Meanwhile, L'Oréal's largest product launch of its 95-year history will land squarely in P&G's domain. L'Oréal's new shampoo and conditioner marketed under its Garnier brand, Fructis, is coming to the U.S. in February. Currently, L'Oréal ranks fourth among shampoo vendors in the U.S. and is No. 5 in conditioners—segments where P&G holds the top two slots with Pantene and Clairol Herbal Essences. P&G played a direct role in Fructis's creation. L'Oréal came up with the new shampoo in France after P&G blindsided it with a breakthrough product in the early 1990s: a silicon-based two-in-one shampoo and conditioner. Now selling in Spain, Germany, Mexico and Canada, the U.S. is Fructis's final hurdle.

Strolling through a Duane Reade drugstore on Manhattan's Fifth Avenue, Karen Fondu, one of L'Oréal's senior U.S. executives, peruses the aisles of lipsticks, eye shadows and hair colorants, pointing out the prime placement of L'Oréal's products. Pausing in the shampoo aisle, she lifts a perfectly manicured finger and points to the top shelf where she wants Fructis to be positioned. "We want to be right there," she says, indicating a spot between bottles of Pantene and Herbal Essences shampoos and conditioners.

L'Oréal executives are enjoying playing the underdog in the U.S. "We're a relative newcomer to this side of the Atlantic," says Joseph Campinell, president of L'Oréal's U.S. consumer-products division. Putting on a mock Southern twang, he says: "There are still a lot of people at Winn-Dixie who want to know what that 'Lowral' brand is."

Knock Knock

In Brazil, an Army Of Underemployed Goes Door-to-Door

Mrs. Carvalheiras Gets Rich Selling Lipstick and Pans For Avon and Local Rivals

Finding Recruits in the Slums

By Miriam Jordan;

Osasco, Brazil—Five years ago, amid one of Brazil's many economic downturns, Marcia Carvalheiras saw her world crumble. Her employer, an appliance distributor, folded. Her husband's bookbinding business was dying. Jobless and desperate, Ms. Carvalheiras sold her car and gave up her family's health insurance. In order to feed her family of four, she collected food handouts from a local church.

Then she got a flier in the mail from a Brazilian direct-sales company. Within two years, she had resumed her middle-class lifestyle. Today, she is practically rich.

Ms. Carvalheiras, 38 years old, is one of Brazil's top Avon representatives. She's also a champion seller for Avon's homegrown Brazilian rival, Natura Cosmeticos, and for 12 other direct-sales firms whose pamphlets tout everything from lingerie to saucepans. From her office in this industrial Sao Paulo suburb, the new entrepreneur subcontracts a small army of people to sell door-to-door for her, primarily in the area's sprawling slums. Her roughly 1,000 workers come from Brazil's large number of unemployed or underemployed women, many of them eager to earn whatever extra cash they can. Ms. Carvalheiras trains her sales force, buys from direct-selling firms for them and splits the commission. Her business earns a monthly profit of $5,000 on revenue of $15,000. The average monthly income in Brazil is just $260.

Door-to-door sales are a bright point in Brazil's volatile economy. While retail sales edged up a lackluster 2.6% last year amidst the latest economic downturn, door-to-door sales jumped 15.8%. Brazil is Avon Products Inc.'s second-biggest market by volume after the U.S., and is home to Avon's largest sales force—800,000 people, up from 150,000 a decade ago—though many, such as Ms. Carvalheiras, split their loyalties with other companies. Avon's U.S. sales force is about 500,000.

"If the economy is strong, we sell because consumers are inclined to buy," says Saulo Nunes, Avon's vice-president for sales in Brazil. "When the economy is weak, sales remain brisk because we attract more representatives to get consumers to buy." In 1999, when a massive currency devaluation traumatized the nation, Avon sales in Brazil jumped 26% in local-currency terms.

Off the Books

Underpinning this resilient market is a ready sales pool born of 12% unemployment and declining real wages. Economists estimate that at least one-third of Brazil's economy is off the books, driven by legions of underemployed people who make ends meet by doing part-time work or freelance jobs, such as selling for Ms. Carvalheiras.

Despite a turnover rate of nearly 30%, Ms. Carvalheiras has little trouble finding replacement workers to peddle lipstick, lotion and lingerie. "Brazil's crises have drawn more and more women to direct selling to supplement their income," says Joao Carlos Basilio, president of a Brazilian cosmetics-industry association. "That has created a market."

In Brazil, about 60% of perfume, 75% of eye makeup and 80% of lipstick sales are made face-to-face rather than in stores. Brazil's Natura, which has a more upmarket image than Avon, has seen its sales swell about 35% a year in the past decade. The country's largest lingerie maker, De Millus, has a door-to-door sales force of 100,000 women, who rang up 75% of the company's $77 million in revenue last year.

Direct sales also get a boost from a Brazilian penchant for mixing business and personal relationships. The intermingling of professional and social affairs permeates everything from big business to politics. Many of Ms. Carvalheiras's customers say they will spend a bit more to buy from someone they know rather than save money at a shop. "Personal relations count more than economic logic in Brazil," says Roberto DaMatta, a University of Notre Dame professor and one of the leading anthropologists studying Brazil.

'Extra Cash'

Ms. Carvalheiras, who started her own direct-selling career when she faced financial hardship, intentionally targeted needy communities. With a loudspeaker attached to her husband's subcompact Fiat, she recruited women in the slums that abut Osasco, promising only "extra cash." It worked. Ms. Carvalheiras enlisted hundreds of women in a matter of weeks.

Lillian Manoel, 20, who has a high-school diploma, lost her job when the bingo parlor where she worked as a receptionist folded six months ago. Since then, she has filled countless job applications, most recently to stock shelves at a pharmaceutical company. But, echoing a common complaint in Brazil, she says her chances of getting hired evaporate when prospective employers learn she recently married. She already has one young daughter out of wedlock, and Ms. Manoel assumes companies won't hire her since they don't want to get stuck with Brazil's generous four-month paid pregnancy leave if she should have another baby.

In Sao Paulo, Brazil's most industrialized state, unemployment hit 19% in 2002. Half of the breadwinners in Ms. Manoel's row of hovels lost their jobs in the last year. Ms. Manoel, who earned about $150 a month at the bingo parlor, now makes about $50 a month selling cosmetics, lingerie, costume jewelry and other items for Ms. Carvalheiras. Her husband, Eurico, works at a construction company, where he earns about $110 a month—enough to feed and clothe the family. The couple and Ms. Manoel's two-year-old, Isabelli, live in the tiny living room of a relative's shack. The cash that Ms. Manoel makes goes to paying a bricklayer, who is building them a home. "Thank God for this freelance work," says Ms. Manoel, as she climbs to the top of the hill where the half-built hovel is precariously perched.

Ms. Manoel counts on her friends to buy something every three weeks, the interval at which companies such as Avon and Natura refresh their catalogs and special offers. One neighbor, Arlene Soares, regularly purchases body lotion and cologne for about $4 each. The single mother of two, who earns about $100 cooking and cleaning for a Sao Paulo family, says that at a local drugstore she can find comparable products for less than half the price of Ms. Manoel's. But, "Lillian is very knowledgeable about what she sells," says Ms. Soares. "And, I know I am helping her out."

Some critics say direct sellers are taking advantage of the high unemployment by inducting armies of part-time salespeople into their organizations without having to shell out benefits. "The companies get high productivity with virtually no expenditure," says Carlos Alonso Barbosa de Oliveira, an expert in labor relations at the University of Campinas.

Ms. Carvalheiras doesn't need to advertise heavily to attract people to sell for her. Outside her main office in the heart of Osasco, two young women wearing aprons emblazoned with "The King of Catalogs"—the name that Ms. Carvalheiras gave her business—distribute fliers to passersby. Recruiters also visit open-air markets and wait outside schools. They stand outside Avon product meetings to lure Avon representatives to work for Ms. Carvalheiras on a freelance basis, selling all the brands that her company represents. Avon tolerates the poaching: Ms. Carvalheiras's Avon sales rose 75% last year to about $50,000. (Avon is one of her most popular brands.)

To handle her large sales force, Ms. Carvalheiras operates three distribution centers. On a recent afternoon, Ms. Carvalheiras's central office in a low-rise, dingy building was packed with women, several with toddlers at their side, who came to place orders, and collect and pay for merchandise. Ms. Carvalheiras knew several of them by name. She helped an illiterate woman fill out an order form. Another wanted help figuring out how much she must sell a month to earn a net of 100 reals, or about $30.

Ms. Carvalheiras's freelance workers, most of whom wouldn't qualify as official representatives for Avon and other brands, are effectively her customers. She buys directly from the company based on orders they place. Then her workers buy the products from her and resell them. In the case of Avon, Ms. Carvalheiras gives two-thirds of the commission to her saleswomen and keeps one-third herself.

Management Fee

Though Avon gives Ms. Carvalheiras 31 days to pay, she demands payment from her saleswomen within 10 days and charges stiff interest penalties—around 3% a month. Though high by U.S. standards, her rate is lower than the nearly 9% a month charged by major Brazilian banks for overdrafts. The time lag benefits Ms. Carvalheiras. She can pay Avon early and get a discount, often about 3% a month, which she keeps as a kind of management fee. "That's more than I would make on any short-term investment," she says.

Ms. Carvalheiras has brought her workers benefits uncommon in Brazil's informal economy. She persuaded a local private hospital to offer group health insurance to about 300 women and their families at a fraction of the normal rate, after learning that many longed for an alternative to the surly service and long lines at government health centers. For the poorest women, she persuaded a bank to waive a minimum-deposit requirement so that they could open accounts.

Ms. Carvalheiras also shoulders risks that a large company wouldn't take. Many of the women selling for her wouldn't pass background checks by a direct-selling firm. Ms. Manoel, for one, appears on a national debtors list because she missed payments on a bed that she had bought in installments after losing her full-time job. Some direct-selling firms require their new representatives to make an initial investment in a demonstration kit, which Ms. Manoel couldn't afford. Also, many women who work for Ms. Carvalheiras sell too little to meet minimum sales targets that companies set for their official representatives. "I like working with Marcia because she doesn't mind if I come in with an order that's as small as one item," says Maria da Guia, 50, after buying just $30 in products to resell in her slum.

Ms. Carvalheiras offers her sales force advice about domestic violence, drug abuse, marital infidelity and other problems that afflict their households. She says she recently escorted a young woman who had been raped to the hospital and the police station. "I have entered a world that people like me normally only read about in the newspapers," says Ms. Carvalheiras, who has a degree from a local college and considers herself middle class.

Even so, it's tough going for the saleswomen on the bottom rung. The turnover remains at 30% a month because many workers fail to earn as much or as quickly as they hoped. Others give up because of personal problems, such as drug addiction and illness in the family.

Ms. Carvalheiras has started devising incentives to motivate her ever-growing sales force and reduce turnover. She has hired 10 women as team leaders, overseeing small groups. Ms. Carvalheiras has also started rewarding top performers—those who sell more than $300 a month—with food items and small appliances. "I learn from Avon and replicate on a smaller scale," she says.

As her empire has expanded, Ms. Carvalheiras has accumulated wealth. She recently bought a three-bedroom apartment in Osasco that she plans to rent out and is building a four-bedroom house. She has also invested in herself: breast implants, a nose job and a hair transplant.

Because of her high sales (she's the third-biggest Avon seller in the country), the company has showered her with prizes, including cars, home appliances and trophies. (Another company awarded her a trip to Disney World.) Several Avon executives have visited The King of Catalogs to see her business close-up and will soon be training freelancers in her new headquarters.

In October, Ms. Carvalheiras opened her first franchise in another city and plans her second one this year. Her husband, who left his bookbinding business, is now her accountant and technology officer, having designed The King of Catalogs Web site. Ms. Carvalheiras will soon launch her own line of skin products, undeterred by Brazil's fickle economy. "I got into this thanks to a crisis," she says. "I intend to grow a lot more."

Out of Control

Oracle's fabled sales culture has broken down. Customers are angry, and Larry Ellison knows it. Here's how he's trying to shape the future of the world's second-largest software maker.

By Ian Mount

Last August, North Dakota state senator Joel Heitkamp was on a commercial flight home from Texas when he struck up a conversation with a professionally dressed woman in the seat next to his. He had no idea what an earful he was about to receive.

The other passenger, it turned out, was Chris Brown, an Oracle Corp. (ORCL) saleswoman who was part of a team trying to sell software to several North Dakota state agencies. According to Heitkamp, she was livid at the prospect that Oracle might lose out in the bidding. She blasted the state's bidding process, which was being managed by Curtis Wolfe—the state's chief information officer and a man Heitkamp respected. And then, in an astonishing move, she said Oracle might sue the state if it lost the bid.

Brandishing lawsuits at customers isn't exactly high on the list of all-time winning sales tactics.

But when Wolfe heard about the conversation, he was not surprised. For months Wolfe had been steaming about other high-pressure moves by Oracle salespeople. In the end the state's $22 million contract went to Oracle archrival PeopleSoft (PSFT) because it had better software, Wolfe says. But the machinations of Oracle's sales team left a sour taste that's sure to linger. "You don't want them to be like used-car salesmen," he says.

Tales of hyperaggressive salespeople are nothing new to Oracle. The company is legendary for a sales culture that combines the fervor of tent revival preachers and the determination of combat Marines. Once the envy of the industry, it's a major reason Oracle became the world's second-largest software company, and its founder, Larry Ellison, one of the world's richest men.

The industry has changed, however, and so has Oracle's place in it. Competitors from IBM (IBM) to Microsoft (MSFT) are challenging the company's once-dominant position in the database software market. Oracle, in turn, is desperately trying to build a presence in applications that run other business processes. That thrusts Oracle's sales team into a much more crowded and nuanced market, face-to-face with seasoned competitors like Siebel Systems (SEBL) and SAP (SAP). The whole strategy has been rendered even more delicate by quality problems in its new business management application suite—called 11i—and by the steepest downturn in IT spending in recent memory.

Episodes like the North Dakota one suggest that Oracle's sales team either doesn't grasp the gravity of the company's situation or is simply unable to adapt its brute-force tactics to the new reality. State officials in places like South Dakota and Wisconsin have joined North Dakota in denouncing Oracle, complaining about everything from heavy-handed sales pitches to gouging on price. Many corporate clients have their own beefs; some say Oracle salespeople have lied about product capabilities. And in its most public debacle, Oracle has been dragged into a California political scandal in which the company is alleged to have stuck the state with as much as $41 million worth of software and services it will never use. There's no evidence yet that the company did anything wrong, and the scandal appears to be more about state politics than about Oracle; still, the headlines only reinforce the image of a sales force that routinely runs roughshod over customers.

Man with a Plan

Larry Ellison say's he's reforming Oracle's famously aggressive sales operation, but some wonder whether the hyper-competitive CEO is right for the job.

Oracle says it has done nothing improper in any of these situations. "It's almost counterintuitive to think that you can behave inappropriately for a long period and be successful," says Kevin Fitzgerald, who runs Oracle's government, education, and health-care sales. "It just doesn't happen that way." But the company admits that bad publicity has cost it business. Indeed, the catalog of complaints is serious enough to have engaged Oracle's sometimes remote founder and CEO. In an interview with *Business 2.0,* the usually defiant Ellison conceded that his

(Cont.)

SELLING MEDICINE

Sick sales cultures can be cured. Here are some time-tested remedies.

Nothing taxes the health of a sales force like a recession. Sales dry up, commissions plunge, top performers walk. Yet tight times are the right times for diagnosing and curing sales force ills. Problems hidden—or caused—by easy growth are exposed, and change is easier because everybody expects it. "Salespeople know the shareholders are screaming, 'Fix something!'" says Andris Zoltners, managing director of sales force consultancy ZS Associates. Luckily, top-line torpor is usually caused by a few highly treatable conditions. And none need be terminal.—Andy Raskin

GREEDOPHILIA: Of all sales force motivators, greed is the worst. "Witness Enron," says Zoltners, who is also a marketing professor at the Kellogg School of Management. "When greed is the driver, salespeople overstate product advantage and do anything to get the sale—not good for long-term customer happiness."

TREATMENT: Go right to the top of the sales team, Zoltners says: "Get rid of the Ken Lay, and changes propagate down. You gotta cut out the heart, and put in a new one."

CALLPHOBIA: It's tough out there for salespeople who got used to the boom-era life of easy deals. And fear of today's more complex selling environment means less pavement-pounding. "Many companies give us a grandiose analysis of their problems, and it turns out their salespeople simply aren't talking to customers," says Sam Reese, CEO of Miller Heiman, a sales training firm. "They show up talking about widgets, and the buyer says, 'I already saw that on your website—I want to discuss financing, customer service, and logistics.'"

TREATMENT: Design a sales process with support from other departments, like finance and engineering. But, Reese warns, establish milestones that a salesperson must hit before resources become available. As Alec Baldwin admonished a poor-performing Jack Lemmon in *Glengarry Glen Ross,* "Coffee is for closers!"

INCENTIVITIS: Compensation plans that don't keep pace with industry changes fail to reward productive behavior. At Microchip Technology, a crucial selling step is getting manufacturing customers to design its microcontrollers into new products. But when Mitch Little became Microchip's VP for worldwide sales in 1999, he saw customers moving assembly overseas. "Our guy in, say, Boston was no longer motivated to get the design win," Little says, "because the customers were purchasing from a plant in Mexico—and the Mexico rep would get the commission."

TREATMENT: Little now compensates everyone on his 300-person team with a salary and an incentive based solely on corporate performance. He credits the move with helping Microchip hold its own in its beleaguered sector, though he admits that it drove some people out. "This takes a different kind of person," Little says. "We found that out real quick."

CHRONIC TEAM ROT: Companies that lowered hiring standards during the boom are paying the price. "A lot of pretenders wound up in sales when it was the land of milk and honey," Reese says. And it doesn't take many bad hires to ruin a quarter. "If you have a bad salesperson, you knock out a territory," Zoltners says. "If you have a bad sales manager, you knock out 10 or 12."

TREATMENT: List the skills your salespeople need—not only selling prowess but also things like industry experience and product knowledge. Then start hiring and firing. "Today is a great time to find out if you have the A team or the B team," Reese says, "and to start muscle-building if it's the latter."

sales operation has in some ways lost its bearings. "Culturally," he says, "Oracle is doing everything it can to operate differently." It has little choice. With its revenues down 11.8 percent for the fiscal year that ended in May and its share price off 90 percent to about $9 since June 2000, Oracle can't afford a sales force that's a liability. Whether Ellison and his team can civilize a program that has been addicted to aggressiveness for two decades—and whether the notoriously competitive Ellison is the person to lead the way—is a question Oracle must answer quickly. At stake are not only Oracle's customer relations, but also its push to become more than just a database vendor. And on that initiative rests the very future of the company.

A fire-breathing sales culture doesn't arise overnight. Oracle's started long ago, with the man Ellison called Genghis Khan.

His real name is Gary Kennedy. A Mormon bishop from a ranching town in the northeast corner of Utah, Kennedy came to Oracle in 1982 and soon built what is acclaimed to this day to be the toughest sales group ever seen in tech. Kennedy's team was heavy on working-class ex-athletes, people Kennedy believed were hungry to make an indelible mark on the world. "I loved to hire policemen's kids," says Kennedy, now semiretired and living outside Salt Lake City. They received the briefest gesture at training—a mere five days—and were unleashed on the world.

Former Kennedy salespeople say he fostered a deeply Darwinian climate. "The motto was 'We Eat Our Young,'" recalls Marc Benioff, a former Oracle sales executive who's now CEO of Salesforce.com. One of Kennedy's blunter motivating tactics was a sales force ranking called "Hail to the Stars." Kennedy didn't just highlight the best salespeople in this regular e-mail—he listed them all, down to the absolute worst, and noted those who'd been canned or had otherwise departed. Each salesperson had a quota and a "commit," essentially a quasi-religious oath to bring in a certain amount of business.

(Cont.)

Written on Post-its stuck in Kennedy's desk, a salesperson's commit hung over him like a sword. "It was basically in blood," says Harry Gould, a former Oracle salesman who's now a top executive at SeeBeyond. "Gary boiled sales down to that one word."

The best salespeople got wealthy in very public ways. In a program he dubbed "Go for the Gold," Kennedy had Brink's truck drivers deliver gold coins to the desks of salespeople who beat quota. Details often got overlooked in the mad push for sales. Former executives say some salesmen who'd missed their quotas got gold by mistake, and Oracle later learned that it had paid out over $10 million more than it meant to because commissions had been miscalculated.

Kennedy's approach moved product: Oracle's sales rose from about $55 million in 1986 to nearly $1 billion in 1990. But that year, the relentless pressure to make quota that had been Kennedy's hallmark caught up with the company. Mired in a slump that made hitting sales targets that much tougher, some of Kennedy's salespeople tried to fill the gap by making under-the-table deals that boosted sales by allowing the customers to return software they didn't want. Oracle was forced to restate earnings, and Kennedy was ousted in a sacrifice to investors.

Today, Kennedy says he regrets some of what happened on his watch. He pushed hard, he says, but always emphasized playing by the rules. "What I didn't say, and wish I'd said, was 'Look, in a world of two bad choices—miss your quota or break the rules—it's much, much better to miss your quota,'" he says.

During the tech boom, rule-breaking was hardly necessary, but Oracle never totally lost its tough-as-nails sales culture. And as times have gotten leaner and the pressure to close deals has grown, some of the old aggression—and the damage it can do to customer relations—has resurfaced.

Wolfe, North Dakota's CIO, says the threatened lawsuit was just one of many instances where Oracle's sales tactics went over the line. For instance, North Dakota had set up a system under which all communication between the 25 or so members of the decision-making committee and the vendors was to be funneled through an independent consultant hired for that purpose. Salespeople from PeopleSoft and the other bidders abided by that rule, Wolfe says. But Oracle's lead salespeople showed up unannounced and repeatedly lobbied committee members directly; in fact, he says, Oracle was so pushy that it learned that one company was going to be dropped from the bidding before the company itself even knew. "They try to go around you, try to go through you," he says. "That oversteps the bounds of propriety, as far as I'm concerned."

Oracle's Fitzgerald downplays the problems in North Dakota. He says Brown, the Oracle saleswoman, might have suggested a lawsuit out of frustration, but adds that Oracle "would never sue a state like North Dakota." Brown declined to comment.

For Infonet Services, a telecom based in El Segundo, Calif., the problem wasn't the pushiness of Oracle salespeople—it was their veracity. In June 2000, an Oracle sales VP started to lean on Infonet to buy its CRM software, says Jim deMin, a technical manager at Infonet. When deMin asked about reference sites, the salesman said the program was indeed up and running—then tried to wriggle free.

"Oracle's salespeople try to go around you, they try to go through you...." North Dakota CIO Curtis Wolfe says. "You don't want them to be like used-car salesmen."

"You guys actually have users of your CRM module, right?" deMin recalls asking him.

"Absolutely," he answered.

"Got a name?" deMin asked.

"Well, no," the salesman admitted.

DeMin says he then conducted his own hunt and finally found a company with the software. It was a rudimentary beta version that the company was testing only because its Oracle sales representative had promised a good deal on other software if it did. DeMin says he suggested that his Oracle rep "have Bob Ballard [the undersea explorer who found the wreckage of the Titanic] look for" an Oracle CRM user. Oracle was "trying to sell us CRM modules that really didn't exist," deMin asserts. In the end, deMin went with software from rival Siebel.

In other instances, distrust was sowed by Oracle's pricing policies. Earlier this year Wisconsin consolidated several of its Oracle databases on a smaller number of servers, to make them easier to manage. It was a minor thing and didn't involve buying more licenses, says Bill Langlois, a state acquisitions specialist, but the state needed recertification that it was in compliance with its Oracle contract. The problem was that Oracle had changed its pricing policy and the salespeople on the Wisconsin deal saw a way to cash in. Langlois recalls a group of three salespeople showing up for a meeting in his office and coming on strong. "They say, 'This is our new policy. This is the way it is,'" he says.

Eventually, Langlois talked down the price, but the negotiations ate up time (five meetings and 25 phone calls, he estimates) and the result wasn't cheap—the state

(Cont.)

coughed up more than $100,000 for what it says is no gain. "This is costing money for me to spend time dealing with these people to give them more money for which we're getting nothing," Langlois says. "There's no more usage, no more people using it, nothing has changed. Except we're paying more."

At least Wisconsin's software works. A recent lawsuit filed by rare-coin broker Wall Street Rarities alleges that Oracle salespeople hard-sold the company an e-commerce inventory program by claiming it had functions that didn't exist. The suit alleges that, on the last day of Oracle's first quarter of 2000, salesmen James Wiberly and Warren Gardner spent three hours trying to get the company's CEO, Bill Anton, to sign a deal, telling him that the discount they were offering was about to expire. Anton demurred, but in November, at the end of the next quarter, Wiberly again pressed Anton to sign up, promising a $300,000 cap on consulting fees. This time Anton agreed—to his chagrin. Wall Street Rarities alleges that the software never worked, causing consigned inventory to back up and driving away sellers. Moreover, the company alleges that it had to spend $500,000 in consulting fees—and still never got a working system. It seeks more than $10 million in damages.

Oracle has disputed Wall Street Rarities's account in court, but won't elaborate. In response to the complaints of Infonet's deMin and Wisconsin's Langlois, an Oracle spokesperson says only, "Oracle does not comment on hearsay or conjecture."

No customer has been publicly angrier than the state of California, causing a PR nightmare for the company. Late on the last day of Oracle's 2001 fiscal year, the state signed off on a $95 million contract for Oracle database software. There were no other bidders—odd for a deal that large—and the state auditor says a rushed decision may have left the state with far more software and services than it can use. (Oracle disputes that.) But what really put the purchase under the microscope was a $25,000 campaign contribution to Gov. Gray Davis from an Oracle lobbyist and sales consultant days after the contract was signed. The check was delivered by Oracle's man to the state's e-government director, a proponent of Oracle getting the deal.

So far, the revelations from state legislative hearings have looked worse for the state's software buyers than for Oracle. Still, the controversy has hurt: Oracle chief financial officer Jeff Henley says the case prompted two potential government clients to put off multimillion-dollar purchases of software last quarter.

From Larry Ellison's perspective, the task of reforming Oracle's sales culture is in very good hands. His.

"This is the first time I've been this directly involved in the sales force," Ellison says. He explains that the sales team has always been the province of people like Kennedy and former chief operating officer Ray Lane, who left after a much-publicized run-in with Ellison over control in June 2000. "That sales aggression ... that was really their style," claims Ellison, a CEO famous for his own hypercompetitive tendencies.

From Larry Ellison's perspective, the task of reforming Oracle's sales culture is in very good hands. His.

But there were worse problems than simple aggression. For years, Oracle has organized its sales force in an "account manager" structure, where one salesperson would be responsible for selling all Oracle products to certain customers. In its infancy, Oracle sold one product—a database. But as it added applications for human resources, supply chains, CRM, and the like, the demands on salespeople for multifaceted expertise have soared. Often, the salespeople haven't been up to it, resulting in them either pushing the wrong software on customers or promising things the applications couldn't deliver. "We can't possibly have salespeople who are experts in everything from our database to our application server," Ellison says. "That's simply impossible."

But Oracle can do a better job by restructuring and changing the way its salespeople handle products. The company has reorganized most of its sales force in recent months. Fitzgerald, Oracle's government sales chief, says that as of June 1, each salesperson in his organization is assigned to specialize in a few particular products so he or she can concentrate on selling a customer the most appropriate software. George Roberts, Oracle's head of North American sales, converted 75 percent of his major-account sales force into specialists by the end of last year, and converted almost all of the rest as of June 1.

Most important, Ellison says he's working to calm down Oracle's aggression in sales by doing the obvious—not rewarding it. He recently eliminated a long-established commission structure, called "accelerators," that rewarded salespeople for deals closed in a quarter's waning days. In some cases the commission was 12 percent if a deal was sealed on the day a quarter closed, compared with 2 percent if it got done the day after. That encouraged furious sales pushes, overpromising, and steep discounts. "You got more into how you were structuring the transaction financially rather than whether this product was right for this given customer," says Ken Martin, who was an

(Cont.)

Oracle sales manager in the late 1990s.

Now, Ellison says, the company is moving to a program that gives salespeople a flat commission of 4 to 6 percent. He calls the old incentives "perverse." "You can argue it's good for the company because the sales force is 'highly motivated' to get the deal into the quarter, but in fact I think it incents behavior that's not in the interest of the company, long-term, or in the interest of the customer," Ellison says. "You really can't reform the sales force until you clean up that problem."

"Oracle does well when the products are good and poorly when they aren't. That's as simple as it gets." —Larry Ellison

Ellison insists that his new, soothing touch will modernize Oracle's sales culture and bring the company greater success than it has ever known. Oracle still has many strengths he can build on. Despite the bust, Oracle's database business remains a profit gusher; the company had operating margins of 44 percent last quarter, second only to Microsoft among major software firms. Oracle earned $656 million in the latest quarter. It has $5.8 billion in cash.

But even if Ellison is right about getting Oracle back on track, there remain questions about where the company will go next. Ellison's vision for the future includes more revenue from outsourcing, perfecting its applications, pushing its application server, selling database clusters, and building subscription revenue from existing customers. All are potentially good businesses, but none have the pop and growth potential of Ellison's original database idea or his as-yet-unfinished push into applications.

The more immediate issue is whether Ellison is really the man to permanently reform Oracle's sales culture. Contrary to Ellison's assertion that Oracle's aggressiveness was in part Ray Lane's "style," Lane was seen by many at the company as a calming influence—a kind of horse whisperer—for the sales force. "Larry is very aggressive and would drive an aggressive sales force," says Nimish Mehta, who spent 11 years at Oracle and is now CEO of Stratify. "Ray kind of buffered that."

Indeed, to many people who know the company, Oracle and Ellison are synonymous, and a change in one would require a change in the other. "Oracle had this culture when it had $25 million in sales. Oracle had this culture when it had $50 million in sales. And Oracle has it today with $10 billion in sales," says Benioff, who was at Oracle for 13 years. "Where did it come from? The guy who's still running the company today."

Ellison has little patience for such analysis. "Everybody talks about selling and the Oracle sales force and all of this other stuff," he says. "Oracle has done well when the products are good and poorly when the products aren't good. That's about as simple as it gets."

For Oracle's sake, he'd better be right.

"Out of Control: Oracle's Fabled Sales Culture Has Broken Down, Customers Are Angry...," *Business 2.0,* August 2002, pp. 38–44.

MTV'S WORLD

Mando-Pop. Mexican Hip Hop. Russian Rap. It's all fueling the biggest global channel

It's the Suit vs. the Tattoo Set. Foggy Bottom and the Hip Hop Crowd. The General and the Veejay. It's, it's . . . well, it's another weird but fascinating cultural moment on MTV, the Viacom-owned music network that supplements its core mission of delivering 150-decibel music to the world's teens with straight-talking programs on issues such as AIDS, drugs, and racism. On Feb. 14, U.S. Secretary of State Colin L. Powell will lead *Be Heard,* a no-holds-barred talk show on MTV Networks, where he will field questions on the crisis in Afghanistan from teens from Boston to Berlin to Bombay. The program will air on MTV's 33 channels worldwide and reach almost 375 million households. MTV's video jockeys—the ones who usually deliver wall-to-wall Hindi film music, German hard rock, Mando-pop, and Mexican hip hop to local viewers—will moderate the meeting, and translators will be on hand to turn questions into English. It will be, in other words, an Event.

Powell's appearance is a media moment that only MTV could pull off. Media moguls can babble on about the global village, about how CNN or BBC can reach out and touch the world. But those news shows are bush league operations compared with MTV's clout. Thanks to the roaring success of its subsidiary, MTV Networks International, the music channel and its sister operations, VH1 and Nickelodeon, reach 1 billion people in 18 different languages in 164 countries. Eight out of ten MTV viewers live outside the U.S. CNN reaches an international audience less than half the size of MTV's. Its impressive global reach has earned MTV membership in that elite of such globally transcendent brands as Coke and Levi's.

MTV seems not to have missed a beat as turmoil roils the executive ranks at parent Viacom, whose board in late January called upon CEO Sumner Redstone and Chief Operating Officer Mel Karmazin to cease feuding. The stock is down almost 20% since early January, but analysts say the strife should have no impact on operating units like MTV. MTV Networks International makes buckets of money year after year from a potent combination of cable subscriber fees, advertising, and increasingly, new media. Few other transnational media operations can claim to make profits at all. But revenues at MTV Networks International increased 19% in 2001, to $600 million, while operating profits grew a hefty 50%, to $135 million. They are expected to more than double by 2004, according to Merrill Lynch & Co. media analyst Jessica Reif Cohen. In the past three years, the growth of MTV Networks International has outpaced the domestic network, accounting for 16% of MTV Networks' revenues, says cofounder and Chairman Tom Freston. He aims to increase that to 40% within five years, as MTV in the U.S. starts to plateau. MTV's international success is attracting a host of imitators, one of them spawned by the relentless Rupert Murdoch. But for now, MTV's version of globalization rocks.

MTV Networks International owes its success to a lot of factors. First, demographics: There were 2.7 billion people between the ages of 10 and 34 in 2000. By 2010, there will be 2.8 billion. Increasingly, this age group is acquiring the bucks to buys CDs, jeans, acne cream—whatever brands are hot in each country. That means advertisers increasingly love MTV International. Second, music: All that stuff about music being a universal language is true, and rock is the universal language for Planet Teen. What MTV does is customize the offering in a brilliant way. Third, television: The number of sets in the world's living rooms—especially in such places as China, Brazil, Russia, and India—is exploding. So are the globe's cable networks. "Everyone who has a TV knows there's something called MTV," says Chantara Kapahi, a 17-year-old student at Jai Hind College in Bombay. The fourth reason: Bill Roedy.

Roedy, a 53-year-old West Point grad, is president of MTV Networks International and, theoretically, is based in London. Theoretically, since his real office is more of a semi-perpetual airborne state involving him, his trademark army green pen and paper, and a business-class round-trip ticket to wherever. To give kids their dose of rock, he has breakfasted with former Israeli Prime Minister Shimon Peres, dined with Singapore founder Lee Kuan Yew, and chewed the fat with Chinese leader Jiang Zemin. Roedy even met with El Caudillo himself—Cuban leader Fidel Castro, who wondered if MTV could teach Cuban kids English. Says Roedy: "We've had very little resistance once we explain that we're not in the business of exporting American culture."

Roedy & Co. are shrewd enough to realize that while the world's teens want American music, they really want the local stuff, too. So, MTV's producers and veejays scour their local markets for the top talent. The result is an endless stream of overnight sensations that keep MTV's global offerings fresh.

On the Move

NORTH AMERICA	
HOUSEHOLDS REACHED	84.6 million
CHANNELS	6
WEB SITES	2
LANGUAGES	2
HOTTEST MARKET/ REVENUE GROWTH	United States/ 5%
ARTIST TO WATCH	Jennifer Lopez

EUROPE	
HOUSEHOLDS REACHED	124.1 million
CHANNELS	15
WEB SITES	9
LANGUAGES	7
HOTTEST MARKET/ REVENUE GROWTH	Russia/ 80%
ARTIST TO WATCH	Alsou

LATIN AMERICA	
HOUSEHOLDS REACHED	28.1 million
CHANNELS	4
WEB SITES	2
LANGUAGES	2
HOTTEST MARKET/ REVENUE GROWTH	Mexico/ 27%
ARTIST TO WATCH	Alejandro Sanz

ASIA/PACIFIC	
HOUSEHOLDS REACHED	137.9 million
CHANNELS	8
WEB SITES	6
LANGUAGES	8
HOTTEST MARKET/ REVENUE GROWTH	China/ 80%
ARTIST TO WATCH	Na Ying

Data: Viacom Inc.

(Cont.)

Just over a year ago, for example, Lena Katina and Yulia Volkova were no different than most Moscow schoolgirls. Today, Katina, 16, and Volkova, 15, make up Tatu, one of the hottest bands ever to come out of Russia. Tatu has won a cult following among local teens since their debut single, *Ya Soshla s Uma* (*I've Gone Crazy*), first aired on MTV Russia 15 months ago. Universal even plans to promote Tatu's next recordings in the U.S. "Our producers could have signed a contract with Sony or Warner, too. We had offers from all of them," says Katina.

Tatu is just one of a slew of emerging local music groups gaining international exposure through MTV and a wider audience in the U.S., too. Colombian rock singer Shakira, unknown outside Latin America until she recorded an MTV Unplugged CD—the acoustic live concerts recorded by MTV—in 1999, is now the winner of one U.S. Grammy and two Latin Grammy awards. Her CD has gone platinum, selling more than 2 million copies worldwide. After releasing four CDs in just three years, Taiwanese pop star Jolin Tsai, 21, is gaining popularity in mainland China thanks to heavy airplay on MTV.

Viacom is now counting on MTV to be one of its biggest growth drivers in the next decade. There's plenty of room to launch new channels on cable and satellite outside the U.S., where penetration, at 38%, is about where the American market was in 1983. As digital television takes off in Europe, MTV plans to introduce more music channels, such as the seven it has in Britain that focus on such genres as rhythm-and-blues and dance. Another part of the strategy: make MTV "a vehicle to develop business [for other Viacom brands]," says Viacom COO Karmazin. "Let's face it, the way people know Viacom is through MTV." Viacom can parlay growth abroad for its lesser-known VH1, Nickelodeon, and TV Land brands "off MTV's reputation."

MTV also is betting heavily on emerging technologies. In Scandinavia, it recently premiered MTV Live, which goes to homes with broadband cable. Viewers can play virtual games, such as *Trash Your Hotel Room,* where users get the chance to be a rock star and wreak virtual havoc. Meanwhile, in July, 2000, MTV Asia launched LiLi, a virtual animated veejay who interacts with viewers on air and online in five Asian languages. An actor behind the image controls LiLi's responses, letting her interview artists and offer viewers tips on pop culture in real time. LiLi is now so popular with Asian teens that Ericsson has launched a line of LiLi mobile phones. In Japan, an MTV wireless Internet service lets users download entertainment news, vote for their favorite veejays, or choose music. MTV "tries to make a lot of noise off the channel," says Nigel Robbins, CEO of MTV Group Japan.

MTV's early international expansion—it got into Moscow in 1993, for example—puts it ahead of the competition in nearly every market. Hong Kong-based Channel V's 24-hour music channel, owned by Rupert Murdoch's Star TV, reaches nearly 47 million homes but has yet to make a profit. VIVA—owned 45.9% by AOL Time Warner, EMI, and Vivendi Universal—is MTV's biggest rival in Europe. It reported a net loss of $9.4 million on sales of $40 million in the first nine months of 2001 but expects to be in the black in 2002. "The market is big enough for both of us," says VIVA CEO Dieter Gorny.

MTV faces some risks in a handful of countries, such as Italy and Brazil, where it operates with a local partner. "It's really a question of whether they can maintain distribution on outlets they don't own," says Sanford C. Bernstein & Co. media analyst Tom Wolzien. Wolzien says News Corp. and Vivendi have much stronger relations with local regulators, giving them an edge in launching music channels they can control.

MTV's best response to these threats is to make its programming as strong as possible. Its policy of 70% local content has resulted in some of the network's most creative shows, such as MTV Brasil's monthlong *Rockgol,* a soccer championship that pits Brazilian musicians against record industry executives. In Russia, the locally produced *Twelve Angry Viewers* was voted one of Russia's top three talk programs. In a colorful studio amid bright blue steps and large green cushions, a dozen teens watch and discuss the latest videos. Periodically, they break into spontaneous dance or pop one another over the head with inflatable lollipops. O.K., it's not Chekhov. But Russian groups beg to be featured on it. Says producer Piotr Sheksheyev: "MTV trusts that we Russians know best what works."

Ceding so much control to local channels does result in the occasional misstep. While watching MTV in Taiwan, Roedy was aghast to see nude wrestling. That was one time he had to intervene. When MTV first entered the Indian market in 1996, Hindi film music—the romantic soundtracks of Bollywood movies—was wildly popular, but the channel's locally hired programmers disdained it as uncool. Viewers abandoned the channel, forcing it to air Bollywood music. Since then its ratings have soared by some 700%.

India is one of the giant markets that MTV is determined to dominate. The other big-country play is China. Analysts believe it is likely to be some time before the government grants 24-hour broadcasting licenses to foreigners on a nationwide basis. Still, in 2001, MTV's advertising revenue in China almost doubled—even though the network airs only a maximum of six hours daily through Chinese cable systems.

Roedy has spent the past decade cultivating relationships in China. At one long dinner with Chinese cable operators, he desperately attempted to hold his own through countless toasts and karaoke songs. After his Chinese counterparts sang Chinese opera arias, Roedy sang a few songs from *Madame Butterfly,* while MTV Chairman Freston belted out *House of the Rising Sun,* the bluesy ballad about a New Orleans whorehouse. They must have been in tune: MTV Mandarin is seen in 60 million homes in China via 40 Chinese cable systems. Last year, more than 10,000 teens came from all over China to audition to become the next veejay on MTV Mandarin. One finalist, who had traveled 18 hours to Beijing, was so distraught at losing that MTV offered to let her veejay for a day. Anything to keep a viewer.

By Kerry Capell in London, with Catherine Belton in Moscow, Tom Lowry in New York, Manjeet Kripalani in Bombay, Brian Bremner in Tokyo, Dexter Roberts in Beijing, and bureau reports

The Medium Is the Instant Message

A New York software company is the first to deliver custom ads via IM, the last great untapped mass-market channel.

By: Marc Weingarten

By some estimates, about 75 million people—not all of them teenage girls—already have access to instant messaging, that addictive hybrid of e-mail and old-fashioned telephone party line. So it comes as no surprise that somebody has finally found a way to turn the technology into a tool of marketing.

The somebody in question is a New York software company called ActiveBuddy. On behalf of corporate clients, ActiveBuddy creates custom bots, or intelligent agents—software applications that connect IM users to data they want, all the while mimicking, in a crude way, the banter of a fellow IM user at the other end of the data link. The databases can convey a client's marketing messages, or the client's ads can appear in the bot's IM dialogue box. It doesn't matter to ActiveBuddy CEO Peter Levitan, as long as major clients like Keebler's, Capitol Records, and Warner Bros. Records keep signing up. "People have got that IM screen up on their desktop seven hours a day," he says. "We think we're just scratching the surface of its potential."

ActiveBuddy bots are elegantly simple applications to use. After you add the name of one to your IM buddy list, type "Hi" or ask it a question to get things rolling. The bot is programmed to respond to natural-language questions in something approaching age-appropriate prose. For example, if you type "Hi" to LindsayBuddy, an ActiveBuddy bot launched in August to promote Warner Bros. Records's new teen artist Lindsay Pagano, it responds, "Wassup yournamehere0434! Glad to see u again. What can i help u with?" The bot, essentially a front for a Pagano website, goes on to field questions about the singer ("Click this link to read Lindsay's bio!"), her tour dates, and, of course, where to buy her new CD. To keep fans amused, it also plays hangman and trivia games and provides Web links to streaming audio and video clips of Pagano. LindsayBuddy won't initiate a conversation, but that's not because it's trying to mimic a sullen teen; like all ActiveBuddy bots, it "speaks" only when spoken to. You can find all of the bots on ActiveBuddy.com, but most people hear about them from other IM users.

For Warner Bros. (which is owned by AOL Time Warner (*AOL*), *Business 2.0's* corporate parent), LindsayBuddy is an experiment. Looking to generate publicity for Pagano before her debut CD's December release, the music label decided a bot might be an effective way to reach the 13 million teens who use IM. So far, so good. By late November, 600,000 people had added LindsayBuddy to their buddy lists, and the bot had received more than 38 million messages. "It's been amazing for us," says Betty Lin, Warner Bros.'s senior manager of new media. "We've generated a ton of traffic for an unknown artist."

Equally impressive to Lin is the fact that LindsayBuddy—like most bots ActiveBuddy creates—is a word-of-mouth phenomenon. Traditional advertising contributed

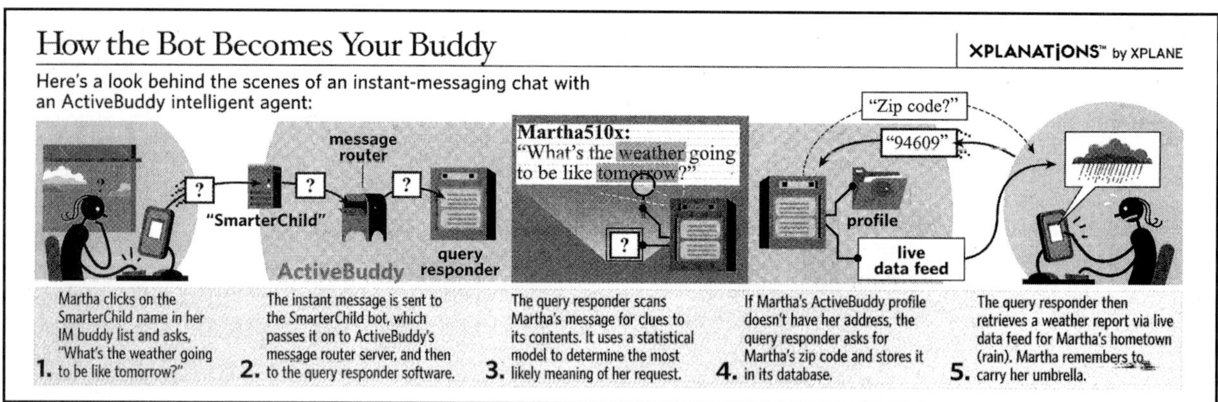

(Cont.)

somewhat to the bot's popularity: LindsayBuddy was advertised on ActiveBuddy's other bots, and Pagano appeared in a commercial on network television last fall. But the lion's share of LindsayBuddy signups come from fans who, having discovered the bot, pass word of it along to their friends.

There's even more buzz around SmarterChild, ActiveBuddy's newest creation. The general-interest bot can answer questions about anything from news and stock quotes to sports scores, movie showtimes, and biblical trivia. Unlike other bots, it's sponsored by multiple advertisers and runs ads on its message screens. Last June, when ActiveBuddy posted a beta version of SmarterChild on its site, 3 million people added it to their buddy lists. Within months it was the company's most popular program.

Grown-Ups With Buddy Lists (Adult IM Users)

GENDER	
Men	50%
Women	50%
AGE*	
18-29	30%
30-49	50%
50+	19%
EDUCATION	
No college	36%
Some college	34%
College graduate	30%
ANNUAL HOUSEHOLD INCOME*	
Less than $50,000	45%
$50,000-$75,000	19%
More than $75,000	24%

Source: Pew Internet & American Life Project, March 2001

*Some respondents didn't know or declined to answer.

Advertisers are pleased with it too. Snack-food giant Keebler's recently placed a two-line advertisement and Web link on SmarterChild to promote a sweepstakes for its Cheez-Its brand. Some 6.5 percent of IMers followed the link to the Cheez-Its website—a very good response rate, considering that the average click-through for e-mail newsletters is just 2.5 percent.

Granted, there are still some bugs to be worked out. As conversationalists, the best that can be said about ActiveBuddy bots is that they get to the point. There's certainly no mistaking their canned responses for human conversation. And their comprehension skills leave a lot to be desired. For example, a query about the New York Yankees on the Sporting News bot referred me to a fantasy football website. Sometimes you have to repeat or rephrase your question several times to get a relevant answer.

Still, ActiveBuddy is clearly on to a rapidly growing medium. And with as many as 150 million potential IM users projected by 2004, others are likely to catch on too. In fact, a competitor called FaceTime has recently popped up, offering customer-service bots for high-profile clients such as Alaska Airlines (*ALK*), Dell (*DELL*), and FAO Schwartz. ActiveBuddy, meanwhile, has plans to create an IM bot for Reuters news agency later this year. "For some reason," Levitan says, "we've discovered that people really like to talk to computers."

"The Medium Is the Instant Message," *Business 2.0,* February 2002, pp. 98–99.

THE TOP 5 RULES OF THE AD GAME WITH AD SPENDING RISING SLOWLY, THIS WON'T BE A BOFFO YEAR. HERE'S HOW IT WILL PLAY OUT

Sure, an advertising recovery is under way, but even the copywriting geniuses on Madison Avenue would have trouble pegging it as the "biggest" or the "best." After eking out a 2.6% gain in 2002, ad spending should see a 5% rise this year, to $249.3 billion, bringing it back to levels seen before the dire 6.5% plunge of 2001, says ad-buying agency Universal McCann. Although TV demand was first to kick in starting last fall, the pickup is now trickling out even to harder hit media such as magazines and the Internet. But the severity of the downturn, coupled with the remaining uncertainties, has left marketers and their agencies scarred in ways that will temper any exuberance as they get back in the game. Remember all the millennium talk of innovative new ways to reach consumers? With caution now the watchword, many marketers have put those ideas on the back burner. Any groundbreaking ads or new products are vulnerable to instant veto by that most ruthless of arbiters, the focus group. "There's huge research before anything goes anywhere," laments Cheryl Berman, chairman and chief creative officer of ad agency Leo Burnett USA. "A housewife in Ohio can make or break a new product or ad concept. It's cowardly, but people are fearful of taking a risk."

How will this all play out? Here are some rules for the new year.

1. The Tube is Still King

It may not be perfect, but TV will continue to sell

Here's the central paradox of the recent ad revival: It has been led by frenzied demand among advertisers for network TV time, even though the medium's ratings continue to erode and marketers increasingly question whether their ads even get noticed amid the clutter of commercials. For the first time last year, cable TV drew a larger audience than network TV.

So why the bidding frenzy? Ironically, it's partly because the inventory of 30- and 60-second time slots has been tightened by TV's poor ratings. Networks were forced to set aside airtime for "make-goods," free ads owed to advertisers who didn't get the audiences they were promised. Then there is the question of the alternatives to network TV, which are even more fragmented. "In a way they're being rewarded for their poor results," concedes David Burwick, senior vice-president and chief marketing officer of Pepsi-Cola North America, which plans a big presence on this month's Super Bowl. "But communal TV events are much rarer these days. There are still only a few ways to reach a lot of people at one shot."

There's another factor, too: Just as there was a time when you'd never get fired for buying IBM computers, TV is still marketers' default choice. A direct-mail offer may be a more efficient way of reaching serious sales prospects, but you know a TV ad will be seen by your CEO. "It seems there ought to be more money invested in customer retention and things like that," says branding consultant Michael Mesic, of Strategic Solutions Group Consulting in Evanston, Ill. "But it's a question of mindset—and TV is visible, if nothing else." Bottom line: Network TV is dead. Long live network TV.

2. The Net: No Ad Boom at Hand

Marketers will build brands online—but not necessarily with ads

It's not quite like that old saw one used to hear about Brazil, that "it's the nation of the future—and always will be." But the promised blossoming of the Internet as an advertising medium continues to recede. By now, boring banner ads have been discredited, and pop-ups seem to aggravate users even more than TV spots during *Everybody Loves Raymond.* And it's likely to be years before most Americans have the broadband "pipes" into their homes that can support the delivery of full-motion TV-style ads—assuming Netizens have any patience for those in the first place.

That may be bad news for companies that are banking on selling lots of online ads, but it doesn't mean that marketers are shunning the Internet altogether. Many have come to recognize that the beauty of the Internet is that it can put lots of information about products and how to buy them in reach of any potential customer. Everything from nutritional information to product specs is readily available for any consumer who wants it—without forcing it on those who don't.

That makes the Internet a powerful marketing tool—but not when it's used to carry pop-ups and banners. Instead, marketers are using traditional techniques like packaging, promotions, and print ads to steer consumers to company Web sites packed with product information, entertainment, and branding messages. That can mean mini-films stashed at BMW's site and gaming tips at Sony Corp.'s PlayStation site, but even makers of more mundane products like Dannon Yogurt are making it a priority to drive traffic to the home URL. The twin paybacks, says Dannon Co.'s marketing vice-president, Eric Leventhal: The company can forge direct relationships with those who visit to gather recipes and participate in promotions. At the same time, it can build a database of its best consumers whose loyalty it can cement with more targeted efforts like coupons and direct mail offers. Bottom line: The Internet's day as a marketing venue may yet come, but that still won't mean big ad sales.

3. Show Us the Numbers

Advertisers will demand results that they can measure

Marketers no longer have to convince top management that marketing is a necessity. But if they want their budgets approved, they'd better be able to show that those dollars are working. Corporations are starting to demand the same accountability for marketing investments that they do for capital investments like machines or trucks, at a time when such gauges are still pretty much a black art.

Still, marketers are making headway. Before it goes national with a new ad, Pepsi-Cola now uses Information Resources Inc.'s BehaviorScan service to pipe different TV ads to different households in test markets in Eau Claire, Wis., and Cedar Rapids, Iowa. Then it measures those ads against the households' actual purchase activity to see if the commercials work.

Similarly, when MasterCard USA concluded that off-the-shelf solutions were not up to the job of measuring whether or not the company's commercials resulted in consumers using their cards more often, MasterCard invested five years in developing a proprietary system that can assess the effects of hundreds of variables. "It's important to show the ROI on every dollar we spend and where the good investment areas are," says Larry Flanagan, executive vice-president and chief marketing officer. "Our management and board of directors are made up of bankers who like to see the numbers." Warning to marketers: This time around, it won't just be bankers who demand to see the numbers.

4. Is Bigger Really Better?

When it comes to choosing an agency, one-stop shopping is out

For years, the major agency holding companies have been trying to convince their clients of the advantages of parking all their marketing needs within the same global company—and have used that as a rationale for accumulating scores of promotion agencies, public-relations firms, package-design consultancies, Web site developers, and direct-mail houses to provide those services.

But is bigger really better? Few marketers are buying that. Instead they're more apt to look for the best provider in each discipline. The argument that the ad agency's sister company will have a better handle on the brand just doesn't cut it these days. Parking all the business with a single company "becomes a very homogeneous experience," says Debbie Myers, head of media services, licensing, and entertainment for YUM! Brands Inc.'s Taco Bell restaurants. The fast food chain prefers to parcel out media buying and promotions to one holding company and national planning to another.

The single-shop strategy hasn't worked out so well for the holding companies, either. Although they insist their model isn't broken, financial pressures have forced them to put the brakes on major acquisitions, and some are even looking to shed assets. Some ad experts even think that the independent ad agency—still on the endangered species list—may be ready for a comeback as clients clamor for greater creativity and less bureaucracy.

5. Aiming For the Bulls-Eye

Magazines with loyal readers and tight focus will come back

After swelling during the boom to the thickness of Russian novels, magazines have been a mixed bag during the bust. Well-targeted publications with an advertising base of consumer products and services have often thrived through the downturn. Business and tech magazines, meanwhile, have taken it on the chin, as finance and tech companies cut back on advertising and corporations in all sectors decided there was no point spending money on image ads during a bear market. Still, for marketers looking to reach a specific kind of consumer, there's a magazine that can deliver the audience, whether it's the shopping fanatics who flock to Conde Nast's *Lucky* or the skateboarding enthusiasts drawn to AOL Time Warner's *TransWorld Skateboarding*.

Even if the ad recovery doesn't succumb to war in the Mideast or other shocks, it's likely to be a gradual climb, not a boom. But at least the money that's spent may be spent more wisely. "We're seeing some rationality come back to the market," says Sam Hill, president of marketing consultant Helios Consulting Group. After the excesses of the sock-puppet years, that's not such a bad thing.

By Gerry Khermouch in New York.

NBC Olympic Campaign Sports Plugs Inside Plugs

Network's Ads Show Athletes Zooming Past Movie Posters That Were Put in Digitally

BY VANESSA O'CONNELL

In the theater, there's sometimes a play within a play. Now Madison Avenue has the plug within a plug.

To lower its costs amid the crippling advertising recession, **General Electric** Co.'s NBC is bringing commercial marketing to a new level by inserting other companies' products into its own promotions for the Winter Olympics. In a new ad campaign to promote the games, for example, NBC has inserted several prominent mentions of the rerelease of the 1982 movie "E.T. The Extra-Terrestrial" from **Vivendi Universal SA's** Universal Studios. For viewers, the result is in effect two ads in one, and they see billboards that don't really exist.

The ad campaign, which is aimed at drawing young viewers, was created by the network's internal agency. It revolves around a chase scene involving two Olympians, the snowboarder Chris Klug and Cammi Granato, a hockey player who helped the U.S. team win the gold medal at the 1998 games.

In the spots, Mr. Klug zooms through a mountain of fresh powder as police and state troopers chase him for speeding. After a pretty girl shows up on the slopes, Mr. Klug crashes through a window into a hockey arena, disrupting a game being played by Ms. Granato, then boards away down the mountain and runs into the pretty girl again. As the police zero in on him, a helicopter appears. "Meet me in February in Salt Lake City," Mr. Klug tells the girl as he grabs a rope thrown to him by his helicopter rescue team and is whisked away.

Careful viewers are likely to notice a billboard on the mountain plastered with an enormous ad for "E.T. The Extra-Terrestrial." Halfway through the chase, Mr. Klug slides by another sign for the movie on the side of the ice rink. The technique, called "virtual video advertising," is commonly used to project stadium billboards during baseball games, but hasn't been widely used in commercials. It allows advertisers to reach viewers who avoid commercial breaks.

"I have never seen this done in ads," says David Sitt, chief executive of **Princeton Video Image** Inc., which creates virtual signs for sporting events. Madison Avenue has previously shied away from adding signs to commercials, he says, partly because advertisers feared that the networks might charge them extra for promoting two companies at the same time.

Barbara Blangiardi, vice president of marketing, NBC, says the network invited outside companies to pitch their brands in the Olympic promotion—and pick up part of the tab—to offset its costs to make the ads and air them in movie theaters and on a home video. NBC paid $545 million for the rights to broadcast the XIX Winter Games in the U.S., and it has been hurt by the ad slowdown and the enormous costs of covering the war on terrorism. Beginning Feb. 8, NBC intends to broadcast 375.5 hours of figure skating, ice hockey, snow boarding and other events.

Ms. Blangiardi says NBC is considering using virtual signage and other product-placement deals more broadly to offset the cost of advertising. She says the network may even consider inserting other products into ads for its fall lineup of TV shows or for other big sports events.

A similar ad for the Olympics appears on home rentals of the movie "A Knight's Tale" from **Sony** Corp.'s Columbia TriStar unit, but viewers see plugs for the home-video release of "The Animal" instead of "E.T." In exchange, NBC gave Sony some commercial time on the network to promote its home video division.

In baseball—and some international broadcasts of soccer, football and bullfights—inserting virtual ads has become quite common. Princeton Video Image created virtual signs for Radio Shack, Claritin, Century 21 and other brands during **Walt Disney** Co.'s ESPN Sunday night baseball package last year. The signs changed every half inning to reflect a new commercial message from different advertisers.

But NBC won't be able to line up advertisers for any kind of billboards at the Olympics because the International Olympic Committee prohibits such ads.

"All Olympic venues are clean venues, and there will be no advertising allowed, even for our Olympic sponsors," says Caroline Shaw, chief communications officer for the Salt Lake Organizing Committee. The rules are intended to keep the focus on the athletes and not on advertisers, she notes. The only signs people will see in the background will be pictures of the athletes, signs to promote the Salt Lake Organizing Committee, which uses a snowflake logo, and the five Olympic rings.

"E.T" and "The Animal" aren't the only products that get some time during the NBC Olympic promotions. In the ads, NBC arranged for the snowboarder to have this sign added to the bottom of his board: "How's my boarding? Hot Snow." Hot Snow is a Web site that was created by MSNBC.com to help young viewers follow the game.

NBC's Olympics marketing scheme is one of the network's most expensive in recent years. It spent close to $800,000 just to make the stunt-packed snowboarder-chase ad. That's far more than the $150,000 to $300,000 NBC typically spends to make its promotions.

Part of the reason for the high cost is the fact that NBC chose to run the spot in movie theaters, beginning Jan. 4, at an additional cost of several hundred thousand dollars. Some shorter versions of the movie commercials were broadcast on the network late at night starting last month.

John Miller, president of NBC's internal agency, says the network was able to create the virtual sign in the ads using a so-called "green screen" on the shoot locale that could carry any message the network wanted to add. Initially, he says, NBC wasn't sure whether it would enlist a movie theater, consumer-products company, or job-placement firm as a partner.

"We only had so much money to promote the Olympics and we had a bunch of big ideas," he says. "One of the reasons we were able to pull this off is that we have some currency: our own air time, the inventory we sometimes use for our own promotional purposes."

Mr. Miller notes that while many middle-aged viewers aren't conditioned to notice virtual signs, the young people NBC is chasing spot them easily.

Mr., Mrs., Meet Mr. Clean

Young Couples Starting Out Are Every Marketer's Dream; 'The Names Are Like Gold'

BY SARAH ELLISON AND CARLOS TEJADA

Every wedding has its awkward guests. Marcus Smith's came courtesy of **AOL Time Warner** Inc.

The interlopers showed up two years ago when Mr. Smith and Sylvia Cziglenyi applied for their marriage license and were weighing the big questions: What's the secret to a happy marriage? What would the future hold?

Then the county clerk handed them a plastic bag labeled "Newlywed Kit" in reassuring pastel letters. "I thought I was being handed our secret married-life membership," says Mr. Smith, a 30-year-old Hollywood, Calif., videogame designer. But the bag offered samples of Mr. Clean cleaner and Tide detergent and a trial disc for America Online.

"We were a little let down," he says.

Mr. Smith and Ms. Cziglenyi didn't realize it, but they were at a "change point." Corporate marketers say certain points in life make consumers especially vulnerable to sales pitches, with the soon-to-be married often being the most susceptible. It's a time when they aren't just choosing a marriage partner, but also are making brand decisions about toothpaste, detergent and appliances that could last even longer.

Unless a couple has been living together for years, weddings represent a moment when two sets of habits and brand preferences meet and usually only one survives. "Newlyweds," says James Stengel, global marketing officer at **Procter & Gamble** Co. in Cincinnati, "are in some ways the ultimate consumer."

Companies including Procter & Gamble, **Clorox** Co., Oakland, Calif., **Colgate-Palmolive** Co., New York, and Germany's **Beiersdorf** AG have all had their products included in Newlywed Kits. They've seen the research: About 67% of women wear the same fragrance they wore when they got married, according to a study by **Firmenich,** Plainsboro, N.J., a leading fragrance maker. A study from Conde Nast's *Bride's* magazine showed that after three years of marriage, 96% of women still shop at the same stores they used when they were engaged; 81% are using the same brands.

U.S. newlyweds spend a total of $70 billion in the first year after marriage for their household, Conde Nast estimates. Most notably, consumers buy more in the first six months of marriage than a settled household does in five years.

But some couples awash in a romantic glow are wary of the hard reality the kits represent. Andrew Heckman, 41, a free-lance financial writer, received a Newlywed Kit when he and his wife registered for their marriage license in Dixon, Ill. They were bewildered by the kit's ration of Tide, Folgers coffee, Secret deodorant and an offer for a new checkbook. For Mr. Heckman the message was grim: Marriage is about body odor, laundry and financial tangles. "Now that I think about it, this stuff seems better suited for a 'divorce kit,'" Mr. Heckman says.

Barbara Kent and Doug Krebs recently got a kit when they visited the Huntington, N.Y., town hall for their marriage license. Ripping open the bag, the two 20-something post-office workers pulled out a sample-size Secret and a pack of Pepto Bismol tablets. "I thought there was going to be sexy lingerie," Mr. Krebs says with disappointment in his voice.

Such reactions don't trouble the marketers, who are stepping up their efforts. Marriages are expected to climb roughly 14% in the coming four years as "echo boomers" reach knot-tying age. AOL Time Warner, whose Parenting Group magazine unit bundles and distributes the kits (including other companies' products for a fee), this year plans to boost their distribution beyond the current 1.45 million packets it gives out annually.

Jo-Ann Raia, the town clerk in Huntington, on Long Island, distributed 1,463 marriage licenses, and roughly as many Newlywed Kits, last year. "I think it's a great idea," she says. "It's a nice little gift to give the couple." The town doesn't charge AOL to hand out the kits, she says, adding, "I'm big on gifts. I'm a party kind of a person."

Nearly every marketer is wooing the newlywed market: With one-fifth of marriage proposals being made in December, it's no coincidence that January bridal magazines are bulging with even more than the regular complement of ads for everything from wedding gowns to shampoos and cars.

"One of the major initiatives" at **Williams-Sonoma** Inc. is to expand contact with newlyweds, says Patrick Connolly, the San Francisco retailer's chief marketing officer. **Whirlpool** Corp., Benton Harbor, Mich., last year commissioned focus groups with newlyweds to better market to young couples. **J.C. Penney** Co., Plano, Texas, has become so smitten with newlyweds that the retailer identifies "Starting Outs" as one of its two major customer groups. Meanwhile, No. 1 auto maker **General Motors** Corp. is marketing its new Saturn ION car to younger consumers with an ad called "Wedding," depicting brides and grooms getting married on the street, in parking garages and on rooftops.

At Conde Nast, owned by closely held **Advance Publications** and publisher of the two biggest U.S. bridal magazines, *Bride's* and *Modern Bride,* researchers studying the buying habits of newlyweds compile a database of roughly 250,000 couples. Other companies, such as closely held marketing firm **American List Counsel**, gather names of newlyweds from county clerk's offices, wedding videographers and photographers, and then sell them to marketers. Newlywed lists go for about $95 per 1,000 names, says Margaret Iadeluca, vice president of sales at ALC, of Monmouth Junction, N.J. Other types of lists bring in less, at roughly $65 per 1,000 names.

Newlywed names "are like gold," says Pete Hunsinger, president of Conde Nast's bridal group.

Price

As airline losses mount, what amenities should a ticket buy?

Carriers add fees for food, heavy bags, paper tickets

By Chris Woodyard
USA TODAY

Full-service airlines are going a la carte.

Reeling from their worst financial crisis in decades, the oldest, take-you-almost-anywhere giants of the airline industry—American, United, Delta, Northwest, Continental, US Airways—are slashing fares while introducing new fees and higher service charges for seemingly everything.

Service fees for paper tickets are now standard for passengers who demand more than an electronic reservation. Checking an extra bag, or a really heavy one, may cost you more than cab fare to the hotel. This month, America West and Northwest airlines are testing whether passengers will actually pay for what has long been a staple of stand-up comedy: airline food.

What exactly should an airline ticket buy—besides a seat? Airline executives are trying to figure that out, and the fate of three-quarters of the nation's airline industry may hinge on the answer.

Reinvention is critical because the full-service giants are fighting two problems at once. Revenue has plummeted 28% in two years as business travelers—the customers whose $1,000-plus airfares paid for these services—have abandoned the giants in droves. Many are now flying mostly profitable discount carriers, such as Southwest, AirTran and ATA, that either don't offer all the services the giants do or charge extra for them. Full-service airlines, which share the bulk of the industry's estimated $9 billion in losses for 2002, are laboring to find new revenue without sacrificing the market strengths they've spent decades building.

The pricing strategy is "a trial balloon," says Michael Taylor, a senior director for J.D. Power and Associates, which does customer-satisfaction surveys in travel and other industries.

Airlines are trying a mishmash of approaches. The least-controversial charges simply increase the prices of things that customers are accustomed to paying for: liquor, headsets and transporting pets.

New charges have been less well received. Continental moved first in August, saying it would start charging for services that were previously free. Among them, the airline added an $80 fee for a third checked bag.

US Airways told its most elite frequent fliers that trips using deeply discounted tickets wouldn't count toward their top-tier status. While it later withdrew that idea after an outcry, US Airways raised its paper ticket fee to $25 and imposed a $100 "standby fee" on US Airways Shuttle fliers who tried to catch flights earlier than the ones they had booked. A few airlines matched the $100 fee, then abandoned it, while Delta added its own version. Starting March 1, it will charge passengers $25 for a confirmed seat on an earlier flight than was booked—if fliers make the request within 3

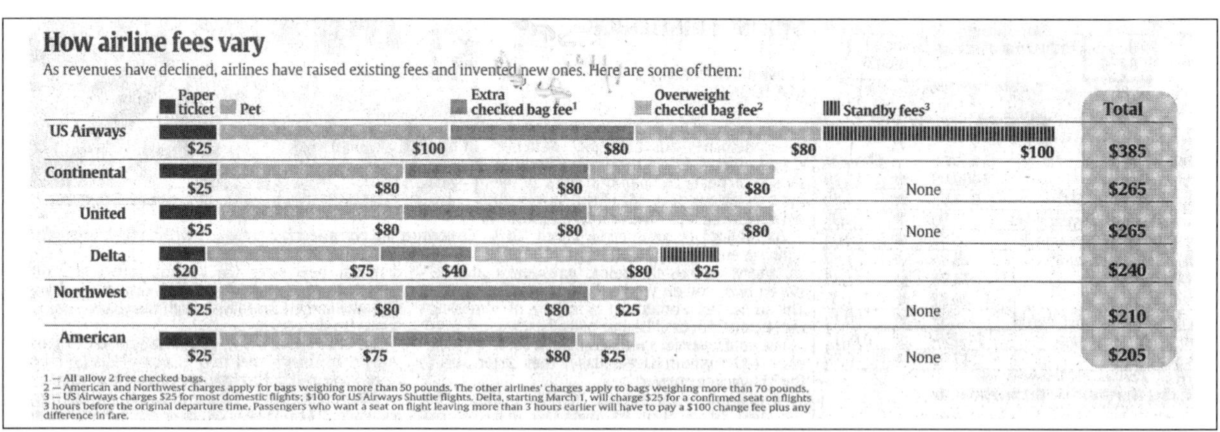

(Cont.)

hours of their scheduled departure—but the fee is waived for top frequent fliers.

"There is some revenue generation" by imposing the fee, says Delta spokesman John Kennedy.

The new charges help make up for revenue lost when fliers booked on flights late in the day change their reservations to more-popular earlier flights. Delta sometimes missed opportunities to sell seats for higher fares by accommodating customers who switched flights, he says.

Airline officials say that charging for specific services allows customers to pick only those that suit their needs.

"We don't want to look upon these as revenue generators," says Scott Bowers, an America West vice president. "We want to look upon these as defraying our costs to keep ticket prices low."

Its plan to sell in-flight meals is meant as a customer convenience. This month, the airline is selling food ranging from a $3 snack box to a $10 hot chicken dinner in tests on 12 flights that previously didn't have food. "We don't want to put $5 into the fare to give you a meal you may or may not want," Bowers says.

Northwest plans to test market food on a few flights starting next week.

Airlines are also using charges as a way to change consumer behavior.

Northwest raised the price of issuing a paper ticket to $25 to move holdouts toward electronic tickets, which saves the airline money. It's worked. Since the fee was raised last year, the percentage of paper tickets issued for domestic flights has fallen to 11% from 20%, says Northwest Vice President Al Lenza.

Likewise, Northwest says it reduced the weight limit for a checked bag to 50 pounds from 70 because of a 27% increase in back-injury claims by employees over a one-year period. Passengers who want to check a bag weighing 50 to 70 pounds pay $25.

On March 1, Northwest will impose a $50 fee for any changes to a frequent-flier ticket. Other airlines charge as much as $100.

When it comes to fees, no U.S. airline has gone as far as a closely watched discount airline in Canada called Tango. Owned by Air Canada, Tango offers fares that are as much as 80% below Air Canada's, but passengers pay extra for amenities, from $10 for an assigned seat to $1 for a cup of coffee.

"Customers really like it," says Ben Smith, Tango's managing director. "They like that they have a choice and can buy as much or as little as they want."

On some flights, almost everyone on the plane buys something, he says.

Bottled water, which costs $1, has proved to be the most popular item.

Tango's U.S. destinations include Las Vegas, Orlando and Fort Lauderdale.

For the full-service carriers, unbundling services from ticket prices may make sense financially, but there's a strategic risk.

"United, American and Delta positioned themselves as creating more comfort and value," says David Aaker, a consultant and author of *Brand Leadership*. Sacrificing that identity means: "Instead of being one of the leaders, you are one of the also-rans."

As airlines' fortunes have sunk, so have travelers' expectations.

"Travelers understand today that the rules of the game have changed," says Peter Yesawich of travel-marketing firm Yesawich Pepperdine Brown & Russell.

"What people want to pay for are the essentials," he says, which could come to mean little more than the airline seat itself.

Making matters worse for airlines: The easy availability of discounts on the Internet has made many travelers more price-conscious. A recognized brand name and complimentary amenities like a cheap snack hold less appeal against saving hundreds of dollars on a plane ride alone.

On the other hand, some fliers still think flying in style is worth paying for.

"The price of the ticket, whether it be first class or the lowest coach fare available, should entitle you to the standard assortment of complimentary items," says Jerry Harris, senior manager for a package-handling company in Poland, Ohio, who travels every week. "On longer flights, that would also include a meal."

Jon Paris, technical manager for an aviation firm in Sudbury, Mass., says the new pricing schemes are "ridiculous." He adds, "Business travelers need a predictable, one-price approach," especially because they often buy full-fare tickets on short notice.

But Chris Shipley, a transportation manager from Aurora, Colo., says he's open to paying for airline meals.

"If I feel like eating or am running late, having the option to purchase on the plane, rather than buying at the inflated airport price, is attractive," he says.

Shipley adds, however, that the more loyalty a passenger shows an airline, the more perks he or she should get.

And there is always a danger that airlines will take the pay-as-you-go concept too far. "What's next," he asks, "pay toilets?"

DRUG PRICES WHAT'S FAIR?

How can we encourage research and still keep prices within reach . . . For Cipro and beyond?

For drugmakers, this fall's Cipro saga contains the germ of a potential nightmare. No, not because of worries that the antibiotic is scarce or that anthrax will bring America to its knees. The scary part for the industry was watching tough-talking Health & Human Services Secretary Tommy G. Thompson bully Cipro manufacturer Bayer into slashing its price by threatening to take away its patent-protected monopoly.

In one fell swoop, Thompson highlighted the fact that Cipro costs about 10 times as much as equally effective drugs, he emboldened Brazil and other countries to break patents to lower drug costs, and he set a worrisome precedent for future government meddling in the cost of medicines. If a free-market Republican Administration can force Bayer to cut its price, how will the government be able to resist stepping in when the soaring cost of a future Medicare drug benefit threatens to break the bank?

Make no mistake: In a few years, America's bill for drugs could well bust the health-care budget because of a triple whammy of expensive new medicines, a tremendous jump in the use of drugs, and the aging of the population. Already, there are drugs such as Pharmacia Corp.'s colon-cancer treatment, Camptosar, that can cost more than $60,000 per patient per year. And as today's gene wizardry becomes tomorrow's amazing new drugs, some of the price tags will be equally amazing.

The nation's drug bill has been rising at 14% to 18% a year, and for 2001 it will be between $160 billion and $170 billion, according to private sector estimates. The bill will climb even faster as seniors' ranks swell with aging baby boomers. The upshot: a clash between soaring costs and payers' ability to foot the bill. "The countdown has already started on the collision course," says Alan L. Hillman, director of the Center for Health Policy at the University of Pennsylvania's Wharton School. "We simply don't have enough money to pay for these future technologies."

The prospect of this collision is already prompting insurers, governments, and other payers to take direct aim at the pharmaceutical industry. To keep costs from soaring even higher, health maintenance organizations (HMOs) and pharmacy benefits managers (PBMs) are trying everything from pushing patients to use generics to demanding that drugmakers prove that their new medicines are cost-effective. States from Florida to Michigan are legislating discounts for residents, and companies like Chrysler are teaming up with others to negotiate lower prices. Meanwhile, a new World Trade Organization agreement gives other countries more leeway to make cheap knockoff drugs in times of medical need. All this comes at a bad time for Big Pharma, which is facing the imminent expiration of patents on many of its blockbusters and fewer-than-expected new drugs in the pipeline. "We are under enormous pressure," says Novartis Chairman and Chief Executive Daniel Vasella.

The industry is fighting back. In an advertising campaign, it is arguing that spending more on drugs actually saves money by reducing costly hospitalizations and other health-care expenses. Companies are also rushing to assure patients who cannot pay that they won't be left out. GlaxoSmithKline PLC announced in October that it would give discounts of 30% to 40% to needy elderly Americans, for instance. Novartis is providing its $28,000-per-year leukemia drug, Gleevec, free to those who can't afford it, as well as discounting other drugs for poor people. And the bioterrorism attack "gave the industry the opportunity to put its white hat back on," says Lehman Brothers Inc. analyst Nancy Myers. Glaxo, Bristol-Myers Squibb, and others rushed to donate antibiotics and expertise to the government. "If industry doesn't make such an effort, we will face a backlash," says Vasella.

Big Pharma's do-gooders, however, can't paper over the underlying issue: Just how will the nation cope with the rising cost of drugs? It's a far from simple question. A close examination shows that this is not a black-and-white case of medical breakthroughs that bust the bank or of lifesaving drugs priced out of reach of ordinary citizens. Instead, the tale is replete with paradoxes and puzzlements. Take one classic example: Some expensive new drugs, such as Gleevec or cholesterol-lowering medicines, do save money by reducing the need for expensive bone-marrow transplants or bypass operations. Yet in terms of overall health-care costs, a quick death is cheap. By living longer, patients will get other diseases that require more costly care. On the other hand, premature deaths rob the economy of productive citizens and workers.

These complexities make it extremely difficult to figure out whether any given drug increases or decreases health-care costs. Add in the larger picture, including productivity and quality-of-life measures, and the economics gets even murkier.

The whole debate is further muddied by the country's schizophrenic attitude toward drugs and drugmakers. Americans want powerful new medicines, along with smashing returns for stockholders. At the same time, people demand that drugmakers deliver their remedies at prices ordinary folks deem reasonable. If drug prices soar, Americans worry that medicines will have to be rationed by the patient's ability to pay, which wounds our sense of social equity.

So how is it possible to understand this complex situation? And more important, what can be done to soften the impact of the collision between soaring costs and ability to pay?

What follows is a step-by-step tour through some of the key questions and answers. The bottom line: The U.S. does spend more than it needs to on drugs, although in certain cases it should be spending more. Drugmakers need big profits to provide the innovative new medicines that the public demands—even though companies also need to boost research and development productivity. Market forces are already beginning to rein in the drug-cost monster, but there are steps the health-care system should take to speed the trend. BusinessWeek estimates that these steps could cut the nation's annual drug bill by as much as $15 billion and reduce other health-care costs as well.

WHY WE SPEND TOO MUCH ON DRUGS. One fact is crystal clear: The U.S. drug bill is higher than need be. Americans take more drugs than necessary, often popping expensive pills such as Cipro when cheaper ones will do. And because of overuse and misuse, studies estimate, the U.S. wastes an extra dollar for every dollar spent on drugs—fixing the ills medicines cause. Some patients don't get, or don't take, the right prescription, for instance, leading to lost work or unnecessary hospitalizations. Others suffer because of dangerous side effects or drug

(Cont.)

THE FORCES THAT MOVE DRUG COSTS

Pharmaceutical costs are pulled in different directions by a panoply of social and economic pressures. Below are some of them:

UPWARD PRESSURE

MARKETING BLITZ

While 80,000 sales reps in the U.S. stoke doctors' interest in drugs, Big Pharma drives demand by ads directed at consumers. Spending on such ads nearly tripled between 1997 and 2000, hitting $2.3 billion. Payers say the strategy pays off—witness the Viagra boom.

PATENT GAMES

Patent-holders use lawsuits to tie up generic-drug makers for years. For some, this wins time to persuade patients to switch to a newer, patented product. AstraZeneca is trying to move users from its $5.8 billion stomach drug Prilosec to the newer Nexium.

UNPRODUCTIVE RESEARCH

Drugmakers have upped research spending in recent years—Pfizer spends $4.9 billion annually; Merck, about $2.6 billion—but with no big payoff in productivity. Hefty up-front investments in genomics, in particular, have so far failed to yield a big crop of new compounds. Big Pharma is licensing more drugs from biotech companies, but such deals don't come cheap.

PRICEY BREAKTHROUGHS

Breakthrough drugs with hefty price tags are coming to market, including rheumatoid arthritis drugs, which can cost nearly $12,000 a year, and Novartis' cancer agent Gleevec, which can cost $28,000. Other cancer drugs could turn the disease into a chronic condition—prolonging lives but at a tremendous cost.

DOWNWARD PRESSURE

POLITICAL HEAT

When Bayer, under pressure from the U.S. government, slashed the price of Cipro, it was following a well-trodden path. Merck, Bristol-Myers, and others have already cut prices on AIDS medications sold in Africa. Other drug companies will come under similar pressures, in the U.S. and abroad, if their products fit the bill in times of emergency.

PATENT EXPIRATIONS

In the next five years, drugs with U.S. sales of $35 billion will lose patents or other forms of market exclusivity. In August, when a generic version of the antidepressant Prozac was launched, pharmacy benefits manager Merck-Medco switched 80% of the patients in its massive mail-order operation to the generic in just one week.

PHARMACO-ECONOMICS

Insurers, government agencies, and other payers are trying to figure out which drugs offer the most bang for the buck. Now the military is requiring that all new allergy patients be started on Allegra, which is less than half the price of competing Claritin, saving millions per year. Another example: substituting cheap ibuprofen for expensive Vioxx.

MARKET FORCES

In addition to pushing doctors to prescribe generics, payers are giving consumers more incentive to pick cheaper alternative drugs by requiring that they pay more out of pocket for the more expensive choices. Already, 50% of people in HMOs have such "tiered co-pays," up from 5% three years ago.

interactions. One famous 1998 study in the *Journal of the American Medical Association* estimates that adverse reactions to drugs in U.S. hospitals may cause more than 100,000 deaths a year. "When you see someone taking 14 drugs, the last seven are typically to treat the side effects of the first seven," observes Albert I. Wertheimer, director of Temple University's Center for Pharmaceutical Health Services Research.

Reduce these problems, and the savings are huge. If the estimated $150 billion spent each year to fix drug havoc could be cut to $50 billion, "we'd save enough to afford a Medicare drug benefit," says J. Lyle Bootman, dean of the University of Arizona's College of Pharmacy.

For each of these problems, there's plenty of blame to go around. Employers, doctors, and health insurers often fail to steer patients toward the drugs that offer the best value or to teach them to take the medicines properly, experts say. Meanwhile, Americans too readily seek pharmaceutical solutions to ailments that are better tackled through prevention. Public-health officials warn that we are on the cusp of a budget-busting diabetes epidemic, triggered by Americans' couch-potato habits. The incidence of the disease has jumped more than 33% since 1990, mirroring a similar rise in obesity.

Drugmakers are culpable, too—although not necessarily because of the prices they charge. Selling drugs is, after all, a business, and companies have a duty to shareholders to maximize profits, observes Dr. Alan M. Garber, professor of medicine and health policy at Stanford University. "It would be unfair to portray the industry as greedy or irresponsible if they charge what they can get," he says. But companies may cross an ethical line when they market expensive drugs to those who don't need them or manipulate the patent system to extend their patent-protected monopolies.

Today, the rise in drug spending is not being fueled by headline-grabbing, $15,000-a-year AIDS or cancer drugs, which are used by too few people to add up to megabucks. Instead, Merck-Medco, a large PBM, figures that more than half of the projected doubling in its spending over the next five years will come from just two main types of drugs: cholesterol-lowering and other heart-related medications, and neurological medications, such as psychiatric drugs or painkillers, that are used by tens of millions of people.

When they develop new classes of drugs, companies typically price them far higher than the older medicines used for the same conditions—even if the extra benefits are small. Expensive drugs called calcium channel blockers, for example, are routinely prescribed for patients with high blood pressure, even though studies show that cheaper beta-blocker and diuretic drugs can work as well or better.

What's more, drugmakers market many medicines directly to consumers, spending billions on ads that critics say are often misleading. "Pharmaceutical companies are coming out with these very expensive new drugs to replace existing drugs, sometimes in the absence of good evidence that their value is worth the extra costs," charges Dr. Sharon Levine, associate director of Kaiser Permanente's physician unit. For instance, the heavily advertised painkillers Celebrex and Vioxx, with combined worldwide sales of $5.6 billion, "are not more effective than Motrin, but they cost up to 60 times as much," Levine says. The new drugs do offer an important benefit for some patients: less stomach bleeding. But most people have no problem taking the older drugs. The Food & Drug Administration has cracked down on Pharmacia for painting too-rosy pictures of its drug's merits in consumer-focused ads.

Meanwhile, one study found that as many as two-thirds of people taking Schering-Plough Corp.'s heavily advertised Claritin and other allergy medicines don't even have allergies. Schering responds that patients wouldn't take Claritin if it didn't work. But "there's no doubt that the direct-to-consumer advertising increases drug consumption," says Barrett A. Toan, chairman and CEO of Express Scripts Inc., a PBM. Claritin sales? About $2.2 billion per year.

WHY DRUGS COST SO MUCH. Investors won't fault companies for persuading consumers to buy more products than they actually need. And the more money drug companies make, the more they can spend developing tomorrow's lifesaving medicines. Indeed, industry execs argue that if prices were squeezed, the world can forget about new and better drugs.

Many economists agree—up to a point. Consider today's protease-inhibitor drugs for AIDS, which have dramatically cut deaths and hospital costs for those with HIV. If Congress had put price controls in place back in the early 1990s when lawmakers were screaming about high prices, "there would be no protease inhibitors now," says Eugene M. Kolassa, professor of pharmacy at the University of Mississippi. While drugmakers would have tried to develop AIDS drugs anyway, they would not have moved as quickly as they did without the promise of blockbuster revenues.

On the other hand, drugmakers wouldn't need to charge such high prices if they could boost R&D productivity. Overall, the average tab for developing a new drug is $500 million to $880 million, the industry says. But the amount actually spent on any one marketable product is roughly one-quarter of that.

To understand why, just look at the drug-development process. In the past, scientists made many variations of existing chemicals and tested them to see which ones had the ability to fight a particular disease. Now, with the explosion of information about genes and biology, the process has gotten more complicated—and oddly enough, more difficult. Researchers try to identify the best target in a particular disease—for instance, a damaged gene that causes cancer—then they make a drug to hit the target and cure the disease.

That process can take 10 years or more. Such a long period means that about half of the calculated $500 million to $880 million total isn't actually spent at all. Instead, it's the opportunity cost—the measure of what the money tied up in the drug for so many years could have earned with alternative investments.

Moreover, there are pitfalls every step of the way. Making drugs from previously unexplored types of chemicals increases the chances of problematic side effects, explains John F. Niblack, R&D chief at Pfizer Inc. And new targets that look great in the test tube or in animals often don't pan out in humans. "If you develop a drug that hits one of those unvalidated targets, you are likely to spend a lot of money and find out that it doesn't work," says Niblack.

That's why, of the thousands of potential drugs that start development, only a tiny percentage make it into animal tests. Only a few of those will be given to people in so-called Phase I trials to test for safety. Then come Phase II trials for safety and the first hints that a drug works. And then Phase III: wide-scale tests to gather proof of safety and efficacy. Only about 1 in 10 of the drugs that enter human trials makes it through Phase III.

The high attrition rate means that about half of drugmakers' actual R&D spending represents the price of all the failed projects. The corollary, therefore, is that reducing the failure rate and the overall development time can dramatically cut total R&D costs. Pfizer's Niblack, for one, believes that new technologies for screening drugs, smarter clinical trials, and other measures will soon slash the attrition rate. But for now, industry productivity is going down and R&D costs are going up. With all the advances in biology, "we had expected a lot more [new drugs] by this time," admits Fred Hassan, chairman and CEO of Pharmacia. "The reason is that the new stuff is difficult to find."

That's why drugmakers are increasingly letting others take the big risks. More and more, they're filling their pipelines by picking up drugs from biotech corporations and startups—after the medicines have already shown promise in clinical trials. Case in point: Bristol-Myers Squibb's $1 billion investment in ImClone Systems' promising cancer drug, C225.

Although drugmakers spend billions on R&D, they also rake in huge profits. Too big, some analysts believe. Since 1988, the return on equity of the five biggest U.S.-based drugmakers—Merck, Eli Lilly, Pfizer, Pharmacia, and Schering-Plough—has averaged 30% a year. Last year, it was 36%, compared with 27% for Microsoft Corp. and 21% for companies in the Standard & Poor's 500-stock index.

Industry execs say that the high returns are justified on the basis of the high risks they take to develop drugs. But economists point out that such risks ought to translate into variable returns—and drugmakers show a consistent high return on equity compared with companies in other sectors. Merck's return, for example, has not fallen below 28% since 1988. "If you went to Vegas with $1,000 and routinely came back with $1,400, could your family accuse you of gambling?" asks Alan Sager, co-director of the Health Reform Program at Boston University.

By this analysis, Big Pharma's prices are higher than needed to cover R&D costs and risks. But that's not surprising, because the price set for a drug typically has little to do with its development cost. Instead, pharmaceuticals are just like any other product: The producers charge what the market will bear. The usual price calculation includes an assessment of the medical benefits the drug brings and how much competition it faces.

If a new drug offers a lifesaving treatment where none existed before, or if it helps avoid costly hospital procedures, the price can be astronomical. An example is Genzyme's drug Cerezyme for the rare Gaucher disease, which has an average price tag of $170,000 a year. The alternative, after all, is severe disability or death. "In reality, if a drug is going to save a life, we will find a way to afford it," says C. Daniel Mullins, associate director of the Center on Drugs & Public Policy at the University of Maryland School of Pharmacy.

And when it comes to new painkillers or other drugs, Big Pharma has been able to get away with charging high prices because

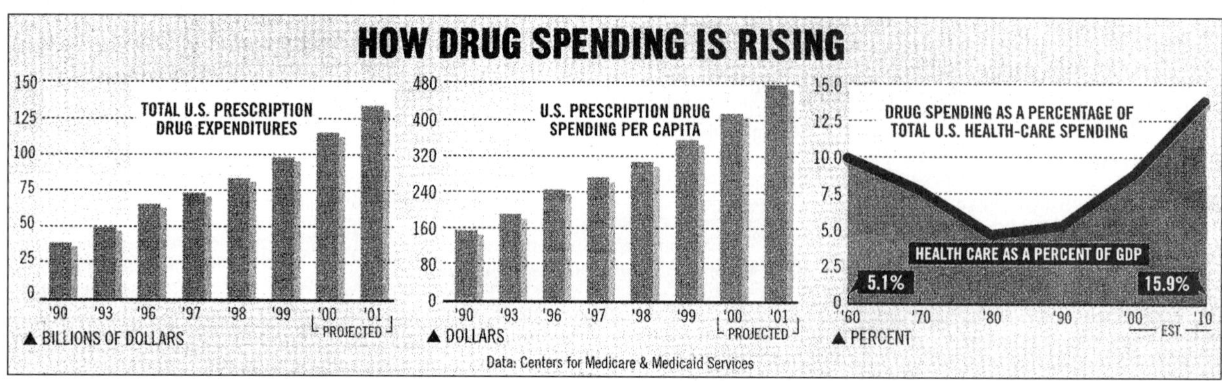

most consumers, shielded by their insurance coverage, have little or no incentive to pick cheaper options, explains Kenneth L. Sperling, head of health-care analysis at Hewitt Associates LLC. That, however, is beginning to change, as the health-care system takes a harder look at the value of drugs.

SO WHAT IS THE VALUE OF DRUGS? AND CAN WE AFFORD THEM? Despite the concern over drug costs, pharmaceuticals represent only about 9.5% of the nation's $1.4 trillion health-care bill. In the U.S., drug spending is less, per person, than it is in many European countries, which have lower per capita medical bills. To economist H.E. Frech III of the University of California at Santa Barbara, the conclusion is clear: If the U.S. spent more on drugs, health-care costs would be lower. Argues the University of Mississippi's Kolassa: "We should be happy that pharmaceuticals are the fastest-growing component of the health-care budget, because it means that other components aren't growing as fast."

There's some merit to the argument. Health experts can point to case after case in which a new drug or a boost in drug use replaces hospital outlays. The advent of stomach-acid blockers, for instance, dramatically slashed the number of ulcer surgeries. Even at $28,000 per year, the leukemia drug Gleevec is cheaper than a bone-marrow transplant. And a newly updated study by Columbia University economist Frank R. Lichtenberg finds that for every extra dollar spent replacing many older drugs with new, costlier ones, four dollars are saved in medical costs.

Even WellPoint Health Networks Inc. in California, which has been particularly aggressive at trying to curtail drug spending, has learned that additional drug use sometimes can save money. In 1998, WellPoint became concerned about rising emergency-room and hospitalization costs for its asthma patients. For help, the company turned to Kathleen A. Johnson, a pharmaceutical economist at the University of Southern California. She helped set up a program to identify patients at risk and train them to monitor their symptoms and use drug inhalers when needed. "We found that even though drug costs went up [about 20%], hospital admissions and emergency-room visits went down by 80%—and overall costs by 48%," says Johnson.

But as usual, the story is more complex than it seems. Many drugs don't replace costly procedures. Glaxo's new flu drug, Relenza, simply shortens flu symptoms by a day or so. Other drugs may cut some costs but raise others. Do AIDS drugs save money, for instance? "The jury is still out," answers Maryland's Mullins. Yes, AIDS-related hospitalizations and deaths are down. But the drugs also have serious side effects. HIV-infected patients are now getting cancer, heart disease, and other diseases that are costly to treat.

Even drugs that help prevent hospitalizations or surgeries may increase health-care costs—because so many people take them. Cholesterol-lowering "statin" drugs reduce the need for bypass and other heart operations. But they are now used by millions of Americans, and scientists estimate that only a minority would have needed operations without the drugs. The total statin bill: $15.5 billion this year, rising to $24.6 billion by 2005, predicts SG Cowen Securities Corp. Economists say it's not clear whether the health-care savings would be greater than that.

The problem of paying will grow even more complicated. Companies are experimenting with genes that help build new blood vessels to the heart, for instance, or cancer treatments where patients' own tumor cells are used to boost the immune system's ability to fight the disease. These approaches, some customized for each individual, will be hugely expensive. Yet if they work, Americans will demand them. "The limiting factor will be affordability," says Dr. August M. Watanabe, executive vice-president for science and technology at Eli Lilly & Co. "Can society afford them for its citizens?"

The nation can easily pay the tab, economists generally agree. "We're a long ways from reaching any limit," says Harvard University economist David Cutler. After all, he points out, GDP is rising faster than total health-care costs. That leaves a bigger and bigger piece of the pie to pay for drugs.

But while a rich nation like the U.S. can foot the bill, many Americans will be left out. In fact, de facto rationing is already common. Look at two of the latest drugs for rheumatoid arthritis, Immunex Corp.'s Enbrel and Johnson & Johnson's Remicade, both of which cost $10,000 to $12,000 a year. The companies do offer some assistance to poor patients. But, says Dr. John H. Klippel, medical director of the Arthritis Foundation, "just because of the expense, they are largely limited to people who have insurance plans that pay for them."

Overall, when it comes to health care, "we're moving to a three-tier system: the haves, the have-littles, and the have-nots," says Wharton's Hillman. "The more technology we have and the more that it costs, the more we have to ration it."

WHAT WE SHOULD DO. For Americans worried that they will be among the have-nots, the good news is that the market has begun to rein in drug costs. Insurers and payers will also get a break because blockbuster drug after blockbuster drug, from Claritin to stomach drug Prilosec, is coming off patent or other monopoly protection. Overall, drugs that are now worth $35 billion per year in U.S. sales could face competition from generics by 2005.

Large employers such as General Motors Corp. stand to reap windfalls. "If you take a look at three of the drugs that will lose exclusivity—Prilosec, Claritin, and Glucophage—we are talking about $75 million in potential savings for GM over a three-year period," says Cynthia Kirman, GM's director of pharmacy. That's why insurers and PBMs are already pushing generic drugs hard. When Prozac went off patent recently, Merck-Medco was able to convert 80% of mail-order customers within a week—an amazingly quick substitution. The savings from the coming flood of generics? Up to $3 billion per year.

Drugmakers are responding as many other companies would—by protecting their profits. For example, they're doing everything in their power to delay competition from generics, sometimes using tactics that even some drug company execs call "brazen" and "embarrassing". Generic competition is not the only threat, however. In the past couple of years, the market has also begun to generate another set of checks and balances on drug prices, called pharmaco-economics. In essence, experts scrutinize the value of individual drugs, aiming to get more bang for the buck.

Pharmaco-economics is already slowing the rise in drug costs for insurers and other payers. In Britain, for instance, a government panel made the controversial recommendation

TOMORROW'S BLOCKBUSTERS

New medicines with mass appeal will keep drug costs soaring

PRODUCT AND APPLICATION	COMPANY	2005 PROJECTED SALES MILLIONS
CIALIS Erectile dysfunction	Eli Lilly/ICOS	$2,000
ARCOXIA Arthritis and pain	Merck	2,000
VANLEV Hypertension	Bristol-Myers Squibb	2,000
BEXTRA Arthritis and pain	Pharmacia/Pfizer	2,000
CLARINEX Allergy	Schering-Plough	2,000
CRESTOR Cholesterol reduction	AstraZeneca	3,500

Data: SG Cowen Securities Corp.

(Cont.)

Rx for Drug Costs

The following steps might help to slow America's rising tab

- ▶ Close legal loopholes that Big Pharma uses to delay generic competition.
- ▶ Lower unnecessary health-care and drug costs—from adverse drug reactions to overprescriptions—by curbing drug misuse.
- ▶ Require insured patients to pay a percentage of a prescription's cost out of pocket, with percentages rising for more expensive choices.
- ▶ Disseminate information on the value of drugs—i.e. how well one drug works compared to the alternatives.
- ▶ Reduce hospitalizations and later drug costs by promoting preventative steps against heart disease, diabetes, and other problems.
- ▶ Tighten rules on advertising drugs directly to consumers. The ads often encourage consumers to select pricey drugs over cheaper ones that work just as well.

that Glaxo's Relenza not be made available to the public through the National Health Service. The benefits didn't justify the cost, the panel said. Similarly, U.S. military pharmacists have decided that all new patients with allergies will be put on only one allergy drug, Allegra. The government has negotiated a price of 60 cents per daily dose for Allegra, less than half the cost of competing Claritin. The savings: $7 million in fiscal 2001.

Kaiser Permanente is another believer in pharmaco-economics. Under its plans, only 6% of arthritis patients—those at higher risk for gastric bleeding—get expensive Cox-2 inhibitor painkillers like Vioxx. The rest take cheap ibuprofen. Nationwide, the ratio is 50-50. "If people can be switched from drugs of very little marginal benefit to drugs that are as good and a lot cheaper, there is an opportunity to save many millions of dollars," says Stanford emeritus professor Alain C. Enthoven. With seed money from BlueCross BlueShield, Enthoven is helping to set up an institute, RxIntelligence, to provide drug-effectiveness data that insurers can use to save money.

Meanwhile, insurers are giving patients incentives to choose cheaper drugs. According to a spring, 2001, survey by market researcher Scott-Levin, 50% of people enrolled in HMOs tracked by the firm were in three-tiered prescription drug plans, up from 5% just three years previously. In such plans, patients typically pay little or nothing for a generic drug. They have a bigger co-pay for the brand-name product, and a still higher co-pay for the most expensive drug.

Some cost-cutting tactics can be risky, leaving some patients with substandard treatments. Economists have shown that simpleminded measures, such as capping drug benefits, can actually raise overall costs since patients may not get the medicines that work best. But done correctly, with the emphasis on effective treatments instead of drug costs alone, this type of scrutiny can lead to better care.

One model, pharmacists say, is the approach used by Active Health Management for companies such as Merrill Lynch and Sears, Roebuck & Co. The idea: Give people more medical attention, not less. When doctors find and treat diabetes, heart disease, or other illnesses early, hospitalizations decline, yielding savings of more than $100 per person per year, calculates Dr. Lonny Reisman, CEO of Active Health Management.

Inevitably, the nation's drug bill will continue to rise, fueled by the introduction of new drugs and by aging baby boomers, now reaching their prime prescription years. "I think we will pay more for drugs and we will have less available for other things," says Express Scripts' Toan. But it is within America's power to use those drugs more effectively.

Health-care experts say there are some simple remedies. The nation's doctors and hospitals should be able to trim scores of billions per year by avoiding health-care costs that occur when drugs are used incorrectly. Steps include computer systems to spot dangerous drug interactions and better patient education about the need to take medicines as prescribed. Health care must also harness market forces more effectively. Back in the 1960s, when Americans paid out of their own pockets for drugs, consumers had a strong incentive to pick the medications that offered the best value. That incentive vanished when insurers began to pick up the tab. But it could be restored and boosted by expanding use of tiered co-pay plans, saving about $1 billion annually. Or for more savings, insurers could require patients to shoulder a specified percentage of each drug's cost; the percentage would increase for more expensive drugs. The nation could also educate consumers, doctors, and payers about which drugs deliver the most for the money, by setting up an independent pharmaco-economic institute. The information it provides could shave $10 billion or more off the annual drug bill, economists estimate. In addition, Congress could close loopholes that drugmakers use to delay introduction of generics. Tightening rules for advertising drugs directly to consumers could reduce overuse of expensive drugs. And Big Pharma must learn to cope with the flood of new knowledge about biology to boost its productivity.

The future could get ugly—not just for have-nots. Maryland's Mullins, for instance, fears that the health-care system may decide not to pay as much for treatment for those who helped bring on their own illnesses, such as smokers. Medical progress, though, will clearly continue on its current fast track. "America is in love with innovation—and it wants new drugs," says Jean Paul Gagnon, director of public policy at Aventis Pharmaceuticals. Now, we need to figure out how to pay for those drugs without breaking the bank.

By John Carey and Amy Barrett

With Arlene Weintraub in Los Angeles, Catherine Arnst in New York, Kerry Capell in London, and Michael Arndt in Chicago

A Rare Chance to Take Back a Market

Johnson & Johnson's New Stent May Dominate Angioplasties

By REED ABELSON

Few companies ever get a second chance once they fall behind the competition on a pivotal product. Johnson & Johnson is about to become an exception to that rule.

Early this year, **Johnson & Johnson,** the giant health care conglomerate that sells everything from Band-Aids to birth control pills, is expected to receive regulatory approval in the United States for a new medical device—a drug-coated stent that promises drastic changes in the way that hundreds of thousands of patients with heart disease are treated.

The stent, called the Cypher, keeps coronary arteries open more successfully and much longer than the plain metal devices now used, sharply reducing the need for repeated angioplasties and for heart bypass surgery. Even at a price likely to be around $3,000 each—more than double the cost of current devices—the stents are expected to take over much of the market for angioplasties.

"It has the potential to change the landscape, not only for patients but also the economics," said Michael Dake, a professor at Stanford University School of Medicine. "It's a really big business."

"If you get a little complacent in the market, you're going to get hammered."

Robert W. Croce

Johnson & Johnson, in 1994, pioneered the stent, a meshlike device inserted in coronary arteries that serves as scaffolding to help overcome the constrictions that cause heart attacks. But the company squandered its lead. Failing to recognize just how important the device was, the company did not invest enough in developing better designs. It also alienated doctors and hospitals by charging $1,600 for each stent without making sure insurers would reimburse the cost. By the late 1990's, Johnson & Johnson's share of the market had fallen sharply.

Robert W. Croce, the chairman of Cordis, the unit at Johnson & Johnson responsible for making stents, vows not to make the same mistakes again. Even before the Food and Drug Administration approves the new stent, the company has been lining up insurance coverage and meeting with hospitals about the device's potential impact on their finances. Cordis is also already at work on new versions of the stent.

"We feel like we're staying ahead of our competitors and will be a moving target," Mr. Croce said. **Guidant** and **Boston Scientific** are already readying their own devices.

The market for the drug-coated stents is worth fighting for. Kurt Kruger, an analyst with Banc of America Securities, says the new stents could lead to a doubling of the existing American market, to $3.2 billion, in 2003. The overwhelming majority of those sales are expected to be of the drug-coated stent, with Johnson & Johnson capturing $2.8 billion of the total, compared with an estimated $415 million in stent sales in 2002.

"It's going to be an absolute gold mine for Johnson & Johnson," said Mr. Kruger, who estimates the market could reach nearly $4 billion by 2004.

While Johnson & Johnson is a huge company, expected to have $36 billion in sales this year, drug-coated stents are by far its most promising product. Recapturing the stent business will give the company a highly profitable franchise in cardiology devices, a rapidly growing market. Sales of the stents could approach those of Johnson & Johnson's most popular product, the Procrit/Eprex anemia drug.

If all goes as expected, Mr. Kruger said, the company's earnings growth in 2003 should reach the high double digits, largely because of the stents.

Because expectations are so high, however, if anything goes wrong Johnson & Johnson risks disappointing doctors and patients, not to mention the investors who have bid up its stock this year.

"Whenever there is a lot of hype surrounding a product launch, sometimes it's setting up for possible problems," said Michael Krensavage, an analyst for Raymond James.

Johnson & Johnson's original stent revolutionized angioplasty, a procedure that involves threading a catheter through a clogged artery and then inflating a balloon to unblock the vessel. The stents made angioplasty more effective, and Johnson & Johnson had the market to itself for about three years. But the company failed to anticipate how quickly the device would catch on, Mr. Croce said, and stumbled. Hospitals shouldered the extra cost of the new devices because Medicare was slow to reimburse them.

By the time competitors like Guidant entered the market in 1997, Johnson & Johnson was vulnerable. The company refused to drop the price of its stents, and the competing devices proved much more flexible and easier for doctors to use.

"If you get a little complacent in the market, you're going to get hammered," said Mr. Croce, who took over Cordis just as the company was losing its grip on the stent market.

Now, Johnson & Johnson is doing what it can to make sure the new device is paid for. Last year, Medicare took the highly unusual step of agreeing to pay for the drug-coated stent even before it received F.D.A. approval.

"I believe, and my staff believes, this is really a revolutionary new technology," said Thomas A. Scully, the head of Medicare, who said he had responded to concern from hospitals that they would lose significant sums if the new devices were not paid for.

While Johnson & Johnson has not yet said what it plans to charge for the new stent, analysts and others expect the price to be about $3,000. Company officials argue that the savings from fewer angioplasties and bypass surgeries easily outweighs the device's costs. While the costs of these procedures vary widely, an average angioplasty with a stent costs some $8,000 and a bypass around $17,500 at the Health Alliance network of hospitals in Cincinnati, for example.

Expansion Plans

With the introduction of its new drug-coated stent, Johnson & Johnson is expected to expand its share of the market for such devices.

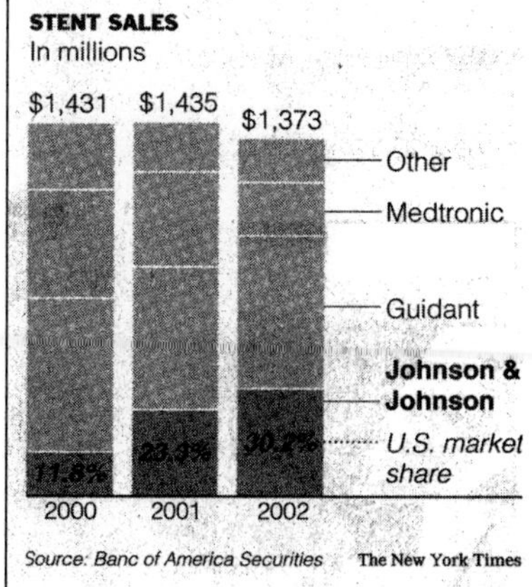

STENT SALES
In millions

$1,431
$1,435
$1,373
Other
Medtronic
Guidant
Johnson & Johnson
U.S. market share
11.8%
23.3%
30.2%
2000
2001
2002

Source: Banc of America Securities
The New York Times

(Cont.)

At Kaiser Permanente, the nation's largest not-for-profit health maintenance organization, the committee studying new procedures has recommended that its doctors consider using drug-coated stents, although it does not analyze the cost of new technologies.

Many private insurers are also deciding their reimbursement policies. **Aetna,** for example, is conducting an expedited review and should decide its reimbursement policy soon after the stent receives approval.

The new stent addresses a fundamental problem: 20 to 40 percent of patients who get the traditional stents experience reblockage of their arteries because of scar tissue. Johnson & Johnson scientists discovered that the scarring could be prevented if stents were coated with a drug licensed from **Wyeth** called Sirolimus, now used in patients getting kidney transplants. The stent releases minute amounts of the drug for the first month or so, when the scarring tends to occur.

In the most recent clinical study, the drug-coated stent sharply reduced the need for a second procedure, and an F.D.A. advisory panel voted unanimously in late October to recommend its approval. The company is expected to get final clearance early this year, although regulators have expressed some concerns about the device.

Johnson & Johnson appears to have the market to itself for at least the first year, although any delay in regulatory approval will shorten that lead. Its competitors, Guidant and Boston Scientific, are scrambling to come up with their own versions of drug-coated stents, and the two have been wrangling over the rights to the drug they want to use, paclitaxel, licensed from **Angiotech Pharmaceuticals.**

Boston Scientific is expected to come to the market at the end of this year. But Guidant, which reported disappointing preliminary results from a study yesterday, is now expected to enter the market sometime in 2005. The company is expected to cancel its plans to merge with the **Cook Group** and instead develop another kind of drug-coated stent.

'It's going to be an absolute gold mine,' one analyst says.

But Johnson & Johnson may not be able to make too much of being first with the new devices. "It will be the best stent that captures the market, not the first," said Dr. William L. Hunter, Angiotech's chief executive.

And many of the factors that gave Johnson & Johnson a second chance also make its lead tenuous, said Gary P. Pisano, a Harvard University business professor who has studied the medical device market.

"The product cycles are very short," he said. "This is a very competitive market," and cardiologists, who tend to be quick to adopt a technology, are also likely to switch to a better device if it becomes available.

"They don't tend to be very brand-loyal," Mr. Pisano said.

While Mr. Croce says he is confident that Sirolimus is the best drug in keeping arteries open, paclitaxel also appears effective. "Neither Johnson & Johnson nor Boston Scientific has been able to deliver a knock-out blow" by producing studies that demonstrate significant superiority, Mr. Kruger of Banc of America said. In 2004, he estimates that Boston Scientific will sell about $1 billion of its drug-coated stents, compared with nearly $3 billion in sales for Johnson & Johnson.

Johnson & Johnson is also working to introduce other versions of its stent in the next few years. The last time around, "we didn't apply enough resources to develop the next generation," Mr. Croce said. Now, the company is planning to introduce an improved stent coated with the same drug in 2004 and another stent that is also coated with heparin, which reduces the chance of blood clots, in 2005.

But the hefty price tag of the Cypher may still prove a stumbling block. The device has already been approved in Europe, but doctors there have been slower than expected to embrace the new stent, and the device has so far captured only 10 percent of the market.

"It's all about reimbursement," said Mr. Croce, who predicted that as next year's budgets take into account more use of the drug-coated stent, more doctors will use it.

But some doctors also say they do not believe that every patient should get the new stent, even though they expect their colleagues to rush to use it. "There's a zeal for popping those things in," said Dean J. Kereiakes, a cardiologist who heads the Ohio Heart Health Center. But the stent may not prove as effective as hoped for in some patients, he said, including patients undergoing a heart attack or diabetics who take insulin.

"I'm an advocate," Dr. Kereiakes said of the new stents, "but I'm also cautious about extrapolating from limited data."

There are also concerns about the impact of the devices on hospitals, many of whom say they will still lose money because the reimbursement for the new stents is not likely to cover all their costs.

It will be years before anyone knows for sure just how lasting a breakthrough Johnson & Johnson's new stent turns out to be.

There will be "a ramp-up of clinical activity over the next few years," said Patrick O'Gara, the medical director of the cardiac service line for **Partners HealthCare,** which includes Brigham & Women's and Massachusetts General Hospitals in Boston, "to see what the limits of the new technology will be and what patients will most benefit."

German Shoppers May Get 'Sale Freedom'

Pressure Mounts to Soften a Strict Law of Competition

BY NEAL E. BOUDETTE
Staff Reporter of THE WALL STREET JOURNAL

BAD HOMBURG, Germany—Despite the best efforts of Hans-Frieder Schoenheit, Germans may soon get to test the theory that they can't tell when a bargain really is a bargain.

Mr. Schoenheit is deputy director at the Competition Center, an organization dedicated to protecting shoppers from the ordeal of discounts. Buy One, Get One Free? Today Only: 20% Off? Those, he says, are gimmicks that dupe consumers and destroy small shops. "If every store had a sale any time it wanted, there would be no price transparency," he says. "It would be totally confusing."

Many Germans used to agree with him, but not anymore—especially after the center pounced when clothing retailer **C&A Mode** announced it would give 20% off credit-card purchases in the first four shopping days after the Jan. 1 debut of the euro.

C&A figured it could ease currency confusion at cash registers that way, but hours after the appearance of advertisements plugging the offer, the center's lawyers took C&A to court and got a restraining order. A judge in Dusseldorf said the lure of a discount for only four days would put consumers under such pressure that they wouldn't be able to make sound buying decisions. Under the 93-year-old Law Against Unfair Competition, C&A was fined 250,000 euros ($221,100).

Many consumers find it silly. "They should just allow the stores to do what they want. It's idiotic," says Kirsten Koob, a mother of a two-year-old in Frankfurt. "If C&A wants to cut prices, let them."

Outraged by the C&A case, state secretaries in both the economics and consumer ministries are now calling for changes to the law, which, among other things, strictly limits when stores can mark down prices.

Big retailers condemn the law as obsolete, although mom-and-pop stores say they could be crushed by mammoth corporations without some amount of protection. Other European countries still have laws limiting sales, but Germany makes claims to maintaining the strictest on the books as well as the tightest enforcement.

Mr. Schoenheit says the center hears "some voices that consumers don't necessarily want this protection," but vows to fight any changes to the competition law. For now, the law remains on his side. It allows price reductions on small lots of merchandise anytime but bans storewide sales unless they occur during one two-week period in the winter and another in the summer. Anniversaries are an exception, but only big ones divisible by 25, such as the 50th or 75th.

Founded in 1912, when Germany still had a kaiser, the center represented family-owned shops and small companies. Mr. Schoenheit acknowledges he is looking out for his members, although the center usually justifies its actions as taken in the interest of consumer protection. For decades, lawmakers and voters agreed with the center, buying the argument that people aren't smart enough to decide for themselves.

The center's objections have prevented bakeries from selling half-price bread at closing time and a pet store from putting goldfish on sale in slow afternoon hours. Suing under another German consumer law, the center fought to stop **Lufthansa** from linking frequent-flier miles to credit cards. The center also went after U.S. retailer **Wal-Mart** Stores Inc. when it advertised it would beat any competitor's price if a shopper showed up with the ad—tantamount to selling one product for two different prices, a court said. Under German law at the time, consumers had to pay the same price.

In a celebrated battle fought all the way to Germany's supreme court, the center and **Land's End** Inc. tussled over the Dodgeville, Wis., mail-order retailer's lifetime guarantee on its outdoorsy shirts and shoes. The center argued that the guarantee was bad for consumers, because it would benefit the company only if customers didn't take advantage of it, making it a ruse that hoodwinked unwitting buyers. The high court ruled that Land's End couldn't advertise the guarantee in Germany because the promise to replace any product any time for any reason amounted to selling two products for one price, a violation of a Nazi-era law against giving shoppers free gifts.

The political winds began to shift when the Competition Center's victories started fueling resentment among Germans who couldn't help but notice that the discounts and deals denied them are widely available outside of Germany.

Last summer, the law against free gifts and another against rebates were repealed. Land's End's guarantee and Lufthansa's frequent-flier-mile credit card are now legal. (Mr. Schoenheit says he is disappointed.)

In its eagerness to protect consumers, the center's actions have ended up ticking them off, instead. In 2000, it sent a letter to Kurt Krummenacher, the head of **Boa Lingua,** a Swiss company that arranges language-instruction vacations across Europe. Boa Lingua's Web site—www.sprachen.ch—uses the German word for languages. The letter said using a general term like that gave Boa Lingua an unfair advantage over other language companies that could have used the word Sprachen.

Threatening a 5,000-mark ($2,261)) fine under German competition law because the Web site can be seen in Germany, the letter said the site had to be changed. Also enclosed was a bank transfer slip—so Boa Lingua could cough up 315 marks to cover the center's legal cost to that point.

"It was ridiculous. I threw it away," Mr. Krummenacher recalls. Weeks later another letter arrived, and soon Swiss lawyers and the media were defending the use of general terms, and ridiculing the notion that Swiss firms should comply with an odd German law. Mr. Krummenacher hasn't heard from the center again.

"Their whole idea about using general terms doesn't make sense," he says. "It's first come, first served. If we don't use Sprachen, then who should? No one?"

Last year, the center picked another target, sending a letter this time to Herbert Huber, a computer administrator in southern Germany whose personal Web site includes a page displaying articles criticizing the center. The letter demanded he stop using its name and threatened to sue if he didn't. The letter contended Web surfers might mistake it for the center's own official site, although Mr. Huber's site was mainly about his family and the town where they live. In the letter, the center demanded 350 marks for legal fees, which Mr. Huber paid.

Now his site refers to "the center who's name I cannot use" and adds, "For details, call me up!"

The clearest sign of how the tide has turned against the center is the aftermath of its fight against C&A, the clothing retailer. The court ruling sparked a torrent of media coverage: TV cameras showed up in C&A stores, and morning and evening news programs covered the sale—the kind of positive publicity even the most lavish ad budget couldn't have achieved.

C&A, which went ahead with the sale while filing an appeal, was mobbed by shoppers. Asked how the fourth and final sale day went, a C&A sales clerk in downtown Frankfurt smacks her palm on her forehead. "Women were buying 10, 15 pairs of pants each," she says. "Sometimes 20."

Middle class buys into lap of luxury. Sort of.

Marketers eager to pump up the bottom line are delivering fancier stuff at cheaper prices

By Bruce Horovitz
USA TODAY

Luxury was once for big tippers. Today, it's also for coupon clippers.

A lifestyle that looks, tastes and feels luxurious is within grasp of most middle-income Americans. Chichi marketers used to ignore Middle America. Now—in search of bottom line growth—they're virtually catering to a middle class that's hungry for the good life.

Average Americans are demanding a taste of luxury at every level. From the fast food they eat to the golf clubs they swing to the vehicles they drive. Americans are living lives of near-luxury but often on silent majority incomes.

Call it the democratization of luxury:

► JetBlue has leather seats and private TVs with 24 channels at coach prices.

► Coach has a line of $120 handbags that sell for not even half the price of the purses that made it a luxury brand name.

► Carnival Cruise Lines carries 3 million passengers a year vs. 100,000 just 25 years ago.

► Callaway Golf markets $500 golf clubs to average golfers.

► Mercedes-Benz sells entry-level cars for $26,000.

► Panera Bread insists on placing its inexpensive, casual food on real china and serving it with honest-to-goodness metal—not plastic—utensils.

"In a society where everything is mass-marketed, there's a need to feel special," says Ronald Shaich, CEO of Panera Bread. The fast, casual food chain nurtures its brand image for quality foods but charges about $2 more for a meal than McDonald's. "It's about delivering something that consumers respect—and that they feel respects them."

Companies that ignore this trend do so at their peril, warns Michael Silverstein, partner at The Boston Consulting Group, co-author of the forthcoming *The New Luxury: Why the Middle Market American Consumer Wants Premium Goods and How Companies Create Them.*

Americans, it seems, have become addicted to luxury. The size of the average house has more than doubled the past 50 years. Nearly one in three home-remodeling projects includes his-and-her vanities. One in 10 features dual dishwashers. Some 12 million Americans traveled to Europe in 2000—12 times the number who traveled there in 1970. And once-high-end features, such as sunroofs, CD players and keyless remote systems, come standard in 80% of cars.

"The biggest mistake any marketer can make is to underestimate the American consumer's aspiration to trade up," says Neil Fiske, co-author of the report.

Behind this New Luxury: gobs of stressed-out, middle-class folks who are only too eager to seek out the highest quality, highest performance goods and services.

Or at least the perception of it.

The trend was in place long before the Sept. 11 terrorist attacks. Starbucks was far ahead of it 30 years ago when it began persuading everyday folks to spend almost as much on a cup of designer coffee as on breakfast. But the events of Sept. 11 appear to have helped accelerate the trend.

Women lead the way

A big driving force behind this bid for luxury: women. They influence 75% of all purchases. As more women enter the workforce, they're seeking the luxury of small rewards to compensate. Luxury was once for Bill and Melinda Gates. Now, it's also for Joe and Jane Six-pack.

"The word 'luxury' is becoming obsolete," says futurist Watts Wacker. "Luxury used to be aspirational. But even on modest incomes, we're living luxurious lives."

And why not? Luxury is more affordable than ever. In 1953, it took 140 hours of work to buy a dishwasher. Today, it takes 28 hours. In 1959, it took 562 hours to buy a color television. Today, it takes 23.

"Value isn't just about price anymore," says Gary Drenik, president of BIGresearch. "The quality has got to be there."

For Hunter Widener, true luxury was leasing his first Mercedes-Benz—at age 29.

(Cont.)

"Why does anyone want a Mercedes?" asks Widener, a private-banking employee at Bank of America in Charlotte. "It's prestigious. It's safe. And it makes you feel good."

So, two years ago, he leased a Mercedes-Benz C240, which sells for about $28,000. "It improves my image with my clients," Widener says.

"My clients are wealthy individuals, and driving a Mercedes makes them see me as more of an equal," he says.

It improves Widener's image of himself, too.

It's not by accident that Mercedes-Benz's domestic sales have tripled since 1994, the model year that its C-Class was introduced. Mercedes has since set domestic sales records for six consecutive years.

The company is on a mission to appeal to middle-income consumers. Its entry-level C230 can be had for $25,670. Total sales of its C-Class cars—all less than $40,000—grew 25% last year, while sales of Mercedes models over $70,000 grew 14%, says Dave Schembri, marketing chief at Mercedes.

Meanwhile, its $37,000 sport-utility vehicle also has brought in new Mercedes buyers. "The luxury segment is being expanded by a recognition that we need to offer our products within a wider range of affordability," Schembri says.

Passion for pampering

Luxury isn't just about pricey items such as homes and cars. It's about the smaller things, too.

Christine Donaldson spends much of her day in the lap of luxury. She inspects resorts across Arizona for AAA.

But she'd rather sleep in her own bed than at a five-star resort. That's because her personal luxury is sleeping on sheets with ultrahigh thread counts. (She prefers 310.) Many fancy hotels don't use sheets as soft as the ones she has. It's not uncommon for her to pay $120 for a single cotton sheet.

"You spend one-third of your life in bed," she points out. "So why not be comfortable there?"

Similarly, when David Pincus wants to treat himself, he splurges for a $50 massage at his health club. For the 54-year-old business professor at the University of Arkansas, that's about once a month. "It's as much a psychological as a physical thing," he says.

He started treating himself better three years ago after bypass surgery. Now, he craves cruises to exotic places—including an around-the-world cruise he has promised his wife.

Perhaps no one understands the national infatuation with cruises better than Bob Dickinson, president of Carnival Cruise Lines, the world's biggest line.

Back in 1970, about 500,000 mostly wealthy Americans took a cruise. This year, upward of 8 million Americans will take a cruise of some sort. Carnival offers a three-day cruise from Miami to Nassau for as little as $179 a person.

Not only are more people cruising, they expect more amenities on the ships.

Seven years ago, only 5% of the rooms on Carnival's boats offered balconies. Because of passenger demand, 64% now do, Dickinson says. Customers pay about $1,000 less for balcony rooms than they did back then, he says.

Two decades ago, a typical Carnival Cruise had simple, cabaret-style entertainment with a few performers. Today, the orchestra alone, on a typical cruise, numbers 15.

"Cruises were once seen as elitist vacations," Dickinson says. "But you no longer need to be one of the beautiful

True top-of-the-line stuff still costs a bunch

Companies have started offering lower-priced versions of their high-end products to satisfy the longings of middle-income consumers. There are key differences, however, between true luxury and near-luxury products.

	Top end	Luxury	Near luxury
Coach	Limited edition alligator carryall, $7,500. Handmade in Italy from alligator skin. Suede lining with internal zip pocket. Nickel hardware.	Ergo spectator zip, $268. Roomy, with three multifunction pockets and a ring to clip an accessory or key fob. Lightweight leather with Coach signature lining.	Hamptons leather Demi pouch, $128. Small. Lightweight leather. Fabric lining.
Mercedes-Benz	CL600 sedan, $125,620. Only 485 sold in the USA last year. Large body. Twin-turbocharged, 5.5-liter V-12 engine, computer-controlled suspension with 20 sensors that adjust to road, built-in hands-free cellphone.	E500 sedan, $55,570. Midsize. Real wood interior trim, 4.9-liter V-8 engine. Suspension uses air chambers as springs at each wheel.	C230 sports coupe, $25,670. Compact. Brushed aluminum interior trim, 1.8-liter four-cylinder engine. Air suspension system uses steel springs.
Callaway Golf	Great Big Bertha II driver, $499. Cutting-edge design. Head crafted of costly titanium. Premium carbon fiber shaft.	Steelhead III Fairway, $249. Less-complex head crafted in cheaper steel. Stock steel or graphite shaft.	Pre-owned, older-design clubs on Web site at about half-price.

(Cont.)

people with a tummy tuck and Botox eyelids."

Here's how others are responding to the demand for luxury:

► **On the golf course.** About 20 years ago, Callaway sold mostly low-end golf clubs and ranked last among the major golf club makers.

Today, it ranks first—mostly by selling top-of-the-line Big Bertha drivers made of titanium that can cost $500 each. A set of Callaway irons can set you back $2,500. Even so, the company targets the average golfer—not elite players, CEO Ronald Drapeau says.

"We make things that nobody really needs. Even golfers don't really need more golf clubs," Drapeau says. "But golfers seem to find a way to support their addiction."

► **At the dinner table.** Panera Bread sales growth has compounded at a rate of 60% over the past four years thanks to consumers' growing need to feel special. Even at a quick meal.

"I call it 'trading up,' " CEO Shaich says. "It's a drive to feel special in a world where not much makes you feel that way."

No matter that the typical diner's check at Panera Bread is $6.15 vs. about $4.50 at fast-food joints. "If it's something they want, they're willing to spend the extra dollar or two for it," Shaich says.

Panera is only too happy to scratch that consumer itch for perceived quality. That requires paying attention to details. The dough for the bread, for example, is always fresh—never frozen. The company trucks the dough 500,000 miles a month to get it to its 500 stores fresh.

And Panera Bread employees never wear uniforms. They wear their own clothes so they don't look like they're part of a megachain. Even the required name tags are crafted by the employees themselves.

► **On the arm.** Coach has long been known as a high-end accessory maker, with its top-end purses selling for up to $7,500.

But four years ago, the brand introduced its Demi handbag line. These leather bags, which sell for as little as $128, are about half the size and half the cost of more typical Coach leather bags. Over the holidays, the Demi line accounted for 10% of Coach sales.

"Accessible luxury is here to stay," says Lew Frankfort, CEO of Coach. "We've broadened the world of Coach to include a wider range of products."

Among them: the Wristlet. These 6-inch-long, leather accessory cases—which some use as handbags—sell for as low as $48. In just two years, the product has evolved into a $25 million business, Frankfort says.

The strategy is working. Coach's second-quarter sales, announced earlier this month, jumped 31%, while its net income rocketed 41%.

► **In the air.** JetBlue's success is due in large part to founder David Neeleman's insistence on giving small luxuries to all. "We brought humanity back to air travel," he says.

Leather seats were a no-brainer, Neeleman says. Leather lasts twice as long as cloth seats, so there's no cost difference in the long haul, he says. And fliers love them.

But Neeleman is utterly convinced that in-flight entertainment is the one luxury for which fliers will happily switch airlines.

One flier recently told Neeleman that even though his firm gave him the option of flying first class on any airline, he picked all-coach JetBlue because of the live, satellite TV.

With that success, JetBlue is also looking into a satellite radio system that would offer live broadcasts of 500 stations. It's in discussions with HBO and Showtime about providing a menu of movies in flight.

No plans for in-flight Broadway shows. Yet.

'Ship Those Boxes, Check the Euro!'

How a Tiny Firm Rides Foreign-Exchange Waves

BY MICHAEL M. PHILLIPS

Plymouth Meeting, Pa. — The first thing Kim Reynolds does each morning is meet with his top factory-floor managers to see if all is well on the production line. The second thing he does is scan the latest intelligence from global currency markets to see if all's well on his bottom line.

It's a routine born of harsh experience: Two years ago, a skyrocketing dollar was one reason why Mr. Reynolds, president of family-owned tubing maker Markel Corp. here in suburban Philadelphia, took a 40% pay cut and had to dip into his savings to cover his two daughters' school tuition. These days when Mr. Reynolds flips through the daily currency report his secretary puts on his desk, he sees a weaker dollar—and stronger euro—that could add as much as a half-million dollars to his profit this year.

To traders, currency ups and downs are a way to make a quick buck. To heads of state, they are referendums on national economies. To corporate giants, they are a fact of life of international production. But for a small company with global aspirations, swings in the $1.2 trillion-a-day world-currency markets are very personal.

Markel, whose Teflon-like tubing and insulated lead wire is used in the automotive, appliance and water-purification industries, got into exporting in the mid-1980s when Mr. Reynolds received a call from a German parts maker asking about one of his best-selling tubes: "Was ist das AR500?"

Now the shipping department at Markel is crowded with cardboard barrels of AR500 destined for German automotive-parts company **W.H. Kuster** GmbH, in Ehringhausen, boxes of automotive tubing for delivery to **Fico Triad** SA in Rubi, Spain, and wooden spools of insulated cables for Simco Japan Inc. in Kobe. Once a week the company sends a 40-foot shipping container to warehouses in Britain, Spain or Holland, and it expects 40% of its $26 million in sales this year will be overseas, mostly in Europe.

"We use a fixed [currency-price] conversion when we quote prices, and we assume the currency loss or gain," says Cheryl Jolly, Markel's export manager, as she supervises the weighing of boxes bound for Germany.

To protect himself and his company—which is unrelated to the New York Stock Exchange-listed insurance company of the same name—Markel's Mr. Reynolds has forged a business strategy that allows it to survive, and perhaps even prosper, when a key element of his profitability is far beyond his control.

Markel's is a four-part approach: charge customers relatively stable prices in their own currencies to build overseas market share; tap "forward" currency markets to provide revenue stability over the next few months; improve efficiency to make it through the times when currency trading turns ugly; and roll the dice and hope things get better.

"You can always change your strategy if it starts to become too painful," says Mr. Reynolds, who is 52 years old and has a Harvard M.B.A. "But I'm not willing to abandon my strategy. We're trying to develop niche businesses where we provide a unique product to customers worldwide."

Mr. Reynolds believes his policy of keeping the prices set in foreign currencies, mainly the euro, has helped him capture 70% of the global market in high-performance, Teflon-based cable-control liners, tubes that allow car accelerator or shift mechanisms to move smoothly.

But it also means that Markel signs contracts that lead to the delivery of wads of euros months or even years down the road, when the value of those euros in dollars may be much less than it was at signing.

To minimize the uncertainty over the span of a few months, Markel's chief financial officer, James A. Hoban, buys forward contracts through PNC Financial Services Group in Pittsburgh. Markel promises the bank say, 50,000 euros in four months, and the bank guarantees a certain number of dollars no matter what happens to the exchange rate.

When he thinks the dollar is on its way up, Mr. Hoban might hedge his entire expected euro revenue stream with a forward contract. When he thinks the dollar is heading down, he will hedge perhaps 50% and take a chance that he will make more dollars by remaining exposed to currency swings.

He doesn't always guess right. Sometime this month, for instance, Markel will have to provide PNC with 50,000 euros from a contract the company bought in early January. The bank will pay $1.05 per euro, or $52,500. Had Mr. Hoban waited, Markel could have sold at the going rate, $1.08 and made an additional $1,500. "We're not in the business of trying to make money on our foreign exchange," Mr. Hoban says. "We're just trying to manage our risks."

To make matters worse, Markel cut the supply deal with Germany's Kuster in 1998 and set the sales price assuming the euro would be at $1.18 by now, just a tad stronger than it traded at when introduced officially at the beginning of 1999. "Dumb us," Mr. Reynolds says. "At the time it was introduced, nobody thought it would immediately plunge."

In fact, the euro sank like a rock, bottoming out near 82 cents on Oct. 26, 2000, and that meant each euro Markel received for its products was worth far less in dollars than the company had expected. In 2001 and 2002 combined, Markel identified more than $625,000 in currency losses, and the company posted overall losses in both years.

The company's seven senior managers took 10% pay cuts in 2001. None of Mr. Reynolds's 63 salaried employees got raises. (His unionized hourly workers were on a five-year contract and were unaffected.) There

A Stronger Euro: the Other Side of the Coin

As the euro has swung to higher than $1.08 this week from $0.83 in October 2000 (first chart), so too have the fortunes of U.S. companies that sell goods in Europe. One such company, family-run manufacturer Markel Corp. in Plymouth Meeting, Pa., has to be as concerned with exchange rates as machine tools. Its revenue has held fairly steady, with $26 million in sales projected for this year. But just as important, the company is projecting a currency gain (second chart) of $400,000 after three years of currency losses, with a loss of $650,000 in 2000.

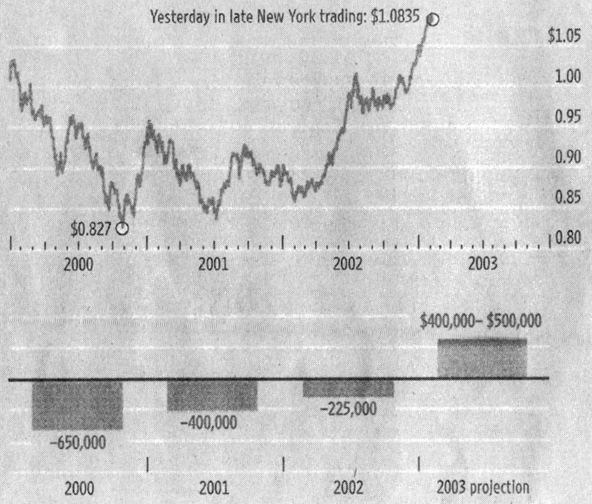

were no year-end bonuses, which usually amount to two or three weeks' pay. And the owners, Mr. Reynolds, his brother-in-law and his father-in-law, received no dividends.

The looming dollar threat also forced Markel to become more efficient. That meant spending on new equipment even when the company was losing money. In 2001, the company paid $250,000 for a new extruder with less down-time, that generates 25% more footage per work shift. Managers cut waste material by 6% in production of high-temperature oxygen-sensor wires, another big seller for the car industry.

In essence, Mr. Reynolds and his team rode out the bad times as best they could. And now they are beginning to enjoy the good times.

Most of Markel's current deals were written assuming that the euro would be valued between 90 cents and 95 cents. But at the current $1.08, helped by worries about the U.S. trade deficit, jittery U.S. financial markets and a possible war in Iraq, it has been a currency windfall for Markel. Company executives figure that if the euro remains between $1.05 and $1.07, and the British pound remains at about $1.60, Markel will post $400,000 to $500,000 in currency gains this year.

"That's the best-case scenario, and it still doesn't get our nut back from the two previous years," Mr. Reynolds says.

The currency gamble goes both ways, however. Mr. Reynolds demands multiyear dollar contracts for his raw materials, meaning that his Japanese supplier takes home fewer yen as the dollar weakens.

"That," Mr. Reynolds says, "is his problem."

Buying on Credit Is the Latest Rage in Russia

BY SABRINA TAVERNISE

New advertisements are appearing on Moscow's streets and subways. Comic-book-style stories portray the new quandaries of the Russian middle class.

"If we buy the car, we can't afford to remodel the apartment," says a woman with a knitted brow, in one ad. Then comes the happy ending. Her husband replies, smiling: "We can do both! If we don't have enough, we'll take a loan!"

In a country that has yet to discover the personal check, where people still pay for apartments and cars with suitcases of cash, Russian consumers are beginning to borrow. This is a new step for Russia's economy, which until now had neither credit cards nor mortgages, and required life's largest purchases to be paid for up front.

For years it was banks, companies and the Russian government that binged on borrowing, careening from one default to the next. But now the government has its financial house in order, and average Russians are beginning to enjoy a basic aspect of a capitalist system. "Consumer credit is about to explode," said Greg Thain, chairman of a Moscow marketing firm called Integrated Marketing Service, which recently conducted a study of 5,000 Russian families' budgets.

Economists offer a range of explanations. As Russia comes out of its fourth year of economic growth, its banking system is beginning to recover from a financial collapse in 1998. After sobering up from the wild currency and bond speculation during the 1990's, banks are regaining the trust of depositors, and are getting down to the more mundane business of lending to consumers.

At the same time, wages are on the rise, and the economy is flush with rubles, partly the effect of an oil boom. Wages are now increasingly paid above the table. Tax changes have drawn more incomes out of the shadows, leaving people more willing to disclose personal details about their financial abilities.

Interest rates, which can range from 15 percent for 10 year mortgages to double that for cars and appliances, would be considered usurious in the United States. But they are attractive in Russia, where the novelty of buying on credit is still so exciting to consumers that most don't even consider how much they are really paying over time when interest is factored into the total.

"The primary driver is increasingly legal incomes," said Aleksei Zabotkine, head economist at United Financial Group, an investment bank in Moscow. "Banks have excess cash and are willing to take on the risky business of lending to the public, and the public is willing to give information."

But eager-to-lend banks do not ask many questions. Nina A. Andreyeva, 41, a manicurist in a fur coat and hat, was filling out her second loan application in a giant home appliance store in northern Moscow on Saturday to help pay for a washing machine and television. She checked boxes indicating her line of work (health worker) and the location of her apartment (on the edge of town). After breezing through the application, she needed only to present her identification card—no proof of employment or verification of income.

Trading suitcases full of cash for the installment plan.

"It's very convenient," she said, pen in hand. "We can start using these things right away, and it's not so hard on our budget."

The borrowing is happening in purchases of home appliances, apartments, cars—even clothes. Mr. Thain said mortgages ranked first in total amount of loans, followed by home appliances and cars. The borrowing, so far, is mostly to consumers in the Moscow area, and has yet to spread to poorer provinces.

While the figures are minuscule compared with developed economies like the United States, they are growing. Russian Standard Bank, one of the largest lenders in the car and home appliance sectors, nearly tripled its client base last year from the previous year, with 550,000 loans at the end of December. The figure was up 63-fold from 1999, the bank's first year in operation. As of November, ruble-denominated loans to consumers in Russia totaled $3.7 billion.

"They told us it was a stupid idea and that we would be put out of business," said Dmitri V. Rudenko, deputy chairman of the bank in his office in northern Moscow. "But we thought, if it worked in Brazil and India, why not in Russia?"

The bank's customers are primarily what Mr. Rudenko described as blue collar. They earn about $250 a month. Few own cars. Still fewer have ever used a credit card. Even so, the default rate is low, 3.5 percent, he said, adding that for many Russians, repaying is a point of pride.

There are, of course, hustles. In one case, a group of vagrant men with passports went individually to each store that offered appliances on credit. They approached bank salesmen, who are based in the stores, asking for loans. Several bank employees noticed the men had traveled together in the same expensive, foreign-made car, and concluded they were being paid by a con artist.

The hustlers "didn't understand the credits all came from the same place—from us," said Dmitri V. Pilnikov, a Russian Standard manager, based at M-Video, the store where Ms. Andreyeva bought her television.

Jaded by a decade of pyramid schemes, Russians were initially wary of the loan offers. Mr. Pilnikov said he struggled at first to get people to take leaflets. Early attempts at advertising were relatively ineffective. Attitudes changed when a relative or neighbor tried it out and liked it.

"When we started, people looked at us like we were robbers," said Mr. Pilnikov. "They were very aggressive. But then their neighbors told them it wasn't a rip-off scheme. Now the thinking has turned around."

Loans are of shorter duration than they are in more developed economies. Russian Standard, for example, charges an annual rate of 29 percent for a standard consumer loan, and says its average span for a loan is between six months and a year. But most borrowers are concerned solely with the size of the monthly payments, and stores have responded. At M-Video, red tags highlight down payments and urge shoppers to buy on credit.

And demand has soared. Mr. Pilnikov said the store had to hire extra security guards to help regulate the rowdy line of loan seekers that, ahead of the Christmas holidays, stretched from his office almost 40 feet to the doors of the store entrance. An age requirement—applicants must be 23 to 65 years old—has forced him to turn away many of the bank's most eager customers: Russian grandmothers.

"They show me their medals of honor as hero workers from World War II," he said, shaking his head. "They say they have good pensions."

Mr. Zabotkine expects that the credit binge will end in crisis. Russians have no experience in the culture of borrowing, and in the current euphoria, few seem to be imagining the consequences of default. A still weak legal system means banks will have difficulties pursuing deadbeats in court. Dasha Malinova, 20, said she and her husband applied for a loan just to see what it was all about.

"It's cool," said Ms. Malinova, flipping her fur-trimmed wrist. "Everyone is taking them."

E-Music Sites Settle on Prices. It's a Start.

BY SAUL HANSELL

Has the music industry found the 99-cent solution to its file-sharing woes?

"Solution" is far too final a term for this business still very much in flux. But after years of denial and confusion, belligerence and panic, most of the big record labels have coalesced around a set of prices at which they will make almost all of their music available to an ever-expanding array of legal online services.

A major step toward a legal mass market for online music came last week when America Online started offering its first online music service to its 27 million members. AOL's plan roughly matches the terms and pricing that have evolved over the last 18 months by about half a dozen other paid music services.

They all now charge $9 or $10 a month for customers to listen to a pool of about 250,000 songs online, using a technology called streaming. And they charge about 99 cents to download a song and copy it onto a CD, where it can be played in a car or on a home stereo, or converted to a computer file format like MP3 to be shared with others (legally or not).

Other variations have also evolved. AOL's service, and others, include an unlimited number of what are known as tethered downloads, where songs can be copied onto a computer and played offline, for example, by a traveling laptop user. (The tethering means a subscriber can listen to the downloads on no more than two computers, and cannot copy the files to other devices or send them to other people.) And others offer variations on Internet radio, where users can pick genres or even specific artists to listen to online.

These options, along with the expanding pool of songs, finally have created online services that might have a chance of appealing to consumers and luring at least some from the free file-sharing services like **KaZaA.**

"We are at a crossover point," said Rob Glaser, the chief executive of **RealNetworks** and the chairman of **MusicNet,** which operates an online music service sold by RealNetworks and AOL. "Everyone doesn't agree on everything, but everyone agrees on enough things that we can start putting products in the market."

This agreement is also helping to frame some of the difficult questions the music industry must confront as it moves, however slowly, into a post-CD world. It is unclear so far whether the dominant digital business model will be selling downloads or renting access to a full catalog. It is clear that consumers are more interested in buying one song at a time than entire albums, an audience preference that is likely to mean major changes for the way the recording industry produces music. What those songs are worth in the long run is very much up in the air—except everyone agrees that eventually the hottest hit and the stalest oldie will not both be worth 99 cents.

But for now at least, the $10-a-month and 99-cent-a-song price list is letting the marketing side of the business take over from the deal makers. And Internet users will start to see increasing promotion for the first time for the online music services.

Listen.com, a privately held service, has attracted quite a bit of attention by discounting the price of burning songs onto CD's to 49 cents, from 99 cents, until March 31. And Internet service providers, including AOL, are looking to bundle stripped-down versions of these music services with their high-speed, or broadband, offerings.

The industry has come a long way since the first legal downloading services were introduced at the end of 2001. Back then Napster, the hugely popular file-sharing service had just been shut down by the courts. With a sense that the threat of free swapping had subsided, the big labels set up paid services, trying to preserve all sorts of advantages for themselves.

Online Jukeboxes

These are some of the fee-based music services available online and what they have to offer.

	SONGS	Download-to-own*	Tethered downloads†	Streamed songs	Internet radio	MONTHLY PACKAGES
Full Audio	200,000+	●	●	●	●	Name changes this week to MusicNow. $4.95, 36 radio channels; $9.95, adds unlimited tethered downloads and streamed songs. Can download songs for 99 cents each.
MusicNet on AOL	250,000+	●	●	●		$3.95, 20 online plays, 20 tethered downloads; $8.95, unlimited number of both. $17.95 allows subscriber to record 10 songs to CD.
PressPlay	250,000	●	●	●	●	$9.95, unlimited tethered downloads and online plays, about 40 digital radio stations.Many other plans add permanent downloading at $1.19 to 50 cents a song.
RealOne MusicPass	100,000+		●	●	●	$4.95, 100 tethered downloads and streamed songs; $9.95 adds 3,200 radio stations.
Listen.com's Rhapsody	292,000	●		●	●	$4.95, 58 radio stations, make custom stations; $9.95, adds unlimited streamed songs and access to burn songs on CD for 49 cents each, 99 cents after March 31.

*Download-to-own allows the buyer to burn a song to CD, or, with some services, transfer it to a compatible portable device or play from a digital file even if the buyer is no longer a subscriber to the music service.

†A tethered download can be played on a computer using the music service's proprietary software and only as long as the user remains a subscriber to the music service.

Source: The companies

(Cont.)

For one, the labels split into two groups. Sony and Universal, the two largest labels, created PressPlay. Warner, **Bertelsmann** and **EMI** along with RealNetworks, created a rival, MusicNet. Neither had access to music of their rival's owners.

Both offered limited numbers of songs that could be listened to online, or through tethered downloads. Only PressPlay allowed songs to be copied onto CD's or portable music players, and only in limited numbers.

Consumers spurned the first services. And indeed America Online refused to introduce the first generation of MusicNet, even though it is part owned by its corporate cousin Warner Music (both part of **AOL Time Warner).**

But as the music industry fiddled, the file-swapping masses were burning more free CD's than ever.

"After Napster shut down, the music-sharing community reassembled like the cyborg in 'Terminator,'" Mr. Glaser said. "It was much more rapid and much more organized than anyone expected."

Indeed, far more people use KaZaA, the largest of the file-sharing services, than ever used Napster. And sales of recorded CD's kept on falling, declining 9 percent in 2002.

So the music companies stopped jockeying for advantage in the music services they owned, and stopped worrying so much about how the paid services would cannibalize their CD sales and started searching for something—anything—that music lovers would actually pay for.

EMI, for instance, first focused on receiving a share of the profits of any online service selling its music, and by the end of last year decided to sell its music to most any online service.

"We moved to the notion that we are a content company and our content will have the greatest value for us and our artists if it's ubiquitously available and we enable the maximum number of business models to thrive," said John Rose, an executive vice president of EMI.

So EMI, which owns part of MusicNet, decided to license its music to PressPlay, Listen.com and others. By the end of last year, all of the labels were available on all of the services.

The music services, meanwhile, were able to use their lack of success to persuade the labels to allow them to offer unlimited streaming and more flexible downloads.

"The industry over the last year has developed a much greater understanding of the viability of this market," said Michael Bebel, chief executive of PressPlay. "We are at a point where a set of fundamental economics has emerged."

For the first time since the demise of the 45 r.p.m. record, the music industry is willing to sell a consumer only a song or two.

A basic wholesale price structure is coming together that online services can use to create product offerings. For example, a download of a song, with a suggested retail price of 99 cents, has a wholesale cost of about 65 cents from the labels, according to music executives.

The streaming services and tethered downloads have a more complicated price structure. Basically, the services pay between two-tenths of a cent and a penny to the label every time a user listens to a song. But there are monthly guarantees to the labels that together make the minimum monthly cost for music licenses to offer an unlimited streaming service about $5, according to music executives.

Internet radio is far cheaper for the online services to offer, costing stations seven-one hundredths of a penny a song for each listener, under a royalty arrangement the federal government set last year. And the services like **MusicMatch's** Radio MX that let users choose the artist they want to listen to but not the song, have a wholesale price that is higher than regular Internet radio and less than services that let users pick each song.

"We found demand drops off quickly after about $5 month," said Dennis Mudd, the chief executive of MusicMatch. Indeed, Radio MX, which has $2.95 and $4.95 a month options, has 120,000 subscribers, more than MusicMatch and PressPlay combined, according to analysts estimates. (Neither releases their subscriber counts, but they admit they are small.)

There is quite a debate about whether $9.95 (or $8.95 on AOL) is the right price for the unlimited streaming services.

Record companies looked for something, anything, that online fans would pay for.

Paul Vidich, an executive vice president of the Warner Music Group, argues that a service that lets users only listen to music—not copy it onto a CD or other device—is likely to be offered free with a broadband Internet subscription.

"At the end of the day we will invite people to listen without charging an admission fee," he said. "We are in the business of selling songs for people to own."

But others argue that in a world where stereo systems and even cars would be hooked up to the Internet with access to every possible song, no one will need to buy any music to keep. If that is true, the value of a monthly music subscription could be far more than $10.

The price of the songs themselves is also very much in question. At first, the labels tried to sell songs for as much as $2.99 each. But a series of experiments showed that consumers were not interested until the price hit 99 cents. That appears to resonate because it is in line with a 12-song CD that costs $15.

For simplicity's sake, the labels started by charging the same price for all their songs. But they are already working on plans to charge more for some and less for others. EMI, for example, is charging a premium of 50 to 75 percent for hot songs when they are released to download services before the albums are available in stores. And others are considering selling older titles in their back catalogs at a discount.

Moving forward, this emphasis on selling one song at a time may substantially hurt the industry. Since the the demise of the two-song 45 r.p.m. record a quarter-century ago, the recording industry has generally been able to charge for a full album on a CD—even if the consumer only wanted a song or two.

But Mr. Rose of EMI argued that the big issue for the music industry is not the subtleties of whether people buy songs or albums, but finding something that music lovers will pay anything for at all. And there is money to be made in volume, he said.

"If all the consumers who pirate tracks today bought them for a buck, that would be a $5 billion a month business," Mr. Rose said, noting that that is twice the size of the music industry today.

Marketing Strategies: Planning, Implementation, and Control

RICK WAGONER'S GAME PLAN

CEO Rick Wagoner has fixed many of GM's problems. But he still has to deal with 30 years of management mistakes

It's a chief executive's nightmare. The better you execute, the more improvements you make—the more your stock drops. That was the position G. Richard Wagoner Jr. found himself in last October. A day after General Motors Corp. announced that it had lifted operating earnings 30% in a stagnant car market, Standard & Poor's downgraded the auto maker's debt with no warning. Surprised investors rushed to sell, and the stock dropped 8%. Credit analysts pointed to GM's $76 billion pension fund, which they estimated at the time to be underfunded by as much as $23 billion. GM will have to plow in billions of dollars for years to keep the fund flush, they said.

The earnings gain was no accounting fluke, either. GM finished the year just as strong, with an operating profit of $3.9 billion, nearly double what it earned in 2001, on 5% higher sales of $186.2 billion. GM clearly leads the rest of the U.S. Big Three car companies, reflecting real operational improvements that Wagoner, 49, helped make in the past decade, starting when he was chief financial officer and later as chief operating officer. After GM lost a staggering $30 billion during a single three-year stretch in the early '90s, Wagoner and Chairman John F. "Jack" Smith Jr. forced GM back to basics. They slashed costs, cut payroll, and overhauled aging plants. Once he took over the corner office in May, 2000, CEO Wagoner pulled the efficiency collar even tighter. Now, GM ranks close to Honda Motor Co. and Toyota Motor Corp. in productivity and has made strides in quality. GM also recaptured leadership of the truck business from rival Ford Motor Co., a coup that made the company billions. Last year, GM even nudged up its share of the U.S. market, to 28.3% from 28.1%.

But as good as those moves are, they pale next to the problems of GM's weak car brands and gargantuan pension payments. In essence, Rick Wagoner is battling 30 years of management mistakes that have left him with immense burdens and very little room to maneuver. Chief executives from Frederic Donner to Roger Smith built up a bloated bureaucracy that cranked out boring, low-quality cars. Turf battles at headquarters sapped resources and diverted attention from a rising threat out of Asia and Europe. Those competitors drove away with the U.S. car market. Now they're aiming to do the same in sport-utility vehicles and trucks—the last bastion of U.S. dominance. GM's most profitable segment is also under attack by environmentalists and safety regulators, and more and more buyers are flocking to smaller crossover SUVs.

Even worse for GM was the buildup of lavish health and retirement benefits for workers that it agreed to in fatter days as a way to buy peace with the United Auto Workers. The company says the gap between its pension funding and future liabilities is now $19.3 billion. That means GM will have to pump as much as $4 billion into the fund over this year and next. Providing health care to former and current workers will drain an additional $5 billion per year. The pension costs alone will cut projected 2003 net income from $4.2 billion to $2.8 billion. Providing for retirees saddles each car rolling off a GM assembly line with a $1,350 penalty vs. a Japanese car built in a new, nonunion U.S. plant, says analyst Scott Hill of Sanford C. Bernstein & Co. That's a daunting handicap in an industry that struggles to make an average operating profit of $800 per vehicle.

Those huge legacy costs explain why Wagoner has kept the heat on his competition with the 0% financing deals he unleashed after September 11, 2001. Closing plants and accepting a smaller chunk of the U.S. market—the route his rival, Ford, has taken—would give GM fewer vehicles over which to spread those big pension and health-care costs. And thanks to an onerous deal it struck in 1990 with the UAW, GM has to pay furloughed workers about 70% of their salary for years after they're laid off. Says Wagoner: "We have a huge fixed-cost base. It's 30 years of downsizing and 30 years of increased health-care costs. It puts a premium on us running this business to generate cash. Our goal is to grow. We don't care who we take it from."

All that would make the outlook for GM pretty bleak, except for one thing: Eventually, those legacy costs start to diminish. Starting around 2008, the ranks of GM's elderly retirees will thin, relieving some of the burden.

Malibu on a Budget

One of Wagoner's biggest accomplishments has been reducing the time and money it takes to build vehicles. Here are some of the savings GM has wrung out of one mainstay car, the 2003 Chevy Malibu, compared with two other midsize sedans, the Oldsmobile Intrigue and Pontiac Grand Prix, that previously were built at the same Fairfax (Kan.) plant.

THE DESIGN — GM designed the Malibu so that fewer workers can assemble more cars. **PAYOFF** GM should be able to build the Malibu with 18 to 19 hours of labor instead of 24 hours.

THE PLATFORM — GM engineers in the U.S., Germany, and Sweden worked together to share the same platform and other parts for the company's Chevrolet Malibu, Opel Vectra, and Saab 9-3 midsize sedans. **PAYOFF** Engineering costs were cut by one-third.

THE INTERIOR — GM gave French interior supplier Faurecia the contract for seats for the Malibu, Vectra, and Saab 9-3. **PAYOFF** GM got seats made of more comfortable and durable materials for the price of cheaper seats.

THE GAS TANK — The Malibu and Saab 9-3 share the same gas tank, saving on engineering and safety tests. **PAYOFF** The tank's cost is 30% lower.

THE SUSPENSION — The Chevy Malibu and Opel Vectra share the same front and rear suspension. **PAYOFF** Development costs are 30% lower for those components.

After that, more of the incremental gains Wagoner has been achieving will fall to the bottom line rather than to retirees. The results could be dramatic.

That makes Wagoner's imperative clear: He has to keep up cash flow to cover those costs until they start to shrink. At the same time, he must continue to rack up improvements in quality, efficiency, design, and brand appeal. If he can come anywhere close, he just might pull off an impressive turnaround. A stock market rebound would help immensely. GM's pension fund holds its own if it earns 9% a year on its investments. Each one-point rise above that is worth $700 million to the fund.

With much of the focus on GM's financial crunch, it's easy to lose sight of Wagoner's greatest achievement—and the best reason to believe that he might beat the legacy monster. Walk around GM's sprawling headquarters complex today and you soon realize that against all odds, Wagoner is making real progress in energizing GM's torpid culture. He broke with GM tradition by recruiting two respected outsiders for key positions—Robert A. Lutz as head of product development and John Devine as vice-chairman and chief financial officer. And he has given them extraordinary leeway to fix the company's problems.

To motivate his team, the self-effacing Wagoner leaves his ego at the door and lets his executives do their jobs. "Rick acts more like a coach than a boss," says David E. Cole, director of the Center for Automotive Research (CAR) in Ann Arbor, Mich. Thus it was Lutz who rolled out Cadillac's lavish Sixteen prototype luxury car at the Detroit auto show earlier this month as Wagoner sat in the background. Afterward, Wagoner chatted with a few reporters while Lutz held court beside the 16-cylinder vehicle, surrounded by a huge crowd, drinking a martini, and wearing someone's lipstick mark on his cheek.

That low-key style has helped Wagoner in tearing down GM's warring fiefdoms. Since giving the swaggering Lutz rule over product development, Wagoner has spiked the design-by-committee system and cut the time it takes to develop a new car to 20 months from nearly four years. GM used to have different studios for each division working on car designs that would get passed on to marketing, then engineering, then manufacturing. Lutz has one committee to cover the entire process. Every Thursday, he hashes out what vehicles should look like and which division will build them, along with a small group that includes Group Vice-President for Advanced Vehicle Development Mark T. Hogan, GM North America President Gary L. Cowger, Design Chief Wayne K. Cherry, and Chief Engineer James E. Queen.

But low-key doesn't mean hands-off. Lutz may make the day-to-day decisions on car design, but Wagoner reserves final say. He meets monthly with top execs, who see car designs much earlier in the process. The ones they think are promising move ahead fast. Says retired executive Richard C. Nerod, who ran GM's Latin America operations: "Rick cut out a lot of the infighting and the bull – – – –."

Wagoner also exerts control by imposing tough performance standards. A legendary number-cruncher who rose up through GM's finance division, he holds top managers to strict measures. GM, like most big companies, always had performance goals. But they never went nearly as deep or into as much detail. Says Cowger: "Everything can be measured."

GM is now the lowest-cost producer among the Big Three—and it's not far behind Toyota and Honda

Everyone, too. Even Lutz, the larger-than-life product czar who flies his own fighter jet and sparked Chrysler's 1990s resurgence with cars such as the Dodge Viper and PT Cruiser, isn't exempt. Lutz was judged on 12 criteria last year, from how well he used existing parts to save money in new vehicles to how many engineering hours he cut from the development process.

Clearly, Wagoner's own ideas on how to fix GM have evolved. He seems to have learned from a brush with grand strategic vision back in the '90s, when, like now-deposed Ford CEO Jacques A. Nasser, he explored ways to grow outside of building cars. Wagoner was behind the decision to pump hundreds of millions into GM's OnStar Corp. telematics business and DirecTV satellite-TV service. Neither produced big revenues for GM. Now, with Devine applying a cold dose of realism to GM's finances, there's little illusion that such diversions can fix the cash crunch. "That was a dream a couple of years ago, but it's not reality," Devine says. "The math will tell you that the principal driver of revenue and profits is the car-and-truck business in North America and Europe."

If Wagoner has brought a new intensity to GM, he probably gets it from his mother, Martha, a onetime school teacher. Family members recall one Christmas several years ago when she doggedly kept baking cookies despite a broken arm. "My mom has a task orientation that you sometimes see in my brother," says Judy Pahren, a financial-services manager who is one of Wagoner's two sisters. Rick had a Norman Rockwell upbringing in Richmond, Va. He picked up a rabid devotion to Duke University basketball from his father, George, an accountant at Eskimo Pie Co. Wagoner got a chance to play for the Blue Devils as a walk-on. He demonstrated a deft shot but learned the limits of his athletic ability. "The knock on Rick was that you couldn't slide a phone book under his jump," says roommate Charles H. McCreary III. The devotion to alma mater remains, though: A few years ago, he ordered a custom "Duke blue" Suburban SUV.

After Duke, Wagoner got his MBA at Harvard Business School, surprising some upon graduation when he chose GM over potentially more lucrative jobs on Wall Street. Wagoner's knack for crunching numbers propelled him through stints at GM units in Canada, Europe, and Brazil. His big break came in 1992, when then-CEO Smith tapped him to be CFO after a boardroom coup. Even as CEO, Wagoner is known for a low-key lifestyle. He prides himself on juggling his work schedule to attend games and other activities of his three sons. And when entertaining, Wagoner is more likely to cook on his backyard grill than hire a caterer.

Wagoner's willingness to let others shine is a classic trait of leaders who have boosted their companies to exceptional performance, says Jim Collins, author of *Good to Great.* As a longtime GM insider, Wagoner has other advantages: He knows what brutal facts need to be confronted, and he can assess which veterans can handle key jobs. Says Collins: "Wagoner has the opportunity to take it back to great." But the odds are stiff—only 11 of 1,435 companies Collins studied made such a lasting transformation. And those that did required an average of seven years to get breakthrough results.

Still, competitors are impressed with the progress Wagoner has made. "I'm a big admirer of his management style," says crosstown rival William C. Ford Jr., chairman and CEO of Ford. He should be—GM's operating profit may not match the $4.6 billion No. 3 Toyota made in just the six months through September. And GM's stock, trading around 37, is down 26% from a year ago. But that performance sure beats Ford's $872 million operating profit and 36% lower stock price.

It's a testament to Wagoner's ability to cut costs that GM managed nearly to double margins in North America last year, to 2.6% of sales. Thanks to efficiency gains, GM is now one of the leanest car builders, with variable costs—labor, parts, outsourced production, etc.—amounting to 62% of revenues, according to UBS Warburg. That puts it ahead of Ford and Chrysler at 68%, and it isn't far behind leaders Toyota and Honda at 60%.

To woo car buyers, GM uses incentives that cost $3,800 per car—twice what Toyota spends

(Cont.)

With lower costs than its domestic competition, GM is better able to withstand the price war it started with 0% financing. But Wagoner is betting that the cars he plans to launch in the next three years will be good enough to sell on merit, not price. A few "niche" vehicles, such as the hulking Hummer H2, are already out. But the assault begins in earnest later this year with the Chevy Malibu family sedan and Equinox car/SUV crossover, Cadillac SRX small SUV, and Pontiac Grand Prix sedan. "This is one major last-ditch effort to save themselves in the car market," says Joseph Phillippi, a former Wall Street analyst who consults for the industry.

Wagoner, who's not a classic Detroit "car guy," seems content to rely on Lutz and his team to fix the lineup. During one trip through the design studio last year, he spotted a sexy two-door version of the Cadillac CTS sports sedan. "I hope you guys figure out a way to build that," Wagoner said, but offered no solutions, recalls one senior designer. "Rick trusts my judgment implicitly," Lutz says, "but if I came up with some wacky product proposals, he'd pull me back."

The most dramatic gains won't come on a sketch pad anyway but in the way GM selects new car designs and then shepherds them through production. In the past, even if a bold design made it off a drawing board, it had little chance of surviving to the showroom. A concept would go from a designer to the marketing staff, which would try to tailor it to consumers. Then it would go to engineers, who would try to figure out how to build it, and so on. Separate teams worked with suppliers, factories, and parts suppliers on their individual slice of the process, with little interaction.

It was a recipe for mediocrity—and often disaster. The Aztek, which emerged in 2000 as a boxy, garish cross between an SUV and a minivan five years after designers first drew it up as a racy bid for younger drivers, is a prime example. Wagoner was determined to tear up that system by the roots. A few months after taking over, he ordered GM's product developers to ready the SSR concept vehicle for production. A combination of hot rod and pickup truck, it had been a big hit at the Detroit auto show. Wagoner thought its distinctive look, with chrome bars splitting the front grille and taillights, would be a great image builder. But the SSR still had to navigate the old GM system. Because it was announced before engineers had a precise blueprint to build it, the program quickly ran over budget. Today, its cost has ballooned way past the original $300 million projection, to almost $500 million. The $42,000 SSR will hit showrooms this summer, a quick turnaround for GM. But with only 5,000 sales projected per year, it makes for a very expensive showcase.

Since then, Wagoner and Lutz have smoothed things out a bit. Lutz, Cowger, Hogan, and the others decide what goes from the design studios into the funnel of cars that will be considered for funding by GM's Automotive Strategy Board, chaired monthly by Wagoner. Lutz says he and Wagoner have disagreed on some product decisions, but he hasn't been turned down yet. Now, 75% of the engineering work is finished when a program manager sits down to build a car.

That's how GM quickly green-lighted plans to resurrect the Pontiac GTO, its famous 1960s muscle car. For years, Pontiac and Chevrolet wanted a brawny car with rear-wheel drive, which is favored by driving enthusiasts. GM's Australian Holden Ltd. subsidiary had a promising candidate in its Monaro sports coupe, but the idea to bring it to the U.S. never made it out of committee. GM execs simply didn't want to spend what little money it would take to alter the Monaro to meet U.S. safety standards and American styling. Says Lutz: "I just asked, 'Why not?'" GM got the program together in less than 18 months. Later this year, Pontiac will roll out the GTO as a 340-horsepower Americanized Monaro.

Wagoner has also streamlined GM's factories. GM is now the most productive domestic auto maker, having cut the time it takes to assemble a vehicle from an average of 32 hours in 1998 to 26 hours in 2001, according to Harbour & Associates. That compares with 27 for Ford, almost 31 at DaimlerChrysler, 22.5 at Toyota, and 17.9 at Nissan. A big factor was expanding parts shared across vehicles. The new Chevy Malibu, for instance, uses the same platform and many of the same parts as the Saab 9-3 sedan. GM's plants are also more flexible—each of seven full-size pickup and SUV plants can make any of the vehicles designed on that platform.

To offset high health and pension costs, GM needs hot cars that bring in cash

The cars rolling off GM's assembly lines today are undeniably better built than they used to be. Once ranked below the industry average, GM trails only Honda and Toyota in J.D. Power & Associates Inc.'s initial quality survey, which measures problems in the first 90 days of ownership. Some cars, such as the Chevrolet Impala, even beat the likes of the Toyota Camry. Last year, *Consumer Reports* recommended 13 GM vehicles—representing 41% of its sales volume—up from 5 last year. But one of GM's most stubborn woes is that many buyers still perceive the Chevy, Pontiac, and Buick brands as musty and second-rate. GM needs incentives averaging $3,800 a vehicle—more than twice what Toyota spends.

The biggest risk to GM's lineup is at the top. Its popular SUVs and pickups accounted for about 90% of profits last year but are under increasing assault from foreign competitors and safety regulators. Like his competitors, Wagoner is banking on crossover vehicles, which combine SUV-like space and looks with a carlike ride and better fuel economy, as a hedge against a big-truck backlash. Cadillac's luxury SRX hits the market this year as a viable rival to the Lexus RX 330 and Mercedes M-class, and Chevy will launch its Equinox as an all-wheel drive crossover. Next year, GM will start offering pickups and SUVs with hybrid gas/electric engines. New designs are also in the works. Lutz has tentatively approved a highly stylized 2007 replacement for the Chevy Silverado and GMC Sierra pickups, which hold a commanding 40% of the pickup market. It will be based on the slick Cheyenne concept truck that GM unveiled in January, which has improved driver and passenger room and doors on each side of the pickup bed to provide easier cargo access. But in small SUVs and gas mileage, GM is playing catch-up to the Japanese.

Wagoner and his team have little choice but to wait out their biggest mess—those massive health and pension costs. Wagoner is brutally realistic: "We'd be accused of a pipe dream if we said in 10 years these issues will go away." GM pays its UAW workers only slightly more per hour than Toyota, Honda, and Nissan pay their American factory workers. But the cost of pension and health-care benefits for current workers is huge—about $24 per hour at GM, vs. $12 at the foreign factories. Pension obligations swelled after the 1990 contract, when then-Chairman Robert Stempel practically guaranteed almost no layoffs. Underestimating the speed of its decline, GM agreed to pay workers for years after a furlough. As losses mounted, GM resorted to early-retirement offers—avoiding billions in unemployment benefits but adding thousands of retirees. Since GM was shrinking faster than Ford, its pension rolls grew more quickly, to 2.5 retirees per worker today, vs. Ford's 1-to-1 ratio. Last year, GM plowed almost $5 billion into the pension fund to shore it up as stock prices fell. But Carol Levenson, an analyst for bond research firm Gimme Credit, points out that GM had to take on $4.6 billion in debt to do it. Until the stock and bond markets spring back, it's three steps forward and two steps back.

That pressure should ease somewhat over the next decade. GM's average worker is 48 years old—five years older than those at Ford or Chrysler. GM's total number of retirees will drop below existing levels by 2010, says CAR's labor and manufacturing analyst, Sean McAlinden. Wagoner believes that even without another bull market to boost the pension fund, GM can handle the drain and maintain its $7 billion capital-spending budget. Meanwhile, to pay down the pension shortfall, Devine is working to

(Cont.)

sell Hughes Electronics' DirecTV business, possibly to News Corp.

Closing the gap on health-care costs will be tougher. This summer, GM and the UAW will start working on a new four-year labor agreement. GM is almost certain to ask for higher co-payments from its 138,000 UAW employees. The union is almost certain to balk. "We don't have an interest in cost-shifting," says Richard Shoemaker, head of the UAW's GM department. GM also is one of many companies pushing to have Medicare pick up a greater share of retiree drug costs. But even Wagoner admits: "I don't see that happening soon."

Can Wagoner return GM to dominance? He has made heroic gains. But he's taking nothing for granted. At a speech in Detroit last year, he told the story of William C. Durant, who pulled together such companies as Buick, Cadillac, and Olds to form GM in 1908. But Durant was more interested in cutting deals than managing, so he wound up running a bowling alley in Flint. "That fate has haunted GM chairmen for decades," Wagoner told his audience. He was joking, of course. But Wagoner will be the first to tell you that his own future is up in the air. It all depends on whether he can save GM from its past.

By David Welch, with Kathleen Kerwin, in Detroit

The Sequel

After Living on Rented Time, Blockbuster Plunges Into Sales

Wal-Mart and Cheaper DVDs Force the Chain to Revamp Its Stores and Marketing

Caught Up in Viacom Tension

By Martin Peers

On a recent visit to a Blockbuster store in Santa Ana, Calif., John Antioco, the chain's chief executive, spotted a customer browsing the videos for sale. Noticing that no clerk had talked to the man, who left empty-handed, the CEO chased him out to the parking lot to ask which movies he wanted. It turned out Blockbuster had one of them, and he ushered the man back inside to make the sale.

Mr. Antioco, who has worked at 7-Eleven Inc. and run Circle K Corp. stores, knows he's going to have to sprint to turn Blockbuster Inc., a rental giant, into more of a retail giant. In little over a decade, Blockbuster changed the face of the entertainment industry by planting big, brightly lit stores nationwide and enticing the masses to do something Americans rarely did, rent something. But now industrywide discounting and the novelty of the DVD have prompted more people to buy their copies of movies, and that's quickly put Blockbuster on the defensive.

Last year, in a major shift, people spent significantly more on movie purchases than rentals. While retail sales for films rose 19% to \$12.26 billion, rental spending slipped 3%, to \$9.92 billion, according to Adams Media Research of Carmel, Calif. And in December Blockbuster's stock plunged 32% after the company disclosed that its fourth-quarter revenue would be weaker than expected, which it blamed on consumers snapping up low-priced DVDs and videos at discount retailers.

Now the 53-year-old Mr. Antioco, who took over Blockbuster in 1997, is steering the company into the retail market—and onto a risky collision course with discount chains such as Wal-Mart Stores Inc., Target Corp. and Costco Corp. A bit player with only a 3% share in video sales, Blockbuster hopes to triple that share by 2006.

This will be the biggest test yet for Mr. Antioco, whose reforms helped the company generate fatter profits even as it struggled with a stagnant rental market. In a masterstroke, he used the Blockbuster clout to renegotiate deals with Hollywood studios in the late 1990s. In the past, they had charged Blockbuster the same price as smaller chains, roughly \$65 for each copy of a movie. But Mr. Antioco got the studios to slash their per-copy charge in exchange for letting Hollywood share in Blockbuster's rental revenue. Blockbuster's cost per movie effectively fell to between \$22 and \$25. The chain also agreed to buy more movies overall. With that and other savvy moves, he was able to revive the Blockbuster cash machine, the very thing that originally enticed its parent, Viacom Inc., to acquire the video chain nine years ago. Under Mr. Antioco, Blockbuster paid off about \$700 million in debt in the past three years, and the company could make enough to repay much of its remaining \$540 million in debt this year.

The predicament Blockbuster finds itself in now is largely Mr. Antioco's doing. His turnaround helped Blockbuster build 1,300 new stores in the U.S. and boost its commanding market share of the movie-rental business to nearly 40% from about 25%, making it a formidable negotiating rival for the Hollywood studios.

Worried they had become too dependent on Blockbuster, some studios cut prices on DVDs in the hope that a thriving retail market would weaken Blockbuster, whose expertise was in rentals. Last year, Warren Lieberfarb, then chief of home video for AOL Time Warner Inc.'s Warner Bros., complained that Blockbuster had used its market share "to increase their margins at the expense of the studios." Mr. Lieberfarb, who left Warner in December, led a drive to offer cheap DVDs to train the public to buy rather than rent them and, he says, to create "an antidote to Blockbuster's dominance" without hurting the studio's profits.

New Rules

About 80% of Blockbuster's annual revenue is in rentals, which the company believes will stay its main business. But as Mr. Antioco begins to alter the Blockbuster stores and culture to emphasize selling, he faces entirely new rules of the game. Blockbuster currently enjoys a fat profit margin on its rental business of 65%, much higher than the 15% it expects in retail. It is going from being the dominant player in a market it pioneered to an also-ran in a business with well-heeled and entrenched retail giants.

On top of it all, Mr. Antioco has to contend with Blockbuster's long-standing role as a misfit stepchild to Viacom, whose main interests have been developing programming and generating advertising for its media empire, which includes CBS and MTV Networks. As the market shifts away from Blockbuster's founding rental business, there's internal debate within Viacom itself over just what to do with the chain of 8,500 stores worldwide.

Mr. Antioco says Blockbuster will have "some real serious choices" about how to spend its cash with a newly clean balance sheet. He may invest more heavily in new areas already being tested, such as videogame retailing or "movie-trading stores," where customers sell their used DVDs and buy new ones. Alternatively, he says he's interested in doing a "sizable acquisition" of a retailer in a sector outside of video. He's coy about his targets; investment bankers believe Blockbuster could merge with a company such as Amazon.com or buy a videogame retailer, such as GameStop Corp.

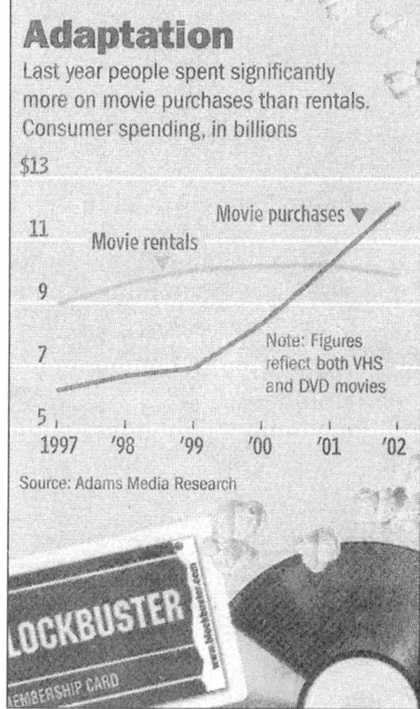

But all this could clash with Viacom's ambitions. In 1997, after Blockbuster ran into problems, Viacom Chairman Sumner Redstone promised shareholders to spin it off. But Viacom changed its mind once the Blockbuster turnaround took hold, selling only 18% to the public. Now Blockbuster's cash flow helps buttress Viacom's own financial statements, dependent on fickle ad revenue. Having Blockbuster diversify further into retail could make Viacom, and some of its big media investors, uneasy.

"What I think is not good for Viacom would be to make us a conglomerate," says

Viacom President Mel Karmazin. He adds that Viacom has more appetite for "acquisitions in our core competencies," such as cable networks and TV stations. He supports Blockbuster's current direction, and doesn't rule out its "doing anything that strategically made sense."

The debate comes amid tension between Mr. Redstone and Mr. Karmazin, who has run the company since it acquired CBS Corp. in 2000. Relations between them were immediately fractious, and the two are now renegotiating Mr. Karmazin's contract, due to expire later this year. Highly regarded as a fiscally disciplined manager, Mr. Karmazin puts a high priority on cash-generating businesses such as Blockbuster and has been a bigger backer of it than Mr. Redstone, arguing against a spinoff.

Mr. Antioco says he and his bosses at Viacom are on the same page, so far. He also stresses that Blockbuster could survive without diversifying away from video rentals. But if that doesn't happen, he adds: "Would we prosper? No."

Since its beginning in the 1980s, Blockbuster has defied predictions. As it expanded rapidly, some analysts were convinced innovations such as video-on-demand would make it obsolete. The forecasts have yet to pan out. But even a decade ago, its then-chairman, Wayne Huizenga, had Blockbuster plow several hundred million dollars into purchases of music retailers, film- and TV-production companies. Under Viacom, Blockbuster hired a Wal-Mart executive in 1996 who decided to remake the stores into "neighborhood entertainment centers," cramming them with candy, T-shirts, toys and books. The result was racks of assorted merchandise clogging the stores and turning off customers. Blockbuster's revenue nosedived.

In 1997, Mr. Redstone hired Mr. Antioco, a Brooklyn-born son of a milkman whose resume outside the convenience-store industry included briefly running the Taco Bell restaurant chain. When he first arrived at the Dallas headquarters, Mr. Antioco knew from his experience as a customer the frustrations of Blockbuster stores. Unable to find a spare copy of the latest movie release, people often left with nothing. At the time, Hollywood studios charged such a high price for each copy of a movie release that the chain could only afford to stock a few copies.

So one of Mr. Antioco's first moves as CEO was to persuade the studios to change its video-supply deals to make it easier for Blockbuster to stock many copies of new-release movies. Blockbuster's revenue skyrocketed so much immediately afterward that Mr. Redstone, on seeing the figures in his New York office, joked to an associate that his computer must have been broken.

Revamped Layouts

Things changed after Hollywood studios began aggressively cutting prices on DVD versions of new and old movies to well below $20. As sales exploded, Mr. Antioco last summer announced plans to plunge Blockbuster into the retail market. It revamped store layouts: Instead of scattering shelves of movies for sale throughout the store, it grouped the shelves together under huge "Buy This" signs hanging from the ceiling. Used tapes and discs, called "previewed," were put in separate racks from new movies.

To ensure that customers can't miss the products for sale, stores are arranged to steer them past racks of for-sale product before they get to the rental wall that usually runs along the perimeter. Blockbuster has also created similar zones dedicated to selling video games.

While online sales of movies so far haven't been much of a threat, Blockbuster must contend with some formidable retail competition, including Wal-Mart and electronics discounters. Circuit City, for instance, recently advertised the "Kate and Leopold" DVD for $12.99—$7 less than Blockbuster's price.

Wal-Mart, the dominant seller of DVDs, has an estimated market share of 20% or more. It seems unconcerned by Blockbuster's plans. "We appreciate competition," says a Wal-Mart spokesman, who won't comment on the share estimate. Along with DVD players, DVDs are part of Wal-Mart's electronics category, he adds, which continues to be a "strong performer."

But taking on Wal-Mart worries some on Wall Street. "That's the current concern if you're looking at Viacom overall," says Tom Wolzien, an analyst with Sanford C. Bernstein & Co., whose parent, Alliance Capital, owns more than 1% of Viacom. Mr. Karmazin says Viacom will ensure that Blockbuster doesn't become a problem for the parent company.

Mr. Antioco says Blockbuster isn't going to compete on cost. "What we are about is convenience, selection," he says.

This past holiday season was tough for Blockbuster. Over Thanksgiving, Mr. Antioco was stunned to see a sharp drop in his rental business. Studios had released more big hit movies priced to buy rather than rent than ever before. Blockbuster, leaning the wrong way, had spent too much on rental product and marketing.

Mr. Antioco and his bosses at Viacom believe the Christmas shortfall was an anomaly. Mr. Antioco expects better financial results this year, partly because Hollywood's marketing on DVDs is lowering costs for Blockbuster. Meanwhile, the rental market continues to be threatened by new technologies such as video-on-demand, more available on cable TV, as well as devices such as Tivo, which allow people to more-easily record their favorite TV shows.

Mr. Antioco addressed Viacom's board at a meeting in late January, updating directors on new business possibilities. He acknowledges an acquisition to expand in retail may not be easy for Viacom.

A "faction of significant shareholders in Viacom" may protest that Viacom is an entertainment company and ask: "Why do you want to get bigger in the retail business?" he says. Indeed, a longtime proponent of spinning off Blockbuster is Gordon Crawford, a senior vice president with Capital Group, one of Viacom's biggest shareholders and among the most influential money managers in the media sector.

But Mr. Karmazin says he likes the fact that Blockbuster helps diversify Viacom's revenue, about half of which comes from advertising. While he makes clear he wouldn't support acquisitions in low-growth areas such as book retailing, "there is a lot of upside" in both the videogame and DVD areas.

Mr. Redstone, the Viacom chairman, sounds a bit less enthusiastic. He told investors at a private meeting last month that "we have decisions to make. Do we spin [it] off? Do we sell it? There are companies who would buy it. Do we keep it? Do we buy it in?" he said. "We don't know the ultimate answer. We should be very careful, skeptical and questioning about the future of Blockbuster."

Under Renovation

A Hardware Chain Struggles to Adjust To a New Blueprint

Home Depot Chief Nardelli Tightens Central Control, And Employees Squawk

Today, He Reveals More Plans

By Dan Morse

ATLANTA — When Bernie Marcus ran Home Depot Inc., he fired up store managers inundated by paperwork from headquarters with this advice: "Get a rubber stamp that says 'Bulls—' on it, stamp it, and send it back to whatever bureaucrat sent it to you." The message: It's your store; do what's best.

Bob Nardelli came to the company from General Electric Co. two years ago with a very different approach: one that increasingly favors directives from headquarters in Atlanta. As chairman and chief executive, he has cut costs, centralized purchasing and tightened control of hiring and store displays. Performance is now measured by lingo that leaves many employees scratching their heads: receiving minutes per bill, percent of E-Velocity and SPR audits, to name a few.

By all accounts, the country's No. 1 home-improvement chain needed at least some tightening. But so far, Mr. Nardelli's swift, aggressive renovations have disrupted employees and spooked many shareholders. Home Depot's once-roaring stock has fallen close to its five-year low, having dropped 51% since Mr. Nardelli arrived.

Sales growth, which started to slacken the year before he took over, has slowed considerably. The company said earlier this month that sales in stores open at least a year will plunge as much as 10% in its fourth quarter, which ends Feb. 2. For the fiscal year, overall sales are expected to rise 10%, compared with 17% the year before.

At a company traditionally known for independent-minded managers and workers, some confusion and resentment have set in. After Mr. Nardelli arrived, "things weren't presented to you; they were told to you," says Tony Calveiro, a former store manager in Kansas City, Mo. He left in July 2001 to become an assistant manager for Costco Wholesale Corp., where he says he has more freedom.

Mr. Marcus says the company lost a lot of talented employees after Mr. Nardelli's arrival, although departures have tapered off. The company plays down the suggestion that it had sizable departures of talented employees because of the changed leadership.

Mr. Nardelli has emphasized hiring more part-timers to handle weekend crowds, but customers are complaining that the quality of service has lagged. The CEO's order to keep store inventory leaner made sense on paper, but in practice it has meant that homeowners and contractors couldn't always find what they were looking for.

Meanwhile, Home Depot is no longer cruising along as it did for nearly two decades, with strong sales and earnings quarter after quarter. Among other factors, the company has blamed cautious consumer spending and big promotions last winter that inflated sales in the same period a year ago. No. 2 Lowe's Cos.—a retailer known for its disciplined operations—has been chipping away at Home Depot's strong lead. (Because the housing market has remained strong, the overall slow economy hasn't hurt home improvement as much as it has other retailers, some industry executives say.)

Three big institutional investors—Fidelity Management & Research Co., Alliance Capital Management Inc. and Janus Capital Management LLC—have dumped Home Depot stock valued at a total of $4.2 billion in recent months, according to FactSet Research Systems Inc. This week, Gary Balter and Neel Gandhi, analysts at Credit Suisse First Boston who have issued a generally favorable rating on the stock, nevertheless fired a broadside at the CEO. Based on their own store visits, the analysts wrote, "Mr. Nardelli in two years at the helm has not yet shown the retail acumen that defines the winners." They cited a lack of skilled employees, poor store displays, missing products and poor purchasing decisions.

'Change Creates Fear'

Mr. Nardelli, 54 years old, is sticking to his strategy. "Change creates fear," he says. The only way for Home Depot to thrive, he adds, is for headquarters to know what's going on. "The naysayers could say, 'Well jeez, you're adding all these metrics.' Well, take all the gauges off the car. Why do you need a gas gauge? Why do you need a speedometer?"

Morale is holding up, he says, given all of the changes and the slumping stock price. "I love the entrepreneurial spirit. I just want to have some compliant entrepreneurial spirit at a certain time," he said in an interview last year.

Since he arrived, margins and cash on hand are up. The balance sheet is strong. The company continues to add stores, so overall sales are still climbing. Ken Langone, an influential board member who helped hire Mr. Nardelli, says the CEO's strategy will pay off. "We think Bob is doing a superb job and is making the changes going forward that are necessary."

Today, the chief executive will spell out more improvement plans at the company's annual investor conference. On tap: continued programs to refurbish stores, more new merchandise and efforts to boost customer service.

A big part of Home Depot's success story has been the energy its managers customarily invested in taking command of their stores, ordering as many hammers and faucets as they thought their customers expected and hiring knowledgeable retired tradespeople and hungry newcomers to work the aisles. "You had these evangelists, if you will, who sold lumber," says consultant Robert Oxley. He used to train Home Depot employees and now teaches vendors trying to sell products to the company. These days, he says, "there's nowhere near the passion as there was under the old guard," saying that's one of the consequences of Mr. Nardelli's approach. "It's not manageable through a computer."

Mr. Marcus, who helped lead the company from its founding in 1978 through early 2001, acknowledges that the old ways sometimes got a little "loosey-goosey." And some of Mr. Nardelli's critics concede that a company that had grown to more than 1,000 stores needed to show more discipline, especially in light of increased competition.

Mr. Nardelli arrived in December 2000, after losing out in the race to replace Jack Welch atop GE. The new Home Depot chief, who lacked any retail experience, burrowed into the new job. Atlanta staffers remember him calling meetings for 8 p.m. on weekdays and 7:30 a.m. on weekends.

A number of executives left, some with strong encouragement, as Mr. Nardelli brought more subordinates under his direct control. He attacked labor costs, setting more structured "wage bands" for specific jobs and limiting merit raises, which he says were "out of control."

Home Depot's deflated stock has weighed on morale, because many employees have received bonuses in the form of stock options whose value has fallen. In break rooms and on the Internet, they grouse about their CEO's $13.8 million in total compensation last fiscal year, not including options.

Mr. Nardelli's challenges are compounded by the reverence with which many employees regard Mr. Marcus and Arthur Blank, the retired founders and longtime executives. Months after Mr. Nardelli arrived, workers who spotted Mr. Marcus in their store would beseech him to come back. But that is fading, says Mr. Marcus, who stresses that Mr. Nardelli is making needed changes that employees are starting to appreciate.

In a 1999 book, Messrs. Marcus and Blank wrote, "We hire people who couldn't work for anybody else, who might otherwise be well-suited to being self-employed or running their own shop, and many of them become store managers." The authors lauded employees for outlandish stunts. Larry Mercer, who would go on to become a top executive, once refunded money to a customer who showed up with a set of car tires, even though Home Depot hadn't sold them. After the customer left, Mr. Mercer hung his tires over the service desk to remind everyone that the customer is always right.

By the time Mr. Nardelli arrived, sales growth had started to slow. On Oct. 12, 2000, Mr. Blank, who was then the CEO, warned that profits would fall short of expectations for the remainder of the fiscal year. Investors bailed out, driving the stock down 28%, its biggest one-day decline ever. Home Depot's board accelerated the succession process that brought Mr. Nardelli aboard.

Purchasing Shift

One of the biggest changes he has pushed involves purchasing. Home Depot had nine regional buying offices, each one acquiring products independently. Mr. Blank had said that the structure helped boost sales 15% to 20%, because the people doing the buying understood so well what customers in their local markets wanted.

But the company's decentralized buying diluted its negotiating clout. And because each region would do things its own way, the company couldn't easily coordinate nationwide buys with nationwide store displays. Some vendors complained that the company was difficult to deal with. "It was like having nine different wives," says one Midwestern tool maker, who requests anonymity.

Mr. Nardelli's solution was to centralize buying in Atlanta. At the same time, he moved to clean out dead and redundant items from store shelves. The company, after all, didn't really need 13 different round-point shovels, he notes.

The buying changes, he says, have yielded better terms from vendors that have widened the company's gross margin, or gross profit as a percentage of sales, to 31.6% in the third quarter, from 30.2% for the same period the year before. Cutting inventory has helped Home Depot amass $4 billion in cash, up from $167 million two years ago.

Mr. Nardelli has forced stores to increase weekend staffing by hiring more part-time workers: college students, for example, and people who have other weekday jobs. Stores went from 30% part-time staffing in December 2001 to 50% just four months later.

But longtime employees say that some part-time workers aren't as committed to Home Depot as full-timers. Customers, meanwhile, have complained that they sometimes can't find knowledgeable sales help—or, in some instances, any help at all.

In Decatur, Ga., Don Schneider, owner of Old Timers Renovations, a residential-contracting business, spent 20 minutes one day, waiting for a forklift operator to arrive and pull out a stack of drywall. "They need to speed up their pit times," Mr. Schneider said, hefting the load into his pickup truck.

Mr. Nardelli has acknowledged he went too far with part-timers. The company has scaled back to a mix of 40% part-time and 60% full-time. He says customer service has had its "ups and downs" but is improving.

Managers also were directed to increase their "inventory velocity," or the speed at which merchandise flows through their stores. When some responded by ordering fewer products, customers couldn't find what they needed. "On paper, all these changes make sense," says Steve Mahurin, a former Atlanta merchandising executive at Home Depot who left voluntarily 14 months after Mr. Nardelli arrived. "Unfortunately, they don't work on the floor of the stores."

The company's buyers "in Atlanta truly do care," Mr. Mahurin says. "They just have 1,500 stores to deal with and it's impossible to give them the attention they need." Home Depot officials counter that they still have plenty of divisional merchants who, while they don't buy, keep tabs on local needs and communicate them to Atlanta.

Many on Wall Street have urged the company to imitate Lowe's, which caters strongly to women shoppers. But some Home Depot veterans chafe at new products purchased by Atlanta, such as crockpots, which don't have much appeal to the company's core customers. Mr. Nardelli also has pushed redesigned large-appliance sections in the stores but says Home Depot will always serve the contractor and serious do-it-yourselfer. And some of the new buys—cleaning products, for example—have been hits.

Mr. Nardelli also says centralized buying will work more smoothly once he gets new computer systems online. He acknowledges that some inventory directives have caused problems and that every buying decision hasn't been flawless.

"Has everything that's happened been perfect? No, this guy has made some errors," says Mr. Marcus, the co-founder. That said, "when he makes an error, he backs off of it, and he isn't ashamed to say, 'I made a mistake.' And he learns from it."

Flying With Panache, and at a Profit, Too

BY JOSEPH B. TREASTER

When Paul Austin, a British executive of a big construction company here on the Persian Gulf, travels by air, he no longer drives to the airport. His favorite airline, **Emirates Airlines,** sends a car to pick him up, as it does for all its business and first-class passengers in London, Paris, Hong Kong and 12 other cities.

In business class, he has a choice of 48 movie cassettes he can load when he wants, and a couple of dozen music and talk programs. Even in economy, passengers may choose from 17 movies and 18 video games available on personal screens.

Mr. Austin dines on meals set on pink linen and sips fine wines. In economy, settings are less plush, but the meals range from stir-fries and curries to lamb stew and Nile perch. Cocktails and wine are free—except for Champagne. When a passenger hesitates over the $5.50 charge for Champagne, flight attendants smile warmly and propose a mixed drink at no charge, easing gracefully out of an awkward situation.

"We want to make the customer feel comfortable," said Gary Chapman, who is in charge of personnel and training for the airline.

Since its start 18 years ago with two Boeing 727's in one of the world's most politically explosive regions, Emirates Airlines has been trying to make flying enjoyable for its passengers and profitable for itself. It has been succeeding nicely, increasing passenger capacity about 20 percent annually, taking trade group awards away from distinguished carriers like **Singapore Airlines** and **Cathay Pacific** and winning the loyalty of business travelers like Mr. Austin.

"They make your entire journey stress-free," he said.

Dubai's location in the Middle East would be enough to stress out some people. To the northwest is Iraq; to the south is Yemen, the ancestral homeland of Osama bin Laden. Only 60 miles across the Strait of Hormuz is Iran. Just offshore in the Persian Gulf, American warships send fighter jets over Iraq every day; in a war, they would probably fire Tomahawk missiles as well.

Yet Dubai successfully promotes itself as a neutral haven, where business flourishes with little interference from government, and tourists from Europe and nearby Arab countries flock to resorts along bone-white beaches. With about one million people and acres of glittering office and hotel towers rising from the desert, Dubai is the commercial and tourism center of the United Arab Emirates, a group of seven city-states set on a crescent of sand at the mouth of the Persian Gulf.

Though Dubai is an Islamic country, it permits drinking and dancing in hotels, creating a party atmosphere for Arabs from stricter regimes and making Dubai reminiscent of Beirut before the Lebanese and their neighbors reduced it to rubble in the 1970's and 80's. The city is also becoming something of a modern Casablanca, a place of international intrigue, spies and smugglers.

Unlike many Middle East airlines, Emirates makes alcoholic drinks an integral part of its service. But, following Islamic dietary practices, it keeps pork off the menu.

With many people still afraid of flying after the Sept. 11, 2001, attacks, and the likelihood of war rising in the Middle East, this is not a good time for airlines. But the little team of managers—from Britain, New Zealand, Ireland and other places—that runs the airline under the direction of Sheik Ahmed bin Saeed al-Maktoum, its chairman and a member of Dubai's ruling family, is pushing to make Emirates one of the world's major airlines. (It is already one of the most profitable, according to Airline Business magazine in England.)

The airline has sidestepped most of the ill effects of the industry's depression. Its plan to inaugurate service to the United States is in limbo because of tensions between Washington and the Arab world. Though it had an alliance with United Airlines, it faces no losses as a result of United's filing for bankruptcy. "We actually owe them money," said Dermot Mannion, the chief financial officer of Emirates, because Emirates carried more of United's passengers.

Fuel costs have risen for many airlines, but Mr. Mannion said "an aggressive hedging strategy" had kept fuel expenses for Emirates at about the same level as last year.

While other airlines have been cutting back on routes, Emirates, which already flies to 64 cities in Europe, Asia, Africa and the Middle East, continues to expand. It is graduating two classes of a dozen or so flight attendants, including some Americans, every six weeks, and plans to put a new wide-body, long-haul jet into service nearly every month this year. Last fall, it opened a route to Osaka, its first destination in Japan. In the summer, it plans to begin flying to Moscow and Shanghai.

Plans to inaugurate service to the United States in June with a 13 1/2-hour nonstop flight from Dubai to New York had to be scrapped when delivery of a new-model Airbus for the route was delayed until next fall. Now Emirates executives say they are not sure when the New York flights will begin.

"One has to be reasonable," Mr. Chapman said. "Is the climate right? The timing has to be right."

In the past, Emirates executives have turned trouble to their advantage. During the Persian Gulf war in 1991, when most airlines grounded flights to the region, Emirates kept going. Its jets burned extra fuel skirting the combat zone, but the airline more than made up the difference in extra passengers and cargo. When some airlines refused to serve Pakistan and Afghanistan last year as American forces were hunting down members of Al Qaeda, Emirates again picked up the slack.

"We know our markets very well," Mr. Mannion said. "We won't go anywhere that is unsafe."

Sometimes, the airline seems to be going for shock effect. Two months after the World Trade Center attack, for example, when the entire airline industry was reeling, Emirates announced that it was buying $15 billion worth of long-haul, wide-body jets from **Boeing** and **Airbus.** The purchase, of about 50 jetliners, some at substantial discounts, was one of the biggest in aviation history.

The airline, said Mike Simon, the company's spokesman, wanted to send a message. "People would continue traveling," he said, "and we would continue expanding."

In an era of penny-pinching, no-frills flying, the experience in the Emirates' passenger cabins is stunning. Its female flight attendants wear elegantly cut jackets and skirts in the crisp tones of the desert, and crimson hats with trailing white gossamer scarves. The men wear double-breasted blazers.

On a mid-December flight from London to Dubai, one attendant paused at an economy passenger's armrest. "Good evening, sir," she said. "How are you feeling tonight? Sir, tonight we are offering a choice of chicken in tandoori paste or rack of lamb. Which would you prefer? Certainly, sir. Can I bring you another glass of wine?"

Compare that with the ambience on a Delta Air Lines flight a week later from Rome to New York, as a sullen flight attendant in a navy skirt and light blue blouse shuffled behind a food cart, barking, "Chicken or pasta? Chicken or pasta?"

Emirates Airlines was created to drive the economy of Dubai. As recently as 1971, when the British withdrew from the area and brokered the formation of the United Arab Emirates among the often warring families that ruled the city-states, Dubai was a dusty village of traders, pearl divers and fishermen. Huge amounts of oil had been discovered

(Cont.)

down the coast in Abu Dhabi, and as the wealthiest of the emirates, it became the capital of the new country.

In 1973, Abu Dhabi and three neighboring gulf states bought control of an airline, which became Gulf Air, but it offered limited service to Dubai. The rulers of Dubai, in control of much less oil, were determined to attract tourists and business, so they started Emirates Airlines. Emirates is now running circles around Gulf Air, which has been losing money for several years.

The Dubai government invites airlines from all over the world to fly to the emirate without restriction. As a result, more than 100 airlines now serve it, but Emirates dominates. In 2001, the last year for which full statistics are available, it carried more than half the 13.5 million passengers who moved through the Dubai airport terminal. The government said about 3.6 million people stayed over as tourists in 2001, and about 4 million in 2002. By 2015, Dubai is hoping for airport traffic of 51 million passengers, including 15 million tourists.

In the first half of 2002, the airline's profit more than doubled over the period a year earlier, rising to $110 million on revenue of $1.17 billion. For all of 2001, profit rose 11 percent over those in 2000, to $127 million on revenue of $1.98 billion.

The airline's executives bristle at competitors' assertions that Emirates is heavily subsidized. But they acknowledge that it does not operate under the same rules as some rivals. Dubai has no income tax, unions or laws that ban age or sex discrimination. Emirates is free to recruit around the world for young, single and attractive flight attendants and to decide at the end of a three-year contract whether to keep them.

The airline is more efficient than many. Chris Tarry, an independent analyst in London, said that the major United States airlines, on average, were flying their planes about 74 percent full but that "they need to sell 90 percent of their seats to break even." Emirates, however, breaks even when its planes are 65 percent full. During the first half of 2002, Mr. Mannion said, Emirates' planes operated at 78 percent of capacity.

Analysts say Emirates also benefits from a small, nimble group of top managers. "What it takes other airlines six months to do, they do in 24 hours," said Anne-Marie Siffroy-Pytlak, an aviation expert at the French bank Credit Agricole Indosuez, which has financed many of Emirates' aircraft deals.

Some executives in Dubai are skeptical about the airline's profitability, saying its financial reports do not have to be as detailed as those required of publicly traded companies. But Ms. Siffroy-Pytlak, who has analyzed the airline's finances, said, "The cash is there."

The decline of service on many airlines has played to Emirates' strengths. In business class on an Emirates flight from Dubai to Rome, Francois Berthier, a perfume maker from Grasse, France, said he preferred Air France's food, but "on this airline they really treat you like a human being, not just a number."

KODAK IS THE PICTURE OF DIGITAL SUCCESS

But can the fast-selling EasyShare alter its profit outlook?

Digital cameras were in demand this Christmas, flying off the shelves along with Microsoft Corp.'s Xbox game consoles and low-cost DVD players. And the supreme hot seller? No, it wasn't Nikon or Canon that came out ahead. Instead, the hit product was from perennial also-ran Eastman Kodak Co. Thanks to its new digital offerings, struggling Kodak was suddenly looking awfully sharp. At Best Buy, Wal-Mart, and countless other stores across the country, Kodak's EasyShare digital cameras, introduced on Apr. 23, were often sold out well before Dec. 25. Says Kodak Chairman Daniel A. Carp: "We'll stay in the game long-term with [EasyShare]."

While the final numbers on 2001 aren't in, EasyShare sales clearly boosted Kodak's market standing. In a December survey of 90 major retailers by Salomon Smith Barney, 50% listed Kodak as their best-selling digital camera, compared with 29% in June. Second-ranked Olympus was a best seller at only about 35% of stores in the December survey, followed by Fuji and Sony. If the trend holds, Kodak will surely gain swiftly on Sony, which had 25% of the digital market in 2001, compared to Kodak's 14% share, according to International Data Corp.

The Kodak digital cameras—there are five in the product line, ranging from about $200 to $400—are a hit because they help resolve significant problems that have plagued digital camera owners. These include difficulty downloading images and short battery life.

The timing couldn't have been better. Kodak hasn't had a big hit in a long time—and never has it needed one more than now. The company relies heavily on sales of traditional film to consumers, a business that has been hit hard by both the recession and September 11, as well as the shift to digital photography. Consumers last year cut back sharply on the use of traditional film—by as much as 5%, according to Goldman, Sachs & Co. In recent weeks, analysts have been steadily dropping Kodak's 2001 profits estimates, to just $667 million, down more than 54% from the prior year, according to UBS Warburg analyst Benjamin A. Reitzes. Now at $29, Kodak's stock is 41% off its high last June.

Having a hot new product line will help—though only so much. Digital cameras accounted for just $500 million of Kodak's estimated $13.1 billion in sales in 2001. That compares with $2.6 billion for the declining film business, according to Warburg's Reitzes. As a result, he contends, digital is chipping away at sales of traditional cameras, film, and photo processing services, but isn't yet boosting the bottom line much. What's more, as sales of digital cameras soar, the prices they command are plummeting. As a whole, camera makers sold nearly 9 million units in 2001, almost triple the number they unloaded in 1999. But the average price per camera has fallen to just under $300, from around $460 two years ago.

It is also unclear whether Kodak can successfully leverage the popularity of its digital cameras into higher margin ancillary lines. Kodak is eyeing future profits from photo-quality inkjet paper and the company's Ofoto.com online photo sharing and printing service. With 2 million members, Ofoto—one of three photo printing services featured in Microsoft's new XP operating system—is now growing 12% a month.

The home photo paper business may be tougher to crack. Right now, only 15% to 20% of digital images are ever printed. Kodak is banking that EasyShare's simplicity could boost demand for home printing, thus spurring sales of high-margin paper. But that in turn could eat into Kodak's existing sales of paper to printing labs.

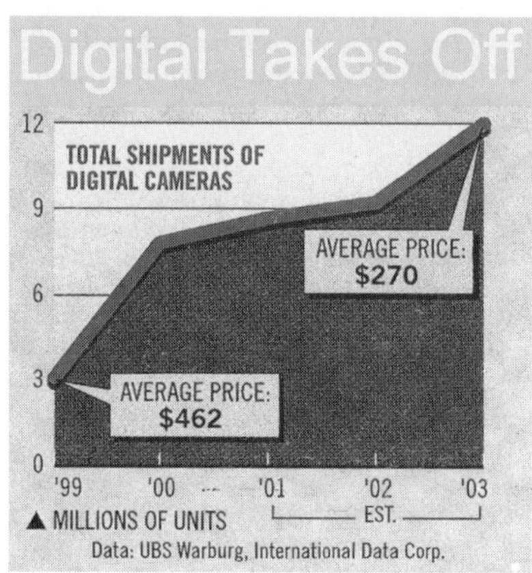

Kodak has avoided the intensely competitive home printer market. Instead, it's pushing printing kiosks in retail stores such as CVS and Kmart. Customers can get their own prints by feeding a CD-ROM or memory card into some 24,000 kiosks that Kodak claims have been profitable since 2000. Add it all up, and as big a success as Kodak's EasyShare cameras are, they may not be enough. Keeping the momentum going—and the profits rolling in—will be no easy task.

By Geoffrey Smith and Faith Keenan in Boston

'Hog' Maker Gets (Financial) Motor Running

By MARILYN ALVA
Investor's Business Daily

Recessions don't faze Spuck Bennett, even though conventional wisdom says they should. After all, he sells high-ticket, discretionary products.

Bennett is a dealer for Harley-Davidson Inc. The century-old motorcycle company, renowned for its heavyweight "hogs," prides itself on being different.

True to form, Bennett's business cruised along even after Sept. 11.

"I've seen no difference . . . as far as sales," he said.

He figures sales at his flagship store in Seaford, Del., were up more than 12% for the year.

One thing did change, though. In December, like other Harley dealers, he started selling Harley's new custom cruiser, the liquid-cooled V-Rod, aimed at a younger crowd.

Suggested price: $17,000. The home office was to ship Bennett eight of the models, but his initial orders totaled 22.

That's nothing new for Harley, which specializes in heavy, air-cooled motorcycles sold to 1,300 dealers from Nebraska to Japan.

Harley officials have long claimed their business is recession-proof, and financials usually back them up. In last year's fourth quarter—a dismal period for many businesses—Harley's sales accelerated 18.3% from the year before to $894.4 million.

Earnings? They blasted ahead nearly 27% to 39 cents a share.

What's the secret?

"It's just like fine wine," said Bennett, who opened his third shop last April on Maryland's eastern shore. "If you have a Harley that's 5 or 10 years old, it's worth almost as much as you paid for it."

That high resale value, along with low interest rates, has made it relatively painless for customers to trade up to new bikes that cost $10,000 to $20,000.

"You would think demand would be a problem in a slow economy (with) a discretionary product, but it hasn't been," said analyst David Cumberland of Robert W. Baird & Co.

History shows the motorcycle industry doesn't follow the crowd even in the best of circumstances.

"It's an industry that's driven by its own cycle, no pun intended," said analyst Rick Fradin of William Blair & Co. "It doesn't seem to track very closely with the economy."

Harley is the leading motorcycle brand in the U.S., though its market share has slipped over the past few years from nearly 50% to about 45%. Its closest rival, Honda Motor Co., commands about a 20% share.

Leaving The Recession In Its Dust

Growth may be slowing some, but Harley-Davidson is still pumping out numbers that leave many recession-weary companies behind

Annual production

	Units	Year-over-year change
1997	132,285	11.4%
1998	150,818	14.0
1999	177,187	17.5
2000	204,592	15.5
2001	234,461	14.6
2002e	258,432	10.2
2003e	289,444	12.0

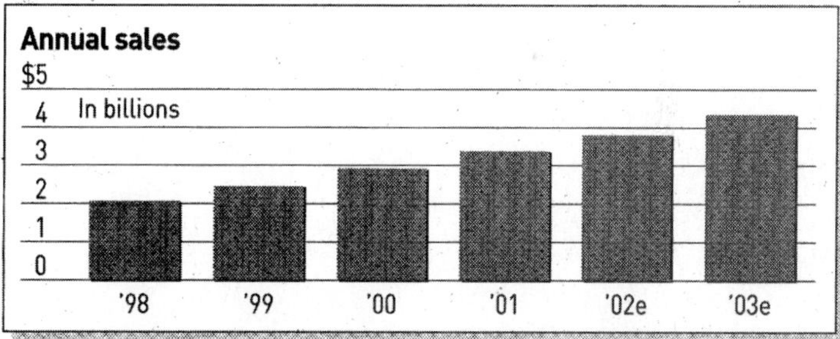

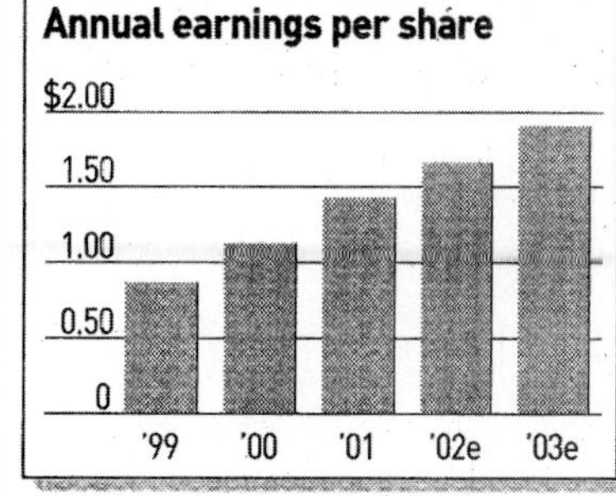

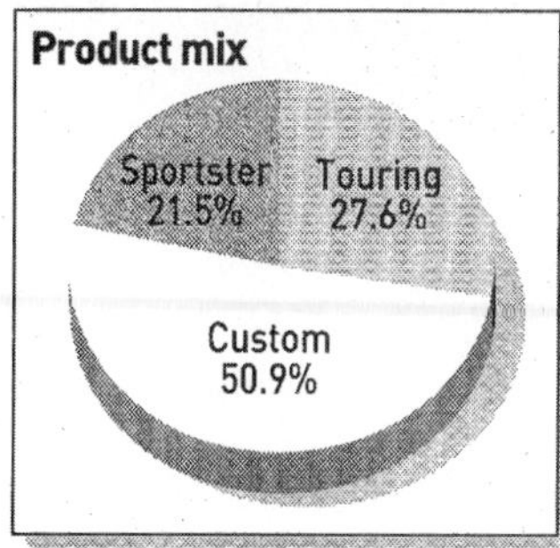

Sources: Company reports, Robert W. Baird & Co., First Call

"We've been capacity-constrained," said James Ziemer, Harley's chief financial officer. "The market is growing faster than our production."

Outside the U.S., Harley's biggest single market is Japan. It's had a tougher time in Europe, where sport bikes are more popular and Honda leads. Harley has lately reduced shipment growth to Europe in favor of the U.S., where margins are better anyway.

Because demand for bikes in the U.S. almost always outstrips supply, Harley's in an enviable spot, analysts say. That helps keep prices high and discounts to a minimum.

Harley could probably sell 30% more motorcycles in a year, Fradin says. "But they couldn't keep the quality up."

And quality has been Chief Executive Jeffrey Bleustein's mantra since taking over the helm in 1997.

Company officials plan a 10% increase in production this year to 258,000 units. But that increase is less than last year's 14.6%.

Earnings growth is heading down, too, analysts figure. Analysts polled by First Call see Harley's earnings this year hitting $1.66 a share. That's 16% above a year ago, when year-over-year earnings were up 27%.

Is there a slowdown on the horizon? Company execs don't see it.

"In a backdrop of 9-11, a recession and what's going on in worldwide economies, I'll tack that record up against most other companies," said Ziemer.

Harley's upcoming 100th anniversary should spark heightened interest in 2003-model products, watchers say. The year-long celebration begins in July.

Dealers already see strong demand for anniversary bikes, even though birthday models haven't yet been disclosed.

"Harley riders have such a strong relationship with the company and the bike, many will want to buy a 2003 bike even if it doesn't have any special insignia on it," said Cumberland.

And while earnings growth might be slowing, he notes the growth is coming up against increasingly tough comparisons.

"As the company grows larger, it's not as easy to put up 25%-type earnings growth," he said. "That said, 2002 and 2003 will be very good years for Harley."

Meanwhile, the firm has begun to attract a younger customer than its typical baby-boomer devotee, whose average age is 46.

Several dealers were asking—and getting—premium prices of up to 30% on the new V-Rod, industry sources say.

"One of my competitors is selling them at $29,000," Bennett said .

Harley shipped just 1,700 V-Rods in the fourth quarter, but plans to send out more than 10,000 this year.

The new Firebolt XB9R, a sports bike, also is expected to spark sales among younger customers. It's slated to hit the market by late March.

Harley is gearing up to bring new riders, including women, into the fold through a new Riders Edge motorcycle training program as well.

"Within a couple of years it will be available at enough dealers to make a difference," said Cumberland. "They're definitely taking steps today that should pay off in the long term."

If at First You Don't Succeed...

Some retailers are finding success in industries long thought off-limits to e-commerce

BY MICHAEL TOTTY AND ANN GRIMES

Are some businesses just not cut out for the Internet?

It certainly seems that way. Consider furniture, which has witnessed the high-profile flameouts of Furniture.com and Living.com, among others. Or groceries, which suffered through the money-burning failure of Webvan Group Inc. and a host of lesser competitors.

These weren't just well-publicized flops of individual companies. Many retail experts saw them as signs that some sectors were doomed to be e-commerce disappointments. Consumers, it was said, won't buy a new sofa or dining-room table without touching the materials and testing the comfort. Online grocers won't be able to crack the brutal economics of food sales. Wine, another e-tail letdown, will never navigate the minefield of state alcoholic-beverage rules.

This conventional wisdom could still prove correct. But despite the dismal history, some retailers are finding ways to crack even the toughest e-commerce cases. They're doing so by avoiding the mistakes of the earlier wave of online-only wrecks and by closely tying their Internet operations with real-world stores and distributors. In most cases, they're also thinking small—in stark contrast with the New Economy hubris of e-tail start-ups—by limiting online sales to a few items or markets.

"It's premature to say these categories don't work," says Mohan Sawhney, professor of e-commerce and technology at Northwestern University's Kellogg School of Management. "The people who emerge from this will emerge stronger and smarter and will emerge as hybrids," combining online and physical stores.

Here's a look at three retail categories—groceries, furniture and wine—and how some companies are finding glimmers of success in these supposedly hopeless sectors.

Groceries

When Louis Borders launched **Webvan** in 1999, it seemed that the start-up may have finally figured out the online grocery puzzle. The company, based in Foster City, Calif., offered free delivery for bigger orders, eliminating one source of customer resistance. It promised to deliver within a 30-minute window, so customers didn't have to hang around the house all afternoon waiting for their orders.

What happened next wasn't pretty: After tearing through $830 million in start-up and IPO funds, the company sought Chapter 11 bankruptcy protection in July and began liquidating its assets. Other online grocers—Streamline.com, HomeRuns.com and ShopLink.com—have joined Webvan in the ash heap of dot-com history.

There are plenty of reasons for the failures, and they point to lingering obstacles for anyone trying to take the grocery business to the Internet. But the flops also offer a road map for companies still trying to make a go of it.

"I think we're getting our second wind," says Robert Rubin, a research director at Forrester Research Inc., in Cambridge, Mass. "The first wave failed as businesses but proved there's a value proposition for consumers. Now it's up to the traditional grocers to execute."

One problem with the first round, Mr. Rubin says, is that buying groceries online requires consumers to make a big change in the way they shop for basic household goods. As a result, the number of households that regularly purchased groceries over the Internet increased far more slowly than promoters had originally expected, to an estimated 5 million in 2001 from 3.7 million in 1999.

In most places, says Ken Cassar, a senior researcher at research firm Jupiter Media Metrix in New York, "going to the grocery store isn't as terrible an experience as companies like Webvan had hoped."

Another problem was price. Online grocers were competing with their storebound competitors by promising to be more convenient, but most consumers were more interested in price, and the online stores weren't any cheaper.

A Forrester survey last year of those who had bought groceries online but stopped found that nearly half said they could find better prices at stores.

This customer resistance led to expensive and devastating solutions. To build up a base of customers from scratch, the newcomers had to spend heavily on advertising and other marketing. Webvan, for instance, spent 25% to 35% of its revenue on advertising, according to its financial statements, compared with an average of about 1% spent by traditional grocers.

Then there were the expensive distribution centers. Webvan officials argued in the company's early stages that the centers, which could handle up to 8,000 orders a day—many times more than a traditional warehouse—would give it a big cost advantage over its bricks-and-mortar competitors. But it never gained the sales volume to take full advantage of the efficiencies, and so its gross margins trailed those of large traditional grocers.

Yet even as the grocery dot-coms fell away, traditional chains have been moving to build up their own online services. That's because grocers increasingly face competition from restaurants, discounters and specialty stores, and the Internet is one way to increase overall sales. And though the online market is small, consumers who are willing to buy groceries online represent the premium customers that companies are most loath to lose.

This time, though, e-grocers are avoiding the world-conquering ambitions of the failures and are proceeding cautiously, taking full advantage of their existing distribution and marketing channels and treating online grocery sales as a niche market.

One path is being taken by Dutch grocery chain **Royal Ahold NV,** which owns the Stop & Shop and Giant chains on the East Coast. In 2000, Ahold bought a majority stake in Peapod Inc., the oldest of the online groceries (last year it purchased the balance of Peapod shares) and proceeded to scale back Peapod's online ambitions.

For Ahold, the purchase "was a way to get into the e-commerce game in groceries without starting from scratch," a Peapod spokeswoman says.

The new owners shut down operations in Dallas, Houston and Austin, Texas; Columbus, Ohio; and San Francisco. Last summer, the owners also eliminated free deliveries.

Now, Peapod offers a scaled-down assortment of the most commonly purchased items, delivered from either its own in-store "warerooms"—areas set aside in existing stores—or distribution centers specially designed to package items for home delivery (as opposed to Stop & Shop's warehouses, which are set up to handle pallet-size delivery to stores). Its target market is busy families, and to encourage shoppers to place larger orders, it charges $9.95 for deliveries of up to $75, with a minimum $50 order, and $4.95 for orders over $75.

With an average order of $132, the service is posting operating profits—excluding marketing costs and some corporate overhead—in one of its five markets, and Peapod officials say the company is "on track with its profitability goals"; before it was taken over by Ahold, the company had projected to show operating profits by the end of 2003. And unlike Webvan, which envisioned expanding to 26 markets in two years, Peapod is taking it slow. "Right now we're focused on current markets," says Andrew Parkinson, Peapod's co-founder and now chief financial officer. "We'll expand when we can do so profitably in each market."

Safeway Inc., a Pleasanton, Calif., grocery chain, is taking a different approach, using a model refined by British grocer **Tesco** PLC, which last June invested more

(Cont.)

Looking for a Foot in the Door

Traffic at selected e-commerce sites. Numbers represent the average number of total unique U.S. visitors per month within the quarter. Figures are in thousands.

FOOD & BEVERAGE	4Q '00	1Q '01	2Q '01	3Q '01	4Q '01
Wine.com	1,043	940	358	161	218
Food.com	583	300	263	170	185
Hickoryfarms.com	531	112	186	238	495
Netgrocer.com	886	264	155	151	154
Omahasteaks.com	646	740	992	508	841
Peapod.com	107	106	117	100	98
Webvan.com	231	679	553	NA	NA
FURNITURE & APPLIANCES					
Furniturefan.com	310	769	764	553	490
Furniturefind.com	146	651	507	396	437
Crateandbarrel.com	330	262	300	298	373
Potterybarn.com	279	278	283	327	381
MAJOR ONLINE RETAIL BENCHMARK					
Amazon.com	23,960	27,100	29,636	31,926	43,204

Source: ComScore Networks

Average monthly sales 2001 (in millions)

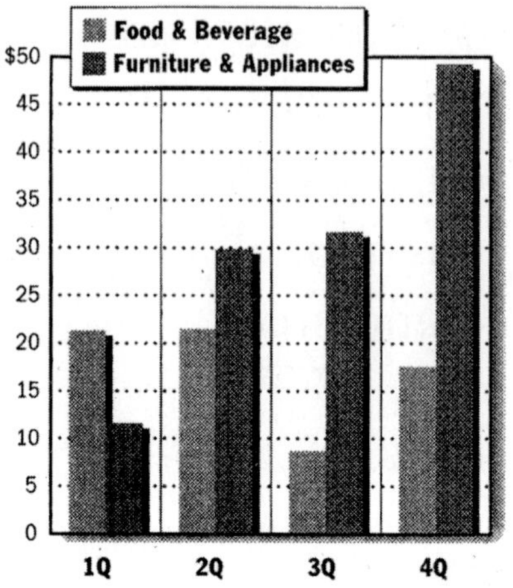

Food & Beverage
Furniture & Appliances
$50
45
40
35
30
25
20
15
10
5
0
1Q
2Q
3Q
4Q

than $22 million in Safeway's online venture, GroceryWorks.com.

In the venture, which started operating last month in Portland, Ore., and Vancouver, Wash., Safeway will avoid expensive centralized distribution centers and instead fill customer orders from existing store inventories.

Using a special shopping cart developed by Tesco with a computer screen that displays a customer's order and shows where in the store ordered items can be found, Safeway says that it can fill orders at a fraction of the cost of using a centralized warehouse. Further, it only needs to invest in new trucks and hire more grocery pickers as demand for the business grows—avoiding the heavy investment costs Webvan incurred with its build-it-and-they-will-come approach.

"The cost of [filling orders] in the store is minimal compared to the warehouse model," says Deborah Lambert, a Safeway spokeswoman.

This "store-pick" model isn't new—it was used and later abandoned by Peapod. Though it holds down the cost of filling orders, Peapod found that as the service grew, its pickers overwhelmed the store aisles. It also led to too many orders going unfilled because items were out of stock and the site couldn't display actual store inventories.

Ms. Lambert says Tesco's technology will help avoid those problems. When a customer places an order, it is automatically routed to a computer in the nearest store, where the order will be filled. Problems with out-of-stock items are avoided because customers can order only items that are in the store's inventory. And she says the company can schedule pickers to work at off-peak hours to sidestep the inconvenience of congested aisles.

Forrester's Mr. Rubin says he prefers Peapod's approach to filling orders, since it's better able to grow without interfering with store operations. But he faults both companies for missing one of the key lessons of the earlier failures: charging for delivery, especially on the high-dollar orders that can make the service pay off. (Safeway charges a flat $9.95 for each delivery.) "By charging for orders over $100," he says, "you're creating a barrier for the customers you want."

Furniture

Selling furniture over the Internet makes the online grocery business look easy.

Few consumers, skeptics insist, will ever want to buy a sofa, chair or dining table without first touching the item and testing it for comfort. "Furniture is a product that consumers need to touch, to feel and to see," says Margaret Whelan, a furniture-industry analyst at UBS Warburg in New York.

Of course, that didn't stop a handful of start-ups from launching home-furnishing e-tail sites. Living.com, based in Austin, Texas, as well as Furniture.com of Framingham, Mass., and at least a half-dozen others plunged into the online furniture business on the notion that they could offer better selection and customer service than the highly fragmented bricks-and-mortar furniture business.

High-powered Internet tools went a long way toward overcoming the touch-and-feel problem. Furniture.com's site enabled browsers to design floor plans combining their existing furniture and items on the site. GoodHome.com used technology that allowed shoppers to alter the appearance of a mocked-up room by changing wallpaper or upholstery. (The San Rafael, Calif., company stopped selling furniture in January 2001 and morphed into a Web site-imaging-technology concern called Scene 7.)

But getting consumers willing to buy wasn't enough. Living.com shut down in August 2000 and is being liquidated in Chapter 11 bankruptcy proceedings. Furniture.com followed a few months later.

Part of the problem was that brand-name furniture manufacturers generally shunned the sites, not wanting to alienate their traditional retail outlets. In addition, delivery problems plagued the online stores. Lisa Poulin, the court-appointed trustee in Living.com's bankruptcy proceeding, says there are "mounds" of disputes and customer complaints over products that were delivered damaged or late.

Where traditional furniture stores can mark down and resell damaged or refused merchandise, the Internet companies didn't have an easy way to move returned pieces. Jerry Epperson, a furniture analyst in Richmond, Va., estimates returns for the online companies represented as much as 35% of sales.

So here's the surprising news: Online furniture sales hit $211 million in the last quarter of 2001 compared with $154 million in the year-earlier period, according to Forrester. Part of the increase came from the sale of furniture at online auctions, such as eBay Inc.'s, where the number of furniture listings doubled in the past year. Further, furniture sales, offline and on, increased in the wake of the Sept. 11 attacks, as shoppers focused more of their spending on the home.

But part of the increase also can be traced to the fact that some retailers are finding success in selling furniture online.

One group, including Houston's **Gallery Furniture, BeHome.com** in Olathe, Kan., and **FurnitureFind.com** in Buchanan, Mich., grew out of mainly regional furniture stores that try to cater to online shoppers from all over the U.S.

FurnitureFind, which according to ComScore Networks Inc., a Reston, Va., market-research firm, averaged almost a half-million visitors a month in last year's fourth quarter, has its roots in a family-owned furniture retailer, Bookout's Furniture, based in southwestern Michigan. Bookout's put up a Web site in 1996 to provide information about its stores but soon found itself flooded with requests from shoppers looking to buy pieces online. By late that year, it began taking orders.

In early 2000, the company was acquired by GoodHome.com, which had hoped to combine its Web technology and FurnitureFind's relationships with manufacturers. But by the end of the year, GoodHome decided to get out of the furniture business to focus on its technology, and FurnitureFind's founders bought back the company. Since then, the site has booked more than $10 million in sales and is "cash-flow positive," says Stephen Antisdel, FurnitureFind's chief executive.

The site, which offers more than 10,000 items from a "master list" of more than 100,000, maintains no inventory, eliminating one costly mistake of the furniture dot-coms. Items aren't built until an order comes in—"just like Dell Computer," says Mr. Antisdel, who is a nephew of Bookout's founder. With an Internet business, he adds, "since you don't have to stock a showroom, what is the point of filling a warehouse?"

To work around the touch-and-feel problem, FurnitureFind sends swatches of materials to anyone who asks for one. And it maintains a call center staffed seven days a week with about a dozen customer-service reps, who train in the local Bookout stores to gain knowledge about furnishings, materials and styles. More than 90% of all sales involve at least one call to customer service.

FurnitureFind also keeps a close eye on deliveries, relying on partnerships with several furniture-moving companies to make sure that items are delivered and set up without damage. As a result, returns are kept at an extremely low 3% of sales, Mr. Antisdel says. The returns that do come in can be sold at the local Bookout outlet store. And it offers free delivery on purchases over $1,400, helping to prevent shopping-cart sticker shock and drive up average sales—which, not coincidentally, are just above $1,400.

The site lacks the kind of fancy technological features, like three-dimensional and design-a-room views, found at Living.com and others. "When we looked at all that cool stuff, we found it didn't translate into meaningful customer benefit," Mr. Antisdel says.

Still, the company is savvy about taking advantage of Internet technology in its marketing. It pays a sponsorship fee so that it is one of the top results when a browser searches for "furniture" at the Yahoo Inc. Web site.

"Anybody can build a Web page," Mr. Antisdel says. "Unless you figure out how this particular [online] world works and how to use this environment, you won't be able to build a viable business online."

For specialty home-furnishing retailers like **Crate & Barrel,** Northbrook, Ill., and **Williams-Sonoma** Inc.'s Pottery Barn unit, the formula is a little different: They offer only a relatively small number of pieces online, complementing their existing store and catalog sales.

Pottery Barn, for instance, lists fewer than 1,000 different pieces online—far fewer than the number of items typically available at a traditional furniture retailer. This means that it ends up selling large numbers of a single item, allowing its manufacturers to stockpile enough frames and other components to turn around orders quickly—and to keep many of the most popular items in stock.

"Many times, on our most popular items, the next day after it's ordered it's going on a truck," says Patrick Connolly, chief marketing officer at San Francisco-based Williams-Sonoma.

Pottery Barn began offering furniture through its catalog in 1994 and moved online in 2000. To get around the touch-and-feel problem, it depicts the furnishings in lavish "lifestyle" settings, in contrast with the warehouse settings of many big bricks-and-mortar furniture retailers. "The customer . . . says, 'My whole life would change if I owned that couch,'" Mr. Connolly says. "It more than makes up for the fact that you're not sitting in it."

The company doesn't disclose online sales. But, Mr. Connolly says, "furniture sales online are good for us."

Wine

Compared with groceries and furniture, wine should have been a snap to sell online. It's easy and relatively inexpensive to ship, and the fragmented retail wine market would seem to be ripe for competition from a national online retailer that could offer thousands of vintages.

It didn't turn out that way, though. In the heady days of dot-com mania, there were nearly a dozen online wine-selling start-ups, including Wine.com, Wineshopper.com and Winebuyer.com. All are now defunct, leaving Wine.com by eVineyard as one of the few survivors.

What happened? It turned out that wine selling was one of the toughest markets for online sellers to break into. A thicket of arcane regulations and laws, designed to support a three-tier distribution system of suppliers, state wholesalers and local retailers, have essentially blocked many Internet entrepreneurs' dreams of cheaper, faster, direct-to-consumer shipping. Blinded by visions of the borderless Internet, most of the newcomers failed to find a profitable way around the rules before their start-up funds ran out.

So, how did eVineyard survive? The company, based in Portland, Ore., expanded slowly, and it methodically complied with the tangle of laws. "It's the tortoise-and-the-hare story," says Brett Lauter, **eVineyard's** vice president and chief marketing officer. "This time last year, if you talked to the analysts, they didn't give us a chance."

Wine is a big business, and online sales still promise to be a key market. There are now about 2,100 U.S. wineries, up from 377 about 30 years ago, and annual sales hover in the $45 billion range. Internet wine sales are expected to account for 5% to 10% of retail wine sales by 2005, according to Salomon Smith Barney.

In general, the current regulatory system requires any company involved in the sale of alcoholic beverages to be licensed by the state as a producer (winery), a wholesaler/distributor or retailer. Generally, wine is purchased from the winery by the licensed wholesaler, which transports it to a particular state, where it is sold to licensed retailers, bars, restaurants, hotels or wine shops. This distribution system dates back to the end of Prohibition in the 1930s and was designed to prevent the consolidation of power that organized crime had over alcohol production and distribution. Supporters say the laws help keep online sales from siphoning off needed state sales taxes and make it harder to sell alcohol to minors.

Twenty-four states, plus the District of Columbia, allow some form of direct interstate shipping between wineries and consumers. Thirteen of these are "reciprocity states" that allow interstate shipments, but several states require various permits and conditions for delivery. The balance prohibit direct shipping.

The peculiarities are confounding. For instance, according to the Wine Institute, a public-policy group in San Francisco, wine cannot be sold in containers larger than one gallon in Florida. In New York and 14 other states, consumers can't buy wine in grocery stores. In Colorado, half-bottles of wine are illegal. Oklahoma prohibits wine sales on Labor Day, Independence Day, Memorial Day, Thanksgiving and Christmas. Minnesota, Missouri, Washington and Wisconsin permit consumers to receive two cases of wine a year directly from out-of-state sellers; some other states allow two cases a month. Minnesota and Utah prohibit the accepting of orders via the Internet. And so on.

"It gets pretty insane," Mr. Lauter says.

Initially, some wine e-tailers responded to the rules by devising elaborate and expensive methods to comply—for instance, by routing

(Cont.)

purchases through local wine stories. Others skirted the rules entirely. Many lobbied—most unsuccessfully—to overturn the laws in state legislatures.

Wine.com, based in Napa, Calif., was typical of the online wine stores, and for a while led the pack. Launched in 1995 by wine experts Peter Granoff and Robert Olson, who called the Web site Virtual Vineyards, the goal was to revolutionize wine shopping by giving consumers direct access to small wineries and high-end limited-production wines not always available though regional distributors.

With $50 million in funding, the company operated like an interstate wine broker, linking customers to suppliers. However, in order to make sales legal the company had to pay high handling fees to wholesalers and local retailers who functioned like fulfillment agents. Those costs were passed on to Wine.com's consumers.

One problem: The company never got enough customers to make the business profitable. Another: Like many Internet companies, Wine.com bought into the build-it-and-they-will come philosophy of the boom, hiring hundreds of employees and burning up capital on advertising.

"It was very difficult for them to aggregate orders in a meaningful way—they had big empty trucks shipping orders all over the country," says Mark Swartzberg, a New York-based analyst for Dutch bank ABN Amro. "They couldn't get critical mass to make the orders meaningful for the retailer or the wholesaler."

Yet another problem: Wine.com was not licensed as a winery, wholesaler or retailer, so it became enmeshed in court battles over whether its approach was legal. "The laws then were not in place for that kind of a success story," says Steve Gross, an analyst with the Wine Institute. The company filed for Chapter 11 bankruptcy protection in the spring of 2001.

San Francisco-based Wineshopper.com took a slightly different approach.

With $46 million in funding from Silicon Valley venture firm Kleiner Perkins Caufield & Byers and Amazon.com Inc., the company also followed a fulfillment model but focused on building a wine-distribution locator database, with the idea of partnering with the Wine & Spirit Wholesalers of America.

Its goal was to build a national inventory of wines on the Web, much like an online book catalog. The problem was many of the wholesalers didn't have the technological infrastructure or the will to participate. High customer-acquisition costs prompted the company to merge in August 2000 with Wine.com.

EVineyard.com, meanwhile, took a more painstaking approach. With $20 million in private equity, the company moved state by state to get licensed as a retailer. It operates basically like a virtual retailer with a virtual inventory, buying wine from wholesalers only when it is ordered, then passing it through packing warehouses before shipping via United Parcel Service.

The hitch, however, is that because the company is in essence a "retailer," it can only offer the wines made available by its regional distributors. "They've filled a niche, but not all of the niche," says Mr. Gross. "You can get product online but the choice still is limited."

Mr. Lauter says, however, that his company serves 77% of the premium wine-drinking market because it operates in 27 states, shipping intrastate as well.

"It took a long time," Mr. Lauter says. "In New York, it took us 10 months. In New Jersey, you cannot get a new license, you have to purchase an existing license and then have a physical presence no more than 100 yards away from the license you bought." To comply with the proximity rule, in New Jersey and 11 other states the company leased packing warehouses along existing wholesaler delivery routes.

The company operates like a retailer, with margins of 25% to 30%, Mr. Lauter says. With only 60 full-time employees, he says, fourth-quarter numbers will show the company turned a profit in December.

In April 2001 eVineyard.com paid $9 million in cash and stock to defunct Wine.com for its domain name, customer list, Web site and other intellectual capital and changed the site's name to Wine.com by eVineyard.

While eVineyard benefited from the demise of its rivals, industry observers like Jeremy Benson, a wine marketing executive in Napa, Calif., say the company did have a better business model. "EVineyard partly benefited from the implosion of the other two," Mr. Benson says. "Wine.com had a tremendous burn rate going on. They had a massive capital investment and spent it quickly." In contrast, he adds, "eVineyard started as a modest investment and didn't bet the farm that there would be an increase in online buyers."

EVineyard's cautionary approach also scored points with the industry's key middlemen. "EVineyard was evolutionary, whereas others were revolutionary," says Edward Maletis, chief executive of Columbia Distributing Co., a Pacific Northwest distributor based in Portland, Ore. "The other guys took a more bullish approach to being able to change the traditional way of how wine gets from the producer into the hands of the consumer. Some wholesalers were rubbed the wrong way."

Mr. Totty is a news editor for The Wall Street Journal Reports based in San Francisco. Ms. Grimes is a deputy chief of The Wall Street Journal's San Francisco bureau.

Europe Presenting Challenges For AOL

FEWER MINUTES SPENT ONLINE

AND THE COUNTRIES DIFFER IN WHAT TYPE OF CONTENT THEY WANT TO SEE ON THE WEB

By Doug Tsuruoka
Investor's Business Daily

Now for the hard part.

It was easy for AOL Time Warner Inc. to cough up $7 billion to buy Bertelsmann AG's 49.5% stake in its European Internet unit, AOL Europe.

The buyback announced Jan. 7 satisfies a condition set by European regulators in clearing America Online's merger with Time Warner last year. It's also a smart move for the company, analysts say, since Europe's a hot Internet growth area.

The number of new subscribers at AOL Europe jumped 40% to 5.5 million last year.

But the ride may get rougher. The world's biggest media company faces a pitched battle for new subscribers and markets in Europe, analysts say. And AOL Europe may not be profitable for some time.

"It's not going to be a walkover for AOL Time Warner in Europe," said Eric Kintz, an e-commerce expert for the consulting firm Roland Berger & Partner LLC. "You have strong local telecom companies that provide Internet services. They know their markets and have brand trust and customer relationships."

AOL's 5.5 million European users are a small fraction of the more than 60 million Internet subscribers in Europe. And the company still has to prove its online business model works in Europe.

Rivals include T-Online, an Internet service provider with 7.5 million members that's owned by German phone company Deutsche Telekom AG. There's also Wanadoo in France, with 2.3 million members. It's owned by France Telecom.

Tactics that worked for AOL in the U.S. may not work in Europe. Why? Europeans spend less time on the Net than Americans.

That's because they pay more to connect to online services, thanks to Europe's costly and tightly regulated phone markets.

While most U.S. consumers pay a flat monthly rate of $10 to $30 for unlimited Net usage, Europeans pay high fees to local telecom firms to access the Net on a minute-by-minute basis.

Culture, Language Gaps

That's the chief reason why only one in four Europeans surf the Net for more than a half-hour a day, says research firm International Data Corp. That compares with over 70 minutes per day of Internet use for the average U.S. AOL subscriber.

European firms also spend less money on online ads than U.S. users. Firms in Western Europe spent $1.5 billion on online ads in 2001, says researcher Jupiter Media Metrix. That compares with $7.3 billion for firms in North America.

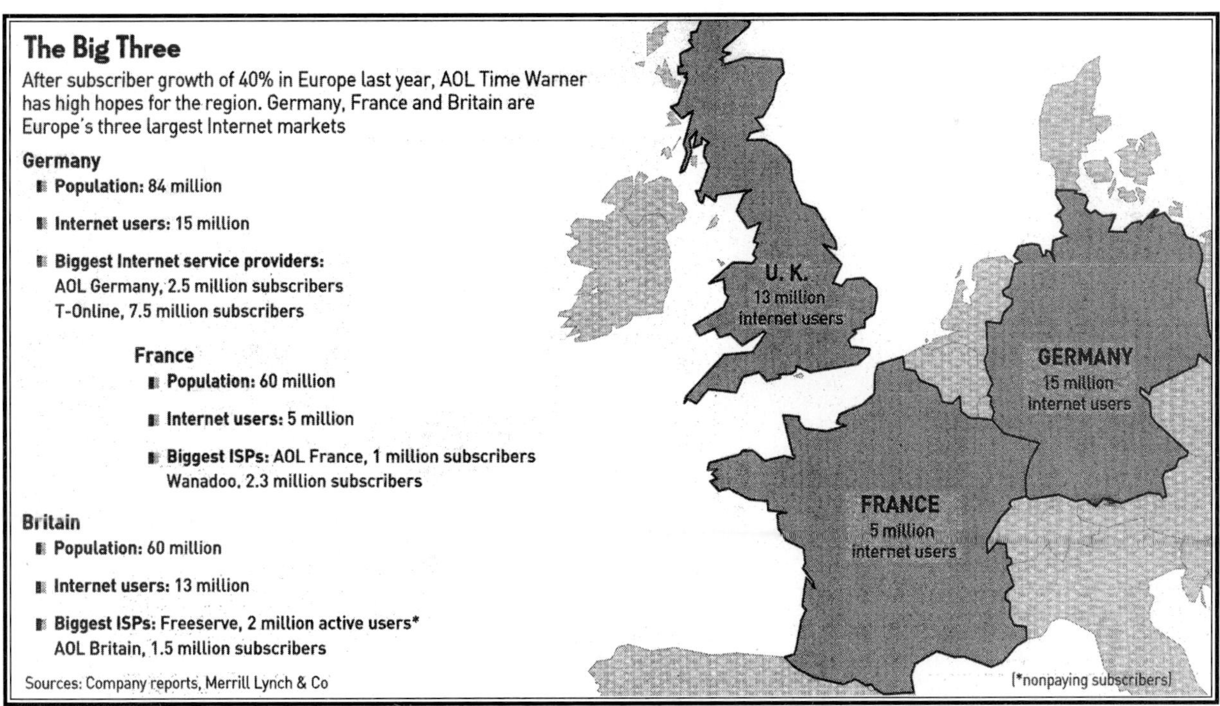

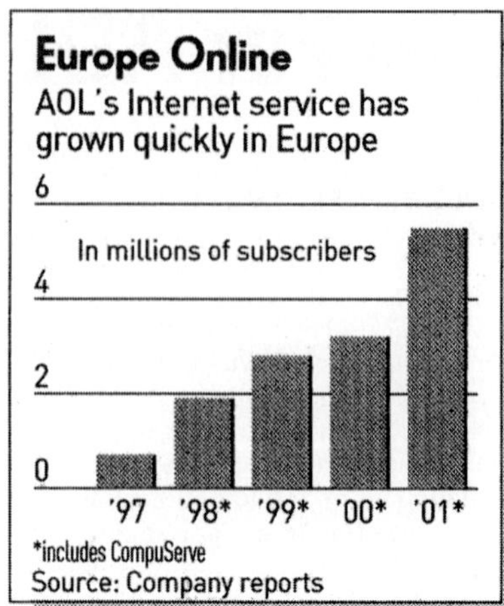

Europe, unlike the U.S., also is stymied by big cultural and language gaps. French and German Internet users prefer different Web site features and content. That tends to stunt the spread of uniform Net technology across Europe.

"It would be a mistake to view Europe as a single market for the Internet," said Barry Parr, an Internet media consultant in San Francisco. "The market won't jell as quickly or as smoothly as the U.S."

More consumers in Europe access the Net through wireless phones rather than personal computers. That could hurt AOL's service, which is designed mainly for PCs rather than wireless devices, Kintz says.

All these factors could make it harder for AOL Time Warner to whip up cash in Europe from Net services.

Robert Pittman, AOL Time Warner's chief operating officer, says the pluses in Europe outweigh the minuses.

The company's ability to offer attractive Internet tech to consumers will keep its subscriber rolls growing, he says. He expects foreign markets like Europe to pick up the slack as dial-up subscriber growth in the U.S. slows.

"AOL Europe will be the foundation for the AOL Time Warner marketing machine in Europe," Pittman said in a conference call with analysts.

Another plus: The bursting of the dot-com bubble swept away many small ISPs in Europe, which were competing against AOL by offering free Internet access.

AOL Europe is the second biggest online service in Europe. It was launched five years ago as a 50-50 joint venture with Bertelsmann, the German media giant.

AOL Europe is the largest ISP in Britain with 1.5 million members. It's second in Germany, behind T-Online, with 2.5 million members. It's second behind Wanadoo in France with nearly 1 million members.

Pittman said last week the slow growth of Internet access in Europe gives the company room to expand.

Household penetration for the Internet in Europe ranges from less than 30% in some countries to less than 40% in others, AOL officials say. That compares with nearly 60% of U.S. households that use the Internet.

"AOL Time Warner has shown it can make good on growth trajectories like this," said Scott Kessler, an analyst with Standard & Poor's Corp. in New York.

Acquiring British Publisher

Pittman also wants to make AOL Europe the keystone for cross-marketing AOL Time Warner's products in Europe.

That means using the online service to hawk products like the European editions of Time Inc.'s magazines and Warner Bros. movies like "Harry Potter."

AOL also is in the process of acquiring IPC Media, Britain's leading magazine publisher, as part of its European push. The idea is to promote subscriptions to AOL Europe in British magazines.

Pittman wants international business to contribute 30% to AOL Time Warner's revenue by 2005. It currently makes up 17% of its estimated 2001 sales of $38 billion.

Others question AOL Time Warner's strategy in Europe.

They say it's spending too much to buy out Bertelsmann. It's paying nearly twice the market value for Bertelsmann's stake. The stiff price is a payback to Bertelsmann, which paid most of the operating costs for AOL Europe.

Still, each AOL Europe subscriber is worth less than half of a U.S. subscriber, says Merrill Lynch & Co. analyst Jessica Reif Cohen. That's because Europeans use the Internet in less cash-generating ways.

With this in mind, the Bertelsmann stake was worth only about $3 billion, not nearly $7 billion, Cohen says.

AOL Europe also is expected to post a loss of $600 million on revenue of $800 million in 2001. That shows the unit has a way to go before breaking even, analysts say.

A Radio Chip in Every Consumer Product

By CLAUDIA H. DEUTSCH AND BARNABY J. FEDER

Here's a tip to thieves: If you are bent on stealing packages of **Gillette** Mach3 razor blades, go someplace other than Tesco's Newmarket Road store in Cambridge, England. There, a "smart shelf" continuously queries tiny radio chips embedded in the packages it holds, and senses the silence when one is removed. The system may soon be programmed to alert security when several are taken at once, Greg Sage, a Tesco spokesman, said.

And, yes, **Procter & Gamble** will notice if a case of Pantene shampoo does not make it to the Wal-Mart Supercenter in Broken Arrow, Okla. Its truck is equipped to monitor signals continuously from chips hidden in each case. If any case stops sending its "Hi, I'm still here" signal, a monitor in the "smart truck" will record exactly when and where.

Such technology, known as radio-frequency identification—the same techniques that enable an electronic sensor to record data from an E-ZPass tag or an office door to open for people with chip-equipped cards in their pockets—could one day stymie pilferers. But it is also capable of doing much more for commerce. Beyond Gillette and Procter & Gamble, companies as diverse as **International Paper** and **Canon USA** are teaming up with retailers and customers to apply R.F.I.D., as it is known, to tracking products from the time they leave an assembly line to the time they leave the store.

The companies are tagging clothes, drugs, auto parts, copy machines and even mail with chips laden with information about content, origin and destination. They are also equipping shelves, doors and walls with sensors that can record that data when the products are near. "We want to track all of our merchandise, and that includes items that people are unlikely to steal," William C. Wertz, a spokesman for **Wal-Mart Stores,** said.

Chip manufacturers are busily spreading that gospel. "That need to have the right product on the right shelf in the right store at the right time—ultimately, that's what will drive our business," said Karsten Ottenberg, a senior vice president at Philips Semiconductor, the leading maker of radio frequency chips and a unit of **Royal Philips Electronics.**

Early tests are encouraging. For three months in 2001, Gap tested radio frequency tags on denim clothes at a store in Atlanta. Sales jumped because the tags prevented the store from running out of popular items, and the tags made it quicker to find any items in stock.

Typically, 15 percent of shoppers leave clothing stores without getting what they want; during the test, fewer than 1 percent of Gap shoppers left empty-handed.

Radio frequency identification still has too many kinks, however, to be an immediate panacea for retailers. Cordless phones, two-way radios, local wireless networks and other communications devices that are widely deployed in factories, warehouses and stores can interfere with the signals. And, although radio tag readers can, under ideal conditions, identify well over 100 tagged items every second from quite a distance, radio waves have a hard time penetrating metals and liquids—something that Procter & Gamble is addressing with the Pantene test.

Tiny chips attached to packages of razor blades can send messages to store managers, alerting them when shelves are depleted.

And costs are still prohibitive. The electronic tags cost at least 30 cents apiece; most experts think anything above 5 cents is too expensive to be widely used for individual packaged goods. Prices would have to fall to less than a penny for virtually everything in stores to be tagged. Sensors, which can be either hand-held or built into walls, can cost $1,000 each.

But costs are coming down fast. **Alien Technology,** for one, says that it can now sell radio frequency identification tags profitably at 5 cents each for orders of a billion tags or more. Just last month, Gillette said it would buy up to 500 million tags over the next few years from Alien.

But Alien's manufacturing capacity is currently just a small fraction of what it would need to fill orders over a billion quickly. And experts warn that while the silicon chips continue to shrink in size and fall in price, making the attached antennas small enough and cheap enough is much harder.

Moreover, most retailers say they are reluctant to invest in the technology until product tags are universally readable, as bar codes are today. That means that every retailer, manufacturer and carrier must agree to standards, and use tags and sensors that speak the same language.

"It's one thing to say something is a great technology, but quite another to say that you're ready to scrap existing systems to accommodate it," said Daniel Butler, vice president for retail operations at the National Retail Federation, a trade association based in Washington.

Consumer privacy is also an issue. It would be easy to combine credit card data with information from the retail chips to know who bought what, and when—and, conceivably, track the product even after it left the store.

"I don't think the average consumer understands the threat to personal privacy that these kinds of technologies can present," said Alan N. Sutin, a partner specializing in information technology at the law firm of Greenberg Traurig.

William H. Steele, a consumer products analyst with Bank of America, doubts companies will "succumb to the temptation to keep tracking products in the consumers' hands," but he, too, stops short of calling the issue specious. "There should be a certain level of skepticism on the part of the U.S. consumer," he said.

Still, companies are increasingly viewing the identification technology as a potential savior. In 1999, Gillette, Procter & Gamble and the Uniform Code Council, which administers bar code standardization, founded the Auto-ID Center at the Massachusetts Institute of Technology to be a standards and research clearinghouse. The center has satellite labs at Cambridge University in England, and in Japan and Australia.

The technological limitations of bar codes makes the growing interest in R.F.I.D. easy to understand. Kevin Ashton, a P. & G. executive who directs the Auto-ID Center, estimates that on average 10 percent of stores are out of items the managers think are in stock—and as many as 40 percent do not realize they are out of a color or size.

The monetary impact of losing track of goods is huge. According to a survey by the University of Florida, shrinkage—the common retailing term for goods that disappear either through theft, misplacement, fraud or just bad record keeping—cost retailers a record $31.3 billion last year. Only a third was a result of shoplifting. Nearly half was employee theft, about 5 percent was vendor theft and 15 percent was paperwork errors.

Suppliers have as much at stake as retailers. Colin Peacock, the leader of a Gillette task force to study shelf availability, said that 73 percent of customers left a store if Mach3 blades were out of stock; 27 percent bought a competitor's blades. He said Mach3 sales had gone up 288 percent at the Cambridge Tesco store that had the smart shelf.

Stores often resort to putting frequently pilfered items behind glass or behind counters.

That means customers must wait for a clerk to get the products. The practice drives away impatient shoppers and all but eliminates impulse buys.

Mr. Peacock suspects that sales are halved when products are hidden away. "The impact of such defensive merchandising can be worse than the problems it solves," he said.

Once it is perfected, radio frequency technology may solve not just those problems, but some that are unrelated to stocking issues. Because the tags, unlike bar codes, are programmable chips, a store like Wal-Mart that frequently changes prices can attach the price to the item and know exactly what a consumer paid if the item is returned—even if the customer lost the receipt.

And then there are product recalls to consider. Radio frequency technology could pinpoint a tainted batch, and—if customers paid with credit cards or used store discount cards—identify customers who purchased such items.

"It would be wonderful to be able to spot just those items that came from a plant that has a flaw, or those perishable items that took too long to arrive and thus might spoil sooner," Mr. Wertz of Wal-Mart said.

Radio-frequency identification chips can track an item from the time it is assembled to the time it is sold. They now cost about 30 cents each, but prices are expected to fall sharply.

Canon USA wants to deploy radio frequency identification to track machines at locations that use dozens of printers and copiers. "It would help us schedule preventive maintenance, and alert us to get equipment back when the lease expires," said James J. Gordon Jr., Canon's vice president for logistics.

Even the United States Postal Service has gotten into the act. Last month, it promoted Charles E. Bravo, until then its chief technology officer, to the new job of senior vice president for intelligent mail and address quality, and charged him with studying tracking technologies.

"We'd love to be able to tell a company that a customer's check is truly in the mail, or that its direct mail flier was just delivered to a customer's door," Mr. Bravo said.

And imagine if the company can also be sure that the item the flier is advertising will be available.

"Increasing productivity, lowering inventories, decreasing theft, all are important," said Paul J. Rieger, Procter & Gamble's associate director of supply chain innovation. "But ending out-of-stock situations, that is still our biggest goal."

The Annoying New Face of Customer Service

Virtual Phone Reps Replace The Old Touch-Tone Menus; Making Claire Less Irritating

By Jane Spencer

Meet the new face of customer service: perky, unflappable—and entirely virtual.

From Amtrak to Sprint PCS, a growing number of companies are ditching their automated service hotlines and replacing them with "virtual agents" that answer customer calls and emails. The phone characters are essentially talking computer programs with human voices—and, in some cases, names and personalities—that ask callers to speak rather than push buttons.

Using speech-recognition technology, the systems try to mimic the experience of talking with an enthusiastic human rep. Yahoo Inc.'s Jenni, who reads e-mails to customers through Yahoo by Phone, says, "Got it!" after nearly everything and quips, "Wow, you're popular!" to callers with crowded in-boxes. Julie, who books Amtrak tickets and offers schedule information, is designed to sound increasingly stressed out each time she misunderstands a customer's speech command.

But many callers aren't entertained by the anthropomorphizing gestures. "It's more annoying to talk to a computer pretending to be a person than just to talk to a computer," says Matthew Vogel, a Boston research analyst. One problem: The characters sometimes don't hear callers correctly. Since the software programs behind the characters match what callers say against a dictionary of possible responses, background noise or a spotty cellphone connection can throw off the entire conversation.

The virtual agents represent the latest push by companies to make customer service more efficient. For more than a decade, the touch-tone menu has ruled the call-center landscape. But the new technology allows companies to automate more-complex transactions. And the speech-recognition calls are 40% faster on average than touch-tone calls, according to Kelsey Group, because customers don't have to listen to lists of menu options. The latest systems understand hundreds of accents and recognize multiple synonyms for common words. (Simon at United Airlines, for example, responds to "mm-hmm" and "yeah, baby" as variations on yes.) And, while speech systems are more expensive than touch-tone automation, they still offer cheap labor. On average, a customer-service call handled by a speech system costs about $2.50, compared with $5 for a call taken by a human, says Gartner Research.

As the technology improves, companies from Aetna to Merrill Lynch are scrambling to replace their touch-tone menus. Total spending on speech-recognition technology in the U.S. topped $680 million in 2002, up 60% from the previous year, according to Kelsey Group.

But the virtual reps aren't popular with some customers, and already, some companies are starting to tweak their agents to make them less annoying. Sprint PCS's Claire has infuriated customers by sounding overly enthusiastic when they call with frustrations like billing or service disruptions. "She sounds completely and utterly thrilled to hear that I have a problem with Sprint," says Carrie Bancroft of New York City. In response to customer complaints, Sprint PCS President Len Lauer ordered phone rep Claire to undergo a personality upgrade, which included making it easier to reach human help through the system. In recent weeks, Claire has stopped introducing herself at the beginning of each conversation. "We're de-emphasizing her character," says a spokesman for Sprint PCS, the mobile unit of Sprint Corp.

Katie, the flirty "virtual skin-care assistant" on the Dove soap Web site, had to be reprogrammed after she was deemed "too aggressive" in her efforts to collect visitors' e-mail addresses, according to NativeMinds, the San Francisco company that built the system. Now, Katie requests an e-mail only if you ask her for free products or coupons.

Katie has plenty of company online. Customer-service "Verbots" or V-reps" now populate Web sites at companies including AT&T Corp., Ford Motor Co. and Coca-Cola Co. These tiny talking heads—usually represented by photos or digital cartoons—lurk in the corner of the Web sites, baiting site visitors with "ask me a question!" The faces front for computer programs that can scan the text of a typed question and generate a response from a dictionary of frequently asked questions. The resulting "chat" sessions mimic an instant message exchange.

Online V-Reps are often more cute than helpful. Some seem more knowledgeable about their personal histories than the company they work for. Hank, the V-rep at Coke.com, can answer questions about his

How to Talk to Your Verbot

The Web's virtual reps remain a work in progress. When we put them to the test, we found that we could stump each one with a seemingly easy question.

CHARACTER/COMPANY	WHAT WE ASKED	THEY SAID	STUMPED BY
Allie AT&T	Where is my remote control?	With your socks.	Can you explain the tax section of my bill.
Mama Ragu	Can you find me a man?	I think always the best place to meet a man is in the pasta section of the grocery store.	Do you use pesticides on your tomatoes?
Hank Coke	Do you ever drink Pepsi?	Never.	Where can I buy Diet Vanilla Coke?
Bill the Brewmaster Miller	Do you like your job?	Imagine working for a company where it's always Miller Time!	Is drinking and driving safe?
Kate Ford	Where do you live?	I live on a server at Ford Headquarters.	My Taurus is making a funny noise.
Katie Dove	Is Dove soap safe to eat?	Yes, Dove products do meet all safety and quality standards.	Is Dove good for dry skin?
Anne IAMS Pet Food	Would you like to go out sometime?	You might want to join a social club and meet some fellow humans.	My dog bites kids.

(Cont.)

sexual orientation but can't tell you where to buy New Vanilla Coke. But since the technology is new, companies are constantly adding new information to the character's answer dictionaries. Ford, for example, employs a small staff devoted to maintaining the online V-rep, Kate. Currently, she can answer at least 8,000 questions.

Some companies create extensive biographies for the characters that include everything from SAT scores to hobbies. Yahoo's Jenni is a free-lance artist who once played guitar in an all-girl rock band. Melinda, at the Internet provider Tiscali, is a British advertising assistant with a glittering Notting Hill social life.

Virtual reps—and the companies creating them—face a formidable challenge: Not all customers are seeking friendship when they call a customer-service line. "I don't want a relationship with a character," declares Sam Berkow, an acoustic designer in Manhattan. "I want an efficient system for buying a train ticket."

Virtual customer-service agents are growing common. But some companies have already had to tweak their virtual reps to make them more customer-friendly.

Jim DiCamillo, an Amtrak passenger, agrees. When Amtrak's Julie starts booking train tickets, unexpected itineraries sometimes begin to unfold. "I say Philadelphia, Pennsylvania, she gives me Billings, Montana!" he says. "She almost convinced me to go there."

Despite the troubles, some customers seem to enjoy their interactions with some of the characters. Lourdes Ayala, a lawyer from Silver Springs, Md., frequently books train tickets through Julie and considers her a friend. "I know what she's going to say before she says it," says Ms. Ayala. "Julie asks all the right questions. She knows me better than my boyfriend."

Ethical Marketing in a Consumer-Oriented World: Appraisal and Challenges

Capitalism Spawns a New Leisure Class: Mall Rats

BY SABRINA TAVERNISE

They come on free shuttle buses and flock together in the food court. They play video games for hours in the Soyuz computer store. They are Moscow mall rats.

The "rats"—and their habitat—are still rarities in Moscow. The first mall—a gaudy tomb of luxury stores that appeared in 1997 underneath a central public square—was more a museum than a place to shop. Later, a Turkish retailer began opening malls in Moscow's thickly settled suburbs.

Now, the Russian capital has 21 malls, one for every 500,000 people, fewer even than in Warsaw, a city one-fifth the size, according to the Moscow office of Jones Lang LaSalle, a real estate consultancy.

But the word is spreading that the mall is the place to be. Benches, tree-lined alleyways and food courts are becoming cold-weather alternatives to traditional hangouts—city parks and the Old Arbat street. In the gray slush of Saturday, teenagers jammed into shuttle buses that run to a new mall in southwestern Moscow. In other neighborhoods, they walked or hitched rides from their parents.

"It's a great place to come and have a rest from my parents," said Anvyar Ilyasov, 16, standing with a cluster of boys at a Sony PlayStation in an electronics store in the Mega mall in southwest Moscow. "My friends told me about it."

In Soviet times, of course, those parents shopped in drab department stores where almost all items were behind glass and lines predominated. Understandably, they were skeptical of malls at first, thinking they were only for rich people. Indeed, after the Soviet Union collapsed in 1991, the older generation switched to outdoor markets, where even in winter clothes flutter on canvas sales stalls and cabbages are hawked out of the backs of trucks.

"People have this impression about malls, they are afraid to walk in," said Stanislav V. Tishenko, a manager at a new Moscow mall.

But the economy is growing, wages—particularly in Moscow—are rising, and the outdoor markets are closing—167 now, down one-third since 1999. Last month, the city authorities closed two of the most popular outdoor markets.

"If that happened five years ago, there would have been a mutiny," said Mariya Volkenshtein, a sociologist at Validata Market Research in Moscow. Malls, she said, are "becoming normal for everyone."

The teenagers remember little or nothing of Soviet shopping agony. Their faces go blank when asked about lines. Instead of the no-frills consumption of their parents' day, young Russians today are surrounded by capitalism at its most raw.

They feast on American culture, but scorn American politics. Aleksei Shulenin, dressed in a knit hat pulled down over his ears, a Nike shirt and baggy jeans, looked as if he had been plucked from the halls of an American high school. He spoke admiringly of American music and movies.

> Malls have become a popular weekend hangout for teenagers, many of whom have no memory of pre-capitalist Russia.

"Americans think they can do anything," he said between bites of a burrito bought at the nearby Mexican fast food restaurant. "Americans believe whatever their government tells them."

But there are other forms of quiet flattery. The word shopping has made its way into the Moscow vernacular. One of the larger malls that opened last year calls itself WayMart, just one letter off from the giant American retailer. The mall's management says the likeness is pure coincidence.

What Moscow malls lack in number they make up for in size. Mega is Eastern Europe's biggest mall, though still smaller than most American malls. It contains an indoor skating rink, and has had 1.5 million visitors since it opened last month, said Olga Starichenko, the mall's spokeswoman.

Mallgoers, according to Mega's marketing surveys, are ages 25 to 45. Most are at the upper end of Moscow's midwage earners, which means they take home monthly salaries of $300 to $400. Muscovites earn more than double the Russian average wage.

Some of the high-schoolers have taken after-school jobs, something unheard of for their parents. Christina Khlystalova, 16, said she earned extra spending money by handing out advertising leaflets outside subway stops, much to the chagrin of her mother, a hairdresser.

"It's easy to find work in Moscow now," said Yevgeniya Kostomarova, who works at a computer store to supplement her finances. "You have to show some initiative, but you can advance without personal connections to the boss."

Almost all the teenage mall-rovers claimed to be from middle-class families, but few could agree on a definition. A group of friends in a mall on Kashirskoye Shosse in southeastern Moscow said their middle-class parents owned foreign luxury cars, like BMW's. Out of a group of five, three had cellphones, every one had an e-mail address, and the girls had nose piercings. Mr. Ilyasov, on the other hand, said his parents could not afford to buy a car.

It is too early to tell if shopping habits will turn around completely. Russians have traditionally traveled to the center of Moscow to shop. Now, as more buy cars, the new malls are reversing the flow, luring people out to the city's edges, much like shopping patterns in the United States.

At the mall on Kashirskoye Shosse, Ms. Khlystalova and her two girlfriends talked about their lives over hamburgers and French fries. There is really nothing special in a mall, they agreed.

"It's a place we go when we're bored," Ms. Khlystalova said.

Web Ads Growing Intrusive

POP-UPS AIM TO DISRUPT

By Doug Tsuruoka
Investor's Business Daily

Everybody's seen them. You click to a Web page and begin reading an item like a film review. Suddenly an ad bloops onto your screen out of nowhere.

The ad blocks the text with a pitch for credit cards or online gambling. It takes an extra mouse click to make it go away.

These pop-ups aren't new. Plenty of advertisers use them. But there's been a blitz of such ads lately. And they're getting bigger, flashier and more disruptive.

"As the downturn drives companies to seek revenue by all available means, it's not surprising to see ads like these emerge into the consumer mainstream," said Panos Anastassiadis, chief executive of Cyveillance Inc., a firm that tracks the Internet.

The most intrusive pop-ups cover the entire screen. They hawk things like movies and use effects such as images that fade in and out.

Others flash their messages across the screen for several seconds before disappearing. There's nothing you can do to make them go away before then.

Among the Web sites featuring them: search engine Yahoo Inc., the Los Angeles Times' latimes.com and entertainment trade paper Daily Variety's variety.com.

Cyveillance estimates that 30% of the Internet's top 100 Web sites use intrusive ads. That's up sharply from six months ago, when analysts say 15% to 20% of sites used them.

Some say this shows how desperate the online ad industry is. With ad revenue slipping, advertisers and Web publishers are going all-out to get a rise out of consumers. Banner ads, which disappear from screens unless you click on them, aren't selling well. Hence the stress on developing ads that consumers can't ignore.

'Banners Are Irrelevant'

Jim Nail, an analyst at Forrester Research Inc., says marketers dislike banners because they have bad click-through rates—a key measure of an ad's success with consumers.

"Banners are irrelevant," Nail said. "They don't grab consumer attention."

Many pop-ups use technology that triggers them as soon as a surfer hits a Web site. They tap into a browser's JavaScript functions, HTML programming codes and Flash animation features to play their interactive effects.

The most common pop-up uses a technology called spawning. It launches a window containing an ad on your screen as soon as you enter a site.

Cyveillance found that spawning was one of the top 10 techniques used by Internet advertisers to expose Web surfers to unsolicited ads.

Another technique is called mousetrapping. It prevents users from backing out or exiting a Web page while the ad's running.

About 5.2% of all sites on the Internet use mousetrapping, according to Cyveillance.

Intrusive ads have another purpose. By making users wait or use extra clicks, Web sites running the ads can raise their visit-time statistics. Higher rankings help attract more advertisers.

Pop-ups aren't the only in-your-face ads these days.

Another is the so-called shoshkele ad. It has animated images that float across your screen when you click onto a Web site. An example is an owl from the recent "Harry Potter" movie. It flew across the screen of anyone who visited the home page of online service about.com recently.

Then there's the pop-under ad. The ad opens on the Web page under your browser and appears on the screen as soon as the browser is closed.

One of the best-known of this type is an ad for the tiny wireless video camera from Seattle-based X10 Wireless Technology Inc.

The X10 ads, which use women models, raised eyebrows when they hit the Web six months ago. They've since been upstaged by more disruptive ads.

The new ads have lots of

Top Tactics

Online merchants have a number of ideas to lure Web surfers to their sites

1. Spawning: Launches a new browser window when Web surfers arrive at a site, or when they leave one.

2. Mousetrapping: Disables the user's ability to go back, exit or close while viewing a page.

3. Invisible seeding: Uses a hidden source code to get an ad to pop up in search engine traffic even though it has nothing to do with what consumers are looking for.

4. Unauthorized software downloads: Invades a consumer's privacy by leaving behind software on the computer that contains embedded advertising or tracking capabilities.

5. Spoof pages: Pages placed on a Web site to attract search engine traffic for higher rankings. These pages can contain selected words, brands, slogans or references to personalities like movie stars. These tactics which draw traffic from consumers who may be searching for information on an altogether different subject.

6. Typo-piracy and cyber-squatting: Web sites that play word games by using misspellings and derivations of a popular brand to divert traffic to their site. It is not uncommon to see thousands of derivations of popular brand names in registered domain names.

7. Changing home pages or favorites: Unauthorized substitution of a new home page setting or changes to a user's "favorites" list while they are visiting a Web site. Approximately 1.4% of sites on the Internet engage in one of these two intrusive tactics.

8. Visible seeding: Mixing ad slogans and mention of popular brands with proprietary content on a site to raise search engine rankings. Placing a brand name in the title bar at the top of a window would be one such example.

9. Mislabeling links: False labeling of hyperlinks that send the shopper to an unintended destination.

10. Framing: The shoppers think they have clicked out of a site, but they haven't. Users are kept on the original site while viewing the content of another, through the original site's window. This way, the original site can increase ad revenue via higher visit time statistics.

(Cont.)

critics. Some consumers have started online clubs and chat rooms with names like "Pop-ups Must Die" to rage against them.

Some tech firms also have found a niche by selling software that filters out pop-ups and other types of unsolicited ads.

The software does this by stopping the ad from running before it has time to download on your screen.

One frequent complaint about pop-up and similar ads is that they steal bandwidth by taking up space in a computer's pipeline to the Web. This clogs the downloading of other data from the Net, and can lead to system crashes.

Intrusive ads may irk some. But Joe Apprendi, executive vice president of Eyeblaster Inc., says they're the wave of the future.

Eyeblaster is an Internet platform provider that lets advertisers visit its site and design pop-ups and other ads. Advertisers then take these ads to Web publishers, which run them.

Like TV Commercials

Apprendi thinks full-page, pop-up ads that run on screens for 10 or 15 seconds will become the norm now that old-fashioned banner ads have failed.

Consumers also will be forced to watch them as part of the trade-off for visiting an otherwise free Web site, such as Yahoo or about.com.

"Online advertising is going to resemble the commercial breaks you have on TV, though the ads will be of much shorter duration," Apprendi said.

He says Web publishers and advertisers will be drawn to these ads because they're one of the few workable ways to grab consumer attention.

Consumers will get used to the new format the same way they got used to TV commercials, he says.

"Using a full-page ad also means you have more screen to deliver engaging and entertaining ad content," Apprendi said.

Greg Stuart, chief executive of the Interactive Advertising Bureau, a trade group, says consumers shouldn't fret about Net ads becoming too intrusive.

Web publishers are still trying to find a balance between meeting the needs of marketers and consumers. Eventually, he says, that balance will be found.

"Web publishers won't run amok with these ads because they'd lose their audience," Stuart said.

"Web Ads Growing Intrusive," *Investor's Business Daily,* January 9, 2002. Reprinted by permission.

Peek-a-Boo, I See You—Clearly

Slumping Eyeglass Business Sets Its Sights on Toddlers; Better for Vision or Profits?

BY NANCY ANN JEFFREY
Staff Reporter of THE WALL STREET JOURNAL

Mallory Tivey used to hate her glasses so much she actually avoided putting them on in the morning. Now, she's so happy with the frames, she slips them on first thing—even before asking her mother for her sippy cup.

"She looks adorable," says Kelly Tivey of her two-year-old daughter, who got her wire specs a few months ago.

The $16 billion-a-year optical industry has set its sights on a new market: tots. With sales to adults slumping, eyeglass companies have stepped up marketing efforts not only to youngsters, but to toddlers and babies. Kids as young as one can now get everything from "Tiny Tot" frames by Fisher-Price to grown-up-looking copper models from OshKosh B'Gosh. A pitchman for Disney's kiddie frames? One-eyed Mike, the ugly but popular star of "Monsters, Inc." And business is doing well, with makers reporting sales increases of 10% to 25% in the past two years.

But do tykes really need glasses? Makers say eye problems in kids tend to get overlooked, and along with many optometrists, they're pushing for state-mandated eye exams for youngsters. But many doctors say the problem is nowhere near as big as manufacturers and optometrists claim, and that only a fraction of the youngest kids need glasses. They point out that many prescriptions often treat mild farsightedness, which is normal in young children and often lessens over time. And then there's the pocketbook issue: The flood of fancy, name-brand frames coming on the market can cost triple generic ones.

"It sounds more to me like a marketing scheme than a public health plan," says James Sprague, a pediatric ophthalmologist in McLean, Va.

Still, the pitch is catching on with parents across the country. For Jacquie Samsel of Roseville, Calif., all it took was the memory of being razzed as "four-eyes" for wearing "cat-eye" frames as a kid. After first getting her son Austin pretty plain glasses when he was just 14 months old, Mrs. Samsel has moved up the fashion chain in recent years. Her latest pick? A pair of $200 wire frames that make Austin look "like the boy from 'Jerry Maguire,'" says the homemaker.

In Falls Church, Va., Don Hammer merely wanted to satisfy his fashion-conscious five-year-old, Kathryn Ellen. When the doctor announced she needed glasses to correct a lazy eye and farsightedness, the kindergartener insisted on a pair of blue, octagonal frames from Esprit. "They're very elegant," says Mr. Hammer of the $250 specs.

Back in the mid-to-late '90s when the optical business was growing at a healthy clip, no one was very interested in kids' glasses, which made up less than 10% of the market. Usually, only children with serious eye problems saw eye doctors, and then only after a pediatrician or a parent noticed something amiss. But with business down 4% last year, and adults buying new glasses only every two years (it used to be every 16 months in the early '90s), the industry needed some help.

Courting the Little People

Their solution? Go after littler people. This spring, Nouveau Eyewear plans to send hundreds of doctors and optical shops copies of the coming book "Magenta Gets Glasses," about how the "Blue's Clues" character got her eyes checked. The Kenmark Group, which makes Hush Puppies' "Pups" line, is giving away stuffed animals to snag kids' loyalties. And then there's ClearVision Optical, makers of the "Tiny Tot" specs: In the past two years, the firm has seen sales of Fisher-Price glasses for infants to four-year-olds rise 15%.

Experts say the moves are well-timed to coincide with an expanding kid population and their parents' obsession with designer logos. Not only do fashion glasses cost between $150 and $300 a pop, but growing tots can need replacement frames as often as three times a year. "It's a very lucrative market if we can catch a young child," says David Friedfeld, president of the company that makes Fisher-Price glasses.

But how can doctors even tell if kids too small to read have vision problems? Creatively. Glen Steele, an optometrist in Memphis, Tenn., moves Mom and Dad around the exam room and watches to see if baby's eyes follow. Jim Rooney, an optician in St. Louis, entertains little customers with a Mickey Mouse hand puppet while he adjusts their frames. And when Wendy James of Canton, Texas, recently brought her 2 1/2-year-old quadruplets to have their eyes checked (three wear glasses), the doctor turned on a dancing Santa Claus figure to attract the focus of his little patients.

Performing Better in School

Advocates for mandatory eye exams, largely optometrists and eyeglass makers, say such tactics help catch problems early and ensure normal development. "When a child gets frustrated in the classroom, he doesn't do well," says Joel Zaba, an optometrist in Virginia Beach, Va. And the

Specs for Toddlers

Eyeglass outfits are stepping up their efforts to court younger and younger kids, including one- and two-year olds. Here are some of today's choices (lenses not included).

NAME/MANUFACTURER	AGE	PRICE	COMMENT
Barbie Rem	girls four to 10	$75 to $90	Only one Barbie doll has glasses, but the company is pushing a dozen styles.
Disney Marchon	infant to 9	$90 to $110	The models are plain or have small Mickey Mouse icons at the temples.
Fisher-Price ClearVision	infant to 8	$99 to $129	Frames are among the higher-priced on the market. Infant styles have flexible ear coils to keep frames on heads.
Hush Puppies Pups Kenmark	four to 12	$98	The company makes glasses for both kids and adults, but the kids' "Pups" models are doing best, with sales having doubled in four years.
Osh Kosh B'Gosh Logo of the Americas	one to eight	$99	After company redesigned collection for a more adult look about a year ago, sales grew 10%.
Sesame Street Zyloware	two to eight	$80 to $120	While other companies are going more sophisticated, the company has put Elmo, rubber ducks and musical notes on its frames.

(Cont.)

movement is picking up steam: Kentucky has passed a law requiring parents to have their preschoolers' eyes checked by a specialist before entering public school, and optometrists are pushing for similar laws in at least six other states.

But some experts complain that having a specialist check little kids' eyes is unnecessary, since most pediatricians do that anyway. What's more, though they don't think the wrong glasses would hurt a child's vision, some doctors say getting a prescription too early can cause headaches in a small number of cases.

Using a special eye instrument, ophthalmologist Steven J. Lichtenstein of Louisville, Ky., examined 123 pre-schoolers last year and says he found only two who had problems, both of which had already been flagged by their own doctors. He also says he recently saw a family of five kids, all of whom were wearing spectacles prescribed elsewhere. In his opinion, four didn't need glasses, and the fifth had been given the wrong prescription. "I'm making money on this, and I don't agree with it," says Dr. Lichtenstein.

Indeed, even some manufacturers concede that glasses could be overprescribed to increase profits. But "doctors are the ones prescribing," says Mr. Friedfeld, of ClearVision Optical. For him, that means that doctors—not eyeglass makers—are the responsible party. "I only make the eyewear," says Mr. Friedfeld.

Not that any of that matters to three-year-old Sarah Demsky. The trend-conscious tyke in Chesterfield, Mo., has been bugging her mom, Jamie, for glasses ever since her two best friends started wearing them recently. Mrs. Demsky tried consoling her daughter with a new pair of $5 kiddie sunglasses, but that just hasn't done the trick. "You can't reason with a three-year-old," sighs Mrs. Demsky.

The Cranky Consumer Works on Its Smile

We Test Five Tooth Whiteners, From Gel to Dentist's Chair; Fighting the Drool Factor

By Eleena de Lisser

Sure, the economy is in the dumps and there's war on the horizon. But how white are your teeth?

It's a question obsessing a remarkable number of Americans. Sales of "tooth polishes" more than doubled last year, and Procter & Gamble alone says its dental-bleaching business has gone from nearly nothing to 20% of its $1 billion oral-care sales in three years. The result: A dazzling array of do-it-yourself kits continue to hit the market. With names like Swabplus Advanced Dental Whitening System and Rembrandt Plus Superior Bleaching Kit, they promise to do for as little as $15 what would cost thousands from a Hollywood dentist.

So we decided to donate our smile to science—enduring days of drooling, tooth-swabbing and various other indignities—to see which kit produced the best results. To establish a baseline, we brought in a dentist to check our teeth before and after with a specially designed "shade" guide to measure changes.

Whiteners tend to work best for people who are over 30 since teeth gradually darken as part of the normal aging process. They also generally have more dramatic results for those who smoke or drink a lot of coffee. Journalists being journalists, our testers included some of both—as well as some nonsmokers with passably white teeth.

The whiteners come in several varieties: swabs that look like Q-tips, bottles reminiscent of Liquid Paper and stick-on strips akin to mini Band-Aids for your teeth. The four products we used cost between $14.99 and $44.95, and promised to make our teeth whiter in six to 21 days. To get in touch with our inner Julia Roberts, we also booked an appointment with a private dentist's office (someone other than our dental judge) to get the latest high-tech treatment: the Zoom! Chairside Whitening System, which cost us about $825 and pledged to do the deed in about an hour.

Unfortunately, the road to glamour is covered with drool. It was especially true of Swabplus, but Crest Professional Whitestrips also caused something of a flood.

There were other problems, too. The Whitestrips caused sharp pain in our teeth a few times, like what you get when you bite into freezing-cold ice cream (but without the pleasure). Crest says that sometimes happens and it's nothing to worry about. In fact, it's a possible side effect with other products, too.

The best performer was Discus Dental's Zoom!, the one administered by a dentist. It required two visits, and answering a detailed medical questionnaire. Weirdest question: "Do you sunburn easily?" That's because the bleaching agent gets activated by a bright light that gets shined in your mouth.

Guess what happens once you're sitting in the dentist's chair, wearing protective goggles, your mouth stretched open with a dental expander: Time slows to a crawl. In fact, after about an hour, our volunteer says she had a bout of anxiety. (A spokesman for the American Dental Association says some patients do become claustrophobic.) The treatment took 90 minutes.

It also caused some tooth pain that tapered off after a few days. The dentist called the sensations "zingers" and said that's normal. The good news is that the results were so dramatic, even our volunteer's 3 1/2-year-old daughter noticed. "Mom, what did you do to your teeth? They look so clean!" she said. The disturbing news: Her husband didn't notice.

P&G's Crest Whitestrips are clear plastic strips you stick to your teeth. You must wear four strips a day (two upper, and two lower) a half-hour each for three weeks. You're supposed to be able to wear two strips simultaneously, but that opened the drool floodgates and the strips simply fell off. However, wearing the four strips separately means devoting two hours a day to treatment instead

PRODUCT/PRICE	PITCH	HOW IT WORKS	'HOLLYWOOD SMILE' MOMENT	COMMENT
Zoom! Chairside Whitening System; $825 (price varies by dentist)	Teeth that are at least six to 10 shades lighter in "just over an hour."	Gel is applied to teeth and activated by a special light. (Actual whitening took closer to 90 minutes).	Many compliments from friends (but our volunteer's husband didn't seem to notice).	**Pricey but effective.** By far the costliest of the methods we used, but it did give the best results.
Colgate Simply White; $14.99	"The EASY way to sparkling white teeth"	You apply a gel to individual teeth with a mini brush, twice a day, for 14 days.	Keeping our **jaw clenched** and lips pulled off our teeth while gel dried.	Our volunteer, a wine- and coffee-drinking smoker, got a multishade improvement in his tooth color.
Crest Professional Whitestrips; $44.95	"Take 10 years off your smile."	Plastic strips, akin to a Band-Aid, worn on top and bottom teeth for at least 30 minutes twice a day.	Our volunteer forgot he was wearing one and drank a beer, which not only ruined the beer but washed a strip off, too.	A slight improvement in whiteness, but for us the product caused a bit of a **drool deluge**.
Swabplus Advanced Dental Whitening System; $24.99	"Noticeably whiten your teeth up to 2 shades within 6 days"	A swab is dipped in whitening powder and dabbed on teeth. **Treatment period is brief**—just six days.	Applying it was easy, but for some reason this one caused us to salivate quite heavily.	The liquid-filled "Q-tip" applicator is nifty, but for our tester it didn't produce a change in tooth color.
Rembrandt Plus Superior Bleaching Kit; $32.99	"Clinically proven to lighten teeth up to 10 shades in just two weeks."	Gel is put into plastic mouth trays that must be worn at least 30 minutes, twice a day—according to the outside of the box ...	... but when you open the box, you are told you have to wear the trays twice as long to get the most benefit.	**The conflicting directions** were frustrating. We wore the trays for well over the minimum recommended time; our teeth got one shade whiter.

(Cont.)

of just one hour. After three weeks our tester had a "half-shade" improvement in whiteness, a measurable change but not one a casual observer might notice.

Colgate Simply White, from Colgate-Palmolive, comes in a bottle that looks like white-out. The twist-off cap is an itty-bitty brush for applying gel twice a day. The hard part was keeping your mouth open for 30 seconds while the goop dries. It was among the easiest to use, and got a few shades of improvement for our volunteer, a coffee-drinking smoker.

Rembrandt Plus, made by Den-Mat, was the most confounding product we tried. For starters, the instructions were misleading. The outside of the box talks about making your teeth "10 shades" whiter if you use it twice a day for 30 minutes or more. But when you open the box, you learn you need to wear it twice as long to hope for the full effect.

It works like this: You squirt some whitening gel in a mouth-shaped plastic tray, and pop the tray in your mouth. Our volunteer, a non-smoker, wore it about 40 minutes, twice a day and wound up with a one-shade improvement.

A Rembrandt spokeswoman says the directions are clear, and pointed out that results will vary depending on how discolored the teeth are to begin with.

Swabplus promises to "noticeably whiten your teeth up to 2 shades within six days." It was also the only product to make no measurable difference in our volunteer's teeth. It comes in the form of 24 "applicators," which look like Q-Tips. Application was easy, but sent our volunteer's mouth into saliva overdrive—to the extent that she was concerned that she may be diluting the product. Saliva doesn't affect efficacy, a spokesman said, and he expressed surprise that we saw no whitening.

Swabplus had a faint aftertaste that wasn't exactly minty fresh. So on the first day of treatment, our volunteer admits, she chased it away with a cup of coffee—talk about counterproductive.

Crash tests may make SUVs even more deadly

To get good grades, SUV and pickup makers have built front ends so stiff that they can batter smaller cars to bits. In a TrailBlazer-vs.-Accord test, for example, the Honda's crash test dummy showed nearly 100% chance of death.

By Jayne O'Donnell
USA TODAY

New evidence from the government suggests that key auto crash tests run by the insurance industry and federal regulators might make sport-utility vehicles deadlier to people in small cars. And *USA TODAY* research finds little proof the tests actually lead to vehicles that better protect their own occupants.

The findings call into question the crash-test ratings that millions of consumers rely on when buying cars and trucks and could lead to an overhaul of federal tests to make them better predictors of what really happens when vehicles collide.

New government testing shows that as automakers design SUVs and pickups to score well in insurance industry and government frontal crash tests, they are making front ends so stiff that they might be more dangerous to those riding in small cars.

Getting a good crash-test rating doesn't mean a vehicle will show lower rates of injuries and deaths for its occupants in a crash, according to separate analyses by *USA TODAY* and General Motors.

The issue of "compatibility"—what happens when one type of vehicle crashes into another—has become a growing safety concern, particularly with the increasing popularity of trucks, which sit higher and weigh more than cars.

Jeffrey Runge, head of the National Highway Traffic Safety Administration (NHTSA), says car-truck compatibility in crashes is one of his top priorities. Major automakers held a meeting this month on car-truck mismatches. The Senate Commerce Committee is expected to address the issue today at a hearing on SUV safety.

Safety experts say every crash is unique, so no test can accurately predict what will happen when a car or truck hits a tree or another vehicle.

"The inference that manufacturers design to the crash test is often true," says Miami trauma surgeon Jeffrey Augenstein, president of the Association for the Advancement of Automotive Medicine. "But if it (the test) doesn't accurately represent what goes on in the real world, the cars may not do well in crashes."

What's at stake

At the center of the crash-test controversy:

► The Insurance Institute for Highway Safety's "offset" tests. In such tests, a portion of the front end of a vehicle strikes part of a barrier that crushes as though it were another vehicle of the same size. The 40 mile-per-hour tests, which air regularly on *Dateline NBC,* are supposed to simulate how most cars actually crash, which is not squarely head on. Vehicles are given overall ratings—from poor to good—based on how well a crash-test dummy's head, chest and legs are protected and how well each car's structure and safety restraints perform.

Many automakers say these tests, conducted at 10 mph above government standards, force them to add stiff front ends if they want to score well against what is meant to be a vehicle the same size. But that stiffening, particularly in the case of SUVs and pickups, can make them treacherous in real-world crashes with smaller vehicles.

When NHTSA, for example, crashed a 2002 Chevrolet TrailBlazer SUV into a 1997 Honda Accord as part of its compatibility research, the head injury score for the Honda's crash test dummy showed a nearly 100% chance of death. It was more than four times higher than when the predecessor Blazer model hit an Accord. GM told NHTSA that it had made the

(Cont.)

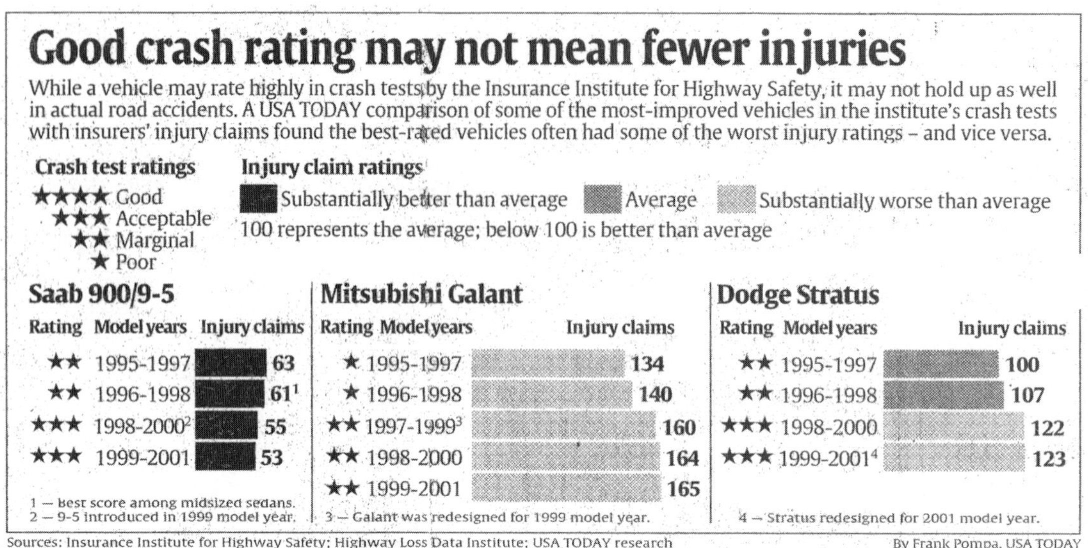

TrailBlazer stiffer partly to perform better in the insurance institute test.

Yet while vehicles that do poorly in the institute test might be expected to have higher injury and death rates, the opposite, surprisingly, is often true.

The Saab 9-5's predecessor, the 1995 Saab 900, "collapsed" in the institute test and was rated marginal. At the same time, it was ranked best among midsize sedans in insurance industry injury claim data that year and "substantially better than average" overall. The redesigned 9-5 has improved its crash-test scores while its injury claims remain about the same.

USA TODAY research found that two other once-poor crash test performers—the Dodge Stratus and Mitsubishi Galant—have improved their test scores but have seen worsening injury claims.

Insurance Institute President Brian O'Neill says insurers' injury claim data are dominated by minor injuries that are not the focus of his test, though he acknowledges that broken legs are.

But critics say that if the institute's test represents the most common serious crashes, evidence of its benefits should be apparent by now. "Nobody has that proof yet," O'Neill acknowledges.

► NHTSA's New Car Assessment Program frontal crash ratings. In this test, vehicles hit a barrier replicating a brick wall head-on at 35 mph. They are given one to five stars (five being best) based on how well driver and passenger-side dummies withstand the crash. In 2007, the test is set to become law. It will have a minimum standard that all automakers would have to meet.

Some automakers say vehicles have to have either very powerful air bags or stiff designs to score well in this severe type of crash. NHTSA statistics show that of all serious two-vehicle frontal crashes, 52% are straight head-on.

Meanwhile, a new GM study, to be presented at an auto engineering meeting next month, concludes that vehicles with higher scores in the NHTSA test do not have fewer deaths and injuries than those that score poorly.

NHTSA would not comment for this story, but officials often cite a 1994 study it did that found fatalities were lower in vehicles that performed well in its tests. The agency is expected to do another such study soon.

NOT 'A FRIENDLY VEHICLE'

The problem with crash tests, says Augenstein, who studies crashes with NHTSA and automaker funding, is that they are designed see how people inside the vehicle being tested are protected.

"So it's not surprising you don't end up with a friendly vehicle that way," he says.

O'Neill says it doesn't have to be so. He says that instead of making SUVs' front ends stiffer, automakers can make the trucks longer and add better-designed passenger compartments.

But GM safety chief Robert Lange says that while the TrailBlazer was made bigger and safer to satisfy customers, adding more length would have added weight, reduced fuel economy and likely offset any safety benefits.

Chris Tinto, Toyota safety regulatory chief, says consumers are demanding better interior space—not longer front ends.

When NHTSA did a compatibility test between

small car Dodge Neon and a Lincoln Navigator SUV redesigned to be safer for occupants and to score better on tests, head-injury scores for the Neon driver more than doubled from what they were in the same test with an older Navigator.

Saeed Barbat, a Ford Motor technical safety specialist, says the 300 extra pounds in the newer model might account for some of the increased head injury score. Safety experts focus most on head injury scores because they are the best way to gauge the likelihood of surviving.

Barbat acknowledges that many automakers, including Ford, make vehicles stiffer to improve crash test scores. But he notes that Ford has also done a number of other things to improve compatibility, including adding front-end beams that cut the risk trucks will ride over the tops of cars.

Lange says the TrailBlazer has bumpers that are level with car bumpers, and its weight is distributed better to reduce the force of impact in front and side crashes.

Barbat, Lange and O'Neill say each of NHTSA's compatibility tests represents just one crash, which might not be repeatable. But O'Neill has made a name for himself and the institute by providing TV networks with tape of tests that also represent just one crash.

Ford, more so than any other automaker, prominently advertises its star ratings in NHTSA's crash tests—despite the fact that it and most automakers used to complain that the tests don't illustrate typical crashes.

What happens in crash tests is clearly important to consumers. Millions of people a year visit NHTSA's site to research safety ratings before they buy a vehicle. The Insurance Institute has recently had more than 8 million visitors a month to its Web site, most of them to check crash-test ratings.

Can tests be more effective?

Many automakers think NHTSA and the institute could improve compatibility and increase the tests' effectiveness by using a movable barrier that crushes just as vehicles do. The barrier could simulate one size of vehicle, and all tested vehicles would have to be sturdy enough to withstand a crash with it. That would force small cars to be made safer but wouldn't force stiffer large trucks.

O'Neill says he isn't considering changing the tests. He says it is the SUVs that are poorly designed for compatibility, not his tests.

NHTSA had been hoping to add a test similar to the institute's to its safety certification or to use as a replacement for its front crash ratings. But this spring, it is expected to announce it is delaying that effort while it continues to test the compatibility of SUVs designed to do well in the institute's tests.

The agency wants to figure out whether requiring offset tests would just shift serious and fatal injuries from one vehicle to another.

Runge doesn't appear to be wedded to any plan for crash tests at the moment. At the recent automaker meeting on compatibility, he challenged the industry to develop its own crash-test proposal for the agency to consider.

"Everything is on the table," he said.

Behind Roses' Beauty, Poor and Ill Workers

By GINGER THOMPSON

Cayambe, Ecuador — In just five years, Ecuadorean roses, as big and red as the human heart, have become the new status flower in the United States, thanks to the volcanic soil, perfect temperatures and abundant sunlight that help generate $240 million a year and tens of thousands of jobs in this once-impoverished region north of Quito.

This St. Valentine's Day, hundreds of American florists and catalogs are offering the roses of this fertile valley. Calyx & Corolla, for instance, bills it as a place "where Andean mists and equatorial sun conspire to produce roses that quickly burst into extravagant bloom, then hold their glory long after lesser specimens have begun to droop."

But roses come with thorns, too. As Ecuador's colorful blooms radiate romance around the world, large growers here have been accused of misusing a toxic mixture of pesticides, fungicides and fumigants to grow and export unblemished pest-free flowers.

As in other industries like garment production, bananas and diamonds, the poor worry about eating first and labor conditions later. They toil here despite headaches and rashes here for the wealthier of the world, who in turn know little of the conditions in which their desires are met.

Doctors and scientists who have worked here say serious health problems have resulted for many of the industry's 50,000 workers, more than 70 percent of them women. Researchers say their work is hampered by lack of access to flower farms because of reluctant growers. But studies that the International Labor Organization published in 1999 and the Catholic University issued here last year showed that women in the industry had more miscarriages than average and that more than 60 percent of all workers suffered headaches, nausea, blurred vision or fatigue.

"No one can speak with conclusive facts in hand about the impact of this industry on the health of the workers, because we have not been able to do the necessary studies,"said Dr. Bolivar Vera, a health specialist at the Health Environment and Development Foundation in Quito. "So the companies have been able to wash their hands of the matter."

In the 20 years since the farms started here, Ecuador has out of nowhere become the fourth-largest producer of roses in the world, with customers from Kazakhstan to Kansas.

St. Valentine's Day is the biggest rose event in the United States, which buys more than 70 percent of its cut flowers from South America and is Ecuador's biggest trading partner. Roses retail for up to $6 a bloom. Last week, workers at RosaPrima, a plantation here, moved at a dizzying pace to cut, wrap and box 70,000 stems a day. Computers help supervisors track each stem and each worker's productivity.

The general manager, Ross Johnson, said he was proud of his business and especially his workers. He said that a doctor visited the farm several times a week and that all workers wore gloves and protective equipment, whether or not handling chemicals. Mr. Johnson said he had cracked down on contractors who hired children as temporary workers.

"We have made a lot of improvements over the years," said Mr. Johnson, who was born in Ecuador and who helped start the farm seven years ago. "I think this is a noble business that does noble things for people here and around the world."

He said roses were typically fumigated 24 hours before being cut. Then they are soaked overnight in a nontoxic chemical solution and shipped at near freezing temperatures.

Dr. Cesar Paz-y-Mino, a geneticist at the Catholic University, said several pesticides used on a farm that was the setting for his research in the late 1990's were restricted as health hazards in other countries, including the United States, and labeled as highly toxic by the World Health Organization.

Among the most notorious are captan, aldicarb and fenamiphos. Dr. Paz-y-Mino refused to identify the flower farm under an agreement that he said he had with the owners.

Roses have become a major Ecuadorean export.

He described the conditions as astonishing and recalled workers' fumigating in street clothes without protective equipment, pesticides stored in poorly sealed containers and fumes wafting over the workers' dining halls. When asked what government agencies monitor worker health and safety, Dr. Paz-y-Mino said, "There are no such checks."

Neither the Labor nor Health Ministries have occupational health departments. In an interview, Labor Minister Felipe Mantilla said he planned to visit flower and banana plantations in a few weeks. Human rights groups, including Human Rights Watch, have criticized Ecuadorean banana growers for using child labor. Mr. Mantilla said the government planned to set up "discussion tables" for workers and managers to discuss competitiveness and labor conditions.

"If there are violations," he said, "we will act firmly. We are drawing up a plan of action on the issue of workers' conditions and we are seeking help from international organizations. The ministry does not have funds to implement plans for progressive control. So that is why we look for international help."

Industry representatives denied that there was a health problem or that unacceptable risks were taken.

"The growers we know are very conscious of environmental issues," said Harrison Kennicott, the chief executive of Kennicott Brothers, a wholesaler in Chicago who is a former president of the Society of American Florists, a trade group.

"They go to lengths to get certified environmentally," Mr. Kennicott said. "The growers take care of the people. They provide housing and medical care.

"Our job is to satisfy our customers, who are the florists and retailers who deliver flowers to the public. Our interest is having the best quality product at a competitive price."

Yet it is hard to erase images of workers like Soledad, 32, and Petrona, 34, both mothers and both looking jaundiced and bony. In interviews after quitting time, they asked not to be fully identified out of fear that they would lose their $156-a-month jobs cutting flowers in greenhouses. The women said they had elementary school educations but did not need high-level science to tell them why their kidneys throbbed at night and heads throbbed in the day.

"There is no respect for the fumigation rules," said Petrona, who has worked on flower farms for four years. "They spray the chemicals even while we are working."

"My hair has begun to fall out," she added, running a hand from the top of her visibly receding hairline down a single scruffy braid. "I am young, but I feel very old."

Soledad, who has worked on flower farms for 12 years, slowly turned her head from side to side.

"If I move my head any faster, I feel nauseous," she said, and then pulled up her sleeve to show her skeletal limbs. "I have no appetite."

When asked whether the farm where they worked had a doctor on duty, the women rolled their eyes.

"He always tells us there is nothing wrong with us and sends us back to work," Petrona said. "He works for the company. He does not help us."

The industry received a helping hand from the Andean Trade Preference Act of 1991. It gives tariff-free access to American markets for farmers in Bolivia, Colombia,

Ecuador and Peru. The law was intended as part of Washington's fight against drug trafficking, offering incentives to abandon coca and poppy growing.

Roses have become one of the top five sources of export revenue for Ecuador. The bloom boom has transformed this once sleepy region of cattle ranches, inhabited primarily by Indians. Much of the heartland has been hollowed out by illegal immigration to Europe and the United States, but the population in the flower regions north and south of Quito has soared. In Cayambe, the population has increased in 10 years, from 5,000 to more than 70,000.

The poor worry about eating first and labor conditions later.

Flowers have helped pave roads and built sophisticated irrigation systems. This year, construction will begin on an international airport between Quito and Cayambe.

The average flower worker earns more than the $120-a-month minimum wage. By employing women, the industry has fostered a social revolution in which mothers and wives have more control over their families' spending, especially on schooling for their children.

As it has grown successful, the industry has come under fire from the green movement in Europe and was the subject of a recent article in Mother Jones magazine. European consumers have pressed for improvements and environmental safeguards, encouraging some growers to join a voluntary program aimed at helping customers identify responsible growers. The certification signifies that dozens of the 460 growers have distributed protective gear, given training in using chemicals and hired doctors to visit at least weekly.

"There are still farms that do not respect fumigation limits or give workers proper training and equipment for handling chemicals," said Gonzalo Luzuriaga, chief executive officer of BellaRosa, another flower grower here. "But many of the farmers are very conscientious about these issues, and we are working to make improvements."

Still numerous signs remain that life for the workers, although better, is far from good. Looking over the town plaza from his second-floor office, Mayor Diego Bonifaz, who also operates a flower farm, said: "It's hard for me to get the wealth out of the plantations and into the community. The farms operate in the first world, selling flowers on the Internet. I am still struggling to pave streets."

Reliable health care, however, seems the most glaring need. Beds have been added to the local hospital, doctors said, but workers often cannot afford services there. The chief of the Red Cross clinic, Dr. Toribio Valladares, said he had seen growing numbers of people with respiratory problems, conjunctivitis, miscarriages and rashes, although he did not have firm numbers.

Like the two women who harvest greenhouse roses, Dr. Valladares voiced deep distrust of doctors who worked on the flower farms.

"When the workers go for help to the doctors on the plantations," he said, "the doctors treat the symptoms but do not examine the workers to try to determine their illnesses. And the doctors always tell them that their illnesses have nothing to do with their work."

In Miami, James Pagano, chief marketing officer of Calyx & Corolla, said he had not been to Ecuador and did not want to comment on environmental or worker conditions.

"We buy what we think consumers will perceive to be a high quality rose at a competitive price," he said. The environment "is not an issue we have any business being in."